THE INWARD JOURNEY

THE INWARD JOURNEY

EDITED BY

JOSEPH F. DOHERTY
WILLIAM C. STEPHENSON
THE UNIVERSITY OF TEXAS AT AUSTIN

HARCOURT BRACE JOVANOVICH, INC.
NEW YORK   CHICAGO   SAN FRANCISCO   ATLANTA

ISBN: 0-15-546945-2

Library of Congress Catalog Card Number: 72-97590

Printed in the United States of America

Cover Photo by Hal Yaeger, Photo Researchers, Inc.

COPYRIGHTS AND ACKNOWLEDGMENTS

For permission to use the selections reprinted in this book, the authors are grateful to the following publishers and copyright holders:

CONTINENTAL TOTAL MEDIA PROJECT For "Suzanne." Words and music by Leonard Cohen. Published by Continental Total Media Project Inc., 515 Madison Avenue, New York, N. Y. 10022. Reprinted by permission.

COWARD, MC CANN & GEOGHEGAN, INC For the excerpt from *Getting Back Together* by Robert Houriet. Copyright © 1971 by Robert Houriet. Reprinted by permission of Coward, McCann & Geoghegan, Inc.

J. M. DENT & SONS LTD For "The Map of Love" from *A Prospect of the Sea* by Dylan Thomas; and for "Poem in October" from *Collected Poems of Dylan Thomas*. Reprinted by permission of the Trustees for the Copyrights of the late Dylan Thomas and J. M. Dent & Sons Ltd.

THE DIAL PRESS For "Sonny's Blues" from *Going to Meet the Man* by James Baldwin. Copyright © 1957 by James Baldwin. Reprinted by permission of the publisher, The Dial Press. Originally appeared in *Partisan Review*.

DOUBLEDAY & COMPANY, INC For "Night-Sea Journey" © 1966 by John Barth (first published in *Esquire* Magazine) from *Lost in the Fun House* by John Barth; for "Four for Sir John Davies," copyright 1952 by the Atlantic Monthly Corporation from *The Collected Poems of Theodore Roethke*; and for "The Myth of Objective Consciousness" from *The Making of a Counter Culture* by Theodore Roszak, copyright © 1968, 1969 by Theodore Roszak. All reprinted by permission of Doubleday & Company, Inc.

E. P. DUTTON & CO., INC For excerpts from the book *Expanded Cinema* by Gene Youngblood. Copyright © 1970 by Gene Youngblood. Published by E. P. Dutton & Co., Inc. and used with their permission.

FABER AND FABER LTD For "Snow" from *Wodwo* by Ted Hughes. Reprinted by permission of Faber and Faber Ltd.

FARRAR, STRAUS & GIROUX, INC For "90 North" from *The Complete Poems* by Randall Jarrell, copyright 1941 by Mrs. Randall Jarrell, copyright renewed 1968 by Mrs. Randall Jarrell; for "Skunk Hour" from *Life Studies* by Robert Lowell, copyright © 1958 by Robert Lowell; and for "The Mild Ones" from *The Pump House Gang* by Tom Wolfe, copyright © 1965 by the New York Herald Tribune, Inc., copyright © 1968 by Tom Wolfe. All reprinted with the permission of Farrar, Straus & Giroux, Inc.

HARCOURT BRACE JOVANOVICH, INC For an excerpt from The Commentary by C. G. Jung to *The Secret of the Golden Flower*, Explained by Richard Wilhelm; for

CONTENTS

CHAPTER SIX

The Lay of the Land: Through Nature   327

CHAPTER SEVEN

Visions for the Future   369

INTRODUCTION

For two centuries prophets of doom have been fearful of the mechanistic, dehumanizing forces at work in our Western culture creating greater and greater spiritual wastelands. Recently many youthful members of the counter culture seem to be seeking secular replacements for the sense of wholeness and purpose which used to be the special property of the religious, mystical imagination. What makes these spiritual revivals so revolutionary is their starting point. Since young people are starting from positions which take them beyond existential despair, they have different expectations, ask different questions, and demand different answers. For large numbers of today's youth the experience of a bleak, shattered, desacralized universe has become so habitual that it no longer stimulates their imagination. Unlike T. S. Eliot, they are not crippled by the question, "After such knowledge, what forgiveness?" Instead, many of the young today view the wasteland as a place from which to begin a journey of exploration, a journey that may lead into man's inner depths or out toward the infinity of the cosmos. There is no easy way to the frontiers of meaning which may lie beyond the wasteland of despair, but a person risks perishing who does not attempt to make the journey.

This anthology explores in twentieth-century literature some attempts to integrate the universe into an experience of totality. Increasingly drawn to the tensions of social and political action (which only feed their sense of the world's turbulence), today's young hunger for such psychic wholeness as was once supplied, for instance, by a universally shared, religious world-view. But for many of the present generation the conventional God of organized religion is dead. And so, whereas many other anthologies address themselves to such public crises as social alienation, racial and sexual injustice, and political frustration, this anthology focuses upon the more personal problem of the formulation and integration of ultimate beliefs. The expression "getting it all together" means exactly that: It makes little sense to continue scratching the wound of America's social conscience if one does not first attempt to come to terms with his own personal anguish. This is perhaps what Bob Dylan decided when he made the shift in the late 1960's from anti-establishment songs of protest to more personal expressions of inner frustration. This book, therefore, centers around the various inward and outward quests for holistic consciousness: Its concern is not just the experience of despair but, more important, explorations out of despair.

The chapter titles themselves suggest the different paths the young have been taking. Judging from the authors and types of books the young are reading, there seem to be at least five fairly distinct avenues which they see leading toward psychic wholeness. The first chapter, "Starting from 'Nothing'," is not one of the avenues, but is the spiritual-philosophic backdrop for the book. That is, it concerns the individual's confrontation with the meaningless void, both interior and cosmic. The second chapter, "Inner Space," surveys the individual's first, and perhaps inevitable, leg of his journey—into the undiscovered self. Strictly speaking, this is not one of the avenues toward integration, but a prerequisite for traveling. Before a person ascends, he must first descend or enter into the spacious domain of his unconscious in order to find himself. This chapter explores some of the hidden caverns of the subrational mind. The third chapter, "Through the Body," has to do with the physical way. The easiest form for understanding this experience is in terms of the drug phenomenon, but psychedelic expansion of mind is just one aspect of a more comprehensive somatic expansion involved in this bodily approach toward integration. Readers familiar with novelists like Henry Miller, William Burroughs, Norman Mailer, Richard Fariña, and Leonard Cohen will sense the meaning of this route: It is through a total heightening of the body, as opposed, for instance, to meditation. The fourth chapter, "The Map of Love," concerns the moment of release which accompanies what is felt to be a merging of oneself with others in an ecstatic experience. The fifth chapter, "The Meditative Way," deals with the route of religious mysticism. As attested to by the large readership of Herman Hesse, D. T. Suzuki, Alan Watts, and poets like Gary Snyder and Allen Ginsberg, this avenue has become increasingly popular. The sixth chapter, "The Lay of the Land," concerns deliverance through a return to nature. The current interest in ecology and camping speaks to the power of this venture. The last chapter, "Visions for the Future," explores man's apocalyptic dreams and his attempt to recover a more primitive form of consciousness.

Such is the overall scope of the anthology. Many of the selections may seem puzzling to readers unfamiliar with contemporary literature. We do not assume that very many freshmen, for example, will know the work of R. D. Laing, Robert Creeley, or John Barth, although they probably will have heard of them. The point, however, is that these are the authors they will be exposed to in their college careers, both in and out of the classroom. Moreover, the chapters deal with experiences and quests students know experientially. Not all freshmen may be acquainted with the philosophic dimensions of existential despair, yet all have experienced the "sound of silence." Some might be naïve about the exact nature of psychedelic expansion of mind, yet all know someone who at least claims to use drugs "to get his head straight." In short, our goal is to provide source material for discussions in which all students can participate because they are all involved with the problem of getting it together, whatever the means.

Our larger educational purpose is to allow the student to translate his emotional experience of the secular, mystical moment into an intellectual experience as well. For this reason, certain popular writers are not represented. Of course not all contemporary writers speak to the subject of the book, and we have courted quality rather than popularity. We have tried to stay away from any more didactic instruction than that afforded by the choice and classification of the selections themselves. While even our chapter divisions may appear somewhat arbitrary—as one would expect for works whose aim is an all-embracing vision of reality—we hope that a good part of our readers' fun will come from dismantling the categories we have created.

We have searched for selections—poems, short stories, and imaginative essays—that illustrate the theme under consideration and yet that also stand on their own. There is no fragment that makes sense only in terms of its chapter. Ideally the teacher will have his students read several works from a chapter to let them modify and complicate each other. We would like to have had space to include more pieces that would question the validity of the particular avenues explored, but we must leave this up to the classroom experience itself. We hope these readings will generate the kind of critical exploration that serves as a springboard to interesting topics for writing as well as discussion.

CHAPTER ONE

Starting from "Nothing": Backgrounds

*The psychological experience of chaos and meaninglessness seems
to be so ruinous to man's mind that he is often tempted to end
his troubles in one destructive gesture. Anthropologists relate a
fascinating story of psychic disintegration among the Achilpa,
a tribe of nomadic Australian primitives, who carried with them
a sacred pole they planted in the center of each new camp; its
leanings revealed the direction of their next migration. For the
Achilpa the pole symbolized the center of the world, or the
opening between heaven and earth through which their god
communicated. Once, however, when the pole was broken, the
tribe felt that chaos had triumphed and the end of the world was
upon them. All meaning, purpose, and direction to their life
collapsed. Utterly befuddled, the entire clan wandered aimlessly
for a time, and then, though food and shelter were near at hand,
they simply lay down and waited for death. Without some access
to the transcendent, life had become intolerable and the world
appeared an unbearable place.*

*Modern man has for some time been nurturing a strong sense
of the utter absurdity of existence. Friedrich Nietzsche's now
famous phrase, "God is dead," expresses what many thinking men
of the nineteenth century in one way or another experienced as
a chill feeling of "zero at the bone." Finding the sense of God
already dead in the hearts of his contemporaries, Nietzsche gave
voice to our modern belief that man no longer lives in a
well-ordered, reasonable universe presided over by a benign
intelligence. (V. S. Pritchett's "The Saint" dramatizes just such a
breakdown of faith.) Instead, the world seems to spin inanely in
the midst of empty space. "Out there" is simply "Nothing,"*

as Kafka's "Conversation With a Supplicant" persuades us.
Moreover, the logical moral consequences of this discovery are just
as frightening: As Ivan announces in The Brothers Karamazov,
"If there is no God, then all things are permissible." Brute chaos,
anarchy, and violence seem to be loosed upon a world which
has lost its sense of sacrality or transcendence. Recognizing this,
Albert Camus has argued that the primary question any thoughtful
man in our time now faces is, why not slit one's throat? Suicide
seems to be the most reasonable response to a universe whose
center will not hold. But rather than capitulate before chaos,
Camus put away his razor blade and chose a much more
precarious and arduous experiment. "I want to know if I can
live with what I know and only with that." Camus knew terrible
things, yet if it is at all possible for us to live in a desacralized
universe, we too must be willing to stare directly into the face of
our despair. Nothing is served by trying to blink away the
invasion of meaninglessness, the inner and outer sense of vacancy
which appears to have taken possession of the world we must
live in—the vacancy being attested to by our selections from
Randall Jarrell, Robert Lowell, Ted Hughes, and Thomas Wolfe.

   The selections in this chapter invite the reader to accept Camus'
challenge to plunge into the center of negation. Only by piercing
to the elemental Nothingness at the core of our being can we
hope to negate the negation and break through to whatever
islands of visionary order, coherence, and meaning may lie on the
other side. This is Camus' great dare, and also one made by
R. D. Laing in his "Transcendental Experience." Can we admit
our orphaned status in the universe, embrace our isolation and
loneliness, and take our start from an awareness of each man's
fundamental alienation imposed upon him as a curse for no less
a crime than the mere fact of his birth? If we shy away from
looking into these abysses, then, like the aborigine Achilpas who
simply lie down to starve when their god abandons them, we will
be choosing death rather than life.

RANDALL JARRELL

90 North

At home, in my flannel gown, like a bear to its floe,
I clambered to bed; up the globe's impossible sides
I sailed all night—till at last, with my black beard,
My furs and my dogs, I stood at the northern pole.

There in the childish night my companions lay frozen,
The stiff furs knocked at my starveling throat,
And I gave my great sigh: the flakes came huddling,
Were they really my end? In the darkness I turned to my
     rest.

—Here, the flag snaps in the glare and silence
Of the unbroken ice. I stand here,   10
The dogs bark, my beard is black, and I stare
At the North Pole . . .
                    And now what? Why, go back.

Turn as I please, my step is to the south.
The world—my world spins on this final point
Of cold and wretchedness: all lines, all winds
End in this whirlpool I at last discover.

And it is meaningless. In the child's bed
After the night's voyage, in that warm world
Where people work and suffer for the end   20
That crowns the pain—in that Cloud-Cuckoo-Land

I reached my North and it had meaning.
Here at the actual pole of my existence,
Where all that I have done is meaningless,
Where I die or live by accident alone—

Where, living or dying, I am still alone;
Here where North, the night, the berg of death
Crowd me out of the ignorant darkness,
I see at last that all the knowledge

I wrung from the darkness—that the darkness flung me—   30
Is worthless as ignorance: nothing comes from nothing,
The darkness from the darkness. Pain comes from the dark-
    ness
And we call it wisdom. It is pain.

ROBERT LOWELL

Skunk Hour

FOR ELIZABETH BISHOP

Nautilus Island's hermit
heiress still lives through winter in her Spartan cottage;
her sheep still graze above the sea.
Her son's a bishop. Her farmer
is first selectman in our village;
she's in her dotage.

Thirsting for
the hierarchic privacy
of Queen Victoria's century,
she buys up all   10
the eyesores facing her shore,
and lets them fall.

The season's ill—
we've lost our summer millionaire,
who seemed to leap from an L. L. Bean
catalogue. His nine-knot yawl
was auctioned off to lobstermen.
A red fox stain covers Blue Hill.

And now our fairy
decorator brightens his shop for fall;   20

his fishnet's filled with orange cork,
orange, his cobbler's bench and awl;
there is no money in his work,
he'd rather marry.

One dark night,
my Tudor Ford climbed the hill's skull;
I watched for love-cars. Lights turned down,
they lay together, hull to hull,
where the graveyard shelves on the town. . . .
My mind's not right.   30

A car radio bleats,
"Love, O careless Love. . . ." I hear
my ill-spirit sob in each blood cell,
as if my hand were at its throat. . . .
I myself am hell;
nobody's here—

only skunks, that search
in the moonlight for a bite to eat.
They march on their soles up Main Street:
white stripes, moonstruck eyes' red fire   40
under the chalk-dry and spar spire
of the Trinitarian Church.

I stand on top
of our back steps and breathe the rich air—
a mother skunk with her column of kittens swills the garbage
    pail.
She jabs her wedge-head in a cup
of sour cream, drops her ostrich tail,
and will not scare.

LEROI JONES

Snake Eyes

That force is lost
which shaped me, spent
in its image, battered, an old brown thing
swept off the streets
where it sucked its
gentle living.
                    And what is meat
to do, that is driven to its end
by words? The frailest gestures
grown like skirts around breathing.   10
                                        We take
unholy risks to prove
we are what we cannot be. For instance,

I am not even crazy.

TED HUGHES

Snow

And let me repeat this over and over again: beneath my feet is the earth, some part of the surface of the earth. Beneath the snow beneath my feet, that is. What else could it be? It is firm, I presume, and level. If it is not actually soil and rock, it must be ice. It is very probably ice. Whichever it may be, it is proof—the most substantial proof possible—that I am somewhere on the earth, the known earth. It would be absurd to dig down through the snow, just to determine exactly what is underneath, earth or ice. This bedded snow may well be dozens of feet deep. Besides, the snow filling all the air and rivering along the ground would pour into the hole as fast as I could dig, and cover me too—very quickly.

This could be no other planet: the air is perfectly natural, perfectly good.

Our aircraft was forced down by this unusual storm. The pilot tried to make a landing, but misjudged the extraordinary power of the wind and the whereabouts of the ground. The crash was violent. The fuselage buckled and gaped, and I was flung clear. Unconscious of everything save the need to get away from the disaster, I walked farther off into the blizzard and collapsed, which explains why when I came to full consciousness and stood up out of the snow that was burying me I could see nothing of either the aircraft or my fellow passengers. All around me was what I have been looking at ever since. The bottomless dense motion of snow. I started to walk.

Of course, everything previous to that first waking may have been entirely different since I don't remember a thing about it. Whatever chance dropped me here in the snow evidently destroyed my memory. That's one thing of which there is no doubt whatsoever. It is, so to speak, one of my facts. The aircraft crash is a working hypothesis, that merely.

There's no reason why I should not last quite a long time yet. I seem to have an uncommon reserve of energy. To keep my mind firm, that is the essential thing, to fix it firmly in my reasonable hopes, and lull it there, encourage it. Mesmerise it slightly with a sort of continuous prayer. Because when my mind is firm, my energy is firm. And that's the main thing here—energy. No matter how circumspect I may be, or how lucid, without energy I am lost on the spot. Useless to think about it. Where my energy ends I end, and all circumspection and all lucidity end with me. As long as I have energy I can correct my mistakes, outlast them, outwalk them—for instance the unimaginable error that as far as I know I am making at this very moment. This step, this, the next five hundred, or five thousand—all mistaken, all absolutely waste, back to where I was ten hours ago. But we recognise that thought. My mind is not my friend. My support, my defence, but my enemy too—not perfectly intent on getting me out of this. If I were mindless perhaps there would be no difficulty whatsoever. I would simply go on aware of nothing but my step by step success in getting over the ground. The thing to do is to keep alert, keep my mind fixed in alertness, recognise these treacherous paralysing, yes, lethal thoughts the second they enter, catch them before they can make that burrowing plunge down the spinal cord. Then gently and without any other acknowledgment push them back—out into the snow where they belong. And that *is* where they belong. They are the infiltrations of the snow, encroachments of this immensity of lifelessness. But they enter so slyly. We are true, they say, or at least very probably true, and on that account you must entertain us and even give us the run of your life, since above all things you are dedicated to the truth. That is the air they have, that's how they come in. What do I know about the truth? As if simpleminded dedication to truth were the final law of existence! I only know more and more clearly what is good for me. It's my mind that has this contemptible awe for the probably true, and my mind, I know, I prove it every minute, is not me and is by no means sworn to help me. Am I a lie? I must survive—that's a truth sacred as any, and as the hungry truths devour the sleepy truths I shall digest every other possible truth to the substance and health and energy of my own, and the ones

I can't digest I shall spit out, since in this situation my intention to survive is the one mouth, the one digestive tract, so to speak, by which I live. But those others! I relax for a moment, I leave my mind to itself for a moment—and they are in complete possession. They plunge into me, exultantly, mercilessly. There is no question of their intention or their power. Five seconds of carelessness, and they have struck. The strength melts from me, my bowels turn to water, my consciousness darkens and shrinks. I have to stop.

What are my facts? I do have some definite facts.

Taking six steps every five seconds, I calculate—allowing for my brief regular sleeps—that I have been walking through this blizzard for five months and during that time have covered something equal to the breadth of the Atlantic between Southampton and New York. Two facts. And a third: throughout those five months this twilight of snow has not grown either darker or brighter.

So.

There seems no reason to doubt that I am somewhere within either the Arctic or the Antarctic Circle. That's a comfort. It means my chances of survival are not uniquely bad. Men have walked the length of Asia simply to amuse themselves.

Obviously I am not travelling in a straight line. But that needn't give me any anxiety. Perhaps I made a mistake when I first started walking, setting my face against the wind instead of downwind. Coming against the wind I waste precious energy and there is always this wearisome snow blocking my eyes and mouth. But I had to trust the wind. This resignation to wind's guidance is the very foundation of my firmness of mind. The wind is not simply my compass. In fact, I must not think of it as a compass at all. The wind is my law. As a compass nothing could be more useless. No need to dwell on that. It's extremely probable indeed and something I need not hide from myself that this wind is leading me to and fro in quite a tight little maze—always shifting too stealthily for me to notice the change. Or, if the sun is circling the horizon, it seems likely that the wind is swinging with it through the three hundred and sixty degrees once in every twenty-four hours, turning me as I keep my face against it in a perfect circle not more than seven miles across. This would explain the otherwise strange fact that in spite of the vast distance I have covered the terrain is still dead level, exactly as when I started.

A frozen lake, no doubt. This is a strong possibility and I must get used to it without letting it overwhelm me, and without losing sight of its real advantages.

The temptation to trust to luck and instinct and cut out across wind is to be restricted. The effect on my system of confidence would be disastrous. My own judgment would naturally lead me in a circle. I would have to make deliberate changes of direction to break out of that circle—only to go in a larger circle or a circle in the opposite direction. So more changes. Wilder and more sudden changes, changes of my changes—all to evade an enemy that showed so little sign of itself it might as well not have existed. It's clear where all that would end. Shouting and running and so on. Staggering round like a man beset by a mob. Falling, grovelling. So on. The snow.

No. All I have to do is endure: that is, keep my face to the wind. My face to the wind, a firm grip on my mind, and everything else follows naturally. There is not the slightest need to be anxious. Any time now the Polar night will arrive, bringing a drastic change of climate—inevitable. Clearing the sky and revealing the faultless compass of the stars.

The facts are overwhelmingly on my side. I could almost believe in Providence. After all, if one single circumstance were slightly—only slightly—other than it is! If, for instance, instead of waking in a blizzard on a firm level place I had come to consciousness falling endlessly through snow-cloud. Then I might have wondered very seriously whether I were in the gulf or not. Or if the atmosphere happened to consist of, say, ammonia. I could not have existed. And in the moment before death by asphyxiation I would certainly have been convinced I was out on some lifeless planet. Or if I had no body but simply arms and legs growing out of a head, my whole system of confidence would have been disoriented from the start. My dreams, for instance, would have been meaningless to me, or rather an argument of my own meaninglessness. I would have died almost immediately, out of sheer bewilderment. It wouldn't need nearly such extreme differences either. If I had been without these excellent pigskin boots, trousers, jacket, gloves and hood, the cold would have extinguished me at once.

And even if I had double the clothing that I have, where would I be without my chair? My chair is quite as important as one of

my lungs. As both my lungs, indeed, for without it I should be
dead. Where would I have slept? Lying in the snow. But lying
flat, as I have discovered, I am buried by the snow in just under
a minute, and the cold begins to take over my hands and my
feet and my face. Sleep would be impossible. In other words, I
would very soon collapse of exhaustion and be buried. As it is,
I unsnap my chair harness, plant the chair in the snow, sit on it,
set my feet on the rung between the front legs, my arms folded
over my knees and my head resting on my arms, and am able in
this way to take a sleep of fully ten minutes before the snow
piles over me.

The chain of providential coincidences is endless. Or rather,
like a chain mail, it is complete without one missing link to be-
tray and annul the rest. Even my dreams are part of it. They are
as tough and essential a link as any, since there can no longer be
any doubt that they are an accurate reproduction of my whole
previous life, of the world as it is and as I knew it—all without
one contradictory detail. Yet if my amnesia had been only a little
bit stronger!—it needed only that. Because without this evidence
of the world and my identity I could have known no purpose in
continuing the ordeal. I could only have looked, breathed and
died, like a nestling fallen from the nest.

Everything fits together. And the result—my survival, and my
determination to survive. I should rejoice.

The chair is of conventional type: nothing in the least mysti-
fying about it. A farmhouse sort of chair: perfectly of a piece with
my dreams, as indeed are my clothes, my body and all the inclina-
tions of my mind. It is of wood, painted black, though in places
showing a coat of brown beneath the black. One of the nine struts
in the back is missing and some child—I suppose it was a child—
has stuck a dab of chewing-gum into the empty socket. Obviously
the chair has been well used, and not too carefully. The right
foreleg has been badly chewed, evidently by a puppy, and on the
seat both black and brown paints are wearing through showing
the dark grain of the pale wood. If all this is not final evidence
of a reality beyond my own, of the reality of the world it comes
from, the world I re-dream in my sleeps—I might as well lie down
in the snow and be done with.

The curious harness needn't worry me. The world, so far as
I've dreamed it at this point, contains no such harness, true. But

since I've not yet dreamed anything from after my twenty-sixth birthday, the harness might well have been invented between that time and the time of my disaster. Probably it's now in general use. Or it may be the paraphernalia of some fashionable game that came in during my twenty-seventh or later year, and to which I got addicted. Sitting on snow peaks in nineteenth-century chairs. Or perhaps I developed a passion for painting polar scenery and along with that a passion for this particular chair as my painting seat, and had the harness designed specially. A lucky eccentricity! It is perfectly adapted to my present need. But all that's in the dark still. There's a lot I haven't dreamed yet. From my twenty-third and twenty-fourth years I have almost nothing—a few insignificant episodes. Nothing at all after my twenty-sixth birthday. The rest, though, is about complete, which suggests that any time now I ought to be getting my twenty-third and twenty-fourth years in full and, more important, my twenty-seventh year, or as much of it as there is, along with the accurate account of my disaster and the origin of my chair.

There seems little doubt of my age. Had I been dreaming my life chronologically there would have been real cause for worry. I could have had no idea how much was still to come. Of course, if I were suddenly to dream something from the middle of my sixtieth year I would have to reorganise all my ideas. What really convinces me of my youth is my energy. The appearance of my body tells me nothing. Indeed, from my hands and feet—which are all I have dared to uncover—one could believe I was several hundred years old, or even dead, they are so black and shrunken on the bone. But the emaciation is understandable, considering that for five months I have been living exclusively on will-power, without the slightest desire for food.

I have my job to get back to, and my mother and father will be in despair. And God knows what will have happened to Helen. Did I marry her? I have no wedding ring. But we were engaged. And it is another confirmation of my youth that my feelings for her are as they were then—stronger, in fact, yes a good deal stronger, though speaking impartially these feelings that seem to be for her might easily be nothing but my desperate longing to get back to the world in general—a longing that is using my one-time affection for Helen as a sort of form or model. It's possible, very possible, that I have in reality forgotten her, even that I am sixty years old, that she has been dead for thirty-four years. Certain things may be very different from what I imagine. If I were to take this drift of thoughts to the logical extreme there is no absolute proof that my job, my parents, Helen and the whole world are not simply my own invention, fantasies my imagination has improvised on the simple themes of my own form, of clothes, my chair and the properties of my present environment. I am in no position to be sure about anything.

But there is more to existence, fortunately, than consideration of possibilities. There is conviction, faith. If there were not, where would I be? The moment I allow one of these "possibilities" the slightest intimacy—a huge futility grips me, as it were physically, by the heart, as if the organ itself were despairing of this life and ready to give up.

Courageous and calm. That should be my prayer. I should repeat that, repeat it like the Buddhists with their "O jewel of the lotus." Repeat it till it repeats itself in my very heart, till every heartbeat drives it through my whole body. Courageous and calm. This is the world, think no more about it.

My chair will keep me sane. My chair, my chair, my chair—I might almost repeat that. I know every mark on it, every grain. So near and true! It alone predicates a Universe, the entire Universe, with its tough carpentering, its sprightly, shapely design— so delicate, so strong. And while I have the game I need be afraid of nothing. Though it is dangerous. Tempting, dangerous, but— it is enough to know that the joy is mine. I set the chair down in the snow, letting myself think I am going to sleep, but instead of sitting I step back a few paces into the snow. How did I think of that? The first time, I did not dare look away from it. I had never before let it out of my hand, never let it go for a fraction between unbuckling it and sitting down on it. But then I let it go and stepped back into the snow. I had never heard my voice before. I was astonished at the sound that struggled up out of me. Well, I need the compensations. And this game does rouse my energies, so it is, in a sense, quite practical. After the game, I could run. That's the moment of danger, though, the moment of overpowering impatience when I could easily lose control and break out, follow my instinct, throw myself on luck, run out across the wind.

But there is a worse danger. If I ran out across the wind I

would pretty soon come to my senses, turn my face back into the wind. It is the game itself, the stage of development it has reached, that is dangerous now. I no longer simply step back. I set the chair down, turn my face away and walk off into the blizzard, counting my steps carefully. At fourteen paces I stop. Fifteen is the limit of vision in this dense flow of snow, so at fourteen I stop, and turn. Let those be the rules. Let me fix the game at that. Because at first I see nothing. That should be enough for me. Everywhere, pouring silent grey, a silence like a pressure, like the slow coming to bear of some incalculable pressure, too gradual to detect. If I were simply to stand there my mind would crack in a few moments. But I concentrate, I withdraw my awe from the emptiness and look pointedly into it. At first, everything is as usual—as I have seen it for five months. Then my heart begins to thump unnaturally, because I seem to make out a dimness, a shadow that wavers deep in the grey turmoil, vanishes and darkens, rises and falls. I step one pace forward and using all my will-power stop again. The shadow is as it was. Another step. The shadow seems to be a little darker. Then it vanishes and I lunge two steps forward but immediately stop because there it is, quite definite, no longer moving. Slowly I walk towards it. The rules are that I keep myself under control, that I restrain all sobs or shouts though of course it is impossible to keep the breathing regular—at this stage at least, and right up to the point where the shadow resolves into a chair. In that vast grey dissolution—my chair! The snowflakes are drifting against the legs and gliding between the struts, bumping against them, clinging and crawling over the seat. To control myself then is not within human power. Indeed I seem to more or less lose consciousness at that point. I'm certainly not responsible for the weeping, shouting thing that falls on my chair, embracing it, kissing it, bruising his cheeks against it. As the snowflakes tap and run over my gloves and over the chair I begin to call them names. I peer into each one as if it were a living face, full of speechless recognition, and I call to them—Willy, Joanna, Peter, Jesus, Ferdinand, anything that comes into my head, and shout to them and nod and laugh. Well, it's harmless enough madness.

The temptation to go beyond the fourteen paces is now becoming painful. To go deep into the blizzard. Forty paces. Then come back, peering. Fifteen paces, twenty paces. Stop. A shadow.

That would not be harmless madness. If I were to leave my chair like that the chances are I would never find it again. My footprints do not exist in this undertow of snow. Weeks later, I would still be searching, casting in great circles, straining at every moment to pry a shadow out of the grey sameness. My chair meanwhile a hundred miles away in the blizzard, motionless—neat legs and elegant back, sometimes buried, sometimes uncovering again. And for centuries, long after I'm finished, still sitting there, intact with its toothmarks and missing strut, waiting for a darkening shape to come up out of the nothingness and shout to it and fall on it and possess it.

But my chair is here, on my back, here. There's no danger of my ever losing it. Never so long as I keep control, keep my mind firm. All the facts are on my side. I have nothing to do but endure.

FRANZ KAFKA

Conversation with the Supplicant

There was a time when I went every day into a church, since a girl I was in love with knelt there in prayer for half an hour in the evening and I was able to look at her in peace.

Once when she had not come and I was reluctantly eyeing the other supplicants I noticed a young fellow who had thrown his whole lean length along the floor. Every now and then he clutched his head as hard as he could and sighing loudly beat it in his upturned palms on the stone flags.

Only a few old women were in the church, and they kept turning their shawled heads sideways to watch the young man at his devotions. Their awareness of him seemed to please him, for before each of his pious outbursts he cast his eyes around to see whether many of them were looking. This I found unseemly, and I made up my mind to accost him as he left the church and to ask him why he prayed in such a manner. Yes, I felt irritable because my girl had not come.

But an hour elapsed before he stood up, crossed himself punctiliously and strode jerkily towards the basin of holy water. I set myself in a direct line between the basin and the door, knowing that I was not going to let him pass without an explanation. I screwed up my mouth as I always do when I want to speak decisively, I advanced my right leg and rested all my weight upon it, balancing my left leg carelessly on the points of my toes; that too gives me a sense of firmness.

Now it is possible that the young man had already caught sight of me when he was sprinkling himself with the holy water, or he might even have remarked me sooner with some dismay, for he made a sudden unexpected dash out through the doorway. The

glass door banged shut. And when I came out immediately behind him I could not see him anywhere, for there were several
narrow streets and plenty of traffic.

He stayed away for the next few days, but my girl was there.
She was wearing her black dress with the transparent lace top
over the shoulders—the crescent of her petticoat showed under
it—from the lower edge of which the silk hung down in a beautifully cut ruffle. And since she had come I forgot the young man
and did not even concern myself with him when he continued
to appear regularly to do his devotions in the usual manner. Yet
whenever he passed me he always seemed in a great hurry and
turned his face away. Perhaps it was only that I could not think
of him except in motion and so even when he was standing still
he seemed to me to be slithering past.

One evening I stayed too long in my room. All the same, I
went along to the church. My girl was not in it, and I thought
of going home again. But there was the young fellow lying on the
floor. I was reminded of my first encounter with him and my
curiosity revived.

I went on tiptoe to the doorway, gave a coin to the blind beggar
who sat there and squeezed in beside him behind the open half
of the door; and for a whole hour there I sat, perhaps with a
crafty look on my face. I liked being there and made up my mind
to come again often. In the second hour I began to think it
foolish to sit there because of a man at his prayers. Yet for a third
hour in growing irritation I let the spiders creep over my clothes
while the last of the people came, drawing deep breaths, out of
the darkness of the church.

And then he too came. He was walking cautiously, trying the
ground lightly with his feet before setting them down.

I rose up, took a large stride forward and seized him.

"Good evening," I said, and with my hand on his collar pushed
him down the steps into the lighted square.

When we were down on the level he said in a fluttering voice:
"Good evening, my dear, dear sir, don't be angry with me, your
most devoted servant."

"Well," said I, "I want to ask you some questions, sir; you
slipped through my fingers the other time but you'll hardly do
that tonight."

"Sir, you are a compassionate man and you'll let me go home. I'm a poor creature, that's the truth."

"No," I cried, against the noise of a passing tram, "I won't let you go. This is the kind of encounter I like. You're a lucky catch for me. I congratulate myself."

Then he said: "Oh God, your heart is alive but your head is a block of wood. You call me a lucky catch, what good luck you must be sure of! For my bad luck is like a seesaw teetering on a very fine point, and it will fall on anyone's head who lays a questioning finger on it. Good night, sir."

"Right," said I, and held his right hand fast, "if you don't give me an answer I'll begin to yell here in the street. And all the shopgirls that are coming out now and all their sweethearts waiting for them so happily will come running up, for they'll think a carriage horse has fallen down or some accident has happened. And then I'll point you out to the people."

At that he tearfully kissed my hands, one after the other. "I'll tell you what you want to know, but please let us rather go into the side street over there." I nodded, and we crossed to it.

But it was not enough for him to be in the dusk of the little street where only a few yellow lamps hung at wide intervals, he drew me into the low hallway of an old house underneath a tiny lamp that hung dripping before a wooden stair. There he took out his handkerchief gravely and spread it on a step, saying: "Do sit down, my dear sir, and you will be better able to ask questions, while I stand here, for so I'll be better able to answer them. Only don't torment me."

So I sat down and said, looking up at him with narrowed eyes: "You're an utter lunatic, that's what you are! Look at the way you carry on in the church! How irritating it is and how unpleasant for onlookers! How can anyone compose himself to worship if he has to look at you."

He kept his body pressed against the wall, only his head could move freely to and fro. "Don't be angry—why should you be angry about things that don't concern you. I get angry when I behave badly; but if someone else does the wrong thing I am delighted. So don't be angry if I tell you that it is the aim of my life to get people to look at me."

"What a thing to say," I cried, much too loudly for the low-roofed hallway, but I was afraid to let my voice die away again, "truly, what a thing to say. Of course I can guess, of course I guessed the first time I saw you, what kind of state you are in. I've had some experience, and I don't mean it as a joke when I tell you it's like being seasick on dry land. It's a condition in which you can't remember the real names of things and so in a great hurry you fling temporary names at them. You do it as fast as you can. But you've hardly turned your back on them before you've forgotten what you called them. A poplar in the fields which you called 'the tower of Babel,' since you either didn't or wouldn't know that it was a poplar, stands wavering anonymously again, and so you have to call it 'Noah in his cups.' "

I was somewhat disconcerted when he said: "I'm thankful to say that I don't understand what you've been talking about."

With annoyance I answered quickly: "Your saying that you're thankful shows that you do know what I was talking about."

"Of course it shows that, my dear sir, but what you said was rather peculiar too."

I laid my hands on a step above me, leaned right back and in this almost untacklable position, which is the last resource of a wrestler, asked him: "Haven't you a comic way of wriggling out of things, projecting your own state of mind like that on other people?"

That made him pluck up courage. He clasped his hands together to give his body unity, and put up some resistance, saying: "No, I don't do that with anybody, not even with you for instance, because I can't. But I should be glad if I could, for then I wouldn't need to make people look at me in church. Do you know why I need to?"

This question rather dished me. Of course I didn't know, and I believe I didn't want to know. I never wanted to come here, I said to myself, but the creature forced me to give him a hearing. So all I had to do was to shake my head, to convey that I didn't know, yet I found myself unable to move my head at all.

The young man standing opposite me smiled. Then he dropped on his knees and with a dreamy look on his face told me: "There has never been a time in which I have been convinced from within myself that I am alive. You see, I have only such a fugitive awareness of things around me that I always feel they were once real and are now fleeting away. I have a constant longing, my dear sir, to catch a glimpse of things as they may have been before they show themselves to me. I feel that then they were calm and beautiful. It must be so, for I often hear people talking about them as though they were."

Since I made no answer and only through involuntary twitchings in my face betrayed my uneasiness, he asked: "Don't you believe that people talk like that?"

I knew I ought to nod assent but could not do it.

"You don't really believe it? Why, listen; once when I was a child and just waking up from a short afternoon nap, still half asleep, I heard my mother calling down from the balcony in the most natural voice: 'What are you doing, my dear? It's so hot.' And a woman answered from the garden: 'I'm reveling in the grass.' She said it quite simply and without insistence, as if it were to be taken for granted."

I thought an answer was expected from me, so I felt in my hip trouser pocket as if I were looking for something. But I wasn't looking for anything, I only wanted to shift my position to show that I was paying attention. And then I said that the incident was remarkable enough and quite beyond my comprehension. I added also that I didn't believe it was true and that it must have been invented for some special purpose which I could not fathom. Then I shut my eyes for they were hurting me.

"Oh, how glad I am that you agree with me, and it was most unselfish of you to stop me in order to let me know it. Why indeed should I feel ashamed—or why should we feel ashamed—because I don't walk upright and ponderously, striking my walking stick on the pavement and brushing the clothes of the people who pass by so loudly. Shouldn't I rather venture to complain with justified resentment at having to flit along the house walls like a shadow with hunched shoulders, many a time disappearing from sight in the plate glass of the shop windows.

"What dreadful days I have to live through! Why are all our buildings so badly put together that tall houses sometimes collapse without any discernible external cause? I go clambering over the ruins asking everyone I meet: 'Now how could such a thing happen! In our town—a brand new house—that's the fifth one today—just think of it.' And nobody can give me an answer.

"And people often fall down in the street and lie there dead. Then all the tradesmen open their doors that are hung with a litter of goods, come trotting out, carry the dead man into a house, and then appear again, with smiling eyes and lips, saying: 'Good morning—the sky is overcast—I'm selling a lot of kerchiefs —yes, the war.' I go slinking into the house and after timidly raising my hand several times with the fingers ready crooked knock at last on the porter's little glass window. 'My dear fellow,' I say to him in a friendly way, 'a dead man was just brought in here. Do let me see him, please.' And when he shakes his head as if undecided, I say positively: 'My dear chap. I'm from the secret police. Show me that dead man at once.' 'A dead man?' he asks, almost in an injured voice. 'No, there's no dead man here. This is a respectable house.' And I take my leave and go.

"And then if I have to cross a large open space I forget everything. The difficulty of this enterprise confuses me, and I can't help thinking: 'If people must build such large squares out of pure wantonness why don't they add a stone balustrade to help one across. There's a gale from the southwest today. The air in the square is swirling about. The tip of the Town Hall is teetering in small circles. All this agitation should be controlled. Every window pane is rattling and the lamp posts are bending like bamboos. The very robe of the Virgin Mary on her column is fluttering and the stormy wind is snatching at it. Is no one aware of this? The ladies and gentlemen who should be walking on the paving stones are driven along. When the wind slackens they come to a stop, exchange a few words and bow to each other, but when the wind blows again they can't help themselves, all their feet leave the ground at the same moment. They have to hold on to their hats, of course, but their eyes twinkle merrily as if there were only a gentle breeze. No one's afraid but me.'"

Smarting as I was, I said: "The story you told me about your mother and the woman in the garden seems to me not in the least remarkable. Not only have I heard many like it and experienced them, but I've even played a part in some of them. It was quite a natural incident. Do you think that if I had been on the balcony I couldn't have said the same thing and got the same answer from the garden? Such a simple affair."

When I said that, he seemed very delighted. He remarked that I was well dressed and he particularly liked my tie. And what a fine skin I had. And admissions became most clear and unequivocal when one withdrew them.

V. S. PRITCHETT

The Saint

When I was seventeen years old I lost my religious faith. It had been unsteady for some time and then, very suddenly, it went as the result of an incident in a punt on the river outside the town where we lived. My uncle, with whom I was obliged to stay for long periods of my life, had started a small furniture-making business in the town. He was always in difficulties about money, but he was convinced that in some way God would help him. And this happened. An investor arrived who belonged to a sect called the Church of the Last Purification, of Toronto, Canada. Could we imagine, this man asked, a good and omnipotent God allowing his children to be short of money? We had to admit we could not imagine this. The man paid some capital into my uncle's business and we were converted. Our family were the first Purifiers —as they were called—in the town. Soon a congregation of fifty or more were meeting every Sunday in a room at the Corn Exchange.

At once we found ourselves isolated and hated people. Everyone made jokes about us. We had to stand together because we were sometimes dragged into the courts. What the unconverted could not forgive in us was first that we believed in successful prayer and, secondly, that our revelation came from Toronto. The success of our prayers had a simple foundation. We regarded it as "Error"—our name for Evil—to believe the evidence of our senses and if we had influenza or consumption, or had lost our money or were unemployed, we denied the reality of these things, saying that since God could not have made them they therefore did not exist. It was exhilarating to look at our congregation and to know that what the vulgar would call miracles were performed among us, almost as a matter of routine, every day. Not very big miracles, perhaps; but up in London and out in Toronto, we knew that deafness and blindness, cancer and insanity, the great scourges, were constantly vanishing before the prayers of the more advanced Purifiers.

"What!" said my schoolmaster, an Irishman with eyes like broken glass and a sniff of irritability in the bristles of his nose. "What! Do you have the impudence to tell me that if you fell off the top floor of this building and smashed your head in, you would say you hadn't fallen and were not injured?"

I was a small boy and very afraid of everybody, but not when it was a question of my religion. I was used to the kind of conundrum the Irishman had set. It was useless to argue, though our religion had already developed an interesting casuistry.

"I *would* say so," I replied with coldness and some vanity. "And my head would not be smashed."

"You would not say so," answered the Irishman. "You would not say so." His eyes sparkled with pure pleasure. "You'd be dead."

The boys laughed, but they looked at me with admiration.

Then I do not know how or why, I began to see a difficulty. Without warning and as if I had gone into my bedroom at night and had found a gross ape seated in my bed and thereafter following me about with his grunts and his fleas and a look, relentless and ancient, scored on his brown face, I was faced with the problem which prowls at the centre of all religious faith. I was faced by the difficulty of the origin of evil. Evil was an illusion, we were taught. But even illusions have an origin. The Purifiers denied this.

I consulted my uncle. Trade was bad at the time and this made his faith abrupt. He frowned as I spoke.

"When did you brush your coat last?" he said. "You're getting slovenly about your appearance. If you spent more time studying books"—that is to say, the Purification literature—"and less with your hands in your pockets and playing about with boats on the river, you wouldn't be letting Error in."

All dogmas have their jargon; my uncle as a business man loved the trade terms of the Purification. "Don't let Error in," was a favorite one. The whole point about the Purification, he said, was that it was scientific and therefore exact; in consequence it was sheer weakness to admit discussion. Indeed, betrayal. He unpinched his pince-nez, stirred his tea and indicated I must submit or change the subject. Preferably the latter. I saw, to my alarm, that my arguments had defeated my uncle. Faith and doubt pulled like strings round my throat.

"You don't mean to say you don't believe that what our Lord said was true?" my aunt asked nervously, following me out of the room. "Your uncle does, dear."

I could not answer. I went out of the house and down the main street to the river where the punts were stuck like insects in the summery flash of the reach. Life was a dream, I thought; no, a nightmare, for the ape was beside me.

I was still in this state, half sulking and half exalted, when Mr. Hubert Timberlake came to the town. He was one of the important people from the headquarters of our Church and he had come to give an address on the Purification at the Corn Exchange. Posters announcing this were everywhere. Mr. Timberlake was to spend Sunday afternoon with us. It was unbelievable that a man so eminent would actually sit in our dining-room, use our knives and forks, and eat our food. Every imperfection in our home and our characters would jump out at him. The Truth had been revealed to man with scientific accuracy—an accuracy we could all test by experiment—and the future course of human development on earth was laid down, finally. And here in Mr. Timberlake was a man who had not merely performed many miracles—even, it was said with proper reserve, having twice raised the dead—but who had actually been to Toronto, our headquarters, where this great and revolutionary revelation had first been given.

"This is my nephew," my uncle said, introducing me. "He lives with us. He thinks he thinks, Mr. Timberlake, but I tell him he only thinks he does. Ha, ha." My uncle was a humorous man when he was with the great. "He's always on the river," my uncle continued. "I tell him he's got water on the brain. I've been telling Mr. Timberlake about you, my boy."

A hand as soft as the best quality chamois leather took mine. I saw a wide upright man in a double-breasted navy blue suit. He had a pink square head with very small ears and one of those torpid, enamelled smiles which were said by our enemies to be too common in our sect.

"Why, isn't that just fine?" said Mr. Timberlake who, owing to his contacts with Toronto, spoke with an American accent. "What say we tell your uncle it's funny he thinks he's funny."

The eyes of Mr. Timberlake were direct and colourless. He had the look of a retired merchant captain who had become decontaminated from the sea and had reformed and made money. His defence of me had made me his at once. My doubts vanished. Whatever Mr. Timberlake believed must be true and as I listened to him at lunch, I thought there could be no finer life than his.

"I expect Mr. Timberlake's tired after his address," said my aunt.

"Tired?" exclaimed my uncle, brilliant with indignation. "How can Mr. Timberlake be tired? Don't let Error in!"

For in our faith the merely inconvenient was just as illusory as a great catastrophe would have been, if you wished to be strict, and Mr. Timberlake's presence made us very strict.

I noticed then that, after their broad smiles, Mr. Timberlake's lips had the habit of setting into a long depressed sarcastic curve.

"I guess," he drawled, "I guess the Almighty must have been tired sometimes, for it says He relaxed on the seventh day. Say, do you know what I'd like to do this afternoon," he said, turning to me. "While your uncle and aunt are sleeping off this meal let's you and me go on the river and get water on the brain. I'll show you how to punt."

Mr. Timberlake, I saw to my disappointment, was out to show he understood the young. I saw he was planning a "quiet talk" with me about my problems.

"There are too many people on the river on Sundays," said my uncle uneasily.

"Oh, I like a crowd," said Mr. Timberlake, giving my uncle a tough look. "This is the day of rest, you know." He had had my uncle gobbling up every bit of gossip from the sacred city of Toronto all the morning.

My uncle and aunt were incredulous that a man like Mr. Timberlake should go out among the blazers and gramophones of the river on a Sunday afternoon. In any other member of our Church they would have thought this sinful.

"Waal, what say?" said Mr. Timberlake. I could only murmur.

"That's fixed," said Mr. Timberlake. And on came the smile as simple, vivid and unanswerable as the smile on an advertisement. "Isn't that just fine!"

Mr. Timberlake went upstairs to wash his hands. My uncle was deeply offended and shocked, but he could say nothing. He unpinched his glasses.

"A very wonderful man," he said. "So human," he apologized.

"My boy," my uncle said. "This is going to be an experience for you. Hubert Timberlake was making a thousand a year in the insurance business ten years ago. Then he heard of the Purification. He threw everything up, just like that. He gave up his job and took up the work. It was a struggle, he told me so himself this morning. 'Many's the time,' he said to me this morning, 'when I wondered where my next meal was coming from.' But the way was shown. He came down from Worcester to London and in two years he was making fifteen hundred a year out of his practice."

To heal the sick by prayer according to the tenets of the Church of the Last Purification was Mr. Timberlake's profession.

My uncle lowered his eyes. With his glasses off the lids were small and uneasy. He lowered his voice too.

"I have told him about your little trouble," my uncle said quietly, with emotion. I was burned with shame. My uncle looked up and stuck out his chin confidently.

"He just smiled," my uncle said. "That's all."

Then we waited for Mr. Timberlake to come down.

I put on white flannels and soon I was walking down to the river with Mr. Timberlake. I felt that I was going with him under false pretences; for he would begin explaining to me the origin of evil and I would have to pretend politely that he was converting me when, already, at the first sight of him, I had believed. A stone bridge, whose two arches were like an owlish pair of eyes gazing up the reach, was close to the landing-stage. I thought what a pity it was the flannelled men and the sunburned girls there did not know I was getting a ticket for *the* Mr. Timberlake who had been speaking in the town that very morning. I looked round for him and when I saw him I was a little startled. He was standing at the edge of the water looking at it with an expression of empty incomprehension. Among the white crowds his air of brisk efficiency had dulled. He looked middle-aged, out of place and insignificant. But the smile switched on when he saw me.

"Ready?" he called. "Fine!"

I had the feeling that inside him there must be a gramophone record going round and round, stopping at that word.

He stepped into the punt and took charge.

"Now I just want you to paddle us over to the far bank," he said, "and then I'll show you how to punt."

Everything Mr. Timberlake said still seemed unreal to me. The fact that he was sitting in a punt, of all commonplace material things, was incredible. That he should propose to pole us up the river was terrifying. Suppose he fell into the river? At once I checked the thought. A leader of our Church under the direct guidance of God could not possibly fall into a river.

The stream is wide and deep in this reach, but on the southern bank there is a manageable depth and a hard bottom. Over the clay banks the willows hang, making their basket-work print of sun and shadow on the water, while under the gliding boats lie cloudy, chloride caverns. The hoop-like branches of the trees bend down until their tips touch the water like fingers making musical sounds. Ahead in midstream, on a day sunny as this one was, there is a path of strong light which is hard to look at unless you half close your eyes, and down this path on the crowded Sundays go the launches with their parasols and their pennants; and also the rowing boats with their beetle-leg oars, which seem to dig the sunlight out of the water as they rise. Upstream one goes, on and on between the gardens and then between fields kept for grazing. On the afternoon when Mr. Timberlake and I went out to settle the question of the origin of evil, the meadows were packed densely with buttercups.

"Now," said Mr. Timberlake decisively when I had paddled to the other side. "Now I'll take her."

He got over the seat into the well at the stern.

"I'll just get you clear of the trees," I said.

"Give me the pole," said Mr. Timberlake, standing up on the little platform and making a squeak with his boots as he did so. "Thank you, sir. I haven't done this for eighteen years but I can tell you, brother, in those days I was considered some poler."

He looked around and let the pole slide down through his hands. Then he gave the first difficult push. The punt rocked pleasantly and we moved forward. I sat facing him, paddle in hand, to check any inward drift of the punt.

"How's that, you guys?" said Mr. Timberlake, looking round at our eddies and drawing in the pole. The delightful water swished down it.

"Fine," I said. Deferentially I had caught the word.

He went on to his second and his third strokes, taking too much water on his sleeve, perhaps, and uncertain in his steering, which I corrected, but he was doing well.

"It comes back to me," he said. "How am I doing?"

"Just keep her out from the trees," I said.

"The trees?" he said.

"The willows," I said.

"I'll do it now," he said. "How's that? Not quite enough? Well, how's this?"

"Another one," I said. "The current runs strong this side."

"What? More trees?" he said. He was getting hot.

"We can shoot out past them," I said. "I'll ease over with the paddle."

Mr. Timberlake did not like this suggestion.

"No, don't do that. I can manage it," he said. I did not want to offend one of the leaders of our Church, so I put the paddle down; but I felt I ought to have taken him farther along away from the irritation of the trees.

"Of course," I said. "We could go under them. It might be nice."

"I think," said Mr. Timberlake, "that would be a very good idea."

He lunged hard on the pole and took us towards the next archway of willow branches.

"We may have to duck a bit, that's all," I said.

"Oh, I can push the branches up," said Mr. Timberlake.

"It is better to duck," I said.

We were gliding now quickly towards the arch, in fact I was already under it.

"I think I should duck," I said. "Just bend down for this one."

"What makes the trees lean over the water like this?" asked Mr. Timberlake. "Weeping willows—I'll give you a thought there. Now Error likes to make us dwell on sorrow. Why not call them *laughing* willows?" discoursed Mr. Timberlake as the branch passed over my head.

"Duck," I said.

"Where? I don't see them," said Mr. Timberlake turning round.

"No, your head," I said. "The branch," I called.

"Oh, the branch. This one?" said Mr. Timberlake, finding a

branch just against his chest, and he put out a hand to lift it. It is not easy to lift a willow branch and Mr. Timberlake was surprised. He stepped back as it gently and firmly leaned against him. He leaned back and pushed from his feet. And he pushed too far. The boat went on, I saw Mr. Timberlake's boots leave the stern as he took an unthoughtful step backwards. He made a last-minute grasp at a stronger and higher branch, and then, there he hung a yard above the water, round as a blue damson that is ripe and ready, waiting only for a touch to make it fall. Too late with the paddle and shot ahead by the force of his thrust, I could not save him.

For a full minute I did not believe what I saw; indeed our religion taught us never to believe what we saw. Unbelieving I could not move. I gaped. The impossible had happened. Only a miracle, I found myself saying, could save him.

What was the most striking was the silence of Mr. Timberlake as he hung from the tree. I was lost between gazing at him and trying to get the punt out of the small branches of the tree. By the time I had got the punt out there were several yards of water between us and the soles of his boots were very near the water as the branch bent under his weight. Boats were passing at the time but no one seemed to notice us. I was glad about this. This was a private agony. A double chin had appeared on the face of Mr. Timberlake and his head was squeezed between his shoulders and his hanging arms. I saw him blink and look up at the sky. His eyelids were pale like a chicken's. He was tidy and dignified as he hung there, the hat was not displaced and the top button of his coat was done up. He had a blue silk handkerchief in his breast pocket. So unperturbed and genteel he seemed that as the tips of his shoes came nearer and nearer to the water, I became alarmed. He could perform what are called miracles. He would be thinking at this moment that only in an erroneous and illusory sense was he hanging from the branch of the tree over six feet of water. He was probably praying one of the closely reasoned prayers of our faith which were more like conversations with Euclid than appeals to God. The calm of his face suggested this. Was he, I asked myself, within sight of the main road, the town Recreation Ground and the landing-stage crowded with people, was he about to re-enact a well-known miracle? I hoped that he was not. I prayed that he was not. I prayed with all my will that Mr. Timberlake would not walk upon the water. It was my prayer and not his that was answered.

I saw the shoes dip, water rise above his ankles and up his socks. He tried to move his grip now to a yet higher branch—he did not succeed—and in making this effort his coat and waistcoat rose and parted from his trousers. One seam of shirt with its pant-loops and brace-taps broke like a crack across the middle of Mr. Timberlake. It was like a fatal flaw in a statue, an earthquake crack which made the monumental mortal. The last Greeks must have felt as I felt then, when they saw a crack across the middle of some statue of Apollo. It was at this moment I realized that the final revelation about man and society on earth had come to nobody and that Mr. Timberlake knew nothing at all about the origin of evil.

All this takes long to describe, but it happened in a few seconds as I paddled towards him. I was too late to get his feet on the boat and the only thing to do was to let him sink until his hands were nearer the level of the punt and then to get him to change handholds. Then I would paddle him ashore. I did this. Amputated by the water, first a torso, then a bust, then a mere head and shoulders, Mr. Timberlake, I noticed, looked sad and lonely as he sank. He was a declining dogma. As the water lapped his collar—for he hesitated to let go of the branch to hold the punt—I saw a small triangle of deprecation and pathos between his nose and the corners of his mouth. The head resting on the platter of water had the sneer of calamity on it, such as one sees in the pictures of a beheaded saint.

"Hold on to the punt, Mr. Timberlake," I said urgently. "Hold on to the punt."

He did so.

"Push from behind," he directed in a dry businesslike voice. They were his first words. I obeyed him. Carefully I paddled him towards the bank. He turned and, with a splash, climbed ashore. There he stood, raising his arms and looking at the water running down his swollen suit and making a puddle at his feet.

"Say," said Mr. Timberlake coldly, "we let some Error in that time."

How much he must have hated our family.

"I am sorry, Mr. Timberlake," I said. "I am most awfully sorry. I should have paddled. It was my fault. I'll get you home at once.

Let me wring out your coat and waistcoat. You'll catch your death . . ."

I stopped. I had nearly blasphemed. I had nearly suggested that Mr. Timberlake had fallen into the water and that to a man of his age that might be dangerous.

Mr. Timberlake corrected me. His voice was impersonal, addressing the laws of human existence, rather than myself.

"If God made water it would be ridiculous to suggest He made it capable of harming His creatures. Wouldn't it?"

"Yes," I murmured hypocritically.

"O.K.," said Mr. Timberlake. "Let's go."

"I'll soon get you across," I said.

"No," he said. "I mean let's go on. We're not going to let a little thing like this spoil a beautiful afternoon. Where were we going? You spoke of a pretty landing-place farther on. Let's go there."

"But I must take you home. You can't sit there soaked to the skin. It will spoil your clothes."

"Now, now," said Mr. Timberlake. "Do as I say. Go on."

There was nothing to be done with him. I held the punt into the bank and he stepped in. He sat like a bursting and sodden bolster in front of me while I paddled. We had lost the pole of course.

For a long time I could hardly look at Mr. Timberlake. He was taking the line that nothing had happened and this put me at a disadvantage. I knew something considerable had happened. That glaze, which so many of the members of our sect had on their faces and persons, their minds and manners, had been washed off. There was no gleam for me from Mr. Timberlake.

"What's the house over there?" he asked. He was making conversation. I had steered into the middle of the river to get him into the strong sun. I saw steam rise from him.

I took courage and studied him. He was a man, I realized, in poor physical condition, unexercised and sedentary. Now the gleam had left him one saw the veined empurpled skin of the stoutish man with a poor heart. I remember he had said at lunch:

"A young woman I know said, 'Isn't it wonderful. I can walk thirty miles a day without being in the least tired.' I said, 'I don't see that bodily indulgence is anything a member of the Church of the Last Purification should boast about.'"

Yes, there was something flaccid, passive and slack about Mr. Timberlake. Bunched in swollen clothes, he refused to take them off. It occurred to me, as he looked with boredom at the water, the passing boats and the country, that he had not been in the country before. That it was something he had agreed to do but wanted to get over quickly. He was totally uninterested. By his questions —What is that church? Are there any fish in this river? Is that a wireless or a gramophone?—I understood that Mr. Timberlake was formally acknowledging a world he did not live in. It was too interesting, too eventful a world. His spirit, inert and preoccupied, was elsewhere in an eventless and immaterial habitation. He was a dull man, duller than any man I have ever known; but his dullness was a sort of earthly deposit left by a being whose diluted mind was far away in the effervescence of metaphysical matters. There was a slightly pettish look on his face as (to himself, of course) he declared he was not wet and that he would not have a heart attack or catch pneumonia.

Mr. Timberlake spoke little. Sometimes he squeezed water out of his sleeve. He shivered a little. He watched his steam. I had planned when we set out to go up as far as the lock but now the thought of another two miles of this responsibility was too much. I pretended I wanted to go only as far as the bend which we were approaching, where one of the richest buttercup meadows was. I mentioned this to him. He turned and looked with boredom at the field. Slowly we came to the bank.

We tied up the punt and we landed.

"Fine," said Mr. Timberlake. He stood at the edge of the meadow, just as he had stood at the landing-stage—lost, stupefied, uncomprehending.

"Nice to stretch our legs," I said. I led the way into the deep flowers. So dense were the buttercups there was hardly any green. Presently I sat down. Mr. Timberlake looked at me and sat down also. Then I turned to him with a last try at persuasion. Respectability, I was sure, was his trouble.

"No one will see us," I said. "This is out of sight of the river. Take off your coat and trousers and wring them out."

Mr. Timberlake replied firmly:

"I am satisfied to remain as I am.

"What is this flower?" he asked to change the subject.

"Buttercup," I said.

"Of course," he replied.

I could do nothing with him. I lay down full length in the sun; and, observing this and thinking to please me, Mr. Timberlake did the same. He must have supposed that this was what I had come out in the boat to do. It was only human. He had come out with me, I saw, to show me that he was only human.

But as we lay there I saw the steam still rising. I had had enough.

"A bit hot," I said getting up.

He got up at once.

"Do you want to sit in the shade?" he asked politely.

"No," I said. "Would you like to?"

"No," he said. "I was thinking of you."

"Let's go back," I said. We both stood up and I let him pass in front of me. When I looked at him again I stopped dead. Mr. Timberlake was no longer a man in a navy blue suit. He was blue no longer. He was transfigured. He was yellow. He was covered with buttercup pollen, a fine yellow paste of it made by the damp, from head to foot.

"Your suit," I said.

He looked at it. He raised his thin eyebrows a little, but he did not smile or make any comment.

The man is a saint, I thought. As saintly as any of those gold-leaf figures in the churches of Sicily. Golden he sat in the punt; golden he sat for the next hour as I paddled him down the river. Golden and bored. Golden, as we landed at the town and as we walked up the street back to my uncle's house. There he refused to change his clothes or to sit by a fire. He kept an eye on the time for his train back to London. By no word did he acknowledge the disasters or the beauties of the world. If they were printed upon him, they were printed upon a husk.

Sixteen years have passed since I dropped Mr. Timberlake in the river and since the sight of his pant-loops destroyed my faith. I have not seen him since, and today I heard that he was dead. He was fifty-seven. His mother, a very old lady with whom he had lived all his life, went into his bedroom when he was getting ready for church and found him lying on the floor in his shirt-sleeves. A stiff collar with the tie half inserted was in one hand. Five minutes before, she told the doctor, she had been speaking to him.

The doctor who looked at the heavy body lying on the single bed saw a middle-aged man, wide rather than stout and with an extraordinary box-like thick-jawed face. He had got fat, my uncle told me, in later years. The heavy liver-coloured cheeks were like the chaps of a hound. Heart disease, it was plain, was the cause of the death of Mr. Timberlake. In death the face was lax, even coarse and degenerate. It was a miracle, the doctor said, that he had lived so long. Any time during the last twenty years the smallest shock might have killed him.

I thought of our afternoon on the river. I thought of him hanging from the tree. I thought of him, indifferent and golden in the meadow. I understood why he had made for himself a protective, sedentary blandness, an automatic smile, a collection of phrases. He kept them on like the coat after his ducking. And I understood why—though I had feared it all the time we were on the river—I understood why he did not talk to me about the origin of evil. He was honest. The ape was with us. The ape that merely followed me was already inside Mr. Timberlake eating out his heart.

R. D. LAING

Transcendental Experience

We are living in an age in which the ground is shifting and the foundations are shaking. I cannot answer for other times and places. Perhaps it has always been so. We know it is true today.

In these circumstances, we have every reason to be insecure. When the ultimate basis of our world is in question, we run to different holes in the ground, we scurry into roles, statuses, identities, interpersonal relations. We attempt to live in castles that can only be in the air because there is no firm ground in the social cosmos on which to build. We are all witnesses to this state of affairs. Each sometimes sees the same fragment of the whole situation differently; often our concern is with different presentations of the original catastrophe.

. . . [Here] I wish to relate the transcendental experiences that *sometimes* break through in psychosis, to those experiences of the divine that are the living fount of all religion.

. . . I [have previously] outlined the way in which some psychiatrists are beginning to dissolve their clinical-medical categories of understanding madness. If we can begin to understand sanity and madness in existential social terms, we shall be more able to see clearly the extent to which we all confront common problems and share common dilemmas.

Experience may be judged as invalidly mad or as validly mystical. The distinction is not easy. In either case, from a social point of view, such judgements characterize different forms of behavior, regarded in our society as deviant. People behave in such ways because their experience of themselves is different. It is on the existential meaning of such unusual experience that I wish to focus.

Psychotic experience goes beyond the horizons of our common, that is, our communal, sense.

What regions of experience does this lead to? It entails a loss of the usual foundations of the "sense" of the world that we share with one another. Old purposes no longer seem viable; old meanings are senseless; the distinctions between imagination, dream, external perceptions often seem no longer to apply in the old way. External events may seem magically conjured up. Dreams may seem to be direct communications from others; imagination may seem to be objective reality.

But most radical of all, the very ontological foundations are shaken. The being of phenomena shifts and the phenomenon of being may no longer present itself to us as before. There are no supports, nothing to cling to, except perhaps some fragments from the wreck, a few memories, names, sounds, one or two objects, that retain a link with a world long lost. This void may not be empty. It may be peopled by visions and voices, ghosts, strange shapes and apparitions. No one who has not experienced how insubstantial the pageant of external reality can be, how it may fade, can fully realize the sublime and grotesque presences that can replace it, or that can exist alongside it.

When a person goes mad, a profound transposition of his place in relation to all domains of being occurs. His center of experience moves from ego to self. Mundane time becomes merely anecdotal, only the eternal matters. The madman is, however, confused. He muddles ego with self, inner with outer, natural and supernatural. Nevertheless, he can often be to us, even through his profound wretchedness and disintegration, the heirophant of the sacred. An exile from the scene of being as we know it, he is an alien, a stranger signaling to us from the void in which he is foundering, a void which may be peopled by presences that we do not even dream of. They used to be called demons and spirits, and they used to be known and named. He has lost his sense of self, his feelings, his place in the world as we know it. He tells us he is dead. But we are distracted from our cosy security by this mad ghost who haunts us with his visions and voices which seem so senseless and of which we feel impelled to rid him, cleanse him, cure him.

Madness need not be all breakdown. It may also be breakthrough. It is potentially liberation and renewal as well as enslavement and existential death.

There are now a growing number of accounts by people who have been through the experience of madness.

The following is part of one of the earlier contemporary accounts, as recorded by Karl Jaspers in his *General Psychopathology*.[1]

> I believe I caused the illness myself. In my attempt to penetrate the other world I met its natural guardians, the embodiment of my own weaknesses and faults. I first thought these demons were lowly inhabitants of the other world who could play me like a ball because I went into these regions unprepared and lost my way. Later I thought they were split-off parts of my own mind (passions) which existed near me in free space and thrived on my feelings. I believed everyone else had these too but did not perceive them, thanks to the protective successful deceit of the feeling of personal existence. I thought the latter was an artifact of memory, thought-complexes, etc., a doll that was nice enough to look at from outside but nothing real inside it.
>
> In my case the personal self had grown porous because of my dimmed consciousness. Through it I wanted to bring myself closer to the higher sources of life. I should have prepared myself for this over a long period by invoking in me a higher, impersonal self, since "nectar" is not for mortal lips. It acted destructively on the animal-human self, split it up into its parts. These gradually disintegrated, the doll was really broken and the body damaged. I had forced untimely access to the "source of life," the curse of the "gods" descended on me. I recognized too late that murky elements had taken a hand. I got to know them after they had already too much power. There was no way back. I now had the world of spirits I had wanted to see. The demons came up from the abyss, as guardian Cerberi, denying admission to the unauthorized. I decided to take up the life-and-death struggle. This meant for me in the end a decision to die, since I had to put aside everything that maintained the enemy, but this was also everything that maintained life. I wanted to enter death without going mad and stood before the Sphinx: Either thou into the abyss or I!

[1] Manchester: Manchester University Press, 1962, pages 417–18.

Then came illumination. I fasted and so penetrated into the true nature of my seducers. They were pimps and deceivers of my dear personal self which seemed as much a thing of naught as they. A larger and more comprehensive self emerged and I could abandon the previous personality with its entire entourage. I saw this earlier personality could never enter transcendental realms. I felt as a result a terrible pain, like an annihilating blow, but I was rescued, the demons shriveled, vanished and perished. A new life began for me and from now on I felt different from other people. A self that consisted of conventional lies, shams, self-deceptions, memory images, a self just like that of other people, grew in me again but behind and above it stood a greater and more comprehensive self which impressed me with something of what is eternal, unchanging, immortal and inviolable and which ever since that time has been my protector and refuge. I believe it would be good for many if they were acquainted with such a higher self and that there are people who have attained this goal in fact by kinder means.

Jaspers comments:

Such self-interpretations are obviously made under the influence of delusion-like tendencies and deep psychic forces. They originate from profound experiences and the wealth of such schizophrenic experience calls on the observer as well as on the reflective patient not to take all this merely as a chaotic jumble of contents. Mind and spirit are present in the morbid psychic life as well as in the healthy. But interpretations of this sort must be divested of any casual importance. All they can do is to throw light on content and bring it into some sort of context.

This patient has described, with a lucidity I could not improve upon, a very ancient quest, with its pitfalls and dangers. Jaspers still speaks of this experience as morbid and tends to discount the patient's own construction. Yet both the experience and the construction may be valid in their own terms.

Certain *transcendental experiences* seem to me to be the original wellspring of all religions. Some psychotic people have transcendental experiences. Often (to the best of their recollection) they have never had such experiences before, and frequently they will never have them again. I am not saying, however, that psychotic experience necessarily contains this element more manifestly than sane experience.

We experience in different modes. We perceive external realities, we dream, imagine, have semiconscious reveries. Some people have visions, hallucinations, experience faces transfigured, see auras and so on. Most people most of the time experience themselves and others in one or another way that I shall call *egoic*. That is, centrally or peripherally, they experience the world and themselves in terms of a consistent identity, a me-here over against a you-there, within a framework of certain ground structures of space and time shared with other members of their society.

This identity-anchored, space-and-time-bound experience has been studied philosophically by Kant, and later by the phenomenologists, e.g. Husserl, Merleau-Ponty. Its historical and ontological relativity should be fully realized by any contemporary student of the human scene. Its cultural, socioeconomic relativity has become a commonplace among anthropologists and a platitude to the Marxists and neo-Marxists. And yet, with the consensual and interpersonal confirmation it offers, it gives us a sense of ontological security whose validity we *experience* as self-validating, although metaphysically-historically-ontologically-socioeconomically-culturally we know its apparent absolute validity as an illusion.

In fact all religious and all existential philosophies have agreed that such *egoic experience* is a preliminary illusion, a veil, a film of *maya*—a dream to Heraclitus, and to Lao Tzu, the fundamental illusion of all Buddhism, a state of sleep, of death, of socially accepted madness, a womb state to which one has to die, from which one has to be born.

The person going through ego-loss or transcendental experiences may or may not become in different ways confused. Then he might legitimately be regarded as mad. But to be mad is not necessarily to be ill, notwithstanding that in our culture the two categories have become confused. It is assumed that if a person is mad (whatever that means) then *ipso facto* he is ill (whatever that means). The experience that a person may be absorbed in, while to others he appears simply ill-mad, may be for him veritable manna from heaven. The person's whole life may be changed, but it is difficult not to doubt the validity of such vision. Also, not everyone comes back to us again.

Are these experiences simply the effulgence of a pathological process or of a particular alienation? I do not think they are.

In certain cases, a man blind from birth may have an operation performed which gives him his sight. The result—frequently misery, confusion, disorientation. The light that illumines the madman is an unearthly light. It is not always a distorted refraction of his mundane life situation. He may be irradiated by light from other worlds. It may burn him out.

This "other" world is not essentially a battlefield wherein psychological forces, derived or diverted, displaced or sublimated from their original object-cathexes, are engaged in an illusionary fight —although such forces may obscure these realities, just as they may obscure so-called external realities. When Ivan in *The Brothers Karamazov* says, "If God does not exist, everything is permissible," he is *not* saying, "If my super-ego, in projected form, can be abolished, I can do anything with a good conscience." He *is* saying, "If there is *only* my conscience, then there is no ultimate validity for my will."

Among physicians and priests there should be some who are guides, who can educt the person from this world and induct him to the other. To guide him in it and to lead him back again.

One enters the other world by breaking a shell: or through a door: through a partition: the curtains part or rise: a veil is lifted. Seven veils: seven seals, seven heavens.

The "ego" is the instrument for living in *this* world. If the "ego" is broken up or destroyed (by the insurmountable contradictions of certain life situations, by toxins, chemical changes, etc.), then the person may be exposed to other worlds, "real" in different ways from the more familiar territory of dreams, imagination, perception or fantasy.

The world that one enters, one's capacity to experience it, seem to be partly conditional on the state of one's "ego."

Our time has been distinguished, more than by anything else, by a drive to control the external world, and by an almost total forgetfulness of the internal world. If one estimates human evolution from the point of view of knowledge of the external world, then we are in many respects progressing.

If our estimate is from the point of view of the internal world and of oneness of internal and external, then the judgement must be very different.

Phenomenologically the terms "internal" and "external" have little validity. But in this whole realm one is reduced to mere verbal expedients—words are simply the finger pointing at the moon. One of the difficulties of talking in the present day of these matters is that the very existence of inner realities is now called in question.

By "inner" I mean our way of seeing the external world and all those realities that have no "external," "objective" presence—imagination, dreams, fantasies, trances, the realities of contemplative and meditative states, realities of which modern man, for the most part, has not the slightest direct awareness.

For example, nowhere in the Bible is there any argument about the *existence* of gods, demons, angels. People did not first "believe in" God: They experienced His presence, as was true of other spiritual agencies. The question was not whether God existed, but whether this particular God was the greatest god of all, or the only God; and what was the relation of the various spiritual agencies to each other. Today, there is a public debate, not as to the trustworthiness of God, the particular place in the spiritual hierarchy of different spirits, etc., but whether God or such spirits *even exist* or ever have existed.

Sanity today appears to rest very largely on a capacity to adapt to the external world—the interpersonal world, and the realm of human collectivities.

As this external human world is almost completely and totally estranged from the inner, any personal direct awareness of the inner world already has grave risks.

But since society, without knowing it, is *starving* for the inner, the demands on people to evoke its presence in a "safe" way, in a way that need not be taken seriously, etc., is tremendous—while the ambivalence is equally intense. Small wonder that the list of artists, in say the last 150 years, who have become shipwrecked on these reefs is so long—Hölderlin, John Clare, Rimbaud, Van Gogh, Nietzsche, Antonin Artaud. . . .

Those who survived have had exceptional qualities—a capacity for secrecy, slyness, cunning—a thoroughly realistic appraisal of the risks they run, not only from the spiritual realms they frequent, but from the hatred of their fellows for anyone engaged in this pursuit.

Let us *cure* them. The poet who mistakes a real woman for his

Muse and acts accordingly. . . . The young man who sets off in a yacht in search of God. . . .

The outer divorced from any illumination from the inner is in a state of darkness. We are in an age of darkness. The state of outer darkness is a state of sin—i.e., alienation or estrangement from the *inner light*.[2] Certain actions lead to greater estrangement; certain others help one not to be so far removed. The former used to be called sinful.

The ways of losing one's way are legion. Madness is certainly not the least unambiguous. The countermadness of Kraepelinian psychiatry is the exact counterpart of "official" psychosis. Literally, and absolutely seriously, it is as *mad*, if by madness we mean any radical estrangement from the totality of what is the case. Remember Kierkegaard's objective madness.

As we experience the world, so we act. We conduct ourselves in the light of our view of what is the case and what is not the case. That is, each person is a more or less naïve ontologist. Each person has views of what is and what is not.

There is no doubt, it seems to me, that there have been profound changes in the experience of man in the last thousand years. In some ways this is more evident than changes in the patterns of his behavior. There is everything to suggest that man experienced God. Faith was never a matter of believing He existed, but of trusting, in the presence that was experienced and known to exist as a self-validating datum. It seems likely that far more people in our time experience neither the presence of God, nor the presence of his absence, but the absence of his presence.

We require a history of phenomena, not simply more phenomena of history.

As it is, the secular psychotherapist is often in the role of the blind leading the half-blind.

The fountain has not played itself out, the frame still shines, the river still flows, the spring still bubbles forth, the light has not faded. But between *us* and It, there is a veil which is more like fifty feet of solid concrete. *Deus absconditus*. Or we have absconded.

Already everything in our time is directed to categorizing and segregating this reality from objective facts. This is precisely the

[2] M. Eliade, *The Two and the One* (London: Harvill Press, 1965), especially Chapter I.

concrete wall. Intellectually, emotionally, interpersonally, organizationally, intuitively, theoretically, we have to blast our way through the solid wall, even if at the risk of chaos, madness and death. For from *this* side of the wall, this is the risk. There are no assurances, no guarantees.

Many people are prepared to have faith in the sense of scientifically indefensible belief in an untested hypothesis. Few have trust enough to test it. Many people make-believe what they experience. Few are made to believe by their experience. Paul of Tarsus was picked up by the scuff of the neck, thrown to the ground and blinded for three days. This direct experience was self-validating.

We live in a secular world. To adapt to this world the child abdicates its ecstasy. ("*L'enfant abdique son extase*": Malarmé.) Having lost our experience of the spirit, we are expected to have faith. But this faith comes to be a belief in a reality which is not evident. There is a prophecy in Amos that a time will come when there will be a famine in the land, "not a famine for bread, nor a thirst for water, but of *hearing* the words of the Lord." That time has now come to pass. It is the present age.

From the alienated starting point of our pseudosanity, everything is equivocal. Our sanity is not "true" sanity. Their madness is not "true" madness. The madness of our patients is an artifact of the destruction wreaked on them by us and by them on themselves. Let no one suppose that we meet "true" madness any more than that we are truly sane. The madness that we encounter in "patients" is a gross travesty, a mockery, a grotesque caricature of what the natural healing of that estranged integration we call sanity might be. True sanity entails in one way or another the dissolution of the normal ego, that false self competently adjusted to our alienated social reality; the emergence of the "inner" archetypal mediators of divine power, and through this death a rebirth, and the eventual re-establishment of a new kind of ego-functioning, the ego now being the servant of the divine, no longer its betrayer.

THOMAS WOLFE

God's Lonely Man

My life, more than that of anyone I know, has been spent in solitude and wandering. Why this is true, or how it happened, I cannot say; yet it is so. From my fifteenth year—save for a single interval—I have lived about as solitary a life as a modern man can have. I mean by this that the number of hours, days, months, and years that I have spent alone has been immense and extraordinary. I propose, therefore, to describe the experience of human loneliness exactly as I have known it.

The reason that impels me to do this is not that I think my knowledge of loneliness different in kind from that of other men. Quite the contrary. The whole conviction of my life now rests upon the belief that loneliness, far from being a rare and curious phenomenon, peculiar to myself and to a few other solitary men, is the central and inevitable fact of human existence. When we examine the moments, acts, and statements of all kinds of people —not only the grief and ecstasy of the greatest poets, but also the huge unhappiness of the average soul, as evidenced by the innumerable strident words of abuse, hatred, contempt, mistrust, and scorn that forever grate upon our ears as the manswarm passes us in the streets—we find, I think, that they are all suffering from the same thing. The final cause of their complaint is loneliness.

But if my experience of loneliness has not been different in kind from that of other men, I suspect it has been sharper in intensity. This gives me the best authority in the world to write of this, our general complaint, for I believe I know more about it than anyone of my generation. In saying this, I am merely stating a fact as I see it, though I realize that it may sound like arrogance or vanity. But before anyone jumps to that conclusion, let him consider how strange it would be to meet with arrogance in one who has lived alone as much as I. The surest cure for vanity is loneliness. For, more than other men, we who dwell in the heart of solitude are always the victims of self-doubt. Forever and forever in our loneliness, shameful feelings of inferiority will rise up suddenly to overwhelm us in a poisonous flood of horror, disbelief, and desolation, to sicken and corrupt our health and confidence, to spread pollution at the very root of strong, exultant joy. And the eternal paradox of it is that if a man is to know the triumphant labor of creation, he must for long periods resign himself to loneliness, and suffer loneliness to rob him of the health, the confidence, the belief and joy which are essential to creative work.

To live alone as I have lived, a man should have the confidence of God, the tranquil faith of a monastic saint, the stern impregnability of Gibraltar. Lacking these, there are times when anything, everything, all or nothing, the most trivial incidents, the most casual words, can in an instant strip me of my armor, palsy my hand, constrict my heart with frozen horror, and fill my bowels with the gray substance of shuddering impotence. Sometimes it is nothing but a shadow passing on the sun; sometimes nothing but the torrid milky light of August, or the naked, sprawling ugliness and squalid decencies of streets in Brooklyn fading in the weary vistas of that milky light and evoking the intolerable misery of countless drab and nameless lives. Sometimes it is just the barren horror of raw concrete, or the heat blazing on a million beetles of machinery darting through the torrid streets, or the cindered weariness of parking spaces, or the slamming smash and racket of the El, or the driven manswarm of the earth, thrusting on forever in exacerbated fury, going nowhere in a hurry.

Again, it may be just a phrase, a look, a gesture. It may be the cold, disdainful inclination of the head with which a precious, kept, exquisite princeling of Park Avenue acknowledges an introduction, as if to say: "You are nothing." Or it may be a sneering reference and dismissal by a critic in a high-class weekly magazine. Or a letter from a woman saying I am lost and ruined, my talent vanished, all my efforts false and worthless—since I have forsaken the truth, vision, and reality which are so beautifully her own.

And sometimes it is less than these—nothing I can touch or see or hear or definitely remember. It may be so vague as to be a kind of hideous weather of the soul, subtly compounded of all the hunger, fury, and impossible desire my life has ever known. Or, again, it may be a half-forgotten memory of the cold wintry red of waning Sunday afternoons in Cambridge, and of a pallid, sensitive, æsthetic face that held me once in earnest discourse on such a Sunday afternoon in Cambridge, telling me that all my youthful hopes were pitiful delusions and that all my life would come to naught, and the red and waning light of March was reflected on the pallid face with a desolate impotence that instantly quenched all the young ardors of my blood.

Beneath the evocations of these lights and weathers, and the cold, disdainful words of precious, sneering, and contemptuous people, all of the joy and singing of the day goes out like an extinguished candle, hope seems lost to me forever, and every truth that I have ever found and known seems false. At such a time the lonely man will feel that all the evidence of his own senses has betrayed him, and that nothing really lives and moves on earth but creatures of the death-in-life—those of the cold, constricted heart and the sterile loins, who exist forever in the red waning light of March and Sunday afternoon.

All this hideous doubt, despair, and dark confusion of the soul a lonely man must know, for he is united to no image save that which he creates himself, he is bolstered by no other knowledge save that which he can gather for himself with the vision of his own eyes and brain. He is sustained and cheered and aided by no party, he is given comfort by no creed, he has no faith in him except his own. And often that faith deserts him, leaving him shaken and filled with impotence. And then it seems to him that his life has come to nothing, that he is ruined, lost, and broken past redemption, and that morning—bright, shining morning, with its promise of new beginnings—will never come upon the earth again as it did once.

He knows that dark time is flowing by him like a river. The huge, dark wall of loneliness is around him now. It encloses and presses in upon him, and he cannot escape. And the cancerous plant of memory is feeding at his entrails, recalling hundreds of forgotten faces and ten thousand vanished days, until all life seems as strange and insubstantial as a dream. Time flows by him like a river, and he waits in his little room like a creature held captive by an evil spell. And he will hear, far off, the murmurous drone of the great earth, and feel that he has been forgotten, that his powers are wasting from him while the river flows, and that all his life has come to nothing. He feels that his strength is gone, his power withered, while he sits there drugged and fettered in the prison of his loneliness.

Then suddenly, one day, for no apparent reason, his faith and his belief in life will come back to him in a tidal flood. It will rise up in him with a jubilant and invincible power, bursting a window in the world's great wall and restoring everything to shapes of deathless brightness. Made miraculously whole and secure in himself, he will plunge once more into the triumphant labor of creation. All his old strength is his again: he knows what he knows, he is what he is, he has found what he has found. And he will say the truth that is in him, speak it even though the whole world deny it, affirm it though a million men cry out that it is false.

At such a moment of triumphant confidence, with this feeling in me, I dare now assert that I have known Loneliness as well as any man, and will now write of him as if he were my very brother, which he is. I will paint him for you with such fidelity to his true figure that no man who reads will ever doubt his visage when Loneliness comes to him hereafter.

The most tragic, sublime, and beautiful expression of human loneliness which I have ever read is the Book of Job; the grandest and most philosophical, Ecclesiastes. Here I must point out a fact which is so much at variance with everything I was told as a child concerning loneliness and the tragic underweft of life that, when I first discovered it, I was astounded and incredulous, doubting the overwhelming weight of evidence that had revealed it to me. But there it was, as solid as a rock, not to be shaken or denied; and as the years passed, the truth of this discovery became part of the structure of my life.

The fact is this: The lonely man, who is also the tragic man, is invariably the man who loves life dearly—which is to say, the joyful man. In these statements there is no paradox whatever. The one condition implies the other, and makes it necessary. The essence of human tragedy is in loneliness, not in conflict, no matter what the arguments of the theater may assert. And just as the great tragic writer (I say, "the tragic writer" as distinguished from "the writer of tragedies," for certain nations, the Roman and

French among them, have had no great tragic writers, for Vergil and Racine were none, but rather great writers of tragedy): just as the great tragic writer—Job, Sophocles, Dante, Milton, Swift, Dostoevski—has always been the lonely man, so has he also been the human who loved life best and had the deepest sense of joy. The real quality and substance of human joy is to be found in the works of these great tragic writers as nowhere else in all the records of man's life upon the earth. In proof of this, I can give here one conclusive illustration:

In my childhood, any mention of the Book of Job evoked instantly in my mind a long train of gloomy, gray, and unbrokenly dismal associations. This has been true, I suspect, with most of us. Such phrases as "Job's comforter," and "the patience of Job," and "the afflictions of Job," have become part of our common idiom and are used to refer to people whose woes seem uncountable and unceasing, who have suffered long and silently, and whose gloom has never been interrupted by a ray of hope or joy. All these associations had united to make for me a picture of the Book of Job that was grim, bleak, and constant in its misery. When I first read it as a child, it seemed to me that the record of Job's tribulations was relieved only by a kind of gloomy and unwilling humor— a humor not intended by the author, but supplied by my own exasperation, for my childish sense of proportion and justice was at length so put upon by this dreary tidal flood of calamities that I had to laugh in protest.

But any reader of intelligence and experience who has read that great book in his mature years will realize how false such a picture is. For the Book of Job, far from being dreary, gray, and dismal, is woven entire, more than any single piece of writing I can recall, from the sensuous, flashing, infinitely various, and gloriously palpable material of great poetry; and it wears at the heart of its tremendous chant of everlasting sorrow the exulting song of everlasting joy.

In this there is nothing strange or curious, but only what is inevitable and right. For the tragic writer knows that joy is rooted at the heart of sorrow, that ecstasy is shot through with the sudden crimson thread of pain, that the knife-thrust of intolerable desire and the wild, brief glory of possession are pierced most bitterly, at the very instant of man's greatest victory, by the premonitory sense of loss and death. So seen and so felt, the best and worst that the human heart can know are merely different aspects of the same thing, and are interwoven, both together, into the tragic web of life.

It is the sense of death and loneliness, the knowledge of the brevity of his days, and the huge impending burden of his sorrow, growing always, never lessening, that makes joy glorious, tragic, and unutterably precious to a man like Job. Beauty comes and passes, is lost the moment that we touch it, can no more be stayed or held than one can stay the flowing of a river. Out of this pain of loss, this bitter ecstasy of brief having, this fatal glory of the single moment, the tragic writer will therefore make a song for joy. That, at least, he may keep and treasure always. And his song is full of grief, because he knows that joy is fleeting, gone the instant that we have it, and that is why it is so precious, gaining its full glory from the very things that limit and destroy it.

He knows that joy gains its glory out of sorrow, bitter sorrow, and man's loneliness, and that it is haunted always with the certainty of death, dark death, which stops our tongues, our eyes, our living breath, with the twin oblivions of dust and nothingness. Therefore a man like Job will make a chant for sorrow, too, but it will still be a song for joy as well, and one more strange and beautiful than any other that man has ever sung:

> Hast thou given the horse strength? hast thou clothed his neck with thunder?
> Canst thou make him afraid as a grasshopper? the glory of his nostrils is terrible.
> He paweth in the valley, and rejoiceth in his strength: he goeth on to meet the armed men.
> He mocketh at fear, and is not affrighted; neither turneth he back from the sword.
> The quiver rattleth against him, the glittering spear and the shield.
> He swalloweth the ground with fierceness and rage; neither believeth he that it is the sound of the trumpet.
> He saith among the trumpets, Ha, ha; and he smelleth the battle afar off, the thunder of the captains, and the shouting.

That is joy—joy solemn and triumphant; stern, lonely, everlasting joy, which has in it the full depth and humility of man's wonder, his sense of glory, and his feeling of awe before the mystery of the universe. An exultant cry is torn from our lips as we read the lines about that glorious horse, and the joy we feel is wild and strange, lonely and dark like death, and grander than the delicate and lovely joy that men like Herrick and Theocritus described, great poets though they were.

Just as the Book of Job and the sermon of Ecclesiastes are, each in its own way, supreme histories of man's loneliness, so do all the books of the Old Testament, in their entirety, provide the most final and profound literature of human loneliness that the world has known. It is astonishing with what a coherent unity of spirit and belief the life of loneliness is recorded in those many books—how it finds its full expression in the chants, songs, prophecies, and chronicles of so many men, all so various, and each so individual, each revealing some new image of man's secret and most lonely heart, and all combining to produce a single image of his loneliness that is matchless in its grandeur and magnificence.

Thus, in a dozen books of the Old Testament—in Job, Ecclesiastes, and the Song of Solomon; in Psalms, Proverbs, and Isaiah; in words of praise and words of lamentation; in songs of triumph and in chants of sorrow, bondage, and despair; in boasts of pride and arrogant assertion, and in stricken confessions of humility and fear; in warning, promise, and in prophecy; in love, hate, grief, death, loss, revenge, and resignation; in wild, singing jubilation and in bitter sorrow—the lonely man has wrought out in a swelling and tremendous chorus the final vision of his life.

The total, all-contributary unity of this conception of man's loneliness in the books of the Old Testament becomes even more astonishing when we begin to read the New. For, just as the Old Testament becomes the chronicle of the life of loneliness, the gospels of the New Testament, with the same miraculous and unswerving unity, become the chronicle of the life of love. What Christ is saying always, what he never swerves from saying, what he says a thousand times and in a thousand different ways, but always with a central unity of belief, is this: "I am my Father's son, and you are my brothers." And the unity that binds us all together, that makes this earth a family, and all men brothers and the sons of God, is love.

The central purpose of Christ's life, therefore, is to destroy the life of loneliness and to establish here on earth the life of love. The evidence to support this is clear and overwhelming. It should be obvious to everyone that when Christ says: "Blessed are the poor in spirit: for theirs is the kingdom of heaven," "Blessed are they that mourn: for they shall be comforted," "Blessed are the meek: for they shall inherit the earth," "Blessed are they which do hunger and thirst after righteousness: for they shall be filled," "Blessed are the merciful: for they shall obtain mercy," and "Blessed are the pure in heart: for they shall see God"—Christ is not here extolling the qualities of humility, sorrow, meekness, righteousness, mercy, and purity as virtues sufficient in themselves, but he promises to men who have these virtues the richest reward that men were ever offered.

And what is that reward? It is a reward that promises not only the inheritance of the earth, but the kingdom of heaven as well. It tells men that they shall not live and die in loneliness, that their sorrow will not go unassuaged, their prayers unheard, their hunger and thirst unfed, their love unrequited: but that, through love, they shall destroy the walls of loneliness forever; and even if the evil and unrighteous of this earth shall grind them down into the dust, yet if they bear all things meekly and with love, they will enter into a fellowship of joy, a brotherhood of love, such as no men on earth ever knew before.

Such was the final intention of Christ's life, the purpose of his teaching. And its total import was that the life of loneliness could be destroyed forever by the life of love. Or such, at least, has been the meaning which I read into his life. For in these recent years when I have lived alone so much, and known loneliness so well, I have gone back many times and read the story of this man's words and life to see if I could find in them a meaning for myself, a way of life that would be better than the one I had. I read what he had said, not in a mood of piety or holiness, not from a sense of sin, a feeling of contrition, or because his promise of a heavenly reward meant very much to me. But I tried to read his bare words nakedly and simply, as it seems to me he must have uttered them, and as I have read the words of other men—of Homer, Donne, and Whitman, and the writer of Ecclesiastes— and if the meaning I have put upon his words seems foolish or extravagant, childishly simple or banal, mine alone or not different from what ten million other men have thought, I have only set it down here as I saw it, felt it, found it for myself, and have tried to add, subtract, and alter nothing.

And now I know that though the way and meaning of Christ's life is a far, far better way and meaning than my own, yet I can never make it mine; and I think that this is true of all the other lonely men that I have seen or known about—the nameless, voiceless, faceless atoms of this earth as well as Job and Everyman and Swift. And Christ himself, who preached the life of love, was yet as lonely as any man that ever lived. Yet I could not say that he was mistaken because he preached the life of love and fellowship, and lived and died in loneliness; nor would I dare assert his way was wrong because a billion men have since professed his way and never followed it.

I can only say that I could not make his way my own. For I have found the constant, everlasting weather of man's life to be, not love, but loneliness. Love itself is not the weather of our lives. It is the rare, the precious flower. Sometimes it is the flower that gives us life, that breaches the dark walls of all our loneliness and restores us to the fellowship of life, the family of the earth, the brotherhood of man. But sometimes love is the flower that brings us death; and from it we get pain and darkness; and the mutilations of the soul, the maddening of the brain, may be in it.

How or why or in what way the flower of love will come to us, whether with life or death, triumph or defeat, joy or madness, no man on this earth can say. But I know that at the end, forever at the end for us—the houseless, homeless, doorless, driven wanderers of life, the lonely men—there waits forever the dark visage of our comrade, Loneliness.

But the old refusals drop away, the old avowals stand—and we who were dead have risen, we who were lost are found again, and we who sold the talent, the passion, and belief of youth into the keeping of the fleshless dead, until our hearts were corrupted, our talent wasted, and our hope gone, have won our lives back bloodily, in solitude and darkness; and we know that things will be for us as they have been, and we see again, as we saw once, the image of the shining city. Far flung, and blazing into tiers of jeweled light, it burns forever in our vision as we walk the Bridge, and strong tides are bound round it, and the great ships call. And we walk the Bridge, always we walk the Bridge alone with you, stern friend, the one to whom we speak, who never failed us. Hear:

"Loneliness forever and the earth again! Dark brother and stern friend, immortal face of darkness and of night, with whom the half part of my life spent, and with whom I shall abide now till my death forever—what is there for me to fear as long as you are with me? Heroic friend, blood brother of my life, dark face—have we not gone together down a million ways, have we not coursed together the great and furious avenues of night, have we not crossed the stormy seas alone, and known strange lands, and come again to walk the continent of night and listen to the silence of the earth? Have we not been brave and glorious when we were together, friend? Have we not known triumph, joy, and glory on this earth—and will it not be again with me as it was then, if you come back to me? Come to me, brother, in the watches of the night. Come to me in the secret and most silent heart of darkness. Come to me as you always came, bringing to me again the old invincible strength, the deathless hope, the triumphant joy and confidence that will storm the earth again."

CHAPTER TWO

Inner Space: The Undiscovered Self

According to ancient legend, the Minotaur was a fearsome bull that Minos had enshrined in his artfully constructed labyrinth, from which no one had ever been able to escape. Each year Minos demanded young human sacrifices from the people of Thebes until heroic Theseus decided to stop the senseless slaughter. Slaying the bull was challenge enough for most men, but the real problem was how to get back out of the labyrinth. Fortunately the gods intervened; Ariadne showed Theseus how to trail a golden thread, which he could then follow back to safety. The myth speaks to a real concern of today's youth: how to take the dark trip into the unknown and often frightening corridors of the inner self and then come back safely.

Life for most people is a matter of adjusting—learning what to do, what not to do, when to put on different masks or play different roles. As people grow older they learn to accommodate themselves to such games, and they form their escapes such as drinking or watching television. But everyone sometimes longs to break out of his ordinary, everyday role into another larger and radically different self—somewhere above, below, inside, or outside the world of ordinary consciousness. Later chapters in this book explore some of the different means of escape (or return, as the case may be), but this chapter chronicles the initial awareness born of the realization that another self exists. This realization is typically expressed as a dying of the old self as avenues are opened to the unconscious. Because the movement toward the subrational level of existence is irrational, fantasies, dreamlike sequences of imagery, and surrealistic landscapes replace the familiar world of the daytime consciousness. Like the protagonist of "Clay," *some people never retain enough objectivity to make it safely back home, but those that do attest to the value of the experience. The trip may be compared to a light show that distorts known reality into shadowy appearances; in fact the main metaphoric expressions of the inward trip have to do with light and dark, great distances, unknown dark forces, untapped sexual and psychic energies, and emotionally charged but unrecognizable human figures. In Aiken's poem "Prelude xiv," the inward trip is described in terms of a recognizable landscape; the speaker finds himself on top of a mountain facing the abyss, wondering whether the void he sees is God or Nothingness. To understand accounts of experiences in the undiscovered self, the reader must suspend his habits of normal perception and see with the dreaming mind. In "A Still Moment," Welty's nightmarish landscape turns out on closer inspection to be a recognizable naturalistic setting. Inner space is nonverbal, but this doesn't mean the average person doesn't experience it, for each of us goes slightly mad every night when we dream. Nor does it mean we cannot attempt to articulate and understand the experience. If we are to trust the psychoanalysts, the person who persists in repressing his darker self courts trouble: The trick is going to the verge, but not falling in.*

GARY SNYDER

Through the Smoke Hole

FOR DON ALLEN

I

There is another world above this one; or outside of this one;
   the way to it is thru the smoke of this one, & the hole that
   smoke goes through. The ladder is the way through the
   smoke hole; the ladder holds up, some say, the world
   above; it might have been a tree or pole; I think it is
   merely a way.

Fire is at the foot of the ladder. The fire is in the center.
   The walls are round. There is also another world below or
   inside this one. The way there is down thru smoke. It is
   not necessary to think of a series.   10

Raven and Magpie do not need the ladder. They fly thru the
   smoke holes shrieking and stealing. Coyote falls thru; we
   recognize him only as a clumsy relative, a father in old
   clothes we don't wish to see with our friends.

It is possible to cultivate the fields of our own world without
   much thought for the others. When men emerge from
   below we see them as the masked dancers of our magic
   dreams. When men disappear down, we see them as plain
   men going somewhere else. When men disappear up we
   see them as great heroes shining through the smoke. When   20
   men come back from above they fall thru and tumble; we
   don't really know them; Coyote, as mentioned before.

II

Out of the kiva come
masked dancers or

plain men.
     plain men go into the ground.

out there out side all the chores
    wood and water, dirt,
wind, the view across the flat,
here, in the round   30
                no corners
head is full of magic figures—
woman your secrets aren't my secrets
what I cant say I wont
walk round
put my hand flat down.
you in the round too.
gourd vine blossom.
walls and houses drawn up
from the same soft soil.   40

thirty million years gone
        drifting sand.
  cool rooms pink stone
worn down fort floor, slat sighting
  heat shine on jumna river

dry wash, truck tracks in the riverbed
coild sand pinyon.

     seabottom
     riverbank
     sand dunes   50
the floor of a sea once again.

     human fertilizer
     underground water tunnels
     skinny dirt gods
     grandmother berries
               out
through the smoke hole.
    (for childhood and youth *are* vanity)

a Permian reef of algae,

out through the smoke hole   60
swallowd sand
            salt mud
swum bodies,   flap
to the limestone blanket—

lizzard tongue,   lizzard tongue

        wha, wha, wha   flying
in and *out* thru the smoke hole

                plain men
        come out of the ground.

CONRAD AIKEN

Prelude xiv

—You went to the verge, you say, and come back safely?
Some have not been so fortunate,—some have fallen.
Children go lightly there, from crag to crag,
And coign to coign,—where even the goat is wary,—
And make a sport of it. . . . They fling down pebbles,
Following, with eyes undizzied, the long curve,
The long slow outward curve, into the abyss,
As far as eye can follow; and they themselves
Turn back, unworried, to the here and now. . . .
But you have been there, too?—   10

        —I saw at length
The space-defying pine, that on the last
Outjutting rock has cramped its powerful roots.

There stood I too: under that tree I stood:
My hand against its resinous bark: my face
Turned out and downward to the fourfold kingdom.
The wind roared from all quarters. The waterfall
Came down, it seemed, from Heaven. The mighty sound
Of pouring elements,—earth, air, and water,—
The cry of eagles, chatter of falling stones,—   20
These were the frightful language of that place.
I understood it ill, but understood.—

—You understood it? Tell me, then, its meaning.
It was an all, a nothing, or a something?
Chaos, or divine love, or emptiness?
Water and earth and air and the sun's fire?
Or else, a question, simply?—

    —Water and fire were there,
And air and earth; there too was emptiness;
All, and nothing, and something too, and love.   30
But these poor words, these squeaks of ours, in which
We strive to mimic, with strained throats and tongues,
The spawning and outrageous elements—
Alas, how paltry are they! For I saw—

—What did you see?

    —I saw myself and God.
I saw the ruin in which godhead lives:
Shapeless and vast: the strewn wreck of the world:
Sadness unplumbed: misery without bound.
Wailing I heard, but also I heard joy.   40
Wreckage I saw, but also I saw flowers.
Hatred I saw, but also I saw love. . . .
And thus, I saw myself.

    —And this alone?

—And this alone awaits you, when you dare
To that sheer verge where horror hangs, and tremble

Against the falling rock; and, looking down,
Search the dark kingdom. It is to self you come,—
And that is God. It is the seed of seeds:
Seed for disastrous and immortal worlds.   50

It is the answer that no question asked.

DAVID WEVILL

I Think I Am Becoming Myself

This is life at the marrow,
No-telling and secretive. In this quiet month
All appearance has been merely figurative;
Whatever I touch might prove the prime mover.

Patience is a tact due to time—
Old-fashioned and ungrateful. So my hands
Miss your plain body, every shape of limb
Grows huge exaggerated as eucalyptus'
Smooth wind-sucking dormant tension of sap.

If a tree should wilt and close up,   10
Under the dream and the dream's fantasy
And under that, in a detritus quicksand of blind
Thick wanting—
What? There life is cold, adequate,
The order bland, the senses blunt as dead tools.

No, this is life at the core, time single.
Beyond this is just a waiting on dates: time
Told by clocks is not time of blood.
Bare objects attend and listen—
Our reunion will be slow and cautious and final.   20

PATRICK WHITE

Clay

FOR BARRY HUMPHRIES AND ZOE CALDWELL

When he was about five years old some kids asked Clay why his mother had called him that. And he did not know. But began to wonder. He did, in fact, wonder a great deal, particularly while picking the bark off trees, or stripping a flower down to its core of mystery. He, too, would ask questions, but more often than not failed to receive the answer because his mother could not bring herself to leave her own train of thought.

Mrs Skerritt said: "If only your father hadn't died he'd still be putting out the garbage the bin is too much for me the stooping not to mention the weight in anyone short of breath but you Clay I know will be good to your mum and help when you are older stronger only that is still a long way off."

So that it was Clay's turn not to answer. What could you say, anyway?

Mrs Skerritt said: "I wouldn't ask anything of anyone but there are certain things of course I wouldn't expect a gentleman to stand up for me in the tram while I have my own two legs only it's the sort of thing a gentleman ought to do and ladies take Mrs Pearl for instance what she expects of her husband and him with the sugar-diabetes too."

Clay mooned about the house listening to his mother's voice boring additional holes in the fretwork, for fretwork had been Dadda's hobby: There was fretwork just about everywhere, brackets and things, even a lace of fretwork hanging from table-top and doorway. Stiff. Sometimes while his mother's voice bored and sawed further Clay would break off pieces of the brown fretwork and hide it away under the house. Under the house was full of fretwork finally.

Or he would moon about the terraces of the garden, amongst the collapsing lattices, flowerpot shards crackling underfoot, legs slapped by the straps of dark, leathery plants, lungs filled with suffocating bursts of asparagus fern. He would dawdle down to the harbour, with its green smell of sea-lettuce, and the stone wall, scribbled with the white droppings of gulls. The house itself leaned rather far towards the harbour, but had not fallen, because some men had come and shored it up. There it hung, however.

So Clay mooned. And would return often to the photograph. It was as though his childhood were riveted to the wedding group. There was his father, those thick thighs, rather tight about the serge crutch (unlike the Dadda he remembered lying Incurable in bed), and the influential Mr Stutchbury, and Auntie Ada, and Nellie Watson (who died), and someone else who was killed in action. But it was to his mum that Clay was drawn, before and after all, into the torrential satin of the lap, by the face which had just begun to move out of its fixture of fretted lace. And the shoe. He was fascinated by the white shoe. Sometimes its great boat would float out from the shore of frozen time, into the waters of his imagination, rocking his cargo of almost transparent thoughts.

Once Mrs Skerritt came into the room and caught him at it, though she did not exactly see Clay for looking at herself.

"Ah dear," she said, "in the end things is sad."

She would often half cry, and at such moments her hair would look more than ever like so many lengths of grey string, or on windy days, a tizz of frayed dish-cloth.

On this particular day when she caught Clay looking at the photograph, his throat swelled, and he dared to ask:

"Why is my name Clay, Mum?"

Because by that time he was seven, and the kids were asking worse than ever, and bashing him up (they were afraid that he was different).

"Why," she said, "let me think your father wanted Percival that is after Mr Stutchbury but I could not bring myself I said there are so many things you don't do but want take a name a name is yours take pottery I said I've half a mind to try my hand if I can find some feller or lady you never know I may be artistic but didn't because well there isn't the time always so much to do the people who have to be told and who have to be told and then Dadda's incurable illness so I did not do that only thought and thought about it and that I believe is why you was called Clay."

Then she went out the back to empty the teapot on a bed of maidenhair which tingled perpetually with moisture.

So the kids continued to bash Clay up, and ask him why he was called that, and he couldn't tell them, because how could you even when you knew.

There were times when it got extra bad, and once they chased him with a woman's cast-off shoe. He ran like a green streak, but not fast enough in the end—they caught him at the corner of Plant Street, where he had been born and always lived, and the heel of their old shoe bored for ever in his mind.

Later, when he had let himself in, into the garden of the leaning house, lost amongst collapsing lattices and the yellow fuzz of asparagus fern, he cried a bit for the difference to which he had been born. But smeared his eyes dry at last, and his nose. The light was rising from the bay in all green peacefulness, as if the world of pointed objects did not exist alongside that of the dreamy bridal shoe.

But he did not embark. Not then. His ribs had not subsided yet.

Once Clay dreamed a dream, and came down into the kitchen. He had meant to keep the dream to himself. Then it was too late, he heard he was telling it to his mum. Even though his mouth was frozen stiff he had to keep on, to tell.

"In this dream," he said, "the steps led on down."

His mum was pushing the rashers around, which went on buckling up in the pan.

"Under the sea," said Clay. "It was beautiful."

He was sorry, but he could not help it.

"Everything drawn out. Hair and things. And weeds. The knotted ones. And the lettucy kind. Some of the fish had beards, Mum, and barked, well, like dogs."

His mum had put the fried bread on a plate to one side, where the little squares were already stiffening.

"And shells, Mum," he said, "all bubbles and echoes as I went on down. It felt good. It felt soft. I didn't have to try. But just floated. Down."

He could see his mother's behind, how it had begun to quiver, and he dreaded what might happen when he told. There was no avoiding it, though, and his mum went on prodding the bacon in the pan.

"When I got to the bottom," he said, "and the steps ended, you should have seen how the sea stretched, over the sand and broken bottles. Everything sort of silvery. I don't remember much else. Except that I found, Mum," he said.

"What?" she asked.

He dreaded it.

"A cloud, Mum," he said, "and it was dead."

Then Mrs Skerritt turned round, it was dreadful, how she looked. She opened her mouth, but nothing came out at first, only Clay saw the little thing at the back. Raised. When suddenly it began to act like a clapper. She began to cry, she began to create.

"Whatever are you gunna do to me?" she cried, as she pummelled and kneaded the moist grey dough of her cheeks.

"On top of everything else I never ever thought I'd have a freak!"

But Clay could only stand, and receive the blows her voice dealt. It was as though someone had taken a stick and drawn a circle round him. Him at the centre. There was no furniture any more.

The bacon was burning in the pan.

When Mrs Skerritt had thought it over, and used a little eau-de-Cologne, she took him up to McGillivray's. It was late by then, on a Saturday morning too. All the way Clay listened to her breathing and sometimes the sound of her corset. McGillivray was already closing, but agreed to do Mrs Skerritt's lad. McGillivray was kind.

"We want it short short Mr McGillivray please," Mrs Skerritt said.

As the barber snipped Clay could hear his mum breathing, from where she sat, behind his back, under the coloured picture of the King.

Mr McGillivray did his usual nice job, and was preparing to design the little quiff when Mrs Skerritt choked.

"That is not short Mr McGillivray not what I mean oh no oh dear but it is difficult to explain there is too much involved and I left school when I turned fourteen."

McGillivray laughed and said: "Short is not shorn!"

"I don't care," she said.

Clay could only look at the glass, and suck his cheeks in.

"Short is what I said and mean," Mrs Skerritt confirmed. "I was never one for not coming to the point."

McGillivray was a gentle man, but he too began to breathe, he took the clippers, and shore a path through his subject's hair. He shore, and shore. Till there Clay was. Exposed.

"That suit?" McGillivray asked.

"Thank you," she said.

So meek.

Then they went home. They crunched over the asphalt. They were that heavy, both of them.

As they went down the hill towards the turn where the milko's cart had plunged over, Mrs Skerritt said:

"There Clay a person is sometimes driven to things in defence of what we know and love I would not of done this otherwise if not to protect you from yourself because love you will suffer in life if you start talking queer remember it doesn't pay to be different and no one is different without they have something wrong with them."

Clay touched his prickly hair.

"Let me remind you," she said, "that your mum loves you that is why."

But Clay could no longer believe in love, and the kids bashed him up worse than ever, because his no-hair made him a sort of different different.

"Wot was you in for?" the kids asked, and did windmills on his stubble. "Old Broad Arrer!" they shouted, and punched.

Actually Clay grew up narrow. He was all knuckle, all wrist. He had those drawn-out arms. He had a greenish skin from living under too many plants. He was long. And his eyes overflowed at dusk, merged with the street lights, and the oil patches on lapping water.

"Are you lonely, Clay?" Mrs Skerritt asked.

"No," he said. "Why?"

"I thought perhaps you was lonely you should get out and meet other young people of your own age you should get to know nice girls otherwise it is not normal."

Then she drew in her chin, and waited.

But Clay stroked his prickly hair. For he went to McGillivray's every so often since it was ordained. When his voice broke the others no longer bashed him up, having problems of their own. The blackheads came, the pimples and moustaches.

Sometimes Mrs Skerritt would cry, sitting on the rotten veranda overlooking the little bay in which cats so often drowned.

"Oh dear Clay," she cried, "I am your mother and have a responsibility a double one since Dadda went I will ask Mr Stutchbury but cannot rely totally do you know what you want to do?"

Clay said: "No."

"Oh dear," she moaned worse than ever, "how did I deserve a silent boy who loves what I would like to know himself perhaps himself."

In fact Clay did not know what he loved. He would have liked to think it was his mother, though it could have been Dadda. So he would try to remember, but it was only cold yellow skin, and the smell of sick sheets. When he had been forced to approach his father, lying Incurable in the bed, his heart could have tumbled down out of the belfry of his body.

Once his mother, it was evening, clutched his head against her apron, so that she must have pricked her hands.

"You are not my son," she clanged, "otherwise you would act different."

But he could not, did not want to. Sometimes, anyway, at that age, he felt too dizzy from growing.

"How?" his voice asked, or croaked.

But she did not explain. She flung his long body away.

"It's not a matter," she said, "that anybody can discuss I will ask Mr Stutchbury to see what we must do and how."

Mr Stutchbury was so influential, as well as having been a mate of Herb Skerritt's all his life. Mr Stutchbury was something, Mrs Skerritt believed, in the Department of Education, but if she did not clear the matter up, it was because she considered there was not all that necessity.

She bought a T-bone steak, and asked him round.

"What," she asked, "should we do with Clay I am a widow as you know and you was his father's friend."

Mr Stutchbury drew in his moustache.

"We will see," he said, "when the time comes."

Then he folded his moist lips over a piece of yellow fat from the not so tender T-bone steak.

When it was time, Mr Stutchbury thought up a letter to some fellow at the Customs and Excise.

Dear Archie (he composed)
This is to recommend the son of an old friend. Herb Skerritt, for many years in the Tramways, died in tragic circumstances— of cancer to be precise . . .

(Clay, who of course opened the letter to see, got quite a shock from a word his mother never on any account allowed to be used in the home.)

. . . it is my duty and wish to further the interests of the above-mentioned boy. In brief, I would esteem it a favour if you could see your way to taking him "under your wing." I do not predict wonders of young Skerritt, but am of the opinion, rather, that he is a decent, average lad. In any event, wonders are not all that desirable, not in the Service anyway. It is the steady hand which pushes the pen a lifetime.
I will not expiate further, but send you my
                                            Salaams!

The young lady whom Mr Stutchbury had persuaded to type the letter had barely left the room, when his superior called, with the result that he forgot to add as he intended: "Kindest regards to Mrs Archbold." Even persons of influence have to consider the ground they tread on.

But Clay Skerritt started at the Customs, because Mr Archbold was not the sort to refuse Mr Stutchbury the favour he asked. So Clay took the ferry, mornings, in the stiff dark suit his mother had chosen. His long thin fingers learned to deal in forms. He carried the papers from tray to tray. In time he grew used to triplicate, and moistened the indelible before writing in his long thin hand the details, and the details.

Clay Skerritt did not complain, and if he was ignored he had known worse. For he was most certainly ignored, by the gentlemen who sat amongst the trays of papers, by the young ladies of the Customs and Excise, who kept their nails so beautifully, who took their personal towels to the toilet, and giggled over private matters and cups of milky tea. If they ever laughed at the junior in particular, at his tricky frame, his pimples, and his stubble of hair, Clay Skerritt was not conscious of it. Why should he be? He was born with inward-looking eyes.

That all was not quite in order, though, he began to gather from his mother.

"When I am gone, Clay," she said—it was the evening the sink got blocked up, "you will remember how your mother was a messer but found she only scraped the dishes into the sink because her mind was otherwise engaged with you Clay your interests always some practical young lady will rectify anything your mother ever did by good intention I would not force you but only advise time is not to be ignored."

But on days when the wind blew black across the grey water Mrs Skerritt might remark, peering out from the arbours of asparagus fern:

"Some young woman clever with her needle lighter-handed at the pastry-board will make you forget your poor mum well it is the way."

Her son was bound to ignore what he could not be expected to believe. He would take a look at the wedding group. All so solidly alive, the figures appeared to announce a truth of which he alone could be the arbiter, just as the great white shoe would still put out, into the distance, for destinations of his choice.

His mother, however, continued in her mistaken attempts to celebrate the passing of reality. There was the day she called, her voice intruding amongst the objects which surrounded him:

"Take my grey costume dear up to the dry cleaner at the Junction tomato sauce is fatal when a person is on the stoutish side."

Clay acted as he had been told. Or the streets were acting round him, and the trams. It was a bright day. Metal sang. The brick homes were no longer surreptitious, but opened up to disclose lives. In one window a woman was looking into her armpit. It made Clay laugh.

At the cleaner's a lady finished a yarn with the young girl. The lady said from alongside her cigarette:

"I'll leave you to it, Marj. I'm gunna make tracks for home and whip me shoes off. My feet are hurting like hell."

Then the bell.

Clay was still laughing.

The young girl was looking down at the sheets of fresh brown paper, through the smell of cleaning. She herself had a cleaned, pallid skin, with pores.

"What's up?" she asked, as the client continued laughing.

She spoke so very flat and polite.

"Nothing," he said, but added: "I think perhaps you are like my mother."

Which was untrue, in a sense, because the girl was flat, still, and colourless, whereas his mother was rotund, voluble, and at least several tones of grey. But Clay had been compelled to say it.

The girl did not reply. She looked down at first, as though he had overstepped the mark. Then she took the costume, and examined the spots of tomato sauce.

"Ready tomorrow," she said.

"Go on!"

"Why not?" the girl replied. "We are a One-day."

But flat and absent she sounded.

Then Clay did not know why, but asked: "You've got something on your mind."

She said: "It's only that the sink got blocked yesterday evening."

It sounded so terribly grey, and she looking out with that expression of permanence. Then at once he knew he had been right, and that the girl at the dry cleaner's had something of his mother: it was the core of permanence. Then Clay grew excited. For he did not believe in impermanence, not even when his mother attempted to persuade, nor even when he watched the clods of earth tumble down on the coffin lid. Not while he was he.

So he said: "Tomorrow."

It sounded so firm, it was almost today.

Clay got used to Marj just as he had got used to his mum, only differently. They swung hands together, walking over the dead grass of several parks, or staring at animals in cages. They were already living together, that is, their silences intermingled. Each had a somewhat clammy palm. And if Marj spoke there was no necessity to answer, it was so flat, her remarks had the colour of masonite.

Marj said: "When I have a home of my own, I will turn out the lounge Fridays. I mean, there is a time and place for everything. There are the bedrooms too."

She said: "I do like things to be nice."

And: "Marriage should be serious."

How serious, Clay began to see, who had not told his mum.

When at last he did she was drying the apostle spoons, one of which she dropped, and he let her pick it up, on seeing that it was necessary for her to perform some therapeutic act.

"I am so glad Clay," she said, rather purple, after a pause, "I cannot wait to see this nice girl we must arrange some we must come to an agree there is no reason why a young couple should not hit it off with the mother-in-law if the home is large it is not so much temperament as the size of the home that causes friction."

Mrs Skerritt had always known herself to be reasonable.

"And Marj is so like you, Mum."

"Eh?" Mrs Skerritt said.

He could not explain that what was necessary for him, for what he had to do, was a continuum. He could not have explained what he had to do, because he did not know, as yet.

All Mrs Skerritt could say was: "The sooner we see the better we shall know."

So Clay brought Marj. Their hands were clammier that day. The plants were huge, casting a fuscous tinge on the shored-up house.

Mrs Skerritt looked out of the door.

"Is this," she said, "I am not yet not yet ready to see."

Clay told Marj she must go away, for that day at least, he would send for her, then he took his mother inside.

Mrs Skerritt did not meet Marj again, except in the mirror, in which she saw with something of a shock there is no such thing as permanence.

Shortly after she died of something. They said it was her ticker.

And Clay brought Marj to live in the house in which he had been born and lived. They did not go on a honeymoon, because, as Marj said, marriage should be serious. Clay hoped he would know what to do as they lay in the bed Mum and Dadda had used. Lost in that strange and lumpy acre Clay and Marj listened to each other.

But it was good. He continued going to the Customs. Once or twice he pinched the lobe of Marj's ear.

"What's got into you?" she asked.

He continued going to the Customs. He bought her a Java sparrow in a cage. It was a kind of love poem.

To which Marj replied: "I wonder if it's gunna scatter its seed on the wall-to-wall. We can always spread a newspaper, though."

And did.

Clay went to the Customs. He sat at his own desk. He used his elbows more than before, because his importance had increased.

"Take this letter away, Miss Venables," he said. "There are only two copies. When I expected five. Take it away," he said.

Miss Venables pouted, but took it away. She, like everybody, saw that something had begun to happen. They would watch Mr Skerritt, and wait for it.

But Marj, she was less expectant. She accepted the houseful of fretwork, the things the mother-in-law had put away—sets of string-coloured doilies for instance, once she came across a stuffed canary in a cardboard box. She did not remark, but accepted. Only once she failed to accept. Until Clay asked:

"What has become of the photo?"

"It is in that cupboard," she said.

He went and fetched out the wedding group, and stuck it where it had been, on a fretwork table. At least he did not ask why she had put the photo away, and she was glad, because she would not have known what to answer. The bits of your husband you would never know were bad enough, but not to understand yourself was worse.

So Marj stuck to the carpet-sweeper, she was glad of the fluff under the bed, she was glad of the pattern on the lino, the cartons of crispies that she bought—so square. Even light is solid when the paths lead inward. So she listened to the carpet-sweeper.

All this time, she realized, something had been happening to Clay. For one thing his hair had begun to grow. Its long wisps curled like feather behind his ears. He himself, she saw, was not yet used to the silky daring of hair, which formerly had pricked to order.

"Level with the lobes of the ears, Mr McGillivray, please," Clay would now explain.

McGillivray, who was old by this, and infallibly kind, always refrained from commenting.

So did the gentlemen at the Customs—it was far too strange. Even the young ladies, who had been prepared to giggle at first, got the shivers for something they did not understand.

Only when the hair had reached as far as Mr Skerritt's shoulders did Mr Archbold send for Clay.

"Is it necessary, Mr Skerritt?" his superior asked, who had the additional protection of a private office.

Clay replied: "Yes."

He stood looking.

He was allowed to go away.

His wife Marj decided there is nothing to be surprised at. It is the only solution. Even if the fretwork crackled, she would not hear. Even if the hanging basket sprouted hair instead of fern, she would not see. There were the chops she put in front of her husband always so nicely curled on the plate. Weren't there the two sides of life?

One evening Clay came up out of the terraced garden, where the snails wound, and the sea smells. He stood for some considerable time in front of his parents' wedding group. The great shoe, or boat, or bridge, had never appeared so structural. Looking back he seemed to remember that this was the occasion of his beginning, the poem, or novel, or regurgitation, which occupied him for the rest of his life.

Marj was certain that that was the evening he closed the door.

She would lie and call: "Aren't you gunna come to bed, Clay?"

Or she would stir at the hour when the sheets are greyest, when the air trembles at the withheld threat of aluminium, Marj would ungum her mouth to remark: "But Clay, the alarm hasn't gone off yet!"

From now on it seemed as though his body never stayed there long enough to warm the impression it left on the bed. She could hardly complain, though. He made love to her twice a year, at Christmas, and at Easter, though sometimes at Easter they might decide against—there was the Royal Agricultural Show, which is so exhausting.

All this is beside the point. It was the sheets of paper which counted, on which Clay wrote, behind the door of that little room which his wife failed to remember, it was soon so long since she had been inside. One of the many things Marj Skerritt learned to respect was another person's privacy.

So Clay wrote. At first he occupied himself with objects, the mysterious life which inanimacy contains. For several years in the beginning he was occupied with this.

. . . the table standing continues standing its legs so permanent of course you can take an axe and swing it cut into the flesh as Poles do every once in a while when they shriek murder murder but mostly nothing disturbs the maps the childhood journeys on the frozen wave of wooden water no boat whether wood or iron when you come to think satin either ever sails from A to B except in the mind of the passenger so the table standing standing under an electric bulb responds unlikely unless to determination or desperation of a Polish kind . . .

One night Clay wrote:

I have never observed a flowerpot intimately until now its hole is fascinating the little down of green moss it is of greater significance than what is within though you can fill it if you decide to if you concentrate long enough . . .

Up till now he had not turned his attention to human beings, though he had been surrounded by them all his life. In actual fact he did not turn his attention to them now, he was intruded on. And Lova was not all that human, or not at first, a presence rather, or sensation of possession.

That night Clay got the hiccups, he was so excited, or nervous. The reverberations were so metallic he failed to hear his wife Marj, her grey voice: "Aren't you gunna come to bed, Clay?"

Lova was, by comparison, a greenish-yellow, of certain fruits, and plant-flesh.

Lova Lova Lova, he wrote at first, to try it out.

He liked it so much it surprised him it had not come to him before. He could have sat simply writing the name, but Lova grew more palpable.

. . . her little conical breasts at times ripening into porepores detachable by sleight of hand or windy days yet so elusive fruit and shoes distributed amongst the grass . . .

In the beginning Lova would approach from behind glass, her skin had that faint hothouse moisture which tingles on the down of ferns, her eyes a ferny brown that complemented his own if he had known. But he knew no more than gestures at first, the floating entanglement of hair in mutual agreement, the slight shiver of skin passing over skin. She would ascend and descend the flights of stone steps, inhabiting for a moment the angles of landings of old moss-upholstered stone. The leaves of the *monstera deliciosa* sieved her at times into a dispersed light. Which he alone knew how to reassemble. On rare occasions their mouths would almost meet, at the bottom of the garden, where the smell of rotting was, and the liquid manure used to stand, which had long since dried up. She was not yet real, and might never be. No. He would make her. But there were the deterrents. The physical discords.

Marj said: "My hands are that chapped I must ask Mr Todd's advice. You can enjoy a chat with a chemist, doctors are most of them too busy pushing you out."

And Lova got the herpes. Clay could not look at her at first. As she sat at her own little table, taking the fifteen varieties of pills, forcing them into her pig's snout, Lova would smile still, but it was sad. And soon the sore had become a scab. He could not bring himself to approach. And breath, besides.

For nights and nights Clay could not write a word. Or to be precise, he wrote over several nights:

. . . a drying and a dying . . .

If he listened, all he could hear was the rustle of Lova's assorted pills, the ruffling of a single sterile date-palm, the sound of Marj turning in the bed.

Then it occurred to his panic the shored-up house might break open. It was so rotten, so dry. He could not get too quickly round the table, scattering the brittle sheets of paper. Motion detached itself from his feet in the shape of abrupt, leather slippers. Skittering to reach the door.

Clay did not, in fact, because Lova he now saw locking locking locked it, popping the key afterwards down between.

Lova laughed. And Clay stood. The little ripples rose up in her throat, perhaps it was the cold key, and spilled over, out of her mouth, her wet mouth. He knew that the private parts of babies tasted as tender as Lova's mouth.

He had never tried. But suspected he must.

She came to him.

"Bum to you!" Lova said.

She sat in his lap then, and with his free hand he wrote, the first of many white nights:

At last my ryvita has turned to velveeta life is no longer a toast-rack.

"Golly," said Lova, "what it is to be an educated feller! Honest, Clay, it must be a great satisfaction to write, if only to keep one of your hands occupied."

She laughed again. When he had his doubts. Does every face wear the same expression unless it is your own? He would have liked to look at the wedding group, to verify, but there were all those stairs between, and darkness. All he could hear was the sound of Marj breaking wind. Marj certainly had said at break-fast: "It is the same. Whatever the manufacturers tell you, that is only to sell the product."

But Lova said: "It is different, Clay, as different as kumquats from pommygranates. You are the differentest of all perhaps. I could lap up the cream of your genius."

She did, in fact, look at moments like a cat crouched in his lap, but would close at once, and open, like a knife.

"I would eat you," she repeated, baring her pointed teeth, when he had thought them broad and spaced, as in Mum or Marj.

Although he was afraid, he wrote with his free right hand:

I would not trust a razor-blade to any but my own . . .

When Lova looked it over.

"Shoot!" she said. "That is what I am!"

He forgot about her for a little, for writing down what he had to write.

. . . Lova sat in my lap smelling of crushed carrot tops she has taken the frizz out of her hair but cannot make it smell less green I would not trust her further than without meaning to cast asper-sions you can't trust even your own thoughts past midnight . . .

"Chip Chip Chip chipped off his finger," Lova said. "Anyway it begins with C."

"Oh dear," C began to cry. "O dear dear dear oh Lova!"

"When does D come in?" she asked.

"D isn't born," he said, "and pretty sure won't be. As for A, A is in bed. No," he corrected. "A am not."

Suddenly he wished he was.

He realized he was eye to eye with Lova their lashes grappling together in gummy agreement but melancholy to overflowing. They were poured into each other.

After that, Clay finished, for the night at least, and experienced the great trauma of his little empty room, for Lova had vanished, and there were only the ink stains on his fingers to show that she had ever been there.

There was nothing for it now but to join Marj in the parental bed, where he wondered whether he would ever be able to rise again. He was cold, cold.

Actually Marj turned over and said: "Clay, I had an argument with Mr Tesoriero over the turnips. I told him you couldn't expect the public to buy them flabby."

But Clay slept, and in fact he did not rise, not that morning, the first in many years, when the alarm clock scattered its aluminium trays all over the house.

Clay Skerritt continued going to the Customs. They had got used to him by then, even to his hair, the streaks in it.

He realized it was time he went to McGillivray's again, but some young dago came out, and said:

"Nho! Nho! McGillivray gone. Dead. How many years? Five? Six?"

So Clay Skerritt went away.

It was natural enough that it should have happened to Mc-Gillivray. Less natural were the substances. The pretending houses. The asphalt which had lifted up.

Then he saw the pointed heel, caught in the crack, wrenching at it. He saw the figure. He saw. He saw.

When she turned round, she said:

"Yes. It's all very well. For you. With square heels. Bum bums."

Wrenching at her heel all the while.

"But Lova," he said, putting out his hands.

She was wearing a big-celled honeycomb sweater.

"Oh, yes!" she said.

And laughed.

"If that's how you feel," he answered.

"If that's how I *feel!*"

His hands were shaking, and might have caught in the oatmeal wool.

"I'm not gunna stand around exchanging words with any long-haired nong in the middle of Military Road. Not on yours!"

"Be reasonable," he begged.

"What is reasonable?" she asked.

He could not tell. Nor if she had asked: what is love?

"Aren't you going to know me then?" he said.

"I know you," she said, sort of flat—two boards could not have come together with greater exactitude.

"And it is time," she said, "to go."

Jerking at her stuck heel.

"I've come here for something," he remembered. "Was it bird-seed?"

"Was it my Aunt Fanny!"

Then she got her heel free and all the asphalt was crackling up falling around them in scraps of torn black tinkly paper.

If he could only have explained that love cannot be explained.

All the while ladies were going in and out, strings eating into their fingers together with their rings. One lady had an alsatian, a basket suspended from its teeth, it did not even scent the trouble.

It was Saturday morning. Clay went home.

That evening, after they had finished their spaghetti on toast, because they were still paying off the Tecnico, Marj said:

"Clay, I had a dream."

"No!" he shouted.

Where could he go? There was nowhere now.

Except on the Monday there was the Customs and Excise. He could not get there quick enough. To sharpen his pencils. To move the paper-clips the other side of the ink eraser.

Then what he was afraid might happen, happened.

Lova had followed him to the Customs.

The others had not spotted it yet, for it could have been any lady passing the day at the Customs in pursuit of her unlawful goods. Only no lady would have made so straight for Mr Skerritt's desk, nor would she have been growing from her big-celled oatmeal sweater quite so direct as Lova was.

She had those little, pointed, laughing teeth.

"Well," she opened, "you didn't reckon on this."

She was so certain of herself by now, he was afraid she might jump out of her jumper.

He sat looking down, at the letter from Dooley and Mann, Import Agents, re the Bechstein that got lost.

"Listen, Lova," he advised. "Not in here. It won't help find the piano."

"Pianner? A fat lot of pianner! You can't play that one on me."

"You may be right," he answered.

"Right!" she said. "Even if I wasn't. Even if I was flippin' wrong!"

She put her handbag on the desk.

"If anyone's gunna play, I'm the one," she said.

Sure enough the old black upright slid around the corner from behind Archbold's glassed-in office, followed by the little leather-upholstered stool, from which the hair was bursting out. Lova seemed satisfied. She laughed, and when she had sat down, began to dish out the gay sad jazz. Playing and playing. Her little hands were jumping and frolicking on their own. The music playing out of every worm hole in the old, sea-changed piano.

Clay looked up, to see Archbold looking down. Miss Titmuss had taken her personal towel, and was having trouble with her heels as she made her way towards the toilet.

When Lova got up. She was finished. Or not quite. She began to drum with her bum on the greasy, buckled-up rashers of keys of the salt-cured old piano.

"There!" she shouted.

She came and sat on the corner of his desk. She had never been so elastic. It was her rage of breathing. He was unable to avoid the pulse of her suspender, winking at him from her thigh.

One or two other of the Customs officials had begun to notice, he observed desperately through the side-curtains of his hair.

So he said: "Look here, Lova, a scene at this stage will make it well nigh impossible for me to remain in the Service. And what will we do without the pension? Marj must be taken into account. I mean to say, it is the prestige as much as the money. Otherwise, we have learnt to do on tea and bread."

Lova laughed then.

"Ha! *Ha!* HA!"

There is no way of writing it but how it was written on the wall. For it was. It got itself printed up on the wall which ran at right angles to Archbold's office.

Clay sat straight, straight. His adam's apple might not endure it much longer.

"Scenes are so destructive," he said, or begged.

So his mum had told him.

"If that is what you want," said Lova, "you know I was never one for holding up procedure for the sake of filling in a form."

And she ripped it off the pad from under his nose. Her hands were so naked, and could get a whole lot nakeder. He was afraid he might be answerable.

"I would never suggest," she shouted, "that the pisspot was standing right end up when it wasn't."

But he had to resist, not so much for personal reasons as for the sake of public decorum, for the honour of the Department. He had to protect the paper-clips.

Because their hands were wrestling, troubling the desk. Him and Lova. At any moment the carton might burst open. At any. It happened quite quickly, breathily, ending in the sigh of scatteration.

"I will leave you for now," she said, getting off the corner of the desk, and pulling down her sweater, which had rucked up.

Almost every one of his colleagues had noticed by this, but all had the decency to avoid passing audible judgement on such a very private situation.

When it was over a little while, Miss Titmuss got down and gathered up the paper-clips, because she was sorry for Mr Skerritt.

He did not wait to thank or explain, but took his hat, treading carefully to by-pass the eyes, and caught the ferry to the other side.

Marj said: "Aren't you early, Clay? Sit on the veranda a while. I'll bring you a cuppa, and a slice of that pound cake, it's still eatable I think."

So he sat on the veranda, where his mother used to sit and complain, and felt the southerly get inside his neckband, and heard the date-palm starting up. Sparrows gathered cautiously.

Marj said: "Clay, if you don't eat up, it'll be tea."

You can always disregard, though, and he went inside the room, which he did not even dread. There she was, sitting in the other chair, in the oatmeal sweater. Her back turned. Naturally.

"Lova," he began.

Then she came towards him, and he saw that she herself might sink in the waters of time she spread before him cunningly the nets of water smelling of nutmeg over junket the steamy mornings and the rather shivery afternoons.

If he did not resist.

She was just about as resistant as water not the tidal kind but a glad upward plume of water rising and falling back as he put his hands gently lapping lapping. She was so gentle.

Marj began to knock on the door.

"Tea's getting cold, Clay," she stammered.

It was, too. That is the way of things.

"I made you a nice devilled toast."

She went away, but returned, and held her ear to the dry rot.

"Clay?" she asked. "Don't you mind?"

Marj did not like to listen at doors because of her regard for privacy.

"Well," she said, "I never knew you to act like this."

It could have been the first time in her life that Marj had opened a door.

Then she began to scream. She began to create. It was unlike her.

She could not see his face because of all that hair. The hair and the boards between them were keeping it a secret.

"This is something I never bargained for," she cried.

For the blood had spurted out of the leg of the table. Just a little.

And that old shoe. He lay holding a white shoe.

"I never ever saw a shoe!" she moaned. "Of all the junk she put away, just about every bit of her, and canaries and things, never a shoe!"

As Clay lay.

With that stiff shoe.

"I don't believe it!" Marj cried.

Because everyone knows that what isn't isn't, even when it is.

EUDORA WELTY

A Still Moment

Lorenzo Dow rode the Old Natchez Trace at top speed upon a race horse, and the cry of the itinerant Man of God, "I must have souls! And souls I must have!" rang in his own windy ears. He rode as if never to stop, toward his night's appointment.

It was the hour of sunset. All the souls that he had saved and all those he had not took dusky shapes in the mist that hung between the high banks, and seemed by their great number and density to block his way, and showed no signs of melting or changing back into mist, so that he feared his passage was to be difficult forever. The poor souls that were not saved were darker and more pitiful than those that were, and still there was not any of the radiance he would have hoped to see in such a congregation.

"Light up, in God's name!" he called, in the pain of his disappointment.

Then a whole swarm of fireflies instantly flickered all around him, up and down, back and forth, first one golden light and then another, flashing without any of the weariness that had held back the souls. These were the signs sent from God that he had not seen the accumulated radiance of saved souls because he was not able, and that his eyes were more able to see the fireflies of the Lord than His blessed souls.

"Lord, give me the strength to see the angels when I am in Paradise," he said. "Do not let my eyes remain in this failing proportion to my loving heart always."

He gasped and held on. It was that day's complexity of horse-trading that had left him in the end with a Spanish race horse for which he was bound to send money in November from Georgia. Riding faster on the beast and still faster until he felt as if he were flying he sent thoughts of love with matching speed to his wife Peggy in Massachusetts. He found it effortless to love at a distance. He could look at the flowering trees and love Peggy in fullness, just as he could see his visions and love God. And Peggy, to whom he had not spoken until he could speak fateful words ("Would she accept of such an object as him?"), Peggy, the bride, with whom he had spent a few hours of time, showing of herself a small round handwriting, declared all in one letter, her first, that she felt the same as he, and that the fear was never of separation, but only of death.

Lorenzo well knew that it was Death that opened underfoot, that rippled by at night, that was the silence the birds did their singing in. He was close to death, closer than any animal or bird. On the back of one horse after another, winding them all, he was always riding toward it or away from it, and the Lord sent him directions with protection in His mind.

Just then he rode into a thicket of Indians taking aim with their new guns. One stepped out and took the horse by the bridle, it stopped at a touch, and the rest made a closing circle. The guns pointed.

"Incline!" The inner voice spoke sternly and with its customary lightning-quickness.

Lorenzo inclined all the way forward and put his head to the horse's silky mane, his body to its body, until a bullet meant for him would endanger the horse and make his death of no value. Prone he rode out through the circle of Indians, his obedience to the voice leaving him almost fearless, almost careless with joy.

But as he straightened and pressed ahead, care caught up with him again. Turning half-beast and half-divine, dividing himself like a heathen Centaur, he had escaped his death once more. But was it to be always by some metamorphosis of himself that he escaped, some humiliation of his faith, some admission to strength and argumentation and not frailty? Each time when he acted so it was at the command of an instinct that he took at once as the word of an angel, until too late, when he knew it was the word of the devil. He had roared like a tiger at Indians, he had submerged himself in water blowing the savage bubbles of the alligator, and they skirted him by. He had prostrated himself to appear dead, and deceived bears. But all the time God would have protected him in His own way, less hurried, more divine.

Even now he saw a serpent crossing the Trace, giving out knowing glances.

He cried, "I know you now!", and the serpent gave him one look out of which all the fire had been taken, and went away in two darts into the tangle.

He rode on, all expectation, and the voices in the throats of the wild beasts went, almost without his noticing when, into words. "Praise God," they said. "Deliver us from one another." Birds especially sang of divine love which was the one ceaseless protection. "Peace, in peace," were their words so many times when they spoke from the briars, in a courteous sort of infection, and he turned his countenance toward all perched creatures with a benevolence striving to match their own.

He rode on past the little intersecting trails, letting himself be guided by voices and by lights. It was battlesounds he heard most, sending him on, but sometimes ocean sounds, that long beat of waves that would make his heart pound and retreat as heavily as they, and he despaired again in his failure in Ireland when he took a voyage and persuaded with the Catholics with his back against the door, and then ran away to their cries of "Mind the white hat!" But when he heard singing it was not the militant and sharp sound of Wesley's hymns, but a soft, tireless and tender air that had no beginning and no end, and the softness of distance, and he had pleaded with the Lord to find out if all this meant that it was wicked, but no answer had come.

Soon night would descend, and a camp-meeting ground ahead would fill with its sinners like the sky with its stars. How he hungered for them! He looked in prescience with a longing of love over the throng that waited while the flames of the torches threw change, change, change over their faces. How could he bring them enough, if it were not divine love and sufficient warning of all that could threaten them? He rode on faster. He was a filler of appointments, and he filled more and more, until his journeys up and down creation were nothing but a shuttle, driving back and forth upon the rich expanse of his vision. He was homeless by his own choice, he must be everywhere at some time, and somewhere soon. There hastening in the wilderness on his flying horse he gave the night's torch-lit crowd a premature benediction, he could not wait. He spread his arms out, one at a time for safety, and he wished, when they would all be gathered in by his tin horn blasts and the inspired words would go out over their heads, to brood above the entire and passionate life of the wide world, to become its rightful part.

He peered ahead. "Inhabitants of Time! The wilderness is your souls on earth!" he shouted ahead into the treetops. "Look about you, if you would view the conditions of your spirit, put here by the good Lord to show you and afright you. These wild places and these trails of awesome loneliness lie nowhere, nowhere, but in your heart."

A dark man, who was James Murrell the outlaw, rode his horse out of a cane brake and began going along beside Lorenzo without looking at him. He had the alternately proud and aggrieved look of a man believing himself to be an instrument in the hands of a power, and when he was young he said at once to strangers that he was being used by Evil, or sometimes he stopped a traveler by shouting, "Stop! I'm the Devil!" He rode along now talking and drawing out his talk, by some deep control of the voice gradually slowing the speed of Lorenzo's horse down until both the horses were softly trotting. He would have wondered that nothing he said was heard, not knowing that Lorenzo listened only to voices of whose heavenly origin he was more certain.

Murrell riding along with his victim-to-be, Murrell riding, was Murrell talking. He told away at his long tales, with always a distance and a long length of time flowing through them, and all centered about a silent man. In each the silent man would have done a piece of evil, a robbery or a murder, in a place of long ago, and it was all made for the revelation in the end that the silent man was Murrell himself, and the long story had happened yesterday, and the place *here*—the Natchez Trace. It would only take one dawning look for the victim to see that all of this was another story and he himself had listened his way into it, and that he too was about to recede in time (to where the dread was forgotten) for some listener and to live for a listener in the long ago. Destroy the present!—that must have been the first thing that was whispered in Murrell's heart—the living moment and the man that lives in it must die before you can go on. It was his habit to bring the journey—which might even take days—to a close with a kind of ceremony. Turning his face at last into the face of the victim, for he had never seen him before now, he would tower up with the sudden height of a man no longer the tale teller but the speechless protagonist, silent at last, one degree nearer the hero. Then he would murder the man.

But it would always start over. This man going forward was going backward with talk. He saw nothing, observed no world at all. The two ends of his journey pulled at him always and held him in a nowhere, half asleep, smiling and witty, dangling his predicament. He was a murderer whose final stroke was over-long postponed, who had to bring himself through the greatest tedium to act, as if the whole wilderness, where he was born, were his impediment. But behind him and before him he kept in sight a victim, he saw a man fixed and stayed at the point of death—no matter how the man's eyes denied it, a victim, hands spreading to reach as if for the first time for life. Contempt! That is what Murrell gave that man.

Lorenzo might have understood, if he had not been in haste, that Murrell in laying hold of a man meant to solve his mystery of being. It was as if other men, all but himself, would lighten their hold on the secret, upon assault, and let it fly free at death. In his violence he was only treating of enigma. The violence shook his own body first, like a force gathering, and now he turned in the saddle.

Lorenzo's despair had to be kindled as well as his ecstasy, and could not come without that kindling. Before the awe-filled moment when the faces were turned up under the flares, as though an angel hand tipped their chins, he had no way of telling whether he would enter the sermon by sorrow or by joy. But at this moment the face of Murrell was turned toward him, turning at last, all solitary, in its full, and Lorenzo would have seized the man at once by his black coat and shaken him like prey for a lost soul, so instantly was he certain that the false fire was in his heart instead of the true fire. But Murrell, quick when he was quick, had put his own hand out, a restraining hand, and laid it on the wavelike flesh of the Spanish race horse, which quivered and shuddered at the touch.

They had come to a great live-oak tree at the edge of a low marsh-land. The burning sun hung low, like a head lowered on folded arms, and over the long reaches of violet trees the evening seemed still with thought. Lorenzo knew the place from having seen it among many in dreams, and he stopped readily and willingly. He drew rein, and Murrell drew rein, he dismounted and Murrell dismounted, he took a step, and Murrell was there too; and Lorenzo was not surprised at the closeness, how Murrell in his long dark coat and over it his dark face darkening still, stood beside him like a brother seeking light.

But in that moment instead of two men coming to stop by the great forked tree, there were three.

From far away, a student, Audubon, had been approaching lightly on the wilderness floor, disturbing nothing in his lightness. The long day of beauty had led him this certain distance. A flock of purple finches that he tried for the first moment to count went over his head. He made a spelling of the soft *pet* of the ivory-billed woodpecker. He told himself always: Remember.

Coming upon the Trace, he looked at the high cedars, azure and still as distant smoke overhead, with their silver roots trailing down on either side like the veins of deepness in this place, and he noted some fact to his memory—this earth that wears but will not crumble or slide or turn to dust, they say it exists in one other spot in the world, Egypt—and then forgot it. He walked quietly. All life used this Trace, and he liked to see the animals move along it in direct, oblivious journeys, for they had begun it and made it, the buffalo and deer and the small running creatures before man ever knew where he wanted to go, and birds flew a great mirrored course above. Walking beneath them Audubon remembered how in the cities he had seen these very birds in his imagination, calling them up whenever he wished, even in the hard and glittering outer parlors where if an artist were humble enough to wait, some idle hand held up promised money. He walked lightly and he went as carefully as he had started at two that morning, crayon and paper, a gun, and a small bottle of spirits disposed about his body. (*Note: "The mocking birds so gentle that they would scarcely move out of the way."*) He looked with care; great abundance had ceased to startle him, and he could see things one by one. In Natchez they had told him of many strange and marvelous birds that were to be found here. Their descriptions had been exact, complete, and wildly varying, and he took them for inventions and believed that like all the worldly things that came out of Natchez, they would be disposed of and shamed by any man's excursion into the reality of Nature.

In the valley he appeared under the tree, a sure man, very sure and tender, as if the touch of all the earth rubbed upon him and the stains of the flowery swamp had made him so.

Lorenzo welcomed him and turned fond eyes upon him. To transmute a man into an angel was the hope that drove him all over the world and never let him flinch from a meeting or with-hold good-byes for long. This hope insistently divided his life into only two parts, journey and rest. There could be no night and day and love and despair and longing and satisfaction to make parti-tions in the single ecstasy of this alternation. All things were speech.

"God created the world," said Lorenzo, "and it exists to give testimony. Life is the tongue: Speak."

But instead of speech there happened a moment of deepest silence.

Audubon said nothing because he had gone without speaking a word for days. He did not regard his thoughts for the birds and animals as susceptible, in their first change, to words. His long playing on the flute was not in its origin a talking to himself. Rather than speak to order or describe, he would always draw a deer with a stroke across it to communicate his need of venison to an Indian. He had only found words when he discovered that there is much otherwise lost that can be noted down each item in its own day, and he wrote often now in a journal, not wanting anything to be lost the way it had been, all the past, and he would write about a day, "Only sorry that the Sun Sets."

Murrell, his cheated hand hiding the gun, could only continue to smile at Lorenzo, but he remembered in malice that he had disguised himself once as an Evangelist, and his final words to this victim would have been, "One of my disguises was what you are."

Then in Murrell Audubon saw what he thought of as "acquired sorrow"—that cumbrousness and darkness from which the naked Indian, coming just as he was made from God's hand, was so lightly free. He noted the eyes—the dark kind that loved to look through chinks, and saw neither closeness nor distance, light nor shade, wonder nor familiarity. They were narrowed to contract the heart, narrowed to make an averting plan. Audubon knew the finest-drawn tendons of the body and the working of their power, for he had touched them, and he supposed then that in man the enlargement of the eye to see started a motion in the hands to make or do, and that the narrowing of the eye stopped the hand and contracted the heart. Now Murrell's eyes followed an ant on a blade of grass, up the blade and down, many times in the single moment. Audubon had examined the Cave-In Rock where one robber had lived his hiding life, and the air in the cave was the cavelike air that enclosed this man, the same odor, flinty and dark. O secret life, he thought—is it true that the secret is withdrawn from the true disclosure, that man is a cave man, and that the openness I see, the ways through forests, the rivers brimming light, the wide arches where the birds fly, are dreams of freedom? If my origin is withheld from me, is my end to be unknown too? Is the radiance I see closed into an interval between two darks, or can it not illuminate them both and discover at last, though it cannot be spoken, what was thought hidden and lost?

In that quiet moment a solitary snowy heron flew down not far away and began to feed beside the marsh water.

At the single streak of flight, the ears of the race horse lifted, and the eyes of both horses filled with the soft lights of sunset, which in the next instant were reflected in the eyes of the men too as they all looked into the west toward the heron, and all eyes seemed infused with a sort of wildness.

Lorenzo gave the bird a triumphant look, such as a man may bestow upon his own vision, and thought, Nearness is near, lighted in a marsh-land, feeding at sunset. Praise God, His love has come visible.

Murrell, in suspicion pursuing all glances, blinking into a haze, saw only whiteness ensconced in darkness, as if it were a little luminous shell that drew in and held the eyesight. When he shaded his eyes, the brand "H.T." on his thumb thrust itself into his own vision, and he looked at the bird with the whole plan of the Mystic Rebellion darting from him as if in rays of the bright reflected light, and he stood looking proudly, leader as he was bound to become of the slaves, the brigands and outcasts of the entire Natchez country, with plans, dates, maps burning like a brand into his brain, and he saw himself proudly in a moment of prophecy going down rank after rank of successively bowing slaves to unroll and flaunt an awesome great picture of the Devil colored on a banner.

Audubon's eyes embraced the object in the distance and he

could see it as carefully as if he held it in his hand. It was a snowy heron alone out of its flock. He watched it steadily, in his care noting the exact inevitable things. When it feeds it muddies the water with its foot. . . . It was as if each detail about the heron happened slowly in time, and only once. He felt again the old stab of wonder—what structure of life bridged the reptile's scale and the heron's feather? That knowledge too had been lost. He watched without moving. The bird was defenseless in the world except for the intensity of its life, and he wondered, how can heat of blood and speed of heart defend it? Then he thought, as always as if it were new and unbelievable, it has nothing in space or time to prevent its flight. And he waited, knowing that some birds will wait for a sense of their presence to travel to men before they will fly away from them.

Fixed in its pure white profile it stood in the precipitous moment, a plumicorn on its head, its breeding dress extended in rays, eating steadily the little water creatures. There was a little space between each man and the others, where they stood overwhelmed. No one could say the three had ever met, or that this moment of intersection had ever come in their lives, or its promise fulfilled. But before them the white heron rested in the grasses with the evening all around it, lighter and more serene than the evening, flight closed in its body, the circuit of its beauty closed, a bird seen and a bird still, its motion calm as if it were offered: Take my flight. . . .

What each of them had wanted was simply *all*. To save all souls, to destroy all men, to see and to record all life that filled this world—all, all—but now a single frail yearning seemed to go out of the three of them for a moment and to stretch toward this one snowy, shy bird in the marshes. It was as if three whirlwinds had drawn together at some center, to find there feeding in peace a snowy heron. Its own slow spiral of flight could take it away in its own time, but for a little it held them still, it laid quiet over them, and they stood for a moment unburdened. . . .

Murrell wore no mask, for his face was that, a face that was aware while he was somnolent, a face that watched for him, and listened for him, alert and nearly brutal, the guard of a planner. He was quick without that he might be slow within, he staved off time, he wandered and plotted, and yet his whole desire mounted in him toward the end (was this the end—the sight of a bird feeding at dusk?), toward the instant of confession. His incessant deeds were thick in his heart now, and flinging himself to the ground he thought wearily, when all these trees are cut down, and the Trace lost, then my Conspiracy that is yet to spread itself will be disclosed, and all the stone-loaded bodies of murdered men will be pulled up, and all everywhere will know poor Murrell. His look pressed upon Lorenzo, who stared upward, and Audubon, who was taking out his gun, and his eyes squinted up to them in pleading, as if to say, "How soon may I speak, and how soon will you pity me?" Then he looked back to the bird, and he thought if it would look at him a dread penetration would fill and gratify his heart.

Audubon in each act of life was aware of the mysterious origin he half-concealed and half-sought for. People along the way asked him in their kindness or their rudeness if it were true, that he was born a prince and was the Lost Dauphin, and some said it was his secret, and some said that that was what he wished to find out before he died. But if it was his identity that he wished to discover, or if it was what a man had to seize beyond that, the way for him was by endless examination, by the care for every bird that flew in his path and every serpent that shone underfoot. Not one was enough; he looked deeper and deeper, on and on, as if for a particular beast or some legendary bird. Some men's eyes persisted in looking outward when they opened to look inward, and to their delight, there outflung was the astonishing world under the sky. When a man at last brought himself to face some mirror-surface he still saw the world looking back at him, and if he continued to look, to look closer and closer, what then? The gaze that looks outward must be trained without rest, to be indomitable. It must see as slowly as Murrell's ant in the grass, as exhaustively as Lorenzo's angel of God, and then, Audubon dreamed, with his mind going to his pointed brush, it must see like this, and he tightened his hand on the trigger of the gun and pulled it, and his eyes went closed. In memory the heron was all its solitude, its total beauty. All its whiteness could be seen from all sides at once, its pure feathers were as if counted and known and their array one upon the other would never be lost. But it was not from that memory that he could paint.

His opening eyes met Lorenzo's, close and flashing, and it was on seeing horror deep in them, like fires in abysses, that he recognized it for the first time. He had never seen horror in its purity and clarity until now, in bright blue eyes. He went and picked up the bird. He had thought it to be a female, just as one sees the moon as female; and so it was. He put it in his bag, and started away. But Lorenzo had already gone on, leaning a-tilt on the horse which went slowly.

Murrell was left behind, but he was proud of the dispersal, as if he had done it, as if he had always known that three men in simply being together and doing a thing can, by their obstinacy, take the pride out of one another. Each must go away alone, each send the others away alone. He himself had purposely kept to the wildest country in the world, and would have sought it out, the loneliest road. He looked about with satisfaction, and hid. Travelers were forever innocent, he believed: that was his faith. He lay in wait; his faith was in innocence and his knowledge was of ruin; and had these things been shaken? Now, what could possibly be outside his grasp? Churning all about him like a cloud about the sun was the great folding descent of his thought. Plans of deeds made his thoughts, and they rolled and mingled about his ears as if he heard a dark voice that rose up to overcome the wilderness voice, or was one with it. The night would soon come; and he had gone through the day.

Audubon, splattered and wet, turned back into the wilderness with the heron warm under his hand, his head still light in a kind of trance. It was undeniable, on some Sunday mornings, when he turned over and over his drawings they seemed beautiful to him, through what was dramatic in the conflict of life, or what was exact. What he would draw, and what he had seen, became for a moment one to him then. Yet soon enough, and it seemed to come in that same moment, like Lorenzo's horror and the gun's firing, he knew that even the sight of the heron, which surely he alone had appreciated, had not been all his belonging, and that never could any vision, even any simple sight, belong to him or to any man. He knew that the best he could make would be, after it was apart from his hand, a dead thing and not a live thing, never the essence, only a sum of parts; and that it would always meet with a stranger's sight, and never be one with the beauty in any other man's head in the world. As he had seen the bird most purely at its moment of death, in some fatal way, in his care for looking outward, he saw his long labor most revealingly at the point where it met its limit. Still carefully, for he was trained to see well in the dark, he walked on into the deeper woods, noting all sights, all sounds, and was gentler than they as he went.

In the woods that echoed yet in his ears, Lorenzo riding slowly looked back. The hair rose on his head and his hands began to shake with cold, and suddenly it seemed to him that God Himself, just now, thought of the Idea of Separateness. For surely He had never thought of it before, when the little white heron was flying down to feed. He could understand God's giving Separateness first and then giving Love to follow and heal in its wonder; but God had reversed this, and given Love first and then Separateness, as though it did not matter to Him which came first. Perhaps it was that God never counted the moments of Time; Lorenzo did that, among his tasks of love. Time did not occur to God. Therefore—did He even know of it? How to explain Time and Separateness back to God, Who had never thought of them, Who could let the whole world come to grief in a scattering moment?

Lorenzo brought his cold hands together in a clasp and stared through the distance at the place where the bird had been as if he saw it still; as if nothing could really take away what had happened to him, the beautiful little vision of the feeding bird. Its beauty had been greater than he could account for. The sweat of rapture poured down from his forehead, and then he shouted into the marshes.

"Tempter!"

He whirled forward in the saddle and began to hurry the horse to its high speed. His camp ground was far away still, though even now they must be lighting the torches and gathering in the multitudes, so that at the appointed time he would duly appear in their midst, to deliver his address on the subject of "In that day when all hearts shall be disclosed."

Then the sun dropped below the trees, and the new moon, slender and white, hung shyly in the west.

E. M. FORSTER

The Other Side of the Hedge

My pedometer told me that I was twenty-five; and, though it is a shocking thing to stop walking, I was so tired that I sat down on a milestone to rest. People outstripped me, jeering as they did so, but I was too apathetic to feel resentful, and even when Miss Eliza Dimbleby, the great educationist, swept past, exhorting me to persevere, I only smiled and raised my hat.

At first I thought I was going to be like my brother, whom I had had to leave by the roadside a year or two round the corner. He had wasted his breath on singing, and his strength on helping others. But I had travelled more wisely, and now it was only the monotony of the highway that oppressed me—dust under foot and brown crackling hedges on either side, ever since I could remember.

And I had already dropped several things—indeed, the road behind was strewn with the things we all had dropped: and the white dust was settling down on them, so that already they looked no better than stones. My muscles were so weary that I could not even bear the weight of those things I still carried. I slid off the milestone into the road, and lay there prostrate, with my face to the great parched hedge, praying that I might give up.

A little puff of air revived me. It seemed to come from the hedge; and, when I opened my eyes, there was a glint of light through the tangle of boughs and dead leaves. The hedge could not be as thick as usual. In my weak, morbid state, I longed to force my way in, and see what was on the other side. No one was in sight, or I should not have dared to try. For we of the road do not admit in conversation that there is another side at all.

I yielded to the temptation, saying to myself that I would come back in a minute. The thorns scratched my face, and I had to use my arms as a shield, depending on my feet alone to push me forward. Halfway through I would have gone back, for in the passage all the things I was carrying were scraped off me, and my clothes were torn. But I was so wedged that return was impossible, and I had to wriggle blindly forward, expecting every moment that my strength would fail me, and that I should perish in the undergrowth.

Suddenly cold water closed round my head, and I seemed sinking down for ever. I had fallen out of the hedge into a deep pool. I rose to the surface at last, crying for help, and I heard someone on the opposite bank laugh and say: "Another!" And then I was twitched out and laid panting on the dry ground.

Even when the water was out of my eyes, I was still dazed, for I had never been in so large a space, nor seen such grass and sunshine. The blue sky was no longer a strip, and beneath it the earth had risen gradually into hills—clean, bare buttresses, with beech trees in their folds, and meadows and clear pools at their feet. But the hills were not high, and there was in the landscape a sense of human occupation—so that one might have called it a park, or garden, if the words did not imply a certain triviality and constraint.

As soon as I got my breath, I turned to my rescuer and said: "Where does this place lead to?"

"Nowhere, thank the Lord!" said he, and laughed. He was a man of fifty or sixty—just the kind of age we mistrust on the road —but there was no anxiety in his manner, and his voice was that of a boy of eighteen.

"But it must lead somewhere!" I cried, too much surprised at his answer to thank him for saving my life.

"He wants to know where it leads!" he shouted to some men on the hillside, and they laughed back, and waved their caps.

I noticed then that the pool into which I had fallen was really a moat which bent round to the left and to the right, and that the hedge followed it continually. The hedge was green on this side—its roots showed through the clear water, and fish swam about in them—and it was wreathed over with dog-roses and Traveller's Joy. But it was a barrier, and in a moment I lost all pleasure in the grass, the sky, the trees, the happy men and women, and realized that the place was but a prison, for all its beauty and extent.

We moved away from the boundary, and then followed a path almost parallel to it, across the meadows. I found it difficult walking, for I was always trying to out-distance my companion, and there was no advantage in doing this if the place led nowhere. I had never kept step with anyone since I left my brother.

I amused him by stopping suddenly and saying disconsolately, "This is perfectly terrible. One cannot advance: One cannot progress. Now we of the road ——"

"Yes, I know."

"I was going to say, we advance continually."

"I know."

"We are always learning, expanding, developing. Why, even in my short life I have seen a great deal of advance—the Transvaal War, the Fiscal Question, Christian Science, Radium. Here for example ——"

I took out my pedometer, but it still marked twenty-five, not a degree more.

"Oh, it's stopped! I meant to show you. It should have registered all the time I was walking with you. But it makes me only twenty-five."

"Many things don't work in here," he said. "One day a man brought in a Lee-Metford, and that wouldn't work."

"The laws of science are universal in their application. It must be the water in the moat that has injured the machinery. In normal conditions everything works. Science and the spirit of emulation—those are the forces that have made us what we are."

I had to break off and acknowledge the pleasant greetings of people whom we passed. Some of them were singing, some talking, some engaged in gardening, hay-making, or other rudimentary industries. They all seemed happy; and I might have been happy too, if I could have forgotten that the place led nowhere.

I was startled by a young man who came sprinting across our path, took a little fence in the fine style, and went tearing over a ploughed field till he plunged into a lake, across which he began to swim. Here was true energy, and I exclaimed: "A cross-country race! Where are the others?"

"There are no others," my companion replied; and, later on, when we passed some long grass from which came the voice of a girl singing exquisitely to herself, he said again: "There are no others." I was bewildered at the waste in production, and murmured to myself, "What does it all mean?"

He said: "It means nothing but itself"—and he repeated the words slowly, as if I were a child.

"I understand," I said quietly, "but I do not agree. Every achievement is worthless unless it is a link in the chain of development. And I must not trespass on your kindness any longer. I must get back somehow to the road, and have my pedometer mended."

"First, you must see the gates," he replied, "for we have gates, though we never use them."

I yielded politely, and before long we reached the moat again, at a point where it was spanned by a bridge. Over the bridge was a big gate, as white as ivory, which was fitted into a gap in the boundary hedge. The gate opened outwards, and I exclaimed in amazement, for from it ran a road—just such a road as I had left—dusty under foot, with brown crackling hedges on either side as far as the eye could reach.

"That's my road!" I cried.

He shut the gate and said: "But not your part of the road. It is through this gate that humanity went out countless ages ago, when it was first seized with the desire to walk."

I denied this, observing that the part of the road I myself had left was not more than two miles off. But with the obstinacy of his years he repeated: "It is the same road. This is the beginning, and though it seems to run straight away from us, it doubles so often, that it is never far from our boundary and sometimes touches it." He stooped down by the moat, and traced on its moist margin an absurd figure like a maze. As we walked back through the meadows, I tried to convince him of his mistake.

"The road sometimes doubles, to be sure, but that is part of our discipline. Who can doubt that its general tendency is onward? To what goal we know not—it may be to some mountain where we shall touch the sky, it may be over precipices into the sea. But that it goes forward—who can doubt that? It is the thought of that that makes us strive to excel, each in his own way, and gives us an impetus which is lacking with you. Now that man who passed us—it's true that he ran well, and jumped well, and swam well; but we have men who can run better, and men who can jump better, and who can swim better. Specialization has produced results which would surprise you. Similarly, that girl—"

Here I interrupted myself to exclaim: "Good gracious me! I could have sworn it was Miss Eliza Dimbleby over there, with her feet in the fountain!"

He believed that it was.

"Impossible! I left her on the road, and she is due to lecture this evening at Tunbridge Wells. Why, her train leaves Cannon Street in—of course my watch has stopped like everything else. She is the last person to be here."

"People always are astonished at meeting each other. All kinds come through the hedge, and come at all times—when they are drawing ahead in the race, when they are lagging behind, when they are left for dead. I often stand near the boundary listening to the sounds of the road—you know what they are—and wonder if anyone will turn aside. It is my great happiness to help someone out of the moat, as I helped you. For our country fills up slowly, though it was meant for all mankind."

"Mankind have other aims," I said gently, for I thought him well-meaning; "and I must join them." I bade him good evening, for the sun was declining, and I wished to be on the road by nightfall. To my alarm, he caught hold of me, crying: "You are not to go yet!" I tried to shake him off, for we had no interests in common, and his civility was becoming irksome to me. But for all my struggles the tiresome old man would not let go; and, as wrestling is not my specialty, I was obliged to follow him.

It was true that I could never have found alone the place where I came in, and I hoped that, when I had seen the other sights about which he was worrying, he would take me back to it. But I was determined not to sleep in the country, for I mistrusted it, and the people too, for all their friendliness. Hungry though I was, I would not join them in their evening meals of milk and fruit, and, when they gave me flowers, I flung them away as soon as I could do so unobserved. Already they were lying down for the night like cattle—some out on the bare hillside, others in groups under the beeches. In the light of an orange sunset I hurried on with my unwelcome guide, dead tired, faint for want of food, but murmuring indomitably: "Give me life, with its struggles and victories, with its failures and hatreds, with its deep moral meaning and its unknown goal!"

At last we came to a place where the encircling moat was spanned by another bridge, and where another gate interrupted the line of the boundary hedge. It was different from the first gate; for it was half transparent like horn, and opened inwards. But through it, in the waning light, I saw again just such a road as I had left—monotonous, dusty, with brown crackling hedges on either side, as far as the eye could reach.

I was strangely disquieted at the sight, which seemed to deprive me of all self-control. A man was passing us, returning for the night to the hills, with a scythe over his shoulder and a can of some liquid in his hand. I forgot the destiny of our race. I forgot the road that lay before my eyes, and I sprang at him, wrenched the can out of his hand, and began to drink.

It was nothing stronger than beer, but in my exhausted state it overcame me in a moment. As in a dream, I saw the old man shut the gate, and heard him say: "This is where your road ends, and through this gate humanity—all that is left of it—will come in to us."

Though my senses were sinking into oblivion, they seemed to expand ere they reached it. They perceived the magic song of nightingales, and the odour of invisible hay, and stars piercing the fading sky. The man whose beer I had stolen lowered me down gently to sleep off its effects, and, as he did so, I saw that he was my brother.

THEODORE ROSZAK

The Myth of Objective Consciousness

Objectivity as a state of being fills the very air we breathe in a scientific culture; it grips us subliminally in all we say, feel, and do. The mentality of the ideal scientist becomes the very soul of the society. We seek to adapt our lives to the dictates of that mentality, or at the very least we respond to it acquiescently in the myriad images and pronouncements in which it manifests itself about us during every waking hour. The Barbarella and James Bond who keep their clinical cool while dealing out prodigious sex or sadistic violence . . . the physiologist who persuades several score of couples to undertake coitus while wired to a powerhouse of electronic apparatus so that he can achieve a statistical measure of sexual normalcy . . . the characters of *Last Year At Marienbad* who face one another as impassively as empty mirrors . . . the Secretary of Defense who tells the public without blinking an eye that our country possesses the "overkill" capacity to destroy any given enemy ten times . . . the high-rise glass and aluminum slab that deprives of visual involvement by offering us only functional linearity and massive reflecting surfaces . . . the celebrated surgeon who assures us that his heart transplant was a "success" though of course the patient died . . . the computer technician who blithely suggests that we have to wage an "all-out war on sleep" in order to take advantage of the latest breakthrough in rapid communications . . . the modish expert who seeks (with phenomenal success) to convince us that the essence of communication lies not in the truth or falsehood, wisdom or folly of the message that person transfers to person, but rather in the technical characteristics of the intervening medium . . . the political scientist who settles for being a psephological virtuoso, pretending that the statistics of meaningless elections are the veritable substance of politics . . . all these (or so I would argue) are life under the sway of objective consciousness.

In short, as science elaborates itself into the dominant cultural influence of our age, it is the psychology and not the epistemology of science that urgently requires our critical attention; for it is primarily at this level that the most consequential deficiencies and imbalances of the technocracy are revealed.

We can, I think, identify three major characteristics of the psychic style which follows from an intensive cultivation of objective consciousness. I have called them: (1) the alienative dichotomy; (2) the invidious hierarchy; (3) the mechanistic imperative.

(1) Objective consciousness begins by dividing reality into two spheres, which would seem best described as "In-Here" and "Out-There." By In-Here is meant that place within the person to which consciousness withdraws when one wants to know without becoming involved in or committed to that which is being known. There are many kinds of operations that can be conducted by In-Here. In the natural sciences, the usual activities of In-Here would include those of observing, experimenting, measuring, classifying, and working out quantitative relationships of the most general kind. In the humanities and what we call the behavioral sciences, the operations are more various, but they include numerous activities that seek to imitate the natural sciences by way of tabulating, pigeonholing, applying information theory or game strategies to human affairs, etc. In-Here may be involved, however, in something as simple as the detached scrutiny of a document, a book, an *objet d'art*—meaning the study of this thing as if one's feelings were not aroused by it, or as if such feelings as might arise could be discounted or screened out.

Whatever the scientific method may or may not be, people think they are behaving scientifically whenever they create an In-Here within themselves which undertakes to know without an investment of the person in the act of knowing. The necessary effect of distancing, of estranging In-Here from Out-There may be achieved in any number of ways: by the intervention of various mechanical gadgets between observer and observed; by the elaboration of chilly jargons and technical terms that replace sensuous speech; by the invention of strange methodologies which reach out to the subject matter like a pair of mechanical hands; by the subordination of the particular and immediate experience to a statistical generalization; by appeal to a professional standard which excuses the observer from responsibility to anything other than a lofty abstraction—such as "the pursuit of truth," "pure research," etc. All these protective strategies are especially compatible with natures that are beset by timidity and fearfulness; but also with those that are characterized by plain insensitivity and whose habitual mode of contact with the world is a cool curiosity untouched by love, tenderness, or passionate wonder. Behind both such timidity and insensitivity there can easily lurk the spitefulness of a personality which feels distressingly remote from the rewards of warm engagement with life. It is revealing that whenever a scientific method of study is brought into play, we are supposed to regard it as irrelevant, if not downright unfair, to probe the many very different motivations that may underlie a man's desire to be purely objective. It is little wonder, then, that the ideal of objectivity can easily be invoked to cover a curiosity of callousness or hostility, as well as a curiosity of affectionate concern. In any event, when I convince myself that I can create a place within me that has been cleansed of all those murky passions, hostilities, joys, fears, and lusts which define my person, a place that is "Not-I," and when I believe that it is *only* from the vantage point of this Not-I that reality can be accurately perceived, then I have begun to honor the myth of objective consciousness.

The essential experience of being In-Here is that of being an unseen, unmoved spectator. Abraham Maslow characterizes the situation in this way:

> It means looking at something that is not you, not human, not personal, something independent of you the perceiver. . . . You the observer are, then, really alien to it, uncomprehending and without sympathy or identification. . . . You look through the microscope or the telescope as through a keyhole, peering, peeping, from a distance, from outside, not as one who has a right to be in the room being peeped into.[1]

[1] Abraham Maslow, *The Psychology of Science* (New York: Harper & Row, 1966), p. 49.

The spectating In-Here has been called by many names: ego, intelligence, self, subject, reason. . . . I avoid such designations here because they suggest some fixed faculty or psychic entity. What I prefer to emphasize is the *act* of contraction that takes place within the person, the sense of taking a step back, away from, and out of. Not only back and away from the natural world, but from the inarticulate feelings, physical urges, and wayward images that surge up from within the person. To these "irrationalities" Freud gave the revealing name, "the *it*": a something which is Not-I, but alien, incomprehensible, and only to be known reliably when it, too, is forced Out-There to become an object for analysis.

The ideal of the objective consciousness is that there should be as little as possible In-Here and, conversely, as much as possible Out-There. For only what is Out-There can be studied and known. Objectivity leads to such a great emptying-out operation: the progressive alienation of more and more of In-Here's personal contents in the effort to achieve the densest possible unit of observational concentration surrounded by the largest possible area of study. The very word "concentration" yields the interesting image of an identity contracted into a small, hard ball; hence a dense, diminished identity, something which is less than one otherwise might be. Yet the predilection of In-Here is to remain "concentrated" as long and as often as possible. Curiously, this great good called knowledge, the very guarantee of our survival, is taken to be something that is forthcoming only to this lesser, shriveled-up identity.

The scientific observer who comes to feel that Out-There has begun to implicate him personally—say, in the manner of a lover spellbinding one's sympathies so that one cannot tell clearly where one's self leaves off and the other begins—has begun to lose his objectivity. Therefore, he must fight back this irrational involvement of his personal feeling. Like Odysseus in the presence of the sirens' song, In-Here must be lashed to the mast, or its mission may never be completed. But if body, feelings, emotions, moral sentiment, sensuous enchantment are all to be located Out-There, then who is this In-Here that is so stalwartly struggling against the siren song? It is a weird identity indeed, this In-Here. More and more it looks like Kafka's castle: a stronghold well defended, but manned by . . . parties unknown.

It would be an interesting line of questioning to put to our experts, would it not? Who are "you" when you are being purely objective? How did you manage to bring this purely objective "you" into existence—and how can you be so sure you really pulled it off? Moreover, does this purely objective "you" prove to be an enjoyable identity? Or is that beside the point?

(2) The act of psychic contraction that creates In-Here simultaneously creates Out-There, which is whatever gets left behind in the wake of the contraction. The line which divides In-Here from Out-There now becomes a line between a place where it is desirable and secure to be (In-Here) and a place that is untrustworthy, perhaps downright dangerous (Out-There). In-Here is the center of reliable knowledge; it knows what it is doing; it learns, plans, controls, watches out cunningly for threats and opportunities. The alternative to being in a place of reliable knowledge is, obviously, to be in a place of drift, unpredictability, stupidity. Such is what Out-There becomes.

Now, in fact, anyone, even the most objective scientist, would fall into a state of total paralysis if he *really* believed that Out-There (beginning with his own organism and unconscious processes) was totally stupid. Nevertheless, In-Here is committed to studying Out-There *as if* it were completely stupid, meaning without intention or wisdom or purposeful pattern. In-Here cannot, if it is to be strictly objective, strive to empathize in any way with Out-There. It must not attribute to Out-There what cannot be observed, measured, and—ideally—formulated into articulate, demonstrable propositions for experimental verification. In-Here must maintain its alienative dichotomy at all times. And like the racist who cannot under Jim Crow conditions come to see the segregated black man as anything but a doltish and primitive nigger, so In-Here, as the unmoved spectator, cannot feel that Out-There has any ingenuity or dignity. Under this kind of scrutiny, even the other human beings who inhabit Out-There can be made stupid, for they were not made to function within laboratory conditions or according to the exacting needs of questionnaires and surveys. Under the eyes of an alien observer they also begin to lose their human purposefulness.

As soon as two human beings relate in detachment as observer to observed, as soon as the observer claims to be aware of nothing more than the behavioral surface of the observed, an invidious hierarchy is established which reduces the observed to a lower status. Of necessity he falls into the same category with all the stupid things of the world that fill Out-There. For consider the gross impertinence of this act of detached observation. Psychologist confronting his laboratory subject, anthropologist confronting tribal group, political scientist confronting voting public . . . in all such cases, what the observer may very well be saying to the observed is the same: "I can perceive no more than your behavioral façade. I can grant you no more reality or psychic coherence than this perception allows. I shall observe this behavior of yours and record it. I shall not enter into your life, your task, your condition of existence. Do not turn to me or appeal to me or ask me to become involved with you. I am here only as a temporary observer whose role is to stand back and record and later to make my own sense of what you seem to be doing or intending. I assume that I can adequately understand what you are doing or intending without entering wholly into your life. I am not particularly interested in what *you* uniquely are; I am interested only in the general pattern to which you conform. I assume I have the right to use you to perform this process of classification. I assume I have the right to reduce all that you are to an integer in my science."

At the extreme, this alienated relationship is that of the Nazi physician experimenting upon his human victims, learning interesting new things about pain, suffering, privation. One cringes from the reference and protests, "*That* was an abnormal case. Normally, research involving human subjects stops short of inhumanity. And, in any event, whatever laboratory work is involved takes place in limited episodes; it is not a total way of life for experimenter or subject." Unhappily, however, the ethos of objectivity has gotten well beyond limited research episodes. Already legions of scientists and military men throughout the world, the products of careful training and selection, give themselves to whole lives of ultimate objectivity. They systematically detach themselves from any concern for those lives their inventions and weapons may someday do to death. They do their job as they are ordered to do it . . . objectively. For them the world at large has become a laboratory—in the same sense that when they enter upon their professional capacity, they leave their personal feelings behind. Perhaps they even take pride in their capacity to do so, for indeed it requires an act of iron will to ignore the claims that person makes upon person.

When In-Here observes Out-There, it is with the intention of giving order to what it perceives. The order can be understood to be that of "law," or statistical generalization, or classification. This orderliness is what sometimes leads scientists to speak of the "beauty of nature." . . . But what is important about all these kinds of order is that they may concede no credit to Out-There for being autonomously clever or marvelous. The scientist's nature becomes "beautiful" when it has been tidied up and pigeonholed. The achievement lies in the scientist's "discovery" of this order; the credit belongs to the observing mind. It is a situation which reminds one of the quaint use of the term "discovery" in relationship to the European voyages of discovery. The phrase suggests that the Americas, Africa, and Asia, with all their indigenous peoples, had been waiting eagerly to be found by the white man. We now recognize the comic ethnocentrism of that view; the cerebral anthropocentrism of scientific discovery is less obvious. But Abraham Maslow offers us one lovely example of the subliminal presumption. He mentions the scientist who praised a book on "the difficult problem of woman's sexuality" because it at last took up a subject "about which so little is known"! He goes on to comment on the psychology of the scientist's nomothetic project:

> Organizing experience into meaningful patterns implies that experience itself has no meaningfulness, that the organizer creates or imposes or donates the meaning, . . . that it is a gift from the knower to the known. In other words, "meaningfulness" of this kind is of the realm of classification and abstraction rather than of experience. . . . Frequently I sense also the implication that it is "human-created," i.e., that much of it would vanish if human beings disappeared.[2]

The relationship Maslow describes is obviously a hierarchical one. In-Here is the superior of Out-There. Out-There has no way to lay claim upon In-Here, to appeal for kindness, appreciation, adoration, etc., because it is In-Here that monopolizes meaning.

[2] Maslow, *The Psychology of Science*, pp. 56, 84.

Out-There is left without voice to speak in behalf of its sanctity or in its defense. Moreover, In-Here knows how Out-There works and therefore has power over Out-There. Since In-Here is the sole dispenser of meaning, who then can gainsay In-Here when it grants itself the unabridged right to use that power? The dead and the stupid are objects of contempt—or at best of condescension; they must submit to the scrutiny, experimentation, and exploitation of In-Here. The fact that Out-There seems not to recognize this hierarchical order only proves how dead or stupid it really is. Instead of making life secure for In-Here, Out-There blunders about producing disease, famine, death, riot, protest, and the many misfortunes of existence. Out-There is obviously unreliable. And the unreliability begins very close to home. It begins with those outbursts of fluid, imprecise, distractive imaginings that well up from the "irrational," as well as with this troublesome body, which seems to do almost nothing properly.

If In-Here did not constantly intervene in the behavior of Out-There, what an impossible chaos would ensue! But fortunately In-Here, being vigilant and clever, is able to keep Out-There in line: to conquer it, to manipulate it, to improve upon it—beginning with the witless body, which is forever proving to be incompetent. In-Here must therefore devise forms of surgical and chemical intervention that will make sure the body sleeps, wakes, digests, excretes, grows, relaxes, feels gay, feels blue, has sex, etc., correctly, at the right time and place. In-Here may even devise ways to keep the body functioning indefinitely, so that it does not commit the ultimate incompetence of dying. Similarly, the natural environment must be conquered and subjected to forceful improvement. Climate and landscape must be redesigned. Waste space must be made livable, meaning covered over with an urban expansion into which nothing that is not manmade or man-arranged will intrude itself. Similarly, the social environment—the body politic—must be brought as completely under centralized, deliberative control as the physical body has been brought under the domination of the cerebrum. Unless the order of things is readily apparent to a command and control center—in the individual, it will be the forebrain; in the society, it will be the technocracy—and available for manipulation, it cannot be respected as order at all.

So, at last, Out-There emerges as a pitiful disappointment: an underdeveloped country awaiting the competent management of In-Here. As Joseph Wood Krutch comments, this reverses the age-old relationship of man to nature and rapidly leads to the un-bridled assertion of human hubris: "Is there anything *we* can't do better?"

> No age before ours would have made such an assumption. Man has always before thought of himself as puny by com-parison with natural forces, and he was humble before them. But we have been so impressed by the achievement of technology that we are likely to think we can do more than nature herself. We dug the Panama Canal, didn't we? Why not the Grand Canyon? [3]

An objective, meaning an alienated, attitude toward the natural environment comes easily these days to a population largely born and raised in the almost totally manmade world of the metropolis. It would be difficult for anyone so raised, including a scientist, *not* to be objective toward a "nature" which he has only known in the form of tidy, if boring, artificialities arranged by the parks and gardens authorities. The flora, fauna, landscape, and, increas-ingly, the climate of the earth lie practically helpless at the feet of technological man, tragically vulnerable to his arrogance. Without question, we have triumphed over them . . . at least until the massive ecological consequences catch up with us.

(3) But there are other areas of nature which pose a more serious problem for the objective consciousness. They appear within the person.

No matter how strenuously In-Here strives to thrust out the "irrational," it continues to intrude itself with its claims in behalf of sensuous contact, fantasy, spontaneity, and concern for the per-son. From somewhere nearby, In-Here continues to feel the pres-sure of a strange need to moralize, to joke, to hate, to love, to lust, to fear. . . . Obviously the citadel of objectivity is a precarious place. This mysterious organism which In-Here pilots about is not a trustworthy machine. Therefore, In-Here, in search of impreg-nable objectivity, takes the final step. It sets about inventing a superior command and control center that will take over whenever

[3] Joseph Wood Krutch, *Grand Canyon* (New York: William Sloane Associates, 1958), p. 25.

In-Here's capacity to achieve perfect impersonality breaks down: an electronic nervous system! Such a device will never lose control of itself, never weaken, never turn unpredictably personal, for it will never have been a person in the first place.

Man's infatuation with the machine is frequently misunderstood as being a love affair with mere power. "Here I sell what all men crave: power!" So said Matthew Boulton, referring to the first steam-engine factory. But the great virtue of the machine lies not only in its power: many mechanisms—like timers or electric eyes or most cybernated systems—are not particularly powerful and yet are highly valued. Is it not the machine's capacity to be severely routinized that we admire quite as much as its sheer strength? Unlike the human organism, the machine can achieve perfect concentration, perfect self-control. It performs the one task to which it is assigned, with no possibility of being distracted. It acts without involvement in what it does. Indeed, the burden which industrialization lifted from men's backs was not physical labor so much as it was deadly routine, with its demand for unrelenting and exhaustive concentration. Thus, the archetypal machine in our society is not the gargantuan steam engine, but the lilliputian clock. For even the steam engine had no industrial significance until it became part of a regulated system of production, a system which ran like "clockwork." As Lewis Mumford reminds us, "the clock . . . is the paragon of automatons. . . . The automation of time, in the clock, is the pattern of all larger systems of automation." [4]

So then: if muscle power can be replaced by a mechanism, how much more desirable still to replace the mind behind the muscle with a mechanism! If In-Here cannot be entirely relied upon to remain objective, then why not design a machine whose In-Here is a totally controlled program which specifies unambiguous objectives and procedures? "Artificial intelligence" is the logical goal toward which objective consciousness moves. Again, it is the clock which anticipates the computer. True time (what Bergson called "duration") is properly the living experience of life itself and therefore radically intuitive. But for most of us, this true time has been hopelessly displaced by the rigid rhythm of clock time. What is

[4] Lewis Mumford, *The Myth of the Machine* (New York: Harcourt Brace Jovanovich, 1967), p. 286. Mumford also calls our attention here to a similar insight on the part of Marx.

fundamentally the vital flow of experience then becomes an arbitrarily segmented, external measuring rod imposed upon our existence—and to experience time in any other way becomes "mystical," or "mad."

If the experience of time can be thus objectified, then why not everything else? Why should we not invent machines that objectify thought, creativity, decision making, moral judgment . . . ? Let us have machines that play games, make poems, compose music, teach philosophy. To be sure, it was once thought that such things were to be done for the joy of the playing, the making, the composing, the teaching. But scientific culture makes no allowance for "joy," since that is an experience of intensive personal involvement. Joy is something that is known only to the person: it does not submit to objectification.

To a mournfully great extent, the progress of expertise, especially as it seeks to mechanize culture, is a waging of open warfare upon joy. It is a bewilderingly perverse effort to demonstrate that nothing, *absolutely nothing* is particularly special, unique, or marvelous, but can be lowered to the status of mechanized routine. More and more the spirit of "nothing but" hovers over advanced scientific research: the effort to degrade, disenchant, level down. Is it that the creative and the joyous embarrass the scientific mind to such an extent that it must try with might and main to degrade them? Consider the strange compulsion our biologists have to synthesize life in a test tube—and the seriousness with which this project is taken. Every dumb beast of the earth knows without thinking once about it how to create life: it does so by seeking delight where it shines most brightly. But, the biologist argues, once we have done it in a laboratory, *then* we shall really know what it is all about. Then we shall be able to *improve* upon it!

GENE YOUNGBLOOD

FROM *Expanded Cinema*

THE AUDIENCE AND
THE MYTH OF ENTERTAINMENT

> "The most important part about tomorrow is not the tech-
> nology or the automation, but that man is going to come
> into entirely new relationships with his fellow men. He
> will retain much more in his everyday life of what we term
> the naïveté and idealism of the child. I think the way to see
> what tomorrow is going to look like is just to look at our
> children."
>
> R. BUCKMINSTER FULLER

As a child of the New Age, for whom "nature" is the solar system
and "reality" is an invisible environment of messages, I am
naturally hypersensitive to the phenomenon of vision. I have come
to understand that all language is but substitute vision and, as
Teilhard de Chardin has observed, "The history of the living
world can be summarized as the elaboration of ever more perfect
eyes within a cosmos in which there is always something more to
be seen." [1]

It is that "something more" that has fascinated me since first I
became aware of the limited range of ordinary consciousness,
chiefly as manifested in the cinema. We are witnessing a metamorphosis in the nature of life on earth. Art, science, and metaphysics, separated for so long in the specialized world of Western
man, are reconverging; the interface reveals a broader and deeper

[1] Pierre Teilhard de Chardin, *The Phenomenon of Man* (New York: Harper
& Row, 1959), p. 31.

reality awaiting our investigation. An increasing number of humans are beginning to understand that man probably never has perceived reality at all, because he has not been able to perceive himself. The realization is not new; only the context is unique: A vast portion of our culture, free of the conditioning of and nostalgia for past environments, has intuited something fundamentally inadequate in prevailing attitudes toward the notion of reality.

In most languages of most cultures throughout history, seeing has been equated with understanding. The entire Indo-European linguistic system is filled with examples: *I see; ya vizhu; je vois.* Yet nearly twenty-four hundred years ago Plato asserted, "The world of our sight is like the habitation in prison." [2] Recent studies in anatomy, physiology, and anthropology have led to a similar conclusion. [3] We have come to see that we don't really see, that "reality" is more within than without. The objective and the subjective are one.

At the same time, science has taught that there is no purely physical reason for the disparity between apprehending and comprehending. We know, for example, that thirty-eight percent of fibers entering or leaving the central nervous system are in the optic nerve. It is estimated that as much as seventy-five percent of information entering the brain is from the eyes. Current research indicates approximately one hundred million sensors in the retina and only five million channels to the brain from the retina. There is a great deal of evidence to suggest that information processing is done in the eye before data are passed to the brain. [4]

The metaphysical space that separates father and son so dramatically in what we call the generation gap was manifested on a global scale on July 20, 1969. In television's elaborate, movie-like, subjective-camera "simulation" of the first moon landing, the history of subjective art with its emphasis on content came into total confrontation with the history of objective art and its emphasis on process. As we saw the event, reality was not half as "real" as the

[2] Plato, *The Republic*, Book VIII, *ca.* 390 B.C.
[3] Extensive research on physiological conditioning is found in *The Influence of Culture on Visual Perception*, by Marshall H. Segall, Donald T. Campbell, and Melville J. Herskovits (Indianapolis: Bobbs-Merrill, 1966).
[4] F. R. Sias, Jr., "The Eye as a Coding Mechanism," *Medical Electronic News*, quoted in: Nels Winkless and Paul Honore, "What Good Is a Baby?" *Proceedings of the AFIPS 1968 Fall Joint Computer Conference.*

simulation because it was the reality of a process of perception. We were seeing nothing but videospace; the simulated reality turned out to be only the reality of a simulation. Objective awareness of a subjective process was all that mattered, and history's simulation suddenly became irrelevant. Thousands of years of theatrical tradition were demolished in two hours before an audience of four hundred million world persons.

In the ascending spiral of evolution each new generation absorbs the experiences of the previous level and expands upon them. Teilhard has termed this *hominization*, the process by which the original protohuman stock becomes increasingly more human, realizing more of its possibilities. This "consciousness expansion" has reached a velocity of evolutionary acceleration at which several transformations occur within the life span of a single generation. Because of mankind's inevitable symbiosis with the mind-manifesting hallucinogens of the ecology on the one hand and his organic partnership with machines on the other, an increasing number of the inhabitants of this planet live virtually in another world. . . .

It is a world infinitely more natural and complete than that of commercial cinema or television, which is used to confirm the existing consciousness rather than to expand it. Art is the language through which we perceive new relationships at work in the environment, both physical and metaphysical. Indeed, art is the essential instrument in the very development of that consciousness. As Hermann Hesse observed, every important cultural gesture comes down to a morality, a model for human behavior concentrated into a gesture. Whitehead found it to be "the ultimate morality of the mind." Perhaps never before has a new model for human behavior been needed so urgently as today.

We who are about to inherit the earth from our fathers will receive it with a brave new design. We see the whole earth and thus we see the illusion that has characterized life upon it. We cannot accept the truths and values of a world in which we no longer live. We are a generation of desperadoes. We move across the landscape with bold abandon because we intuit that the birth certificate is the only credit card. The word "utopian" is not anathema to us because we know that the illusion can be shattered within our own lifetimes, that the industrial equation means practical utopianism for the first time in history.

Our grasp of these realities is inarticulate; we cannot speak it. We are haunted by our own disenchantment and alienation as much as our parents are offended by it. The human condition, as this millennium draws to a close, is one of decreasing intervals between increasing emergencies until nothing but emergency exists. We have nothing to lose. Spiritually we have nothing to lose because there is only sorrow in the values of the past and we have no tears left. Physically we have nothing to lose because we know that wealth can neither be created nor spent, that it goes nowhere and always increases with use.

> In this century alone we have gone from less than one percent of humanity being able to survive in appreciable health and comfort to forty-four percent of humanity surviving at a standard of living unexperienced or undreamed of before. This utterly unpredicted synergetic success occurred within only two-thirds of a century despite continually decreasing metallic resources per each world person. . . . the world total of seventy billion dollars in mined gold represents only three one-thousandths of one percent of the value of the world's organized industrial production resources.[5]

Within the larger context of radical evolution there are many local revolutions. One of them is the revolution of expectations that burns in the minds of the new consciousness. Eskimo children who've never seen a wheeled vehicle can identify the types of aircraft flying over the North Pole. Young Dyaks in the longhouses of equatorial Borneo listen to the Beatles on transistor radios. Teenage Bedouins wandering the Sahara hear Nasser's radio telling how Vietnamese children are being slaughtered half the world away.[6]

Dylan swears he sees his reflection so high above the wall upon which he once drew conclusions. Seeing that reflection is the revolution. It tells us old reasons for doing things that no longer exist. "There's less to do because circumstances do it for us: the earth. Art has obscured the difference between art and life; now

[5] R. Buckminster Fuller, *Operating Manual for Spaceship Earth* (Carbondale, Ill.: Southern Illinois University Press, 1969), pp. 82, 95.
[6] Ritchie Calder, "The Speed of Change," *Bulletin of the Atomic Scientists* (December, 1965).

life will obscure the difference between life and art." [7] We no longer need to prove our right to live. We're struggling in the toil of old realities, stranded from our conscience, doing our best to deny it. We are tragically in need of new vision: Expanded cinema is the beginning of that vision. We shall be released. We will bring down the wall. We'll be reunited with our reflection.

I'm writing at the end of the era of cinema as we've known it, the beginning of an era of image-exchange between man and man. The cinema, said Godard, is truth twenty-four times a second. The truth is this: That with the possibility of each man on earth being born a physical success there is no archetypal Man whom one can use in the culturally elitist manner and each man becomes the subject of his own study. The historical preoccupation with finding the one idea that is Man will give way to the idea that earth is, and then to the idea of other earths. . . .

EVOCATION AND EXPOSITION: TOWARD OCEANIC CONSCIOUSNESS

There is an important distinction to be made between *evocation,* the language of synaesthetic cinema, primarily poetic in structure and effect, and *exposition,* the language of narrative cinema, which chiefly conforms to traditional, literary narrative modes. Intermedia artist and filmmaker Carolee Schneemann has characterized evocation as "the place between desire and experience, the interpenetrations and displacements which occur between various sense stimuli." "Vision is not a fact," Miss Schneemann postulates, "but an aggregate of sensations. Vision creates its own efforts toward realization; effort does not create vision." [8]

Thus, by creating a new kind of vision, synaesthetic cinema creates a new kind of consciousness: oceanic consciousness. Freud spoke of oceanic consciousness as that in which we feel our individual existence lost in mystic union with the universe. Nothing could be more appropriate to contemporary experience, when for the first time man has left the boundaries of this globe. The

[7] John Cage, *A Year from Monday* (Middletown, Conn.: Wesleyan University Press, 1968), pp. 9, 19.
[8] Carolee Schneemann, "Snows," *I-Kon,* Susan Sherman (ed.), Vol. 1, No. 5 (New York: March, 1968).

oceanic effect of synaesthetic cinema is similar to the mystical allure of the natural elements: We stare in mindless wonder at the ocean or a lake or river. We are drawn almost hypnotically to fire, gazing as though spellbound. We see cathedrals in clouds, not thinking anything in particular, but feeling somehow secure and content. It is similar to the concept of *no-mindedness* in Zen, which also is the state of mantra and mandala consciousness, the widest range of consciousness.

Miss Schneemann defines perception as *eye-journey* or *empathy-drawing*. It is precisely through a kind of empathy-drawing that the content of synaesthetic cinema is created jointly by the film and the viewer. The very nature of evocation requires creative effort on the part of the viewer, whereas expository modes do all the work and the viewer becomes passive. In expositional narrative, a story is being *told*; in evocative synaesthesia an experience is being created. . . .

With typical poetic eloquence, Hermann Hesse has summarized the evocative effects of oceanic consciousness in this memorable passage from *Demian:*

> The surrender to nature's irrational, strangely confused formations produces in us a feeling of inner harmony with the force responsible for these phenomena . . . the boundaries separating us from nature begin to quiver and dissolve . . . we are unable to decide whether the images on our retina are the result of impressions coming from without or from within . . . we discover to what extent we are creative, to what extent our soul partakes of the constant creation of the world.[9]

WILL HINDLE: *CHINESE FIREDRILL*

There have been essentially three generations of personal film-makers in the United States. The first began with the invention of the medium and continued in various stages through the 1940's. The second began approximately in the mid-1950's with the increasing availability of inexpensive 8mm and 16mm equipment. It represented the first popular movement toward personal cinema

[9] Hermann Hesse, *Demian* (New York: Bantam Books, 1968), p. 88.

as a way of life. The third generation has evolved since the mid-1960's, primarily in the San Francisco area, where the latest trend is toward a blending of aesthetics and technology. One reason personal cinema is more eloquent than commercial cinema is that the filmmaker is forced into a closer interaction with his technology.

Will Hindle is exemplary of this recent technological awareness, a combination of engineering and aesthetics. Trained in art, literature, and professional television filmmaking, Hindle has applied his knowledge to personal cinema in a singularly spectacular fashion. His ability to invest a technical device with emotional or metaphysical content is truly impressive. He has, for example, developed the technique of rear-projection rephotography to a high degree of eloquence. He shoots original scenes with wide-angle lenses, then "crops" them by projecting and rephotographing this footage using a special single-frame projector. Thus extremely subtle effects are achieved that would be prohibitively expensive, if not impossible, if done through conventional laboratory optical printing.

Although many synacsthetic films are wonderfully evocative, Hindle's recent works are especially notable for their ability to generate overwhelming emotional impact almost exclusively from cinematic technique, not thematic content. Hindle has an uncanny talent for transforming spontaneous unstylized reality into unearthly poetic visions, as in *Billabong* (1968), a wordless impressionistic "documentary" about a boy's camp in northern California, and *Watersmith* (1969), a spectacular visual fantasy created from footage of an Olympic swimming team at practice.

Chinese Firedrill, unique in Hindle's work, was prestylized and "performed" almost in the traditional sense of a scripted, directed, and acted movie. The difference is that Hindle used the images not for their symbolic or theatrical content, but as ingredients of an almost iconographic nature to be compounded and manipulated through the process of the medium. Although there are "actors" (Hindle plays the principal role), there is no characterization. Although there are sets, we're not asked to suspend our disbelief.

Chinese Firedrill is a romantic, nostalgic film. Yet its nostalgia is of the unknown, of vague emotions, haunted dreams, unspoken words, silences between sounds. It's a nostalgia for the oceanic present rather than a remembered past. It is total fantasy; yet like the best fantasies—8½, *Beauty and the Beast, The Children of Paradise*—it seems more real than the coldest documentary. The "action" occurs entirely within the mind of the protagonist, who never leaves the small room in which he lives. It's all rooms everywhere, all cubicles wherever we find man trapped within his dreams. Through the door/mirror is the beyond, the unreachable, the unattainable, the beginning and the end. Not once in the film's twenty minutes can we pinpoint a sequence or action that might be called "dramatic" in the usual sense. Yet almost immediately an overwhelming atmosphere of pathos is generated. There are moments of excruciating emotional impact, not from audience manipulation, but from Hindle's ability to realize metaphysical substance, stirring the inarticulate conscious. Every effort is made to distance the viewer, to keep us aware of our perceptions, to emphasize the purely cinematic as opposed to the theatrical.

We find Hindle kneeling on the floor of his surrealistic room stuffing thousands of IBM cards into boxes. Over this we hear a strange monologue of fragmented words and sentences in an odd foreign accent. This is punctuated by fierce thunderclaps and howling wind that evolve into ethereal music and tinkling bell sounds. Periodically the screen is slashed across with blinding white flashes, while the central images constantly are transformed through lap-dissolves and multiple superimpositions. There are flash-forwards of images to be encountered later, though we don't recognize them and therefore don't interpret them. We see nude lovers, a small boy bathing, a beautiful woman with candles, a huge eyeball, a battery of glaring lights. These are noted for their inherent psychological connotations and not as narrative devices.

The most memorable sequence of *Firedrill*, possibly one of the great scenes in the history of film, involves Hindle lying in anguish on his floor and slowly reaching out with one hand toward the glimmering void beyond his door. Suddenly a mirror-like reflection of his arm and hand appears on the opposite side of the mirror. When he removes his hand we see the vague shadowy figure of a nude woman silhouetted ghostlike, her skin sparkling. In slow motion the silhouette of a nude man enters from an opposite direction and the two gossamer figures embrace in a weightless ballet of graceful motion in some dream of bliss. In the film's final image, the haunted man has become a child once again, splashing in his bath in a series of freeze-frames that grow ever fainter until they vanish.

SYNAESTHETICS AND KINAESTHETICS: THE WAY OF ALL EXPERIENCE

The term *kinetic* generally indicates motion of material bodies and the forces and energies associated with it. Thus to isolate a certain type of film as kinetic and therefore different from other films means we're talking more about forces and energies than about matter. I define *aesthetic* quite simply as: the manner of experiencing something. *Kinaesthetic*, therefore, is the manner of experiencing a thing through the forces and energies associated with its motion. This is called *kinaesthesia*, the experience of sensory perception. One who is keenly aware of kinetic qualities is said to possess a kinaesthetic sense.

The fundamental subject of synaesthetic cinema—forces and energies—cannot be photographed. It's not what we're seeing so much as the process and effect of seeing: that is, the phenomenon of experience itself, which exists only in the viewer. Synaesthetic cinema abandons traditional narrative because events in reality do not move in linear fashion. It abandons common notions of "style" because there is no style in nature. It is concerned less with facts than with metaphysics, and there is no fact that is not also metaphysical. One cannot photograph metaphysical forces. One cannot even "represent" them. One can, however, actually *evoke* them in the inarticulate conscious of the viewer.

The dynamic interaction of formal proportions in kinaesthetic cinema evokes cognition in the inarticulate conscious, which I call *kinetic empathy*. In perceiving kinetic activity, the mind's eye makes its empathy-drawing, translating the graphics into emotional-psychological equivalents meaningful to the viewer, albeit meaning of an inarticulate nature. "Articulation" of this experience occurs in the perception of it and is wholly nonverbal. It makes us aware of fundamental realities beneath the surface of normal perception: forces and energies. . . .

CHAPTER THREE

Through the Body: The Physical Way

We may never be certain but a plausible guess is that, among our nearest simian neighbors in the branched tree of evolution, it is a rare orangutan who spends any time brooding over such questions as: Who am I? Where do I come from? Where am I bound? When that first ape swung to earth and began walking upright as homo sapiens, we like to believe that he stepped into self-consciousness. You have all, no doubt, seen copies at least of August Rodin's famous statue, The Thinker. Rapt in brooding intensity over his fist, the concentrated inward-seeking figure represents all that we point to, with an almost arrogant pride, as separating us from the "brute" beasts. In our self-awareness lies our uniquely human (and, we usually add, superior) status. But Rodin's Thinker has the disturbed look of a deeply troubled man. His thoughts do not appear to make him very happy. Can it be that man's greatest power is also a curse? Can it be that the more his intelligence turns toward the deeper recesses of his own brain, the more Rodin's figure secretly comes to feel himself increasingly cut off from his body and the world about him? He would seem to be schizoid, divided between mind and body.

To contemplate life intellectually seems inevitably to involve standing aside from participating in its events, as when we must stand back from a painting before our eyes can bring it into focus. Conversely, to plunge instinctively into the total experience of a physical movement—the swing of a bat, the return of a tennis serve—is to feel oneself fully alive through the body in a way that would collapse if we consciously began to think through the steps of what we were doing. Physical and mental, we are stretched between poles which seem locked in an eternal war whose strain appears on the verge of rending us apart. Thus, for Freud, man is by definition the neurotic animal, precisely because he is self-aware. Ironically, therefore, his unique intelligence makes man the only animal who can truly be said to be capable of madness.

Something close to this realization of the predicament of consciousness prompted Ralph Waldo Emerson's melancholy remark, "It is very unhappy but too late to be helped, the discovery we have made that we exist. That discovery is called the Fall of Man." Notice that it is not existence Emerson laments, but rather the conscious awareness of it. To taste the fruit of the tree of knowledge is to lose that sense of the ecstatic harmony between the self and all other beings that characterized Eden. Some, such as Theodore Roszak, would argue that the increasing intellectualization which removes us further and further from a direct participation in the experience of existence is the primal sin by which man dispossessed himself of paradise. Such seems to be the case in "A Blessing," where a city man regains a sense of lost paradise simply by leaving behind his intellect and participating directly in a nonhuman world of horses grazing in a pasture. When we add up the inhuman crimes of intellect that have marred our own century alone—our genius for creating the complex technology responsible for the weaponry of mass warfare or industrial pollution, to cite the most obvious examples—we can only wonder if we haven't sold our birthright to the garden for a mess of pottage or a plot in potter's field. Perhaps the psychiatrist Ferenczi is accurate when he writes, "Pure intelligence is in principle madness." His point is that the more we translate experience into abstract ideas and categories, the more we tend to lose touch with substantial realities. This the beginning premise from which Castaneda undertakes his study of the Yaqui Indians' peyote cult in The Teachings of Don Juan.

Lost in the labyrinth of conceptual nightmares, we sever our connection with elemental verities. This divorce from experience comes very close to a clinical definition of insanity—but who is to lock us up in asylums when we are all "out of our minds" because we are so totally immersed in them? Or perhaps, when such madness is judged the norm, the only "sane" alternative is to choose deliberately to go "out of your mind"—transported by music (Baldwin), a crow's view of reality (Castaneda), a field

with horses (Wright), the explosive lift out of self that can
come through unabashed sex (Dickey), or the throb of a motorcycle
between one's thighs (Wolfe). The selections in this section
beckon us to abandon our so thoroughly mentalized world-view
and slip back into our sheer sensual selves. They invite us to
recover that miraculous sense of physical presence, unencumbered
by the confusion of ideas, which we can still recognize
occasionally in some young children before the loss of innocence
"humanizes" them into those neurotic animals called by e. e.
cummings, "manunkind."

JAMES DICKEY

Cherrylog Road

Off Highway 106
At Cherrylog Road I entered
The '34 Ford without wheels,
Smothered in kudzu,
With a seat pulled out to run
Corn whiskey down from the hills,

And then from the other side
Crept into an Essex
With a rumble seat of red leather
And then out again, aboard   10
A blue Chevrolet, releasing
The rust from its other color,

Reared up on three building blocks.
None had the same body heat;
I changed with them inward, toward
The weedy heart of the junkyard,
For I knew that Doris Holbrook
Would escape from her father at noon

And would come from the farm
To seek parts owned by the sun   20
Among the abandoned chassis,
Sitting in each in turn
As I did, leaning forward
As in a wild stock-car race

In the parking lot of the dead.
Time after time, I climbed in
And out the other side, like
An envoy or movie star
Met at the station by crickets.
A radiator cap raised its head,   30

Become a real toad or a kingsnake
As I neared the hub of the yard,
Passing through many states,
Many lives, to reach
Some grandmother's long Pierce-Arrow
Sending platters of blindness forth

From its nickel hubcaps
And spilling its tender upholstery
On sleepy roaches,
The glass panel in between   40
Lady and colored driver
Not all the way broken out,

The back-seat-phone
Still on its hook.
I got in as though to exclaim,
"Let us go to the orphan asylum,
John; I have some old toys
For children who say their prayers."

I popped with sweat as I thought
I heard Doris Holbrook scrape   50
Like a mouse in the southern-state sun
That was eating the paint in blisters
From a hundred car tops and hoods.
She was tapping like code,

Loosening the screws,
Carrying off headlights,
Sparkplugs, bumpers,
Cracked mirrors and gear-knobs,
Getting ready, already,
To go back with something to show   60

Other than her lips' new trembling
I would hold to me soon, soon,
Where I sat in the ripped back seat
Talking over the interphone,

Praying for Doris Holbrook
To come from her father's farm

And to get back there
With no trace of me on her face
To be seen by her red-haired father
Who would change, in the squalling barn,   70
Her back's pale skin with a strop,
Then lay for me

In a bootlegger's roasting car
With a string-triggered 12-gauge shotgun
To blast the breath from the air.
Not cut by the jagged windshields,
Through the acres of wrecks she came
With a wrench in her hand,

Through dust where the blacksnake dies
Of boredom, and the beetle knows   80
The compost has no more life.
Someone outside would have seen
The oldest car's door inexplicably
Close from within:

I held her and held her and held her,
Convoyed at terrific speed
By the stalled, dreaming traffic around us,
So the blacksnake, stiff
With inaction, curved back
Into life, and hunted the mouse   90

With deadly overexcitement,
The beetles reclaimed their field
As we clung, glued together,
With the hooks of the seat springs
Working through to catch us red-handed
Amidst the gray breathless batting

That burst from the seat at our backs.
We left by separate doors

Into the changed, other bodies
Of cars, she down Cherrylog Road   100
And I to my motorcycle
Parked like the soul of the junkyard

Restored, a bicycle fleshed
With power, and tore off
Up Highway 106, continually
Drunk on the wind in my mouth,
Wringing the handlebar for speed,
Wild to be wreckage forever.

JAMES WRIGHT

A Blessing

Just off the highway to Rochester, Minnesota,
Twilight bounds softly forth on the grass.
And the eyes of those two Indian ponies
Darken with kindness.
They have come gladly out of the willows
To welcome my friend and me.
We step over the barbed wire into the pasture
Where they have been grazing all day, alone.
They ripple tensely, they can hardly contain their happiness
That we have come.   10
They bow shyly as wet swans. They love each other.
There is no loneliness like theirs.
At home once more,
They begin munching the young tufts of spring in the dark-
    ness.
I would like to hold the slenderer one in my arms,
For she has walked over to me
And nuzzled my left hand.
She is black and white,

Her mane falls wild on her forehead,
And the light breeze moves me to caress her long ear   20
That is delicate as the skin over a girl's wrist.
Suddenly I realize
That if I stepped out of my body I would break
Into blossom.

JAMES BALDWIN

Sonny's Blues

I read about it in the paper, in the subway, on my way to work. I read it, and I couldn't believe it, and I read it again. Then perhaps I just stared at it, at the newsprint spelling out his name, spelling out the story. I stared at it in the swinging lights of the subway car, and in the faces and bodies of the people, and in my own face, trapped in the darkness which roared outside.

It was not to be believed and I kept telling myself that as I walked from the subway station to the high school. And at the same time I couldn't doubt it. I was scared, scared for Sonny. He became real to me again. A great block of ice got settled in my belly and kept melting there slowly all day long, while I taught my classes algebra. It was a special kind of ice. It kept melting, sending trickles of ice water all up and down my veins, but it never got less. Sometimes it hardened and seemed to expand until I felt my guts were going to come spilling out or that I was going to choke or scream. This would always be at a moment when I was remembering some specific thing Sonny had once said or done.

When he was about as old as the boys in my classes his face had been bright and open, there was a lot of copper in it; and he'd had wonderfully direct brown eyes, and great gentleness and privacy. I wondered what he looked like now. He had been picked up, the evening before, in a raid on an apartment downtown, for peddling and using heroin.

I couldn't believe it: but what I mean by that is that I couldn't find any room for it anywhere inside me. I had kept it outside me for a long time. I hadn't wanted to know. I had had suspicions, but I didn't name them, I kept putting them away. I told myself that Sonny was wild, but he wasn't crazy. And he'd always been a good boy, he hadn't ever turned hard or evil or disrespectful, the way kids can, so quick, so quick, especially in Harlem. I didn't want to believe that I'd ever see my brother going down, coming to nothing, all that light in his face gone out, in the condition I'd already seen so many others. Yet it had happened and here I was, talking about algebra to a lot of boys who might, every one of them for all I knew, be popping off needles every time they went to the head. Maybe it did more for them than algebra could.

I was sure that the first time Sonny had ever had horse, he couldn't have been much older than these boys were now. These boys, now, were living as we'd been living then, they were growing up with a rush and their heads bumped abruptly against the low ceiling of their actual possibilities. They were filled with rage. All they really knew were two darknesses, the darkness of their lives, which was now closing in on them, and the darkness of the movies, which had blinded them to that other darkness, and in which they now, vindictively, dreamed, at once more together than they were at any other time, and more alone.

When the last bell rang, the last class ended, I let out my breath. It seemed I'd been holding it for all that time. My clothes were wet—I may have looked as though I'd been sitting in a steam bath, all dressed up, all afternoon. I sat alone in the classroom a long time. I listened to the boys outside, downstairs, shouting and cursing and laughing. Their laughter struck me for perhaps the first time. It was not the joyous laughter which—God knows why —one associates with children. It was mocking and insular, its intent was to denigrate. It was disenchanted, and in this, also, lay the authority of their curses. Perhaps I was listening to them because I was thinking about my brother and in them I heard my brother. And myself.

One boy was whistling a tune, at once very complicated and very simple, it seemed to be pouring out of him as though he were a bird, and it sounded very cool and moving through all that harsh, bright air, only just holding its own through all those other sounds.

I stood up and walked over to the window and looked down into the courtyard. It was the beginning of the spring and the sap was rising in the boys. A teacher passed through them every now and again, quickly, as though he or she couldn't wait to get out of that courtyard, to get those boys out of their sight and off their minds. I started collecting my stuff. I thought I'd better get home and talk to Isabel.

The courtyard was almost deserted by the time I got downstairs. I saw this boy standing in the shadow of a doorway, looking just like Sonny. I almost called his name. Then I saw that it wasn't Sonny, but somebody we used to know, a boy from around our block. He'd been Sonny's friend. He'd never been mine, having been too young for me, and, anyway, I'd never liked him. And now, even though he was a grown-up man, he still hung around that block, still spent hours on the street corner, was always high and raggy. I used to run into him from time to time and he'd often work around to asking me for a quarter or fifty cents. He always had some real good excuse, too, and I always gave it to him, I don't know why.

But now, abruptly, I hated him. I couldn't stand the way he looked at me, partly like a dog, partly like a cunning child. I wanted to ask him what the hell he was doing in the school courtyard.

He sort of shuffled over to me, and he said, "I see you got the papers. So you already know about it."

"You mean about Sonny? Yes, I already know about it. How come they didn't get you?"

He grinned. It made him repulsive and it also brought to mind what he'd looked like as a kid. "I wasn't there. I stay away from them people."

"Good for you." I offered him a cigarette and I watched him through the smoke. "You come all the way down here just to tell me about Sonny?"

"That's right." He was sort of shaking his head and his eyes looked strange, as though they were about to cross. The bright sun deadened his damp dark brown skin and it made his eyes look yellow and showed up the dirt in his conked hair. He smelled funky. I moved a little away from him and I said, "Well, thanks. But I already know about it and I got to get home."

"I'll walk you a little ways," he said. We started walking. There were a couple of kids still loitering in the courtyard and one of them said good night to me and looked strangely at the boy beside me.

"What're you going to do?" he asked me. "I mean, about Sonny?"

"Look. I haven't seen Sonny for over a year, I'm not sure I'm going to do anything. Anyway, what the hell *can* I do?"

"That's right," he said quickly, "ain't nothing you can do. Can't much help old Sonny no more, I guess."

It was what I was thinking and so it seemed to me he had no right to say it.

"I'm surprised at Sonny, though," he went on—he had a funny way of talking, he looked straight ahead as though he were talking to himself—"I thought Sonny was a smart boy, I thought he was too smart to get hung."

"I guess he thought so too," I said sharply, "and that's how he got hung. And how about you? You're pretty goddamn smart, I bet."

Then he looked directly at me, just for a minute. "I ain't smart," he said. "If I was smart, I'd have reached for a pistol a long time ago."

"Look. Don't tell *me* your sad story, if it was up to me, I'd give you one." Then I felt guilty—guilty, probably, for never having supposed that the poor bastard *had* a story of his own, much less a sad one, and I asked, quickly, "What's going to happen to him now?"

He didn't answer this. He was off by himself some place. "Funny thing," he said, and from his tone we might have been discussing the quickest way to get to Brooklyn, "when I saw the papers this morning, the first thing I asked myself was if I had anything to do with it. I felt sort of responsible."

I began to listen more carefully. The subway station was on the corner, just before us, and I stopped. He stopped, too. We were in front of a bar and he ducked slightly, peering in, but whoever he was looking for didn't seem to be there. The juke box was blasting away with something black and bouncy and I half watched the barmaid as she danced her way from the juke box to her place behind the bar. And I watched her face as she laughingly responded to something someone said to her, still keeping time to the music. When she smiled one saw the little girl, one sensed the doomed, still-struggling woman beneath the battered face of the semi-whore.

"I never *give* Sonny nothing," the boy said finally, "but a long time ago I come to school high and Sonny asked me how it felt." He paused, I couldn't bear to watch him, I watched the barmaid, and I listened to the music which seemed to be causing the pavement to shake. "I told him it felt great." The music stopped, the barmaid paused and watched the juke box until the music began again. "It did."

All this was carrying me some place I didn't want to go. I certainly didn't want to know how it felt. It filled everything, the people, the houses, the music, the dark, quicksilver barmaid, with menace; and this menace was their reality.

"What's going to happen to him now?" I asked again.

"They'll send him away some place and they'll try to cure him." He shook his head. "Maybe he'll even think he's kicked the habit. Then they'll let him loose"—he gestured, throwing his cigarette into the gutter. "That's all."

"What do you mean, that's *all*?"

But I knew what he meant.

"I *mean*, that's *all*." He turned his head and looked at me, pulling down the corners of his mouth. "Don't you know what I mean?" he asked softly.

"How the hell *would* I know what you mean?" I almost whispered it, I don't know why.

"That's right," he said to the air, "how would *he* know what I mean?" He turned toward me again, patient and calm, and yet I somehow felt him shaking, shaking as though he were going to fall apart. I felt that ice in my guts again, the dread I'd felt all afternoon; and again I watched the barmaid, moving about the bar, washing glasses, and singing. "Listen. They'll let him out and then it'll just start all over again. That's what I mean."

"You mean—they'll let him out. And then he'll just start working his way back in again. You mean he'll never kick the habit. Is that what you mean?"

"That's right," he said, cheerfully. "*You* see what I mean."

"Tell me," I said at last, "why does he want to die? He must want to die, he's killing himself, why does he want to die?"

He looked at me in surprise. He licked his lips. "He don't want to die. He wants to live. Don't nobody want to die, ever."

Then I wanted to ask him—too many things. He could not have answered, or if he had, I could not have borne the answers. I started walking. "Well, I guess it's none of my business."

"It's going to be rough on old Sonny," he said. We reached the subway station. "This is your station?" he asked. I nodded. I took one step down. "Damn!" he said, suddenly. I looked up at him. He grinned again. "Damn if I didn't leave all my money home. You ain't got a dollar on you, have you? Just for a couple of days, is all."

All at once something inside gave and threatened to come pouring out of me. I didn't hate him any more. I felt that in another moment I'd start crying like a child.

"Sure," I said. "Don't sweat." I looked in my wallet and didn't have a dollar, I only had a five. "Here," I said. "That hold you?"

He didn't look at it—he didn't want to look at it. A terrible, closed look came over his face, as though he were keeping the number on the bill a secret from him and me. "Thanks," he said, and now he was dying to see me go. "Don't worry about Sonny. Maybe I'll write him or something."

"Sure," I said. "You do that. So long."

"Be seeing you," he said. I went on down the steps.

And I didn't write Sonny or send him anything for a long time. When I finally did, it was just after my little girl died, he wrote me back a letter which made me feel like a bastard.

Here's what he said:

> Dear brother,
>
> You don't know how much I needed to hear from you. I wanted to write you many a time but I dug how much I must have hurt you and so I didn't write. But now I feel like a man who's been trying to climb up out of some deep, real deep and funky hole and just saw the sun up there, outside. I got to get outside.
>
> I can't tell you much about how I got here. I mean I don't know how to tell you. I guess I was afraid of something or I was trying to escape from something and you know I have never been very strong in the head (smile). I'm glad Mama and Daddy are dead and can't see what's happened to their son and I swear if I'd known what I was doing I would never have hurt you so, you and a lot of other fine people who were nice to me and who believed in me.
>
> I don't want you to think it had anything to do with me being a musician. It's more than that. Or maybe less than that. I can't get anything straight in my head down here

and I try not to think about what's going to happen to me when I get outside again. Sometime I think I'm going to flip and *never* get outside and sometime I think I'll come straight back. I tell you one thing, though, I'd rather blow my brains out than go through this again. But that's what they all say, so they tell me. If I tell you when I'm coming to New York and if you could meet me, I sure would appreciate it. Give my love to Isabel and the kids and I was sorry to hear about little Gracie. I wish I could be like Mama and say the Lord's will be done, but I don't know it seems to me that trouble is the one thing that never does get stopped and I don't know what good it does to blame it on the Lord. But maybe it does some good if you believe it.

> Your brother,
> SONNY

Then I kept in constant touch with him and I sent him whatever I could and I went to meet him when he came back to New York. When I saw him many things I thought I had forgotten came flooding back to me. This was because I had begun, finally, to wonder about Sonny, about the life that Sonny lived inside. This life, whatever it was, had made him older and thinner and it had deepened the distant stillness in which he had always moved. He looked very unlike my baby brother. Yet, when he smiled, when we shook hands, the baby brother I'd never known looked out from the depths of his private life, like an animal waiting to be coaxed into the light.

"How you been keeping?" he asked me.

"All right. And you?"

"Just fine." He was smiling all over his face. "It's good to see you again."

"It's good to see you."

The seven years' difference in our ages lay between us like a chasm: I wondered if these years would ever operate between us as a bridge. I was remembering, and it made it hard to catch my breath, that I had been there when he was born; and I had heard the first words he had ever spoken. When he started to walk, he walked from our mother straight to me. I caught him just before he fell when he took the first steps he ever took in this world.

"How's Isabel?"

"Just fine. She's dying to see you."

"And the boys?"

"They're fine, too. They're anxious to see their uncle."

"Oh, come on. You know they don't remember me."

"Are you kidding? Of course they remember you."

He grinned again. We got into a taxi. We had a lot to say to each other, far too much to know how to begin.

As the taxi began to move, I asked, "You still want to go to India?"

He laughed. "You still remember that. Hell, no. This place is Indian enough for me."

"It used to belong to them," I said.

And he laughed again. "They damn sure knew what they were doing when they got rid of it."

Years ago, when he was around fourteen, he'd been all hipped on the idea of going to India. He read books about people sitting on rocks, naked, in all kinds of weather, but mostly bad, naturally, and walking barefoot through hot coals and arriving at wisdom. I used to say that it sounded to me as though they were getting away from wisdom as fast as they could. I think he sort of looked down on me for that.

"Do you mind," he asked, "if we have the driver drive alongside the park? On the west side—I haven't seen the city in so long."

"Of course not," I said. I was afraid that I might sound as though I were humoring him, but I hoped he wouldn't take it that way.

So we drove along, between the green of the park and the stony, lifeless elegance of hotels and apartment buildings, toward the vivid, killing streets of our childhood. These streets hadn't changed, though housing projects jutted up out of them now like rocks in the middle of a boiling sea. Most of the houses in which we had grown up had vanished, as had the stores from which we had stolen, the basements in which we had first tried sex, the rooftops from which we had hurled tin cans and bricks. But houses exactly like the houses of our past yet dominated the landscape, boys exactly like the boys we once had been found themselves smothering in these houses, came down into the streets for light and air and found themselves encircled by disaster. Some escaped the trap, most didn't. Those who got out always left something of themselves behind, as some animals amputate a leg and leave it in the trap. It might be said, perhaps, that I had escaped, after all, I was a school teacher; or that Sonny had, he hadn't lived in Harlem for years. Yet, as the cab moved uptown through streets which seemed, with a rush, to darken with dark people, and as I covertly studied Sonny's face, it came to me that what we both were seeking through our separate cab windows was that part of ourselves which had been left behind. It's always at the hour of trouble and confrontation that the missing member aches.

We hit 110th Street and started rolling up Lenox Avenue. And I'd known this avenue all my life, but it seemed to me again, as it had seemed on the day I'd first heard about Sonny's trouble, filled with a hidden menace which was its very breath of life.

"We almost there," said Sonny.

"Almost." We were both too nervous to say anything more.

We live in a housing project. It hasn't been up long. A few days after it was up it seemed uninhabitably new, now, of course, it's already rundown. It looks like a parody of the good, clean, faceless life—God knows the people who live in it do their best to make it a parody. The beat-looking grass lying around isn't enough to make their lives green, the hedges will never hold out the streets, and they know it. The big windows fool no one, they aren't big enough to make space out of no space. They don't bother with the windows, they watch the TV screen instead. The playground is most popular with the children who don't play at jacks, or skip rope, or roller skate, or swing, and they can be found in it after dark. We moved in partly because it's not too far from where I teach, and partly for the kids; but it's really just like the houses in which Sonny and I grew up. The same things happen, they'll have the same things to remember. The moment Sonny and I started into the house I had the feeling that I was simply bringing him back into the danger he had almost died trying to escape.

Sonny has never been talkative. So I don't know why I was sure he'd be dying to talk to me when supper was over the first night. Everything went fine, the oldest boy remembered him, and the youngest boy liked him, and Sonny had remembered to bring something for each of them; and Isabel, who is really much nicer than I am, more open and giving, had gone to a lot of trouble about dinner and was genuinely glad to see him. And she's always been able to tease Sonny in a way that I haven't. It was nice to see her face so vivid again and to hear her laugh and watch her make Sonny laugh. She wasn't, or, anyway, she didn't seem to be, at all uneasy or embarrassed. She chatted as though there were no subject which had to be avoided and she got Sonny past his first, faint stiffness. And thank God she was there, for I was filled with that icy dread again. Everything I did seemed awkward to me, and everything I said sounded freighted with hidden meaning. I was trying to remember everything I'd heard about dope addiction and I couldn't help watching Sonny for signs. I wasn't doing it out of malice. I was trying to find out something about my brother. I was dying to hear him tell me he was safe.

"Safe!" my father grunted, whenever Mama suggested trying to move to a neighborhood which might be safer for children. "Safe, hell! Ain't no place safe for kids, nor nobody."

He always went on like this, but he wasn't, ever, really as bad as he sounded, not even on weekends, when he got drunk. As a matter of fact, he was always on the lookout for "something a little better," but he died before he found it. He died suddenly, during a drunken weekend in the middle of the war, when Sonny was fifteen. He and Sonny hadn't ever got on too well. And this was partly because Sonny was the apple of his father's eye. It was because he loved Sonny so much and was frightened for him, that he was always fighting with him. It doesn't do any good to fight with Sonny. Sonny just moves back, inside himself, where he can't be reached. But the principal reason that they never hit it off is that they were so much alike. Daddy was big and rough and loud-talking, just the opposite of Sonny, but they both had— that same privacy.

Mama tried to tell me something about this, just after Daddy died. I was home on leave from the army.

This was the last time I ever saw my mother alive. Just the same, this picture gets all mixed up in my mind with pictures I had of her when she was younger. The way I always see her is the way she used to be on a Sunday afternoon, say, when the old folks were talking after the big Sunday dinner. I always see her wearing pale blue. She'd be sitting on the sofa. And my father would be sitting in the easy chair, not far from her. And the living room would be full of church folks and relatives. There they sit, in chairs all around the living room, and the night is creeping up outside, but nobody knows it yet. You can see the darkness growing against the window-panes and you hear the street noises every now and again, or maybe the jangling beat of a tambourine from one of the churches close by, but it's real quiet in the room. For a moment nobody's talking, but every face looks darkening, like the sky outside. And my mother rocks a little from the waist, and my father's eyes are closed. Everyone is looking at something a child can't see. For a minute they've forgotten the children. Maybe a kid is lying on the rug half asleep. Maybe somebody's got a kid on his lap and is absent-mindedly stroking the kid's head. Maybe there's a kid, quiet and big-eyed, curled up in a big chair in the corner. The silence, the darkness coming, and the darkness in the faces frightens the child obscurely. He hopes that the hand which strokes his forehead will never stop—will never die. He hopes that there will never come a time when the old folks won't be sitting around the living room, talking about where they've come from, and what they've seen, and what's happened to them and their kinfolk.

But something deep and watchful in the child knows that this is bound to end, is already ending. In a moment someone will get up and turn on the light. Then the old folks will remember the children and they won't talk any more that day. And when light fills the room, the child is filled with darkness. He knows that every time this happens he's moved just a little closer to that darkness outside. The darkness outside is what the old folks have been talking about. It's what they've come from. It's what they endure. The child knows that they won't talk any more because if he knows too much about what's happened to *them,* he'll know too much too soon, about what's going to happen to *him.*

The last time I talked to my mother, I remember I was restless. I wanted to get out and see Isabel. We weren't married then and we had a lot to straighten out between us.

There Mama sat, in black, by the window. She was humming an old church song, *Lord, you brought me from a long ways off.* Sonny was out somewhere. Mama kept watching the streets.

"I don't know," she said, "if I'll ever see you again, after you go off from here. But I hope you'll remember the things I tried to teach you."

"Don't talk like that," I said, and smiled. "You'll be here a long time yet."

She smiled, too, but she said nothing. She was quiet for a long time. And I said, "Mama, don't you worry about nothing. I'll be writing all the time, and you be getting the checks. . . ."

"I want to talk to you about your brother," she said, suddenly. "If anything happens to me he ain't going to have nobody to look out for him."

"Mama," I said, "ain't nothing going to happen to you *or* Sonny. Sonny's all right. He's a good boy and he's got good sense."

"It ain't a question of his being a good boy," Mama said, "nor of his having good sense. It ain't only the bad ones, nor yet the dumb ones that gets sucked under." She stopped, looking at me. "Your Daddy once had a brother," she said, and she smiled in a way that made me feel she was in pain. "You didn't never know that, did you?"

"No," I said, "I never knew that," and I watched her face.

"Oh, yes," she said, "your Daddy had a brother." She looked out of the window again. "I know you never saw your Daddy cry. But *I* did—many a time, through all these years."

I asked her, "What happened to his brother? How come nobody's ever talked about him?"

This was the first time I ever saw my mother look old.

"His brother got killed," she said, "when he was just a little younger than you are now. I knew him. He was a fine boy. He was maybe a little full of the devil, but he didn't mean nobody no harm."

Then she stopped and the room was silent, exactly as it had sometimes been on those Sunday afternoons. Mama kept looking out into the streets.

"He used to have a job in the mill," she said, "and, like all young folks, he just liked to perform on Saturday nights. Saturday nights, him and your father would drift around to different places, go to dances and things like that, or just sit around with people they knew, and your father's brother would sing, he had a fine voice, and play along with himself on his guitar. Well, this particular Saturday night, him and your father was coming home from some place, and they were both a little drunk and there was a moon that night, it was bright like day. Your father's brother was feeling kind of good, and he was whistling to himself, and he had his guitar slung over his shoulder. They was coming down a hill and beneath them was a road that turned off from the highway. Well, your father's brother, being always kind of frisky, decided to run down this hill, and he did, with that guitar banging and clanging behind him, and he ran across the road, and he was making water behind a tree. And your father was sort of amused at him and he was still coming down the hill, kind of slow. Then he heard a car motor and that same minute his brother stepped from behind the tree, into the road, in the moonlight. And he started to cross the road. And your father started to run down the hill, he says he don't know why. This car was full of white men. They was all drunk, and when they seen your father's brother they let out a great whoop and holler and they aimed the car straight at him. They was having fun, they just wanted to scare him, the way they do sometimes, you know. But they was drunk. And I guess the boy, being drunk, too, and scared, kind of lost his head. By the time he jumped it was too late. Your father says he heard his brother scream when the car rolled over him, and he heard the wood of that guitar when it give, and he heard them strings go flying, and he heard them white men shouting, and the car kept on a-going and it ain't stopped till this day. And, time your father got down the hill, his brother weren't nothing but blood and pulp."

Tears were gleaming on my mother's face. There wasn't anything I could say.

"He never mentioned it," she said, "because I never let him mention it before you children. Your Daddy was like a crazy man that night and for many a night thereafter. He says he never in his life seen anything as dark as that road after the lights of that car had gone away. Weren't nothing, weren't nobody on that road, just your Daddy and his brother and that busted guitar. Oh, yes. Your Daddy never did really get right again. Till the day he died he weren't sure but that every white man he saw was the man that killed his brother."

She stopped and took out her handkerchief and dried her eyes and looked at me.

"I ain't telling you all this," she said, "to make you scared or bitter or to make you hate nobody. I'm telling you this because you got a brother. And the world ain't changed."

I guess I didn't want to believe this. I guess she saw this in my face. She turned away from me, toward the window again, searching those streets.

"But I praise my Redeemer," she said at last, "that He called your Daddy home before me. I ain't saying it to throw no flowers at myself, but, I declare, it keeps me from feeling too cast down to know I helped your father get safely through this world. Your father always acted like he was the roughest, strongest man on earth. And everybody took him to be like that. But if he hadn't had *me* there—to see his tears!"

She was crying again. Still, I couldn't move. I said, "Lord, Lord, Mama, I didn't know it was like that."

"Oh, honey," she said, "there's a lot that you don't know. But you are going to find it out." She stood up from the window and came over to me. "You got to hold on to your brother," she said, "and don't let him fall, no matter what it looks like is happening to him and no matter how evil you gets with him. You going to be evil with him many a time. But don't you forget what I told you, you hear?"

"I won't forget," I said. "Don't you worry, I won't forget. I won't let nothing happen to Sonny."

My mother smiled as though she were amused at something she saw in my face. Then, "You may not be able to stop nothing from happening. But you got to let him know you's *there*."

Two days later I was married, and then I was gone. And I had a lot of things on my mind and I pretty well forgot my promise to Mama until I got shipped home on a special furlough for her funeral.

And, after the funeral, with just Sonny and me alone in the empty kitchen, I tried to find out something about him.

"What do you want to do?" I asked him.

"I'm going to be a musician," he said.

For he had graduated, in the time I had been away, from dancing to the juke box to finding out who was playing what, and what they were doing with it, and he had bought himself a set of drums.

"You mean, you want to be a drummer?" I somehow had the

feeling that being a drummer might be all right for other people but not for my brother Sonny.

"I don't think," he said, looking at me very gravely, "that I'll ever be a good drummer. But I think I can play a piano."

I frowned. I'd never played the role of the older brother quite so seriously before, had scarcely ever, in fact, *asked* Sonny a damn thing. I sensed myself in the presence of something I didn't really know how to handle, didn't understand. So I made my frown a little deeper as I asked: "What kind of musician do you want to be?"

He grinned. "How many kinds do you think there are?"

"Be *serious*," I said.

He laughed, throwing his head back, and then looked at me. "I *am* serious."

"Well, then, for Christ's sake, stop kidding around and answer a serious question. I mean, do you want to be a concert pianist, you want to play classical music and all that, or—or what?" Long before I finished he was laughing again. "For Christ's *sake*, Sonny!"

He sobered, but with difficulty. "I'm sorry. But you sound so— *scared!*" and he was off again.

"Well, you may think it's funny now, baby, but it's not going to be so funny when you have to make your living at it, let me tell you *that*." I was furious because I knew he was laughing at me and I didn't know why.

"No," he said, very sober now, and afraid, perhaps, that he'd hurt me, "I don't want to be a classical pianist. That isn't what interests me. I mean"—he paused, looking hard at me, as though his eyes would help me to understand, and then gestured help-lessly, as though perhaps his hand would help—"I mean, I'll have a lot of studying to do, and I'll have to study *everything*, but I mean, I want to play *with*—jazz musicians." He stopped. "I want to play jazz," he said.

Well, the word had never before sounded as heavy, as real, as it sounded that afternoon in Sonny's mouth. I just looked at him and I was probably frowning a real frown by this time. I simply couldn't see why on earth he'd want to spend his time hanging around night clubs, clowning around on bandstands, while people pushed each other around a dance floor. It seemed—beneath him, somehow. I had never thought about it before, had never been forced to, but I suppose I had always put jazz musicians in a class with what Daddy called "good-time people."

"Are you *serious?*"

"Hell, *yes,* I'm serious."

He looked more helpless than ever, and annoyed, and deeply hurt.

I suggested, helpfully: "You mean—like Louis Armstrong?"

His face closed as though I'd struck him. "No. I'm not talking about none of that old-time, down home crap."

"Well, look, Sonny, I'm sorry, don't get mad. I just don't altogether get it, that's all. Name somebody—you know, a jazz musician you admire."

"Bird."

"Who?"

"Bird! Charlie Parker! Don't they teach you nothing in the goddamn army?"

I lit a cigarette. I was surprised and then a little amused to discover that I was trembling. "I've been out of touch," I said. "You'll have to be patient with me. Now. Who's this Parker character?"

"He's just one of the greatest jazz musicians alive," said Sonny, sullenly, his hands in his pockets, his back to me. "Maybe *the* greatest," he added, bitterly, "that's probably why *you* never heard of him."

"All right," I said, "I'm ignorant. I'm sorry. I'll go out and buy all the cat's records right away, all right?"

"It don't," said Sonny, with dignity, "make any difference to me. I don't care what you listen to. Don't do me no favors."

I was beginning to realize that I'd never seen him so upset before. With another part of my mind I was thinking that this would probably turn out to be one of those things kids go through and that I shouldn't make it seem important by pushing it too hard. Still, I didn't think it would do any harm to ask: "Doesn't all this take a lot of time? Can you make a living at it?"

He turned back to me and half leaned, half sat, on the kitchen table. "Everything takes time," he said, "and—well, yes, sure, I can make a living at it. But what I don't seem to be able to make you understand is that it's the only thing I want to do."

"Well Sonny," I said, gently, "you know people can't always do exactly what they *want* to do—"

"No, I don't know that," said Sonny, surprising me. "I think people *ought* to do what they want to do, what else are they alive for?"

"You getting to be a big boy," I said desperately, "it's time you started thinking about your future."

"I'm thinking about my future," said Sonny, grimly. "I think about it all the time."

I gave up. I decided, if he didn't change his mind, that we could always talk about it later. "In the meantime," I said, "you got to finish school." We had already decided that he'd have to move in with Isabel and her folks. I knew this wasn't the ideal arrangement because Isabel's folks are inclined to be dicty and they hadn't especially wanted Isabel to marry me. But I didn't know what else to do. "And we have to get you fixed up at Isabel's."

There was a long silence. He moved from the kitchen table to the window. "That's a terrible idea. You know it yourself."

"Do you have a *better* idea?"

He just walked up and down the kitchen for a minute. He was as tall as I was. He had started to shave. I suddenly had the feeling that I didn't know him at all.

He stopped at the kitchen table and picked up my cigarettes. Looking at me with a kind of mocking, amused defiance, he put one between his lips. "You mind?"

"You smoking already?"

He lit the cigarette and nodded, watching me through the smoke. "I just wanted to see if I'd have the courage to smoke in front of you." He grinned and blew a great cloud of smoke to the ceiling. "It was easy." He looked at my face. "Come on, now. I bet you was smoking at my age, tell the truth."

I didn't say anything but the truth was on my face, and he laughed. But now there was something very strained in his laugh. "Sure. And I bet that ain't all you was doing."

He was frightening me a little. "Cut the crap," I said. "We already decided that you was going to go and live at Isabel's. Now what's got into you all of a sudden?"

"*You* decided it," he pointed out. "I didn't decide nothing." He stopped in front of me, leaning against the stove, arms loosely folded. "Look, brother. I don't want to stay in Harlem no more, I really don't." He was very earnest. He looked at me, then over toward the kitchen window. There was something in his eyes I'd never seen before, some thoughtfulness, some worry all his own. He rubbed the muscle of one arm. "It's time I was getting out of here."

"Where do you want to *go*, Sonny?"

"I want to join the army. Or the navy, I don't care. If I say I'm old enough they'll believe me."

Then I got mad. It was because I was so scared. "You must be crazy. You goddamn fool, what the hell do you want to go and join the *army* for?"

"I just told you. To get out of Harlem."

"Sonny, you haven't even finished *school*. And if you really want to be a musician, how do you expect to study if you're in the *army*?"

He looked at me, trapped, and in anguish. "There's ways. I might be able to work out some kind of deal. Anyway, I'll have the G.I. Bill when I come out."

"*If* you come out." We stared at each other. "Sonny, please. Be reasonable. I know the setup is far from perfect. But we got to do the best we can."

"I ain't learning nothing in school," he said. "Even when I go." He turned away from me and opened the window and threw his cigarette out into the narrow alley. I watched his back. "At least, I ain't learning nothing you'd want me to learn." He slammed the window so hard I thought the glass would fly out, and turned back to me. "And I'm sick of the stink of these garbage cans!"

"Sonny," I said, "I know how you feel. But if you don't finish school now, you're going to be sorry later that you didn't." I grabbed him by the shoulders. "And you only got another year. It ain't so bad. And I'll come back and I swear I'll help you do *whatever* you want to do. Just try to put up with it till I come back. Will you please do that? For me?"

He didn't answer and he wouldn't look at me.

"Sonny. You hear me?"

He pulled away. "I hear you. But you never hear anything *I* say."

I didn't know what to say to that. He looked out of the window and then back at me. "OK," he said, and sighed. "I'll try."

Then I said, trying to cheer him up a little, "They got a piano at Isabel's. You can practice on it."

And as a matter of fact, it did cheer him up for a minute. "That's right," he said to himself. "I forgot that." His face relaxed a little. But the worry, the thoughtfulness, played on it still, the way shadows play on a face which is staring into the fire.

But I thought I'd never hear the end of that piano. At first, Isabel would write me, saying how nice it was that Sonny was so serious about his music and how, as soon as he came in from school, or wherever he had been when he was supposed to be at school, he went straight to that piano and stayed there until suppertime. And, after supper, he went back to that piano and stayed there until everybody went to bed. He was at that piano all day Saturday and all day Sunday. Then he bought a record player and started playing records. He'd play one record over and over again, all day long sometimes, and he'd improvise along with it on the piano. Or he'd play one section of the record, one chord, one change, one progression, then he'd do it on the piano. Then back to the record. Then back to the piano.

Well, I really don't know how they stood it. Isabel finally confessed that it wasn't like living with a person at all, it was like living with sound. And the sound didn't make any sense to her, didn't make any sense to any of them—naturally. They began, in a way, to be afflicted by this presence that was living in their home. It was as though Sonny were some sort of god, or monster. He moved in an atmosphere which wasn't like theirs at all. They fed him and he ate, he washed himself, he walked in and out of their door; he certainly wasn't nasty or unpleasant or rude, Sonny isn't any of those things; but it was as though he were all wrapped up in some cloud, some fire, some vision all his own; and there wasn't any way to reach him.

At the same time, he wasn't really a man yet, he was still a child, and they had to watch out for him in all kinds of ways. They certainly couldn't throw him out. Neither did they dare to make a great scene about that piano because even they dimly sensed, as I sensed, from so many thousands of miles away, that Sonny was at that piano playing for his life.

But he hadn't been going to school. One day a letter came from the school board and Isabel's mother got it—there had, apparently, been other letters but Sonny had torn them up. This day, when Sonny came in, Isabel's mother showed him the letter and asked where he'd been spending his time. And she finally got it out of him that he'd been down in Greenwich Village, with musicians and other characters, in a white girl's apartment. And this scared her and she started to scream at him and what came up, once she began—though she denies it to this day—was what sacrifices they were making to give Sonny a decent home and how little he appreciated it.

Sonny didn't play the piano that day. By evening, Isabel's mother had calmed down but then there was the old man to deal with, and Isabel herself. Isabel says she did her best to be calm but she broke down and started crying. She says she just watched Sonny's face. She could tell, by watching him, what was happening with him. And what was happening was that they penetrated his cloud, they had reached him. Even if their fingers had been a thousand times more gentle than human fingers ever are, he could hardly help feeling that they had stripped him naked and were spitting on that nakedness. For he also had to see that his presence, that music, which was life or death to him, had been torture for them and that they had endured it, not at all for his sake, but only for mine. And Sonny couldn't take that. He can take it a little better today than he could then but he's still not very good at it and, frankly, I don't know anybody who is.

The silence of the next few days must have been louder than the sound of all the music ever played since time began. One morning, before she went to work, Isabel was in his room for something and she suddenly realized that all of his records were gone. And she knew for certain that he was gone. And he was. He went as far as the navy would carry him. He finally sent me a postcard from some place in Greece and that was the first I knew that Sonny was still alive. I didn't see him any more until we were both back in New York and the war had long been over.

He was a man by then, of course, but I wasn't willing to see it. He came by the house from time to time, but we fought almost every time we met. I didn't like the way he carried himself, loose and dreamlike all the time, and I didn't like his friends, and his music seemed to be merely an excuse for the life he led. It sounded just that weird and disordered.

Then we had a fight, a pretty awful fight, and I didn't see him for months. By and by I looked him up, where he was living, in a furnished room in the Village, and I tried to make it up. But there were lots of other people in the room and Sonny just lay on his bed, and he wouldn't come downstairs with me, and he treated these other people as though they were his family and I weren't. So I got mad and then he got mad, and then I told him that he might just as well be dead as live the way he was living. Then he stood up and he told me not to worry about him any more in life, that he *was* dead as far as I was concerned. Then he pushed me to the door and the other people looked on as though nothing were happening, and he slammed the door behind me. I stood in the hallway, staring at the door. I heard somebody laugh in the room and then the tears came to my eyes. I started down the steps, whistling to keep from crying, I kept whistling to myself, *You going to need me, baby, one of these cold, rainy days.*

I read about Sonny's trouble in the spring. Little Grace died in the fall. She was a beautiful little girl. But she only lived a little over two years. She died of polio and she suffered. She had a slight fever for a couple of days, but it didn't seem like anything and we just kept her in bed. And we would certainly have called the doctor, but the fever dropped, she seemed to be all right. So we thought it had just been a cold. Then, one day, she was up, playing, Isabel was in the kitchen fixing lunch for the two boys when they'd come in from school, and she heard Grace fall down in the living room. When you have a lot of children you don't always start running when one of them falls, unless they start screaming or something. And, this time, Grace was quiet. Yet, Isabel says that when she heard that *thump* and then that silence, something happened in her to make her afraid. And she ran to the living room and there was little Grace on the floor, all twisted up and the reason she hadn't screamed was that she couldn't get her breath. And when she did scream, it was the worst sound, Isabel says, that she'd ever heard in all her life, and she still hears it sometimes in her dreams. Isabel will sometimes wake me up with a low, moaning, strangled sound and I have to be quick to awaken her and hold her to me and where Isabel is weeping against me seems a mortal wound.

I think I may have written Sonny the very day that little Grace was buried. I was sitting in the living room in the dark, by myself, and I suddenly thought of Sonny. My trouble made his real.

One Saturday afternoon, when Sonny had been living with us, or, anyway, been in our house, for nearly two weeks, I found myself wandering aimlessly about the living room, drinking from a can of beer, and trying to work up the courage to search Sonny's room. He was out, he was usually out whenever I was home, and Isabel had taken the children to see their grandparents. Suddenly I was standing still in front of the living room window, watching Seventh Avenue. The idea of searching Sonny's room made me still. I scarcely dared to admit to myself what I'd be searching for. I didn't know what I'd do if I found it. Or if I didn't.

On the sidewalk across from me, near the entrance to a barbecue joint, some people were holding an old-fashioned revival meeting. The barbecue cook, wearing a dirty white apron, his conked hair reddish and metallic in the pale sun, and a cigarette between his lips, stood in the doorway, watching them. Kids and older people paused in their errands and stood there, along with some older men and a couple of very tough-looking women who watched everything that happened on the avenue, as though they owned it, or were maybe owned by it. Well, they were watching this, too. The revival was being carried on by three sisters in black, and a brother. All they had were their voices and their Bibles and a tambourine. The brother was testifying and while he testified two of the sisters stood together, seeming to say, Amen, and the third sister walked around with the tambourine outstretched and a couple of people dropped coins into it. Then the brother's testimony ended and the sister who had been taking up the collection dumped the coins into her palm and transferred them to the pocket of her long black robe. Then she raised both hands, striking the tambourine against the air, and then against one hand, and she started to sing. And the two other sisters and the brother joined in.

It was strange, suddenly, to watch, though I had been seeing these street meetings all my life. So, of course, had everybody else down there. Yet, they paused and watched and listened and I stood still at the window. *"Tis the old ship of Zion,"* they sang, and the sister with the tambourine kept a steady, jangling beat,

"*It has rescued many a thousand!*" Not a soul under the sound
of their voices was hearing this song for the first time, not one of
them had been rescued. Nor had they seen much in the way of
rescue work being done around them. Neither did they especially
believe in the holiness of the three sisters and the brother, they
knew too much about them, knew where they lived, and how.
The woman with the tambourine, whose voice dominated the air,
whose face was bright with joy, was divided by very little from
the woman who stood watching her, a cigarette between her
heavy, chapped lips, her hair a cuckoo's nest, her face scarred
and swollen from many beatings, and her black eyes glittering
like coal. Perhaps they both knew this, which was why, when, as
rarely, they addressed each other, they addressed each other as
Sister. As the singing filled the air the watching, listening faces
underwent a change, the eyes focusing on something within; the
music seemed to soothe a poison out of them; and time seemed,
nearly, to fall away from the sullen, belligerent, battered faces, as
though they were fleeing back to their first condition, while dreaming of their last. The barbecue cook half shook his head and
smiled, and dropped his cigarette and disappeared into his joint.
A man fumbled in his pockets for change and stood holding it in
his hand impatiently, as though he had just remembered a pressing appointment further up the avenue. He looked furious. Then
I saw Sonny, standing on the edge of the crowd. He was carrying
a wide, flat notebook with a green cover, and it made him look,
from where I was standing, almost like a schoolboy. The coppery
sun brought out the copper in his skin, he was very faintly smiling,
standing very still. Then the singing stopped, the tambourine
turned into a collection plate again. The furious man dropped
in his coins and vanished, so did a couple of the women, and
Sonny dropped some change in the plate, looking directly at the
woman with a little smile. He started across the avenue, toward
the house. He has a slow, loping walk, something like the way
Harlem hipsters walk, only he's imposed on this his own half-beat.
I had never really noticed it before.

I stayed at the window, both relieved and apprehensive. As
Sonny disappeared from my sight, they began singing again. And
they were still singing when his key turned in the lock.

"Hey," he said.

"Hey, yourself. You want some beer?"

"No. Well, maybe." But he came up to the window and stood beside me, looking out. "What a warm voice," he said.

They were singing *If I could only hear my mother pray again!*

"Yes," I said, "and she can sure beat that tambourine."

"But what a terrible song," he said, and laughed. He dropped his notebook on the sofa and disappeared into the kitchen. "Where's Isabel and the kids?"

"I think they went to see their grandparents. You hungry?"

"No." He came back into the living room with his can of beer. "You want to come some place with me tonight?"

I sensed, I don't know how, that I couldn't possibly say No. "Sure. Where?"

He sat down on the sofa and picked up his notebook and started leafing through it. "I'm going to sit in with some fellows in a joint in the Village."

"You mean, you're going to play, tonight?"

"That's right." He took a swallow of his beer and moved back to the window. He gave me a sidelong look. "If you can stand it."

"I'll try," I said.

He smiled to himself and we both watched as the meeting across the way broke up. The three sisters and the brother, heads bowed, were singing *God be with you till we meet again.* The faces around them were very quiet. Then the song ended. The small crowd dispersed. We watched the three women and the lone man walk slowly up the avenue.

"When she was singing before," said Sonny, abruptly, "her voice reminded me for a minute of what heroin feels like sometimes—when it's in your veins. It makes you feel sort of warm and cool at the same time. And distant. And—and sure." He sipped his beer, very deliberately not looking at me. I watched his face. "It makes you feel—in control. Sometimes you've got to have that feeling."

"Do you?" I sat down slowly in the easy chair.

"Sometimes." He went to the sofa and picked up his notebook again. "Some people do."

"In order," I asked, "to play?" And my voice was very ugly, full of contempt and anger.

"Well"—he looked at me with great, troubled eyes, as though, in fact, he hoped his eyes would tell me things he could never otherwise say—"they *think* so. And *if* they think so—!"

"And what do *you* think?" I asked.

He sat on the sofa and put his can of beer on the floor. "I don't know," he said, and I couldn't be sure if he were answering my question or pursuing his thoughts. His face didn't tell me. "It's not so much to *play*. It's to *stand* it, to be able to make it at all. On any level." He frowned and smiled: "In order to keep from shaking to pieces."

"But these friends of yours," I said, "they seem to shake themselves to pieces pretty goddamn fast."

"Maybe." He played with the notebook. And something told me that I should curb my tongue, that Sonny was doing his best to talk, that I should listen. "But of course you only know the ones that've gone to pieces. Some don't—or at least they haven't *yet* and that's just about all *any* of us can say." He paused. "And then there are some who just live, really, in hell, and they know it and they see what's happening and they go right on. I don't know." He sighed, dropped the notebook, folded his arms. "Some guys, you can tell from the way they play, they on something *all* the time. And you can see that, well, it makes something real for them. But of course," he picked up his beer from the floor and sipped it and put the can down again, "they *want* to, too, you've got to see that. Even some of them that say they don't—*some,* not all."

"And what about you?" I asked—I couldn't help it. "What about you? Do *you* want to?"

He stood up and walked to the window and remained silent for a long time. Then he sighed. "Me," he said. Then: "While I was downstairs before, on my way here, listening to that woman sing, it struck me all of a sudden how much suffering she must have had to go through—to sing like that. It's *repulsive* to think you have to suffer that much."

I said: "But there's no way not to suffer—is there, Sonny?"

"I believe not," he said, and smiled, "but that's never stopped anyone from trying." He looked at me. "Has it?" I realized, with this mocking look, that there stood between us, forever, beyond the power of time or forgiveness, the fact that I had held silence— so long!—when he had needed human speech to help him. He turned back to the window. "No, there's no way not to suffer. But you try all kinds of ways to keep from drowning in it, to keep on top of it, and to make it seem—well, like *you*. Like you did something, all right, and now you're suffering for it. You know?" I said nothing. "Well you know," he said impatiently, "why *do* people suffer? Maybe it's better to do something to give it a reason, *any* reason."

"But we just agreed," I said, "that there's no way not to suffer. Isn't it better, then, just to—take it?"

"But nobody just takes it," Sonny cried, "that's what I'm telling you! *Everybody* tries not to. You're just hung up on the *way* some people try—it's not *your* way!"

The hair on my face began to itch, my face felt wet. "That's not true," I said, "that's not true. I don't give a damn what other people do, I don't even care how they suffer. I just care how *you* suffer." And he looked at me. "Please believe me," I said, "I don't want to see you—die—trying not to suffer."

"I won't," he aid, flatly, "die trying not to suffer. At least, not any faster than anybody else."

"But there's no need," I said, trying to laugh, "is there? in killing yourself."

I wanted to say more, but I couldn't. I wanted to talk about will power and how life could be—well, beautiful. I wanted to say that it was all within; but was it? or, rather, wasn't that exactly the trouble? And I wanted to promise that I would never fail him again. But it would all have sounded—empty words and lies.

So I made the promise to myself and prayed that I would keep it.

"It's terrible sometimes, inside," he said, "that's what's the trouble. You walk these streets, black and funky and cold, and there's not really a living ass to talk to, and there's nothing shaking, and there's no way of getting it out—that storm inside. You can't talk it and you can't make love with it, and when you finally try to get with it and play it, you realize *nobody's* listening. So *you've* got to listen. You got to find a way to listen."

And then he walked away from the window and sat on the sofa again, as though all the wind had suddenly been knocked out of him. "Sometimes you'll do *anything* to play, even cut your mother's throat." He laughed and looked at me. "Or your brother's." Then he sobered. "Or your own." Then: "Don't worry. I'm all right now and I think I'll *be* all right. But I can't forget— where I've been. I don't mean just the physical place I've been, I mean where I've *been*. And *what* I've been."

"What have you been, Sonny?" I asked.

He smiled—but sat sideways on the sofa, his elbow resting on the back, his fingers playing with his mouth and chin, not looking at me. "I've been something I didn't recognize, didn't know I could be. Didn't know anybody could be." He stopped, looking inward, looking helplessly young, looking old. "I'm not talking about it now because I feel *guilty* or anything like that—maybe it would be better if I did, I don't know. Anyway, I can't really talk about it. Not to you, not to anybody," and now he turned and faced me. "Sometimes, you know, and it was actually when I was most *out* of the world, I felt that I was in it, that I was *with* it, really, and I could play or I didn't really have to *play*, it just came out of me, it was there. And I don't know how I played, thinking about it now, but I know I did awful things, those times, sometimes, to people. Or it wasn't that I *did* anything to them—it was that they weren't real." He picked up the beer can; it was empty; he rolled it between his palms: "And other times—well, I needed a fix, I needed to find a place to lean, I needed to clear a space to *listen*—and I couldn't find it, and I—went crazy, I did terrible things to *me*, I was terrible *for* me." He began pressing the beer can between his hands, I watched the metal begin to give. It glittered, as he played with it, like a knife, and I was afraid he would cut himself, but I said nothing. "Oh well. I can never tell you. I was all by myself at the bottom of something, stinking and sweating and crying and shaking, and I smelled it, you know? *my* stink, and I thought I'd die if I couldn't get away from it and yet, all the same, I knew that everything I was doing was just locking me in with it. And I didn't know," he paused, still flattening the beer can, "I didn't know, I still *don't* know, something kept telling me that maybe it was good to smell your own stink, but I didn't think that *that* was what I'd been trying to do—and—who can stand it?" and he abruptly dropped the ruined beer can, looking at me with a small, still smile, and then rose, walking to the window as though it were the lodestone rock. I watched his face, he watched the avenue. "I couldn't tell you when Mama died— but the reason I wanted to leave Harlem so bad was to get away from drugs. And then, when I ran away, that's what I was running from—really. When I came back, nothing had changed, *I* hadn't changed, I was just—older." And he stopped, drumming with his fingers on the windowpane. The sun had vanished, soon darkness would fall. I watched his face. "It can come again," he said, almost as though speaking to himself. Then he turned to me. "It can come again," he repeated. "I just want you to know that."

"All right," I said, at last. "So it can come again. All right."

He smiled, but the smile was sorrowful. "I had to try to tell you," he said.

"Yes," I said. "I understand that."

"You're my brother," he said, looking straight at me, and not smiling at all.

"Yes," I repeated, "yes. I understand that."

He turned back to the window, looking out. "All that hatred down there," he said, "all that hatred and misery and love. It's a wonder it doesn't blow the avenue apart."

We went to the only night club on a short, dark street, downtown. We squeezed through the narrow, chattering, jam-packed bar to the entrance of the big room, where the bandstand was. And we stood there for a moment, for the lights were very dim in this room and we couldn't see. Then, "Hello, boy," said a voice and an enormous black man, much older than Sonny or myself, erupted out of all that atmospheric lighting and put an arm around Sonny's shoulder. "I been sitting right here," he said, "waiting for you."

He had a big voice, too, and heads in the darkness turned toward us.

Sonny grinned and pulled a little away, and said, "Creole, this is my brother. I told you about him."

Creole shook my hand. "I'm glad to meet you, son," he said, and it was clear that he was glad to meet me *there*, for Sonny's sake. And he smiled, "You got a real musician in *your* family," and he took his arm from Sonny's shoulder and slapped him, lightly, affectionately, with the back of his hand.

"Well. Now I've heard it all," said a voice behind us. This was another musician, and a friend of Sonny's, a coal-black, cheerful-looking man, built close to the ground. He immediately began confiding to me, at the top of his lungs, the most terrible things about Sonny, his teeth gleaming like a lighthouse and his laugh coming up out of him like the beginning of an earthquake. And it turned out that everyone at the bar knew Sonny, or almost everyone; some were musicians, working there, or nearby, or not working, some were simply hangers-on, and some were there to hear Sonny play. I was introduced to all of them and they were all very polite to me. Yet, it was clear that, for them, I was only Sonny's brother. Here, I was in Sonny's world. Or, rather: his kingdom. Here, it was not even a question that his veins bore royal blood.

They were going to play soon and Creole installed me, by myself, at a table in a dark corner. Then I watched them, Creole, and the little black man, and Sonny, and the others, while they horsed around, standing just below the bandstand. The light from the bandstand spilled just a little short of them and, watching them laughing and gesturing and moving about, I had the feeling that they, nevertheless, were being most careful not to step into that circle of light too suddenly: that if they moved into the light too suddenly, without thinking, they would perish in flame. Then, while I watched, one of them, the small, black man, moved into the light and crossed the bandstand and started fooling around with his drums. Then—being funny and being, also, extremely ceremonious—Creole took Sonny by the arm and led him to the piano. A woman's voice called Sonny's name and a few hands started clapping. And Sonny, also being funny and being ceremonious, and so touched, I think, that he could have cried, but neither hiding it nor showing it, riding it like a man, grinned, and put both hands to his heart and bowed from the waist.

Creole then went to the bass fiddle and a lean, very bright-skinned brown man jumped up on the bandstand and picked up his horn. So there they were, and the atmosphere on the bandstand and in the room began to change and tighten. Someone stepped up to the microphone and announced them. Then there were all kinds of murmurs. Some people at the bar shushed others. The waitress ran around, frantically getting in the last orders, guys and chicks got closer to each other, and the lights on the bandstand, on the quartet, turned to a kind of indigo. Then they all looked different there. Creole looked about him for the last time, as though he were making certain that all his chickens were in the coop, and then he—jumped and struck the fiddle. And there they were.

All I know about music is that not many people ever really hear it. And even then, on the rare occasions when something opens within, and the music enters, what we mainly hear, or hear corroborated, are personal private, vanishing evocations. But the man who creates the music is hearing something else, is dealing with the roar rising from the void and imposing order on it as it hits the air. What is evoked in him, then, is of another order, more terrible because it has no words, and triumphant, too, for that same reason. And his triumph, when he triumphs, is ours. I just watched Sonny's face. His face was troubled, he was working hard, but he wasn't with it. And I had the feeling that, in a way, everyone on the bandstand was waiting for him, both waiting for him and pushing him along. But as I began to watch Creole, I realized that it was Creole who held them all back. He had them on a short rein. Up there, keeping the beat with his whole body, wailing on the fiddle, with his eyes half closed, he was listening to everything, but he was listening to Sonny. He was having a dialogue with Sonny. He wanted Sonny to leave the shore line and strike out for the deep water. He was Sonny's witness that deep water and drowning were not the same thing—he had been there, and he knew. And he wanted Sonny to know. He was waiting for Sonny to do the things on the keys which would let Creole know that Sonny was in the water.

And, while Creole listened, Sonny moved, deep within, exactly like someone in torment. I had never before thought of how awful the relationship must be between the musician and his instrument. He has to fill it, this instrument, with the breath of life, his own. He has to make it do what he wants it to do. And a piano is just a piano. It's made out of so much wood and wires and little hammers and big ones, and ivory. While there's only so much you can do with it, the only way to find this out is to try and make it do everything.

And Sonny hadn't been near a piano for over a year. And he wasn't on much better terms with his life, not the life that stretched before him now. He and the piano stammered, started one way, got scared, stopped; started another way, panicked, marked time, started again; then seemed to have found a direction, panicked again, got stuck. And the face I saw on Sonny I'd never seen before. Everything had been burned out of it, and, at the same time, things usually hidden were being burned in, by the fire and fury of the battle which was occurring in him up there.

Yet, watching Creole's face as they neared the end of the first set, I had the feeling that something had happened, something I hadn't heard. Then they finished, there was scattered applause, and then, without an instant's warning, Creole started into something else, it was almost sardonic, it was *Am I Blue.* And, as though he commanded, Sonny began to play. Something began to happen. And Creole let out the reins. The dry, low, black man said something awful on the drums, Creole answered, and the drums talked back. Then the horn insisted, sweet and high, slightly detached perhaps, and Creole listened, commenting now and then, dry, and driving, beautiful and calm and old. Then they all came together again, and Sonny was part of the family again. I could tell this from his face. He seemed to have found, right there beneath his fingers, a damn brand-new piano. It seemed that he couldn't get over it. Then, for awhile, just being happy with Sonny, they seemed to be agreeing with him that brand-new pianos certainly were a gas.

Then Creole stepped forward to remind them that what they were playing was the blues. He hit something in all of them, he hit something in me, myself, and the music tightened and deepened, apprehension began to beat the air. Creole began to tell us what the blues were all about. They were not about anything very new. He and his boys up there were keeping it new, at the risk of ruin, destruction, madness, and death, in order to find new ways to make us listen. For, while the tale of how we suffer, and how we are delighted, and how we may triumph is never new, it always must be heard. There isn't any other tale to tell, it's the only light we've got in all this darkness.

And this tale, according to that face, that body, those strong hands on those strings, has another aspect in every country, and a new depth in every generation. Listen, Creole seemed to be saying, listen. Now these are Sonny's blues. He made the little black man on the drums know it, and the bright, brown man on the horn. Creole wasn't trying any longer to get Sonny in the water. He was wishing him Godspeed. Then he stepped back, very slowly, filling the air with the immense suggestion that Sonny speak for himself.

Then they all gathered around Sonny and Sonny played. Every now and again one of them seemed to say, Amen. Sonny's fingers filled the air with life, his life. But that life contained so many others. And Sonny went all the way back, he really began with the spare, flat statement of the opening phrase of the song. Then he began to make it his. It was very beautiful because it wasn't hurried and it was no longer a lament. I seemed to hear with what burning he had made it his, with what burning we had yet to make it ours, how we could cease lamenting. Freedom lurked around us and I understood, at last, that he could help us to be free if we would listen, that he would never be free until we did. Yet, there was no battle in his face now. I heard what he had gone through, and would continue to go through until he came to rest in earth. He had made it his: that long line, of which we knew only Mama and Daddy. And he was giving it back, as everything must be given back, so that, passing through death, it can live forever. I saw my mother's face again, and felt, for the first time, how the stones of the road she had walked on must have bruised her feet. I saw the moonlit road where my father's brother died. And it brought something else back to me, and carried me past it, I saw my little girl again and felt Isabel's tears again, and I felt my own tears begin to rise. And I was yet aware that this was only a moment, that the world waited outside, as hungry as a tiger, and that trouble stretched above us, longer than the sky.

Then it was over. Creole and Sonny let out their breath, both soaking wet, and grinning. There was a lot of applause and some of it was real. In the dark, the girl came by and I asked her to take drinks to the bandstand. There was a long pause, while they talked up there in the indigo light and after awhile I saw the girl put a Scotch and milk on top of the piano for Sonny. He didn't seem to notice it, but just before they started playing again, he sipped from it and looked toward me, and nodded. Then he put it back on top of the piano. For me, then, as they began to play again, it glowed and shook above my brother's head like the very cup of trembling.

CARLOS CASTANEDA

FROM *The Teachings of Don Juan*

In the month of December, 1964, don Juan [1] and I went to collect the different plants needed to make the smoking mixture. It was the fourth cycle. Don Juan merely supervised my actions. He urged me to take time, to watch, and to deliberate before I picked any of the plants. As soon as the ingredients had been gathered and stored, he prompted me to meet with his ally again.

Thursday, December 31, 1964

"Now that you know a bit more about the devil's weed and the smoke, you can tell more clearly which of the two you like better," don Juan said.

"The smoke really terrifies me, don Juan. I don't know exactly why, but I don't have a good feeling about it."

"You like flattery, and the devil's weed flatters you. Like a woman, she makes you feel good. The smoke, on the other hand, is the most noble power; he has the purest heart. He does not entice men or make them prisoners, nor does he love or hate. All he requires is strength. The devil's weed also requires strength, but of a different kind. It is closer to being virile with women. On the other hand, the strength required by the smoke is strength of the heart. You don't have that! But very few men have it. That is why I recommend that you learn more about the smoke. He reinforces the heart. He is not like the devil's weed, full of

[1] Don Juan is a Yaqui Indian who instructed Castaneda in the mysteries of his peyote cult.

passions, jealousies, and violence. The smoke is constant. You don't have to worry about forgetting something along the line."

Wednesday, January 27, 1965

On Tuesday, January 19, I smoked again the hallucinogenic mixture. I had told don Juan I felt very apprehensive about the smoke, and that it frightened me. He said I had to try it again to evaluate it with justice.

We walked into his room. It was almost two o'clock in the afternoon. He brought out the pipe. I got the charcoals, then we sat facing each other. He said he was going to warm up the pipe and awaken her, and if I watched carefully I would see how she glowed. He put the pipe to his lips three or four times, and sucked through it. He rubbed it tenderly. Suddenly he nodded, almost imperceptibly, to signal me to look at the pipe's awakening. I looked, but I couldn't see it.

He handed the pipe to me. I filled the bowl with my own mixture, and then picked a burning charcoal with a pair of tweezers I had made from a wooden clothespin and had been saving for this occasion. Don Juan looked at my tweezers and began to laugh. I vacillated for a moment, and the charcoal stuck to the tweezers. I was afraid to tap them against the pipe bowl, and I had to spit on the charcoal to put it out.

Don Juan turned his head away and covered his face with his arm. His body shook. For a moment I thought he was crying, but he was laughing silently.

The action was interrupted for a long time; then he swiftly picked up a charcoal himself, put it in the bowl, and ordered me to smoke. It required quite an effort to suck through the mixture; it seemed to be very compact. After the first try I felt I had sucked the fine powder into my mouth. It numbed my mouth immediately. I saw the glow in the bowl, but I never felt the smoke as the smoke of a cigarette is felt. Yet I had the sensation of inhaling something, something that filled my lungs first and then pushed itself down to fill the rest of my body.

I counted twenty inhalations, and then the count did not matter any longer. I began to sweat; don Juan looked at me fixedly and told me not to be afraid and to do exactly as he said.

I tried to say "alright," but instead I made a weird, howling sound. It went on resounding after I had closed my mouth. The sound startled don Juan, who had another attack of laughter. I wanted to say "yes" with my head, but I couldn't move.

Don Juan opened my hands gently and took the pipe away. He ordered me to lie down on the floor, but not to fall asleep. I wondered if he was going to help me lie down but he did not. He just stared at me uninterruptedly. All of a sudden I saw the room tumbling, and I was looking at don Juan from a position on my side. From that point on the images became strangely blurry, as in a dream. I can vaguely recall hearing don Juan talk to me a great deal during the time I was immobilized.

I did not experience fear, or unpleasantness, during the state itself, nor was I sick upon awakening the next day. The only thing out of the ordinary was that I could not think clearly for some time after waking up. Then gradually, in a period of four or five hours, I became myself again.

Wednesday, January 20, 1965

Don Juan did not talk about my experience, nor did he ask me to relate it to him. His sole comment was that I had fallen asleep too soon.

"The only way to stay awake is to become a bird, or a cricket, or something of the sort," he said.

"How do you do that, don Juan?"

"That is what I am teaching you. Do you remember what I said to you yesterday while you were without your body?"

"I can't recall clearly."

"I am a crow. I am teaching you how to become a crow. When you learn that, you will stay awake, and you will move freely; otherwise you will always be glued to the ground, wherever you fall."

Sunday, February 7, 1965

My second attempt with the smoke took place about midday on Sunday, January 31. I woke up the following day in the early evening. I had the sensation of possessing an unusual power to recollect whatever don Juan had said to me during the experience. His words were imprinted on my mind. I kept on hearing them with extraordinary clarity and persistence. During this attempt another fact became obvious to me: My entire body had become numb soon after I began to swallow the fine powder, which got into my mouth every time I sucked the pipe. Thus I not only inhaled the smoke, but also ingested the mixture.

I tried to narrate my experience to don Juan; he said I had done nothing important. I mentioned that I could remember everything that had happened, but he did not want to hear about it. Every memory was precise and unmistakable. The smoking procedure had been the same as in the previous attempt. It was almost as if the two experiences were perfectly juxtaposable, and I could start my recollection from the time the first experience ended. I clearly remembered that from the time I fell to the ground on my side I was completely devoid of feeling or thought. Yet my clarity was not impaired in any way. I remember thinking my last thought at about the time the room became a vertical plane: "I must have clunked my head on the floor, yet I don't feel any pain."

From that point on I could only see and hear. I could repeat every word don Juan had said. I followed each one of his directions. They seemed clear, logical, and easy. He said that my body was disappearing and only my head was going to remain, and in such a condition the only way to stay awake and move around was by becoming a crow. He commanded me to make an effort to wink, adding that whenever I was capable of winking I would be ready to proceed. Then he told me that my body had vanished completely and all I had was my head; he said the head never disappears because the head is what turns into a crow.

He ordered me to wink. He must have repeated this command, and all his other commands countless times, because I could remember all of them with extraordinary clarity. I must have winked, because he said I was ready and ordered me to straighten up my head and put it on my chin. He said that in the chin were the crow's legs. He commanded me to feel the legs and observe that they were coming out slowly. He then said that I was not solid yet, that I had to grow a tail, and that the tail would come out of my neck. He ordered me to extend the tail like a fan, and to feel how it swept the floor.

Then he talked about the crow's wings, and said they would come out of my cheekbones. He said it was hard and painful. He commanded me to unfold them. He said they had to be extremely long, as long as I could stretch them, otherwise I would not be able to fly. He told me the wings were coming out and were long and beautiful, and that I had to flap them until they were real wings.

He talked about the top of my head next and said it was still very large and heavy, and its bulk would prevent my flying. He told me that the way to reduce its size was by winking; with every wink my head would become smaller. He ordered me to wink until the top weight was gone and I could jump freely. Then he told me I had reduced my head to the size of a crow, and that I had to walk around and hop until I had lost my stiffness.

There was one last thing I had to change, he said, before I could fly. It was the most difficult change, and to accomplish it I had to be docile and do exactly as he told me. I had to learn to see like a crow. He said that my mouth and nose were going to grow between my eyes until I had a strong beak. He said that crows see straight to the side, and commanded me to turn my head and look at him with one eye. He said that if I wanted to change and look with the other eye I had to shake my beak down, and that that movement would make me look through the other eye. He ordered me to shift from one eye to the other. And then he said I was ready to fly, and that the only way to fly was to have him toss me into the air.

I had no difficulty whatsoever eliciting the corresponding sensation to each one of his commands. I had the perception of growing bird's legs, which were weak and wobbly at first. I felt a tail coming out of the back of my neck and wings out of my cheekbones. The wings were folded deeply. I felt them coming out by degrees. The process was hard but not painful. Then I winked my head down to the size of a crow. But the most astonishing effect was accomplished with my eyes. My bird's sight!

When don Juan directed me to grow a beak, I had an annoying sensation of lack of air. Then something bulged out and created a block in front of me. But it was not until don Juan directed me to see laterally that my eyes actually were capable of having a full view to the side. I could wink one eye at a time and shift the focusing from one eye to the other. But the sight of the room and all the things in it was not like an ordinary sight. Yet it was impossible to tell in what way it was different. Perhaps it was lopsided, or perhaps things were out of focus. Don Juan became very big and glowy. Something about him was comforting and safe. Then the images blurred; they lost their outlines, and became sharp abstract patterns that flickered for a while.

Sunday, March 28, 1965

On Thursday, March 18, I smoked again the hallucinogenic mixture. The initial procedure was different in small details. I had to refill the pipe bowl once. After I had finished the first batch, don Juan directed me to clean the bowl, but he poured the mixture into the bowl himself because I lacked muscular coordination. It took a great deal of effort to move my arms. There was enough mixture in my bag for one refill. Don Juan looked at the bag and said this was my last attempt with the smoke until the next year because I had used up all my provisions.

He turned the little bag inside out and shook the dust into the dish that held the charcoals. It burned with an orange glow, as if he had placed a sheet of transparent material over the charcoals. The sheet burst into flame, and then it cracked into an intricate pattern of lines. Something zigzagged inside the lines at high speed. Don Juan told me to look at the movement in the lines. I saw something that looked like a small marble rolling back and forth in the glowing area. He leaned over, put his hand into the glow, picked out the marble, and placed it in the pipe bowl. He ordered me to take a puff. I had a clear impression that he had put the small ball into the pipe so that I would inhale it. In a moment the room lost its horizontal position. I felt a profound numbness, a sensation of heaviness.

When I awakened, I was lying on my back at the bottom of a shallow irrigation ditch, immersed in water up to my chin. Someone was holding my head up. It was don Juan. The first thought I had was that the water in the channel had an unusual quality; it was cold and heavy. It slapped lightly against me, and my thoughts cleared with every movement it made. At first the water had a bright green halo, or fluorescence, which soon dissolved, leaving only a stream of ordinary water.

I asked don Juan about the time of day. He said it was early morning. After awhile I was completely awake, and got out of the water.

"You must tell me all you saw," don Juan said when we got to his house. He also said he had been trying to "bring me back" for three days, and had had a very difficult time doing it. I made numerous attempts to describe what I had seen, but I could not concentrate. Later on, during the early evening, I felt I was ready to talk with don Juan, and I began to tell him what I remembered from the time I had fallen on my side, but he did not want to hear about it. He said the only interesting part was what I saw and did after he "tossed me into the air and I flew away."

All I could remember was a series of dreamlike images or scenes. They had no sequential order. I had the impression that each one of them was like an isolated bubble, floating into focus and then moving away. They were not, however, merely scenes to look at. I was inside them. I took part in them. When I tried to recollect them at first, I had the sensation that they were vague, diffused flashes, but as I thought about them I realized that each one of them was extremely clear although totally unrelated to ordinary seeing—hence, the sensation of vagueness. The images were few and simple.

As soon as don Juan mentioned that he had "tossed me into the air" I had a faint recollection of an absolutely clear scene in which I was looking straight at him from some distance away. I was looking at his face only. It was monumental in size. It was flat and had an intense glow. His hair was yellowish, and it moved. Each part of his face moved by itself, projecting a sort of amber light.

The next image was one in which don Juan had actually tossed me up, or hurled me, in a straight onward direction. I remember I "extended my wings and flew." I felt alone, cutting through the air, painfully moving straight ahead. It was more like walking than like flying. It tired my body. There was no feeling of flowing free, no exuberance.

Then I remembered an instant in which I was motionless, looking at a mass of sharp, dark edges set in an area that had a dull, painful light; next I saw a field with an infinite variety of lights. The lights moved and flickered and changed their luminosity. They were almost like colors. Their intensity dazzled me.

At another moment, an object was almost against my eye. It was a thick, pointed object; it had a definite pinkish glow. I felt a sudden tremor somewhere in my body and saw a multitude of similar pink forms coming toward me. They all moved on me. I jumped away.

The last scene I remembered was three silvery birds. They radiated a shiny, metallic light, almost like stainless steel, but intense and moving and alive. I liked them. We flew together.

Don Juan did not make any comments on my recounting.

Tuesday, March 23, 1965

The following conversation took place the next day, after the recounting of my experience.

Don Juan said: "It does not take much to become a crow. You did it and now you will always be one."

"What happened after I became a crow, don Juan? Did I fly for three days?"

"No, you came back at nightfall as I had told you to."

"But how did I come back?"

"You were very tired and went to sleep. That is all."

"I mean did I fly back?"

"I have already told you. You obeyed me and came back to the house. But don't concern yourself with that matter. It is of no importance."

"What is important, then?"

"In your whole trip there was only one thing of great value—the silvery birds!"

"What was so special about them? They were just birds."

"Not just birds—they were crows."

"Were they white crows, don Juan?"

"The black feathers of a crow are really silvery. The crows shine so intensely that they are not bothered by other birds."

"Why did their feathers look silvery?"

"Because you were seeing as a crow sees. A bird that looks dark to us looks white to a crow. The white pigeons, for instance, are pink or bluish to a crow; sea gulls are yellow. Now, try to remember how you joined them."

I thought about it, but the birds were a dim, disassociated image which had no continuity. I told him I could remember only that I felt I had flown with them. He asked me whether I had joined them in the air or on the ground, but I could not possibly answer that. He became almost angry with me. He demanded that I think about it. He said: "All this will not mean a damn; it will be only a mad dream unless you remember correctly." I strained myself to recollect, but I could not.

Saturday, April 3, 1965

Today I thought of another image in my "dream" about the silvery birds. I remembered seeing a dark mass with myriads of pinholes. In fact, the mass was a dark cluster of little holes. I don't know why I thought it was soft. As I was looking at it, three birds flew straight at me. One of them made a noise; then all three of them were next to me on the ground.

I described the image to don Juan. He asked me from what direction the birds had come. I said I couldn't possibly determine that. He became quite impatient and accused me of being inflexible in my thinking. He said I could very well remember if I tried to, and that I was afraid to let myself become less rigid. He said that I was thinking in terms of men and crows, and that I was neither a man nor a crow at the time that I wanted to recollect.

He asked me to remember what the crow had said to me. I tried to think about it, but my mind played on scores of other things instead. I couldn't concentrate.

Sunday, April 4, 1965

I took a long hike today. It got quite dark before I reached don Juan's house. I was thinking about the crows when suddenly a very strange "thought" crossed my mind. It was more like an impression or a feeling than a thought. The bird that had made the noise said they were coming from the north and going south, and when we met again they would be coming the same way.

I told don Juan what I had thought up, or maybe remembered. He said, "Don't think about whether you remembered it or made it up. Such thoughts fit men only. They do not fit crows, especially those you saw, for they are the emissaries of your fate. You are already a crow. You will never change that. From now on the crows will tell you with their flight about every turn of your fate. In which direction did you fly with them?"

"I couldn't know that, don Juan!"

"If you think properly you will remember. Sit on the floor and tell me the position in which you were when the birds flew to you. Close your eyes and make a line on the floor."

I followed his suggestion and determined the point.

"Don't open your eyes yet!" He proceeded, "In which direction did you all fly in relation to that point?"

I made another mark on the ground.

Taking these points of orientation as a reference, don Juan interpreted the different patterns of flight the crows would observe to foretell my personal future or fate. He set up the four points of the compass as the axis of the crows's flight.

I asked him whether the crows always followed the cardinal points to tell a man's fate. He said that the orientation was mine alone; whatever the crows did in my first meeting with them was of crucial importance. He insisted on my recalling every detail, for the message and the pattern of the "emissaries" were an individual, personalized matter.

There was one more thing he insisted I should remember, and that was the time of day when the emissaries left me. He asked me to think of the difference in the light around me between the time when I "began to fly" and the time when the silvery birds "flew with me." When I first had the sensation of painful flight, it was dark. But when I saw the birds, everything was reddish—light red, or perhaps orange.

He said: "That means it was late in the day; the sun was not down yet. When it is completely dark a crow is blind with whiteness and not with darkness, the way we are at night. This indication of the time places your last emissaries at the end of the day. They will call you, and as they fly above your head, they will become silvery white; you will see them shining against the sky, and it will mean your time is up. It will mean you are going to die and become a crow yourself."

"What if I see them during the morning?"

"You won't see them in the morning!"

"But crows fly all day."

"Not your emissaries, you fool!"

"How about *your* emissaries, don Juan?"

"Mine will come in the morning. There will also be three of them. My benefactor told me that one could shout them back to black if one does not want to die. But now I know it can't be done. My benefactor was given to shouting, and to all the clatter and violence of the devil's weed. I know the smoke is different because he has no passion. He is fair. When your silvery emissaries come for you, there is no need to shout at them. Just fly with them as you have already done. After they have collected you they will reverse directions, and there will be four of them flying away."

Saturday, April 10, 1965

I had been experiencing brief flashes of disassociation, or shallow states of nonordinary reality.

One element from the hallucinogenic experience with the mushrooms kept recurring in my thoughts: the soft, dark mass of pinholes. I continued to visualize it as a grease or an oil bubble which began to draw me to its center. It was almost as if the center would open up and swallow me, and for very brief moments I experienced something resembling a state of nonordinary reality. As a result I suffered moments of profound agitation, anxiety, and discomfort, and I willfully strove to end the experiences as soon as they began.

Today I discussed this condition with don Juan. I asked for advice. He seemed to be unconcerned and told me to disregard the experiences because they were meaningless, or rather valueless. He said the only experiences worth my effort and concern would be those in which I saw a crow; any other kind of "vision" would be merely the product of my fears. He reminded me again that in order to partake of the smoke it was necessary to lead a strong, quiet life. Personally I seemed to have reached a dangerous threshold. I told him I felt I could not go on; there was something truly frightening about the mushrooms.

In going over the images I recalled from my hallucinogenic

experience, I had come to the unavoidable conclusion that I had seen the world in a way that was structurally different from ordinary vision. In other states of nonordinary reality I had undergone, the forms and the patterns I had visualized were always within the confines of my visual conception of the world. But the sensation of seeing under the influence of the hallucinogenic smoke mixture was not the same. Everything I saw was in front of me in a direct line of vision; nothing was above or below that line of vision.

Every image had an irritating flatness, and yet, disconcertingly, a profound depth. Perhaps it would be more accurate to say that the images were a conglomerate of unbelievably sharp details set inside fields of different light; the light in the fields moved, creating an effort of rotation.

After probing and exerting myself to remember, I was forced to make a series of analogies or similes in order to "understand" what I had "seen." Don Juan's face, for instance, looked as if he had been submerged in water. The water seemed to move in a continuous flow over his face and hair. It so magnified them that I could see every pore in his skin or every hair on his head whenever I focused my vision. On the other hand, I saw masses of matter that were flat and full of edges, but did not move because there was no fluctuation in the light that came from them.

I asked don Juan what were the things that I had seen. He said that because this was the first time I was seeing as a crow the images were not clear or important, and that later on with practice I would be able to recognize everything.

I brought up the issue of the difference I had detected in the movement of light. "Things that are alive," he said, "move inside, and a crow can easily see when something is dead, or about to die, because the movement has stopped or is slowing down to a stop. A crow can also tell when something is moving too fast, and by the same token a crow can tell when something is moving just right."

"What does it mean when something is moving too fast, or just right?"

"It means a crow can actually tell what to avoid and what to seek. When something is moving too fast inside, it means it is about to explode violently, or to leap forward, and a crow will avoid it. When it moves inside just right, it is a pleasing sight and a crow will seek it."

"Do rocks move inside?"

"No, not rocks or dead animals or dead trees. But they are beautiful to look at. That is why crows hang around dead bodies. They like to look at them. No light moves inside them."

"But when the flesh rots, doesn't it change or move?"

"Yes, but that is a different movement. What a crow sees then is millions of things moving inside the flesh with a light of their own, and that is what a crow likes to see. It is truly an unforgettable sight."

"Have you seen it yourself, don Juan?"

"Anybody who learns to become a crow can see it. You will see it yourself."

At this point I asked don Juan the unavoidable question.

"Did I really become a crow? I mean would anyone seeing me have thought I was an ordinary crow?"

"No. You can't think that way when dealing with the power of the allies. Such questions make no sense, and yet to become a crow is the simplest of all matters. It is almost like frolicking; it has little usefulness. As I have already told you, the smoke is not for those who seek power. It is only for those who crave to see. I learned to become a crow because these birds are the most effective of all. No other birds bother them, except perhaps larger, hungry eagles, but crows fly in groups and can defend themselves. Men don't bother crows either, and that is an important point. Any man can distinguish a large eagle, especially an unusual eagle, or any other large, unusual bird, but who cares about a crow? A crow is safe. It is ideal in size and nature. It can go safely into any place without attracting attention. On the other hand, it is possible to become a lion or a bear, but that is rather dangerous. Such a creature is too large; it takes too much energy to become one. One can also become a cricket, or a lizard, or even an ant, but that is even more dangerous, because large animals prey on small creatures."

I argued that what he was saying meant that one really changed into a crow, or a cricket, or anything else. But he insisted I was misunderstanding.

"It takes a very long time to learn to be a proper crow," he said.

"But you did not change, nor did you stop being a man. There is something else."

"Can you tell me what the something else is, don Juan?"

"Perhaps by now you know it yourself. Maybe if you were not so afraid of becoming mad, or of losing your body, you would understand this marvelous secret. But perhaps you must wait until you lose your fear to understand what I mean."

TOM WOLFE

The Mild Ones

God knows how many thousands of work-a-daddy citizens of Columbus, Ohio, Tom's own city, drive past the Harley-Davidson agency at 491 West Broad Street every day without ever seeing *Tom's Bomb,* that weird monster in the show window. Yet there are many boys and men, religiosi of a sort, in Los Angeles, Oakland, Chicago, Cleveland, who know of it. They know of this *ecstatic* in Columbus, Tom Reiser—the stud who rides a motorcycle with an automobile engine in it—

Liberation!

Tom's Bomb is up on a platform in one corner of the window. It is a Harley-Davidson 74-XA motorcycle with a Chevrolet V-8 automobile engine in it. Reiser put a whole automobile engine in a motorcycle. He had to put it in crossways, so that half the block sticks out of one side of the bike and half out the other, right out of the frame there, right in front of the rider's legs and just in back of the front wheel. The proportions are like a boulder rammed through a sheet of plywood. The motorcycle frame weighs 300 pounds and the engine weighs 550 pounds, a Chevrolet V-8 with all the headers, the wires, the flywheel, everything showing.

Reiser got the idea from another one of the underground heroes of the motorcycle world, Ed Potter. Ed Potter, in motorcycling, is like what Chuck Berry, Muddy Waters, Hank Williams, or one of these people is in music, a *germinal* folk figure from back 'ere on Route 422 or something. Potter put a whole automobile engine in a motorcycle frame and called the machine the "Bloody Mary." But he didn't have any transmission in it, no gear shift. He couldn't start it off from a dead start and accelerate. He had to go out to the drag strip and get on and have his buddy Jimmy jack the rear wheel up off the ground. Then he would turn the throttle up until the rear wheel was turning at the equivalent of about 110 miles an hour. Then his buddy Jimmy would kick the jack out from under it and—holy jesus—the back wheel would hit the asphalt and shriek like a woman's scream and he would start careening down the strip, fishtailing every way you can think of, including straight into the crowd. There was a true ball buster.

Tom Reiser refined the whole thing. He invented a motorcycle transmission, the kind you operate on the handlebars of the motor-cycle, for the Chevrolet V-8 engine. Reiser is a student of the motorcycle. That is one thing people do not generally understand about the motorcycle crowd. The kids who go in for racing, whether drag racing, like Reiser, or oval track racing or long-dis-tance road racing, hill climbing, or cross-country racing, are very studious. They develop a priestly passion for speed engineering. They are truly religious men, bound by their devotion to Libera-tion through the internal-combustion engine. They are sequestered from most secular concerns. They spend practically all their spare time working on the machines. They seldom drink much because it takes up too much time or even smoke much because it gets in the way when you're working on the machine.

Reiser looks a little like Slats in the comic strip, "Abbie and Slats." He is 29 years old, tall, blond, raw-boned, open, outgoing; Western-looking, one might say. He is married and has two chil-dren. His father, who is retired, was a florist and his mother was a seamstress; he went to South High School in Columbus and later was trained at the Harley-Davidson mechanics school in California. He was always a genius with motorcycles. And cour-age—raw nerve—it seemed like his priestly passion for the motor-cycle, for speed, made it so he would do practically anything to get speed out of a motorcycle. Reiser won the Canadian hill-climbing championship in 1965 and is after the speed record at the Utah salt flats. He put together "Tom's Bomb" in 1961, and thankgod they had just built the superhighway from Columbus west to Cincinnati, Route 71, because that was the chance to try it out.

The federal superhighway program has been a godsend for speed engineering in the state of Ohio. The beautiful time is right after a stretch of highway is built, but before it is opened to cars. Ohio's speed kids, the motorcyclists, the drag racers, both motorcycle and automobile, follow that beautiful superhighway system wherever the road contractors go with it. At night they sneak out onto the great smooth stretches of American superhighway and . . . *go.* Tom Reiser warmed up "Tom's Bomb" out on Route 71 under the moon and then he took it out to the drag strip near Newark, Ohio, for an exhibition. They all saw the machine rolling out toward the starting line, and a shriek went up—

"Well, when I started off," Reiser was saying, "the back wheel bit down so hard it threw me back and it felt like the whole motorcycle was going to go over backward. It was like the whole thing was just going to lift up and go over backward. It was like the whole thing was covered in smoke, me and everything. I couldn't see nothing. The guys thought the engine had exploded or something. It was the rubber burning, but they thought the whole thing was on fire and they were going to have to get me out of there with a fire hose. It was a weird feeling. It started off with a whole row of jerks. I don't know what that was, unless there was so much power, it was just running over the top of itself, and then all of a sudden it shot out of the cloud, and after that there wasn't anything to do but *hang on—*"

By the time he burst out of the cloud, Reiser was already going about 50 miles an hour. By the time he hit 60, he had his head practically down on the handlebars, to lower his body and cut down on the wind resistance. His body was stretched out over the Chevrolet V-8 engine, which was mounted in the frame between the seat and the front wheel. He was stretching more and more flat out with each split second of acceleration until his feet came up off the foot rests and his legs stretched out straight behind—

"When I hit about 90," said Reiser, "it was like the bike wasn't hardly touching the road any more—"

—and when he hit 130, he *knew* it wasn't—

"All of a sudden I was *sailing*—like I wasn't on the ground any more at all. I couldn't hardly see anything or hear anything. There was no gravity or nothing, I was just *sailing*—"

—and as he spoke, I could *see* it, the ultimate vision. I could see his body stretched out and pressing down tighter and tighter upon the V-8 engine until his thoracic cavity was practically bolted onto it. Its fiery combustions were his neural explosions and his neural explosions were its fiery combustions. His body and that roaring engine block were one and the same creature, sailing —at 140—160—180—200 miles an hour—2,000 miles an hour— sailing!—at last, the winged American centaur, the American dream, at last: soaring over God's own good green Great Plains of America bareback aboard a 300-horsepower Chevrolet V-8 engine!

CHAPTER FOUR

The Map of Love: Being with Others

The eighteenth-century French essayist Sebastien Chamfort once wrote: "All is true and all is false in love: love is the only thing about which it is impossible to say anything absurd." Or anything that isn't absurd, we might add, considering the oceans of ink that have been spilled over it. What makes the subject so intriguing, and yet so infuriating, is that many different faces of love stare out at us in paradoxical contradiction. At one extreme, religious mystics, both Christian and Eastern, used the vocabulary of sexual ecstasy to convey the transport they experienced in the ravishing presence of their heavenly vision. At another extreme, medieval troubadours celebrated worldly passions in the language of religious salvation. For the poet W. B. Yeats, the contrarieties were bound together by the ironic absurdity that "Love has pitched his mansion in/The place of excrement." Similarly, in "Suzanne" the lover speaks of wedding body and soul, junkyard and religious ecstasy in a total act of love. On the one hand, love can create a heightened state of sensibility and a more complete possession of all one's faculties. On the other, love can lead to a loss of one's separate selfness or self-possession—perhaps even to a surrender of selfishness—as in Williams' "The Dance."

Something like these last considerations has led the philosopher and mystic Martin Buber to distinguish between I-it and I-Thou relationships. In an I-it relationship the self looks upon another being as an object to be studied and exploited, but not to be felt in a genuine experience of communication. In turning others into objects we objectify them, hence dehumanizing them. Pornography, for example, is objectionable precisely because it objectifies other human beings. I-it relationships are only juxtapositions of the self against others, and therefore are fundamentally alienating. Conversely, I-Thou relationships are personalized acts of reciprocity that involve (literally, to enwind or enroll within) both participants in what Buber calls "being-for-the-other"; in amplifying each other, every I and every Thou also augments his own uniqueness. Thus, a total relationship is created greater than the mere sum of the parts of those entering into it. Such a union occurs in "The Map of Love," where a young boy and girl encounter and transcend their own naked sexuality. I-Thou relationships are those extremely rare unions of love in which the self participates in the being of another without abandoning its own sense of individual identity.

At the core of love is the mystery of sex which both fascinates and terrifies us. Perhaps in a discussion of the symbolism latent in sexual coupling we will be able to move into a deeper understanding of the function of love as an act of expanded consciousness. In his Symposium, *Plato recounts an ancient myth explaining the origin of Male and Female as the splitting asunder of a once complete hermaphrodite physiology (a coupling of the gods Hermes and Aphrodite in a single name and body). Originally each individual was a totally self-sufficient sexual organization possessing the reproductive apparatus of both male and female—as certain monoecious plants still do today. Myths are stories man tells to dramatize symbolically and indirectly some of his most deeply buried perplexities. Plato's myth engenders a yearning for a former sense of wholeness and higher unity imagined to have existed outside of history and prior to "the battle of the sexes." This racial memory, longing for a more complete experience of wholeness beyond what is now possible since mankind's Fall into separate masculine and feminine sexuality, can only come about through the fusion of opposites. This is the case in "Someone Talking to Himself," where man and woman achieve an experience of wholeness transcending their own personal identities and linking them up with the primal bed of humanity. In sexual congress, the male and female components of that once organically integral hermaphrodite are again welded together into a unity. The coupling enacted through sexual intercourse unites such opposites as male with female, body with spirit, self with other, and farcical physicality with ecstatic (even mystic) transcendence. It becomes a symbol of all those acts of fusion by which we combine oppositions in a dialectical process, creating a synthesis greater than the simple sum of the parts. Perhaps every creative gesture is fundamentally procreative which involves the reconciliation of oppositions—a notion at the core of Roethke's poem "Four For Sir John Davies."*

Now we are in a position to elaborate further upon Buber's concept of I-Thou relationships. Love is the name for the act by which we place ourselves in creative relationships, rather than dominating or exploitative ones, with the otherness of a world beyond our own skin and self-absorption. But love, as we said, is not necessarily a loss or surrender of self. Rather, our very individuality, uniqueness, and differentness can be enhanced by meaningfully relating ourselves to what we are not. At the heart of the paradox of love is how we enter into an increased sense of self-possession or self-awareness through the act of bridging outward from ourselves toward another. It would not be too farfetched to say that no man can truly know himself unless he has first known another in a loving way. And yet, what lovers know of each other is not truly the individuality of each within himself nor that of the other, but rather something unique which has been created through the cooperation of both of them and which exceeds what each separately has to contribute.

Love is never easy, however. If we persist in looking upon love symbolically as the act by which a self opens up and pushes beyond the boundaries of its own exclusive enclosure to make contact with the otherness, the mysteriousness, of another, we can appreciate some of the terrible risk involved. Though the gains are great, the dangers are also frightening. When we open up those defenses in which we have carefully encircled ourselves as protection against the hostile threats of the outer world—the world of otherness—we leave ourselves exposed to the possibility of great personal hurt. Self-exposure, in every sense of the word, is the hazard we must chance. Only through the nakedness implicit in this opening to the self may the others of the world enter our being in the name of love. But we can never be certain, until it is too late, that they don't come in the name of destruction. It is a risk that must be accepted, however, because only when we pass through this threat of destruction is the possibility of our being truly alive ever made real. As Norman O.

Brown has written, "selfishness is shellfishness"; that is, total self-enclosure is to live like a clam entombed in the cave of one's own shell. Every leap beyond the self becomes an opportunity for procreative exchange with another. And every act of love increases our possibility of having a love affair with the entire world, as is suggested in a variety of ways by the Toomer, Houriet, and Williams selections. That world, however, confronts us as an immense frontier of mysterious otherness. To venture into that darkness is to enter into an experience, to quote Emerson, "of tremendousness to the brink of fear."

LEONARD COHEN

Suzanne

Suzanne takes you down
To her place near the river.
You can hear the boats go by,
You can stay the night beside her,
And you know that she's half-crazy
But that's why you want to be there,
And she feeds you tea and oranges
That come all the way from China,
And just when you mean to tell her
That you have no love to give her,   10
Then she gets you on her wave-length
And she lets the river answer
That you've always been her lover.

And you want to travel with her,
And you want to travel blind,
And you know that she can trust you
'Cause you've touched her perfect body
With your mind.

And Jesus was a sailor
When he walked upon the water   20
And he spent a long time watching
From a lonely wooden tower
And when he knew for certain
That only drowning men could see him,
He said, "All men shall be sailors, then,
Until the sea shall free them,"
But he, himself, was broken
Long before the sky would open.
Forsaken, almost human,
He sank beneath your wisdom   30
Like a stone.

And you want to travel with him,
And you want to travel blind,

And you think you'll maybe trust him
'Cause he touched your perfect body
With his mind.

Suzanne takes your hand
And she leads you to the river.
She is wearing rags and feathers
From Salvation Army counters,   40
And the sun pours down like honey
On our lady of the harbor;
And she shows you where to look
Among the garbage and the flowers.
There are heroes in the seaweed,
There are children in the morning,
They are leaning out for love,
And they will lean that way forever
While Suzanne, she holds the mirror.

And you want to travel with her,   50
You want to travel blind,
And you're sure that she can find you
'Cause she's touched her perfect body
With her mind.

THEODORE ROETHKE

Four for Sir John Davies

1   THE DANCE

Is that dance slowing in the mind of man
That made him think the universe could hum?
The great wheel turns its axle when it can;
I need a place to sing, and dancing-room,
And I have made a promise to my ears
I'll sing and whistle romping with the bears.

For they are all my friends: I saw one slide
Down a steep hillside on a cake of ice,—
Or was that in a book? I think with pride:
A caged bear rarely does the same thing twice   10
In the same way: O watch his body sway!—
This animal remembering to be gay.

I tried to fling my shadow at the moon,
The while my blood leaped with a wordless song.
Though dancing needs a master, I had none
To teach my toes to listen to my tongue.
But what I learned there, dancing all alone,
Was not the joyless motion of a stone.

I take this cadence from a man named Yeats;
I take it, and I give it back again: 20
For other tunes and other wanton beats
Have tossed my heart and fiddled through my brain.
Yes, I was dancing-mad, and how
That came to be the bears and Yeats would know.

2   THE PARTNER

Between such animal and human heat
I find myself perplexed. What is desire?—
The impulse to make someone else complete?
That woman would set sodden straw on fire.
Was I the servant of a sovereign wish,
Or ladle rattling in an empty dish?   30

We played a measure with commingled feet:
The lively dead had taught us to be fond.
Who can embrace the body of his fate?
Light altered light along the living ground.
She kissed me close, and then did something else.
My marrow beat as wildly as my pulse.

I'd say it to my horse: we live beyond
Our outer skin. Who's whistling up my sleeve?

I see a heron prancing in his pond;
I know a dance the elephants believe.   40
The living all assemble! What's the cue?—
Do what the clumsy partner wants to do!

Things loll and loiter. Who condones the lost?
This joy outleaps the dog. Who cares? Who cares?
I gave her kisses back, and woke a ghost.
O what lewd music crept into our ears!
The body and the soul know how to play
In that dark world where gods have lost their way.

3   THE WRAITH

Incomprehensible gaiety and dread
Attended what we did. Behind, before,   50
Lay all the lonely pastures of the dead;
The spirit and the flesh cried out for more.
We two, together, on a darkening day
Took arms against our own obscurity.

Did each become the other in that play?
She laughed me out, and then she laughed me in;
In the deep middle of ourselves we lay;
When glory failed, we danced upon a pin.
The valley rocked beneath the granite hill;
Our souls looked forth, and the great day stood still.   60

There was a body, and it cast a spell,—
God pity those but wanton to the knees,—
The flesh can make the spirit visible;
We woke to find the moonlight on our toes.
In the rich weather of a dappled wood
We played with dark and light as children should.

What shape leaped forward at the sensual cry?—
Sea-beast or bird flung toward the ravaged shore?
Did space shake off an angel with a sigh?
We rose to meet the moon, and saw no more.   70

It was and was not she, a shape alone,
Impaled on light, and whirling slowly down.

4 THE VIGIL

Dante attained the purgatorial hill,
Trembled at hidden virtue without flaw,
Shook with a mighty power beyond his will,—
Did Beatrice deny what Dante saw?
All lovers live by longing, and endure:
Summon a vision and declare it pure.

Though everything's astonishment at last,
Who leaps to heaven at a single bound?   80
The links were soft between us; still, we kissed;
We undid chaos to a curious sound:
The waves broke easy, cried to me in white;
Her look was morning in the dying light.

The visible obscures. But who knows when?
Things have their thought: they are the shards of me;
I thought that once, and thought comes round again;
Rapt, we leaned forth with what we could not see.
We danced to shining; mocked before the black
And shapeless night that made no answer back.   90

The world is for the living. Who are they?
We dared the dark to reach the white and warm.
She was the wind when wind was in my way;
Alive at noon, I perished in her form.
Who rise from flesh to spirit know the fall:
The word outleaps the world, and light is all.

WILLIAM CARLOS WILLIAMS

The Dance

When the snow falls the flakes
spin upon the long axis
that concerns them most intimately
two and two to make a dance

the mind dances with itself,
taking you by the hand,
your lover follows
there are always two,

yourself and the other,
the point of your shoe setting the pace,   10
if you break away and run
the dance is over

Breathlessly you will take
another partner
better or worse who will keep
at your side, at your stops

whirls and glides until he too
leaves off
on his way down as if
there were another direction   20

gayer, more carefree
spinning face to face but always down
with each other secure
only in each other's arms

But only the dance is sure!
make it your own.
Who can tell
what is to come of it?

in the woods of your
own nature whatever   30
twig interposes, and bare twigs
have an actuality of their own

this flurry of the storm
that holds us,
plays with us and discards us
dancing, dancing as may be credible.

RICHARD WILBUR

Someone Talking to Himself

Even when first her face,
Younger than any spring,
Older than Pharaoh's grain
And fresh as Phoenix-ashes,
Shadowed under its lashes
Every earthly thing,
There was another place
I saw in a flash of pain:
Off in the fathomless dark
Beyond the verge of love   10
I saw blind fishes move,
And under a stone shelf
Rode the recusant shark—
Cold, waiting, himself.

Oh, even when we fell,
Clean as a mountain source
And barely able to tell
Such ecstasy from grace,
Into the primal bed
And current of our race,   20

We knew yet must deny
To what we gathered head:
That music growing harsh,
Trees blotting the sky
Above the roaring course
That in the summer's drought
Slowly would peter out
Into a dry marsh.

Love is the greatest mercy,
A volley of the sun   30
That lashes all with shade,
That the first day be mended;
And yet, so soon undone,
It is the lover's curse
Till time be comprehended
And the flawed heart unmade.
What can I do but move
From folly to defeat,
And call that sorrow sweet
That teaches us to see   40
The final face of love
In what we cannot be?

JEAN TOOMER

Fern

Face flowed into her eyes. Flowed in soft cream foam and plaintive ripples, in such a way that wherever your glance may momentarily have rested it immediately thereafter wavered in the direction of her eyes. The soft suggestion of down slightly darkened,
like the shadow of a bird's wing might, the creamy brown color
of her upper lip. Why after noticing it you sought her eyes, I
cannot tell you. Her nose was aquiline, Semitic. If you have heard
a Jewish cantor sing, if he has touched you and made your own
sorrow seem trivial when compared with his, you will know my
feeling when I follow the curves of her profile, like mobile rivers,
to their common delta. They were strange eyes. In this, that they
sought nothing—that is, nothing that was obvious and tangible
and that one could see, and they gave the impression that nothing
was to be denied. When a woman seeks, you will have observed,
her eyes deny. Fern's eyes desired nothing that you could give her;
there was no reason why they should withhold. Men saw her eyes
and fooled themselves. Fern's eyes said to them that she was easy.
When she was young, a few men took her, but got no joy from it.
And then, once done, they felt bound to her (quite unlike their
hit and run with other girls), felt as though it would take them a
lifetime to fulfill an obligation which they could find no name
for. They became attached to her, and hungered after finding the
barest trace of what she might desire. As she grew up, new men
who came to town felt as almost everyone did who ever saw her:
that they would not be denied. Men were everlastingly bringing
her their bodies. Something inside of her got tired of them, I
guess, for I am certain that for the life of her she could not tell
why or how she began to turn them off. A man in fever is no

195

trifling thing to send away. They began to leave her, baffled and ashamed, yet vowing to themselves that someday they would do some fine thing for her: send her candy every week and not let her know whom it came from, watch out for her wedding day and give her a magnificent something with no name on it, buy a house and deed it to her, rescue her from some unworthy fellow who had tricked her into marrying him. As you know, men are apt to idolize or fear that which they cannot understand, especially if it be a woman. She did not deny them, yet the fact was that they were denied. A sort of superstition crept into their consciousness of her being somehow above them. Being above them meant that she was not to be approached by anyone. She became a virgin. Now a virgin in a small southern town is by no means the usual thing, if you will believe me. That the sexes were made to mate is the practice of the South. Particularly, black folks were made to mate. And it is black folks whom I have been talking about thus far. What white men thought of Fern I can arrive at only by analogy. They let her alone.

Anyone of course could see her, could see her eyes. If you walked up the Dixie Pike most any time of day, you'd be most like to see her resting listless-like on the railing of her porch, back propped against a post, head tilted a little forward because there was a nail in the porch post just where her head came which for some reason or other she never took the trouble to pull out. Her eyes, if it were sunset, rested idly where the sun, molten and glorious, was pouring down between the fringe of pines. Or maybe they gazed at the gray cabin on the knoll from which an evening folksong was coming. Perhaps they followed a cow that had been turned loose to roam and feed on cotton stalks and corn leaves. Like as not they'd settle on some vague spot above the horizon, though hardly a trace of wistfulness would come to them. If it were dusk, then they'd wait for the searchlight of the evening train which you could see miles up the track before it flared across the Dixie Pike, close to her home. Wherever they looked, you'd follow them and then waver back. Like her face, the whole countryside seemed to flow into her eyes. Flowed into them with the soft listless cadence of Georgia's South. A young Negro, once, was looking at her spellbound from the road. A white man passing in a buggy had to flick him with his whip if he was to get by without

running him over. I first saw her on her porch. I was passing with
a fellow whose crusty numbness (I was from the North and suspected of being prejudiced and stuck-up) was melting as he found
me warm. I asked him who she was. "That's Fern," was all that I
could get from him. Some folks already thought I was given to
nosing around; I let it go at that, so far as questions were concerned. But at first sight of her I felt as if I heard a Jewish cantor
sing. As if his singing rose above the unheard chorus of a folksong.
And I felt bound to her. I too had my dreams: something I would
do for her. I have knocked about from town to town too much
not to know the futility of mere change of place. Besides, picture
if you can this cream-colored solitary girl sitting at a tenement
window looking down on the indifferent throngs of Harlem. Better that she listen to folksongs at dusk in Georgia, you would say,
and so would I. Or suppose she came up North and married. Even
a doctor or a lawyer, say, one who would be sure to get along—
that is, make money. You and I know, who have had experience
in such things, that love is not a thing like prejudice which can
be bettered by changes of town. Could men in Washington, Chicago, or New York, more than the men of Georgia, bring her
something left vacant by the bestowal of their bodies? You and I
who know men in these cities will have to say, they could not.
See her out and out a prostitute along State Street in Chicago.
See her move into a southern town where white men are more
aggressive. See her become a white man's concubine. . . . Something I must do for her. There was myself. What could I do for
her? Talk, of course. Push back the fringe of pines upon new
horizons. To what purpose? And what for? Her? Myself? Men in
her case seem to lose their selfishness. I lost mine before I touched
her. I ask you, friend (it makes no difference if you sit in the
Pullman or the Jim Crow as the train crosses her road), what
thoughts would come to you—that is, after you'd finished with
the thoughts that leap into men's minds at the sight of a pretty
woman who will not deny them; what thoughts would come to
you had you seen her in a quick flash, keen and intuitively, as she
sat there on her porch when your train thundered by? Would
you have got off at the next station and come back for her to take
her, where? Would you have completely forgotten her as soon as
you reached Macon, Atlanta, Augusta, Pasadena, Madison, Chi-

cago, Boston, or New Orleans? Would you tell your wife or sweet-heart about a girl you saw? Your thoughts can help me, and I would like to know. Something I would do for her. . . .

One evening I walked up the Pike on purpose, and stopped to say hello. Some of her family were about, but they moved away to make room for me. Damn if I knew how to begin. Would you? Mr. and Miss So-and-So, people, the weather, the crops, the new preacher, the frolic, the church benefit, rabbit and possum hunt-ing, the new soft drink they had at old Pap's store, the schedule of the trains, what kind of town Macon was, Negro's migration North, boll weevils, syrup, the Bible—to all these things she gave a yassur or nassur, without further comment. I began to wonder if perhaps my own emotional sensibility had played one of its tricks on me. "Let's take a walk," I at last ventured. The sugges-tion, coming after so long an isolation, was novel enough, I guess, to surprise. But it wasn't that. Something told me that men be-fore me had said just that as a prelude to the offering of their bodies. I tried to tell her with my eyes. I think she understood. The thing from her that made my throat catch, vanished. Its passing left her visible in a way I'd thought, but never seen. We walked down the Pike with people on all the porches gaping at us. "Doesn't it make you mad?" She meant the world. Through a canebrake that was ripe for cutting, the branch was reached. Under a sweet-gum tree, and where reddish leaves had dammed the creek a little, we sat down. Dusk, suggesting the almost im-perceptible procession of giant trees, settled with a purple haze about the cane. I felt strange, as I always do in Georgia, particu-larly at dusk. I felt that things unseen to men were tangibly im-mediate. It would not have surprised me had I had a vision. People have them in Georgia more often than you would suppose. A black woman once saw the mother of Christ and drew her in charcoal on the courthouse wall. . . . When one is on the soil of one's ancestors, most anything can come to one. . . . From force of habit, I suppose, I held Fern in my arms—that is, without at first noticing it. Then my mind came back to her. Her eyes, un-usually weird and open, held me. Held God. He flowed in as I've seen the countryside flow in. Seen men. I must have done something—what, I don't know, in the confusion of my emotion. She sprang up. Rushed some distance from me. Fell to her knees, and began swaying, swaying. Her body was tortured with something it could not let out. Like boiling sap it flooded arms and fingers till she shook them as if they burned her. It found her throat, and spattered inarticulately in plaintive, convulsive sounds, mingled with calls to Christ Jesus. And then she sang, brokenly. A Jewish cantor singing with a broken voice. A child's voice, uncertain, or an old man's. Dusk hid her; I could hear only her song. It seemed to me as though she were pounding her head in anguish upon the ground. I rushed to her. She fainted in my arms.

There was talk about her fainting with me in the canefield. And I got one or two ugly looks from town men who'd set themselves up to protect her. In fact, there was talk of making me leave town. But they never did. They kept a watch out for me, though. Shortly after, I came back North. From the train window I saw her as I crossed her road. Saw her on her porch, head tilted a little forward where the nail was, eyes vaguely focused on the sunset. Saw her face flow into them, the countryside and something that I call God, flowed into them. . . . Nothing ever really happened. Nothing ever came to Fern, not even I. Something I would do for her. Some fine unnamed thing. . . . And, friend, you? She is still living, I have reason to know. Her name, against the chance that you might happen down that way, is Fernie May Rosen.

DYLAN THOMAS

The Map of Love

Here dwell, said Sam Rib, the two-backed beasts. He pointed to his map of Love, a square of seas and islands and strange continents with a forest of darkness at each extremity. The two-backed island, on the line of the equator, went in like the skin of lupus to his touch, and the blood sea surrounding found a new motion in its waters. Here seed, up the tide, broke on the boiling coasts; the sand grains multiplied; the seasons passed; summer, in a father's heat, went down to the autumn and the first pricks of winter, leaving the island shaping the four contrary winds out of its hollows.

Here, said Sam Rib, digging his fingers in the hills of a little island, dwell the first beasts of love. And here the get of the first loves mixed, as he knew, with the grasses that oiled their green upgoings, with their own wind and sap nurtured the first rasp of love that never, until spring came, found the nerves' answer in the following blades.

Beth Rib and Reuben marked the green sea around the island. It ran through the landcracks like a boy through his first caves. Under the sea they marked the channels, painted in skeleton, that linked the first beasts' islands with the boggy lands. For shame of the half-liquid plants sprouting from the bog, the pen-drawn poisons seething in the grass, and the copulation in the second mud, the children blushed.

Here, said Sam Rib, two weathers move. He traced with his finger the slightly drawn triangles of two winds, and the mouths of two cornered cherubs. The weathers moved in one direction. Singly they crawled over the abominations of the swamp, content in the shadow of their own rains and snowings, in the noise of their own sighs, and the pleasures of their twin green achings. The weathers, like a girl and a boy, moved through the tossing world, the sea storm dragging under them, the clouds divided in many rages of movement as they stared on the raw wall of wind.

Return, synthetic prodigals, to thy father's laboratory, declaimed Sam Rib, and the fatted calf in a test-tube. He indicated the shift of locations, the pen lines of the separate weathers travelling over the deep sea and the second split between the lovers' worlds. The cherubs blew harder; wind of the two tossing weathers and the sprays of the cohering sea drove on and on; on the single strand of two coupled countries, the weathers stood. Two naked towers on the two-loves-in-a-grain of the million sands, they mixed, so the map arrows said, into a single strength. But the arrows of ink shot them back; two weakened towers, wet with love, they trembled at the terror of their first mixing, and two pale shadows blew over the land.

Beth and Reuben scaled the hill that cast an eye of stone on the striped valley; hand-in-hand they ran down the hill, singing as they went, and took off their gaiters at the wet grass of the first of the twenty fields. There was a spirit in the valley that would roll on when all the hills and trees, all the rocks and streams, had been buried under the West death. Here was the first field wherein mad Jarvis, a hundred years before, had sown his seed in the belly of a bald-headed girl who had wandered out of a distant county and lain with him in the pains of love.

Here was the fourth field, a place of wonder, where the dead might spin all drunken-legged out of the dry graves, or the fallen angels battle upon the waters of the streams. Planted deeper in the soil of the valley than the blind roots could burrow after their mates, the spirit of the fourth field rose out of darkness, drawing the deep and the dark from the hearts of all who trod the valley a score or more miles from the borders of the mountainous county.

In the tenth and the central field Beth Rib and Reuben knocked at the doors of the bungalows, asking the location of the first island surrounded by loving hills. They knocked at the back door and received a ghostly admonishment.

Barefooted and hand-in-hand, they ran through the ten remaining fields to the edge of the Idris water where the wind smelt of seaweed and the valley spirit was wet with sea rain. But night came down, hand on thigh, and shapes in the further stretches

of the now misty river drew a new shape close to them. An island
shape walled round with darkness a half-mile up river. Stealthily
Beth Rib and Reuben tiptoed to the lapping water. They saw the
shape grow, unlocked their fingers, took off their summer clothes,
and, naked, raced into the river.

Up river, up river, she whispered.

Up river, he said.

They floated down river as a current tugged at their legs, but
they fought off the current and swam towards the still growing
island. Then mud rose from the bed of the river and sucked at
Beth's feet.

Down river, down river, she called, struggling from the mud.

Reuben, weed-bound, fought with the grey heads that fought
his hands, and followed her back to the brink of the sea-going
valley.

But, as Beth swam, the water tickled her; the water pressed on
her side.

My love, cried Reuben, excited by the tickling water and the
hands of the weeds.

And, as they stood naked on the twentieth field, My love, she
whispered.

First fear shot them back. Wet as they were, they pulled their
clothes on them.

Over the fields, she said.

Over the fields, in the direction of the hills and the hill-home
of Sam Rib, like weakened towers the children ran, no longer
linked, bewildered by the mud and blushing at the first tickle of
the misty island water.

Here dwell, said Sam Rib, the first beasts of love. In the cool
of a new morning the children listened, too frightened to touch
hands. He touched again the sagging hill above the island, and
pointed the progression of the skeleton channels linking mud
with mud, green sea with darker, and all love-hills and islands
into one territory. Here the grass mates, the green mates, the
grains, said Sam Rib, and the dividing waters mate and are mated.
The sun with the grass and the green, sand with water, and water
with the green grass, these mate and are mated for the bearing
and fostering of the globe. Sam Rib had mated with a green
woman, as Great-Uncle Jarvis with his bald girl; he had mated
with a womanly water for the bearing and fostering of the child

who blushed by him. He marked how the boggy lands lay so near the first beast doubling a back, the round of doubled beasts under as high a hill as Great-Uncle's hill that had frowned last night and wrapped itself in stones. Great-Uncle's hill had cut the children's feet, for the daps and the gaiters were lost forever in the grass of the first field.

Thinking of the hill, Beth Rib and Reuben sat quiet. They heard Sam say that the hill of the first island grew soft as wool for the descent, or smooth as ice for tobogganing. They remembered the tame descent last night.

Tame hill, said Sam Rib, grows wild for the ascending. Lining the adolescents' hill was a white route of stone and ice marked with the sliding foot or sledge of the children going down; another route, at the foot, climbed upwards in a line of red stone and blood marked with the cracking prints of the ascending children. The descent was soft as wool. Fail on the first island, and the ascending hill wraps itself in a sharp thing of stones.

Beth Rib and Reuben, never forgetful of the hump-backed boulders and the flints in the grass, turned to each other for the first time that day. Sam Rib had made her and would mould him, would make and mould the boy and girl together into a double climber that sought the island and melted there into a single strength. He told them again of the mud, but did not frighten them. And the grey heads of the weeds were broken, never to swell again in the hands of the swimmer. The day of ascending was over; the first descent remained, a hill on the map of love, two branches of stone and olive in the children's hands.

Synthetic prodigals returned that night to the room of the hill, through caves and chambers running to the roof, discerning the roof of stars, and happy in their locked hands. There lay the striped valley before them, and the grass of the twenty fields fed the cattle; the night cattle moved by the hedges or lapped at warm Idris water. Beth Rib and Reuben ran down the hill, and the tender stones lay still under their feet; faster, they ran down the Jarvis flank, the wind at their hair, smells of the sea blown to their quivering nostrils from the north and the south where there was no sea; and, slowing their speed, they reached the first field and the rim of the valley to find their gaiters placed neatly in a cow-cloven spot in the grass.

They buttoned on their gaiters, and ran through the falling blades.

Here is the first field, said Beth Rib to Reuben.

The children stopped, the moonlight night went on, a voice spoke from the hedge darkness.

Said the voice, You are the children of love.

Where are you?

I am Jarvis.

Who are you?

Here, my dears, here in the hedge with a wise woman.

But the children ran away from the voice in the hedge.

Here in the second field.

They stopped for breath, and a weasel, making his noise, ran over their feet.

Hold harder.

I'll hold you harder.

Said a voice, Hold hard, the children of love.

Where are you?

I am Jarvis.

Who are you?

Here, here, lying with a virgin from Dolgelley.

In the third field the man of Jarvis lay loving a green girl, and, as he called them the children of love, lay loving her ghost and the smell of buttermilk on her breath. He loved a cripple in the fourth field, for the twist in her limbs made loving longer, and he cursed the straight children who found him with a straight-limbed lover in the fifth field marking the quarter.

A girl from Tiger Bay held Jarvis close, and her lips marked a red, cracked heart upon his throat; this was the sixth and the weather-tracked field where, turning from the maul of her hands, he saw their innocence, two flowers wagging in a sow's ear. My rose, said Jarvis, but the seventh love smelt in his hands, his fingering hands that held Glamorgan's canker under the eighth hedge. From the Convent of Bethel's Heart, a holy woman served him the ninth time.

And the children in the central field cried as ten voices came up, came up, came down from the ten spaces of the half-night and the hedging world.

It was full night when they answered, when the voices of one voice compassionately answered the two-voiced question ringing on the strokes of the upward, upward, and the downward air.

We, said they, are Jarvis, Jarvis under the hedge, in the arms of a woman, a green woman, a woman bald as a badger, on a nun's thigh.

They counted the numbers of their loves before the children's ears. Beth Rib and Reuben heard the ten oracles, and shyly they surrendered. Over the remaining fields, to the whispers of the last ten lovers, to the voice of aging Jarvis, grey-haired in the final shadows, they sped to Idris. The island shone, the water babbled, there was a gesture of the limbs in each wind's stroke denting the flat river. He took off her summer clothes, and she shaped her arms like a swan. The bare boy stood at her shoulder; and she turned and saw him dive into the ripples in her wake. Behind them her fathers' voices slipped out of sound.

Up river, called Beth, up river.

Up river, he answered.

Only the warm, mapped waters ran that night over the edges of the first beasts' island white in a new moon.

CLIFFORD R. BRAGDON

Love's So Many Things

The first four hours out of Cleveland were not bad. The bus was hot as the devil, but almost empty, and I had the whole back seat alone where I could make myself comfortable stretched out. But when we hit Youngstown, it was all over. Everybody in eastern Ohio got on there—fat women with bundles, slick boys with panama hats and several suitcases, girls in couples, and a sailor. I had to sit up to make room for a fellow and his wife.

The man looked as if he thought he were pretty hard—tight blue suit and long hair plastered back and parted in the middle— like a million others; all they seem to care about is how smooth their hair is. When he smoked, he pulled his lips tight and made the smoke spurt out of the corner of his mouth, first up and then down. They all do that, millions of them. They want you to think they are pretty hard. This one's eyes were little and grey. His wife was pretty, poor kid, though sort of pale and thin, it seemed to me.

Anyway, every chair was taken, and the heat was terrific. I began to wonder whether it was worth the twelve or fifteen I would save on it. If it had not been for the sailor and a couple of girls, I don't know how we could have stood it. As it was, everyone was glad to have them along. They sang songs and giggled and carried on almost all night. Sitting right in back of them, I got the bene- fit of the really good part, the hot give and take, so to speak. For instance, the sailor asked the thinnest one where they were going, and she said, "No place, friend. We're just travelling for our health." Then the other one began singing,

> "I wonder how the old folks are to-night.
> Do they miss the little girl who ran away?"

It was like that almost till morning. Sometimes one would sing, sometimes both—harmony—and it really wasn't bad, except once in a while. Then the sailor would groan, and they would laugh it off and get talking.

The fellow next to me—the fellow with the wife—was all ears. Every time one of them would make a wisecrack, he would haw-haw and stamp his feet. His wife would look up at him now and then and smile as if she thought it was pretty good too, and blink her eyes. But as a matter of fact, I don't think she was even listening, because the minute she got on the bus she just curled up in a corner—coughed a few times—she had a pretty bad cough—and closed her eyes. Her husband didn't seem to mind, though. He ate three or four plums and took in the entertainment. He was sitting so that his wife could rest her head on his lap and he had to lean over on me to hear everything the sailor and the girls said.

As soon as he finished the plums, he got friendly. First he winked at me after he had nearly fallen over from laughing once, and then he leaned even closer than he was already, nudging me.

"They're rich, ain't they?" he whispered. His voice didn't sound at all the way he looked.

"Yeah," I said. "Your wife mind if I smoke?"

"No. Where you from?" he said. "Youngstown?"

I told him, no, I was from Cleveland, and he mentioned how bad the Indians were doing. Just then his wife sat up and coughed. She asked him for a cigarette, but he shook his head. Then he kissed her.

When she was curled up again, he turned to me. "It must be swell being a sailor," he said. "Lots of fun, them fellows."

"Yeah," I said, "but they don't get on land only once in so often."

"That's right," he answered, nudging me again, "but when they do, oh, boy—uh?"

I moved over a little. "It's pretty good, I guess."

"You bet," he said. "You know I used to be pretty quick on the pickup myself. I used to have a pretty good line—and they fell for it, too, if I do say it."

Neither of us spoke for a while then. We were scrouging around trying to get a little less cramped and hot than we were, or else listening to the clowns in front of us. Everybody else was doing the same thing or just sitting still with their heads back and their mouths open—especially the fat women. All the women on this bus were fat—except the little girl on the back seat—and they appeared not to mind the heat as much as the thin men. They sat as if they had been dumped down and a few yards of crumpled stuff thrown around them.

My new friend seemed to be turning something over in his mind, and so I had a chance to take a peek at his wife. I couldn't see her very well unless we were passing under a light. It gave a funny effect then, as if she were alive for a second and then dead, about to wake up and then just dropped asleep again. I was getting so I could hardly keep my eyes off her.

When we were pulling out of Pittsburgh where someone got off, leaving us three the back seat to ourselves, he started in again. "Where you bound for, Bud?" he asked me.

I told him New York and asked him where he was going.

"Harrisburg. I got an aunt," he said. "Well, we're getting off the bus at Harrisburg, that is, but we're going up to the Pocono Mountains. We been over two thousand miles on the roads in the last five days. We been out to Denver."

"Is that so?" I said. "Nice out there, they tell me."

He laughed a little. "Well," he said, "yeah, it's a nice enough place, but no work."

I asked him what he'd been doing out there then, thinking he might be one of these auto-hoboes. Neither he nor his wife looked like money at all—even cheap money. He didn't answer my question, so I said, "What did you do, drive out and then take the busses back?"

"No," he answered, "we took the busses both ways. Was you ever in Harrisburg?"

"No," I said.

It was getting late, and the entertainment was off for a while because one of the girls, the less fat one, had paired off with the sailor. The other pretended she didn't care and sang by herself for a minute but not for long. She tried to get hold of a red-headed fellow across the aisle, but there was nothing doing, so she flopped around and pretended to go to sleep. I was ready for sleep myself, but didn't like to sleep sitting up, and besides, I kept glancing over at the girl curled up in the corner. I lit another cigarette and asked the girl's husband what he was going to do in Pocono.

"I don't know," he said.

"A little vacation, maybe?"

"No, I'll get work up there if I can," he said. "One reason for going up there is maybe my uncle can get me some work. I got a trade—glass worker, but I don't care much what I do." He settled himself a little. "It don't make any difference," he went on. "There are some good farms up there—Dutch. Maybe I'd make a good farmer. Yeah, a swell farmer—not. But it's O.K. with me." He stepped carefully on the cigarette I had just tossed on the floor, and smiled.

"Well, but what's the idea going up into the hills though?" I asked him. It was about two in the morning. The time and the heat both must have made me feebleminded. Anyway he didn't answer my question, because his wife woke up just then and sat up and put her fingers through his hair as if she liked the stuff. She was just a kid. He must have been about thirty-one or -two; hard to tell exactly. But she didn't look more than twenty at the most.

Well, for a while then he didn't even know I was alive. A big change came over him. He took out his handkerchief and fanned her like they do a fighter. It seemed funny to see this tiny little kid sitting in a corner of the back seat on a bus, all slumped down like a fighter just saved by the bell, and being fanned like one, too. It made me feel sore at something because I wanted to do something for her. Of course there wasn't anything I could do—I just felt like it ought to have been somebody else fanning her and kissing her. Not that there was anything wrong with this fellow exactly; she ought to have been married to somebody else, that's all. The poor kid must have been boiling hot—though it had cooled off a little by this time—because there were little beads of sweat all over her forehead, and she coughed so much I finally had the sense to quit smoking.

Her husband fanned her like that until she smiled at him and closed her eyes. Then she curled up again, and her husband made her as comfortable as he could. At about the same time the sailor and the girl split up. The girl came back and sat with her friend. At first the fat one pretended she was still asleep, but she soon got over that, and the two of them started in singing again. It was late, and some man up front didn't like it.

"Aw, pipe down, lady," he hollered, "and go to sleep."

The girls came right back at him. "If you don't like it, why don't you get out?" one of them said.

This got a good laugh; we were in the mountains without a house in sight. Just the same the girls quit singing.

"If he was back here, I'd slap his mouth," the fat one said.

The sailor turned around. "Well," he said, "your friend here bit mine."

"Oh, hush up, you big liar," answered the girl he had been sitting with. Then they all three laughed and started another conversation.

The fellow sitting with me laughed so hard at what the sailor said, I thought he would roll off onto the floor.

"That was a fast one," he said, rubbing his nose. "Like I said to a girl friend once." He reached in his pocket as if he wanted a cigarette, but changed his mind. He slid down in his seat so that he was talking up sideways at my chin. "This girl was in swimming, see?" he went on, grinning all over, "so I come up behind her under water and pinched her on the—well, you get me, haw, haw, haw—just kidding, see, but she made out she didn't notice it, and she says to her friend who was standing there with her, she says, 'Oh, wasn't that a big wave, Betty'—or Beth, or whatever her name was. I heard her and came right back, 'Yeah, that was swell,' I says. Swell, see, me pinching her," and he laughed hard and nudged me for the hundredth time. He was looking the way people usually do when they tell a joke—like a kid watching someone else eating a piece of candy. I thought it was a pretty bum joke, but we got talking along those lines for a while. He told a few pretty fair ones about his adventures—just the usual stuff, and then I asked him again how he happened to be going up to the mountains with the hillbillies. I preferred hearing about that though I guess it was really his wife I was interested in.

Every now and then I would look over at her, but she made me feel so foolish, I kept trying to listen to her dumb husband instead. She made me feel like I wanted to hold her like a little kid and give her a drink of water—in little sips. She would sip, I thought, and then look up and catch her breath and smile with her eyes. It made me feel foolish, thinking like that.

Well, her husband said something after a minute, answering me, I guess, but I missed it. Then I heard him say,

"I said she's pretty, ain't she?"

Of course I felt like even a bigger yap then than before; he couldn't have helped noticing me staring at her, not even him. But he didn't seem sore. I said, "Yes, but she don't look very well."

"No," he said, "she's got a cold."

He turned so that he could look at her, and patted her arm. "She's only twenty-two," he went on. "We been married five years, would you believe it? She was seventeen then."

"Is that a fact?" I answered, not knowing what else to say.

"Yeah. She's Irish. Look at that nose and you can tell she's a little mick all right. She's only been in this country five and a half years. She come over six months before I married her."

He just seemed to be talking for talking's sake. I guess he didn't want to fall asleep, either. But I wanted him to keep on about her, so I said, "What's her name? Colleen?"

"No," he said, "Mary. She's not really Irish I guess though. She says she's Manx from the Isle of Man. Sounds like a cat, don't it? There's a cat name Manx, ain't there? Anyway I tell her she ain't got it right. She's a minx, not a Manx, I tell her."

He stopped suddenly and looked at me as if he was afraid I might think he was a sap, and yet as if he wanted me to laugh at the same time. One dirty, stubby hand was still on her arm, stroking it. It was dark, and he didn't know I could see that. But I could. Her arm was so white. It was impossible now to keep from looking at her; I was beginning to think she was the prettiest girl I had ever seen.

Pretty soon her husband started talking again. "She was working at my aunt's house when I was there for a while. They lived in Brooklyn then. That's how I come to meet her. Ever been in Brooklyn?"

"Love at first sight, uh?" I said.

He chuckled. "Hell, no," he said. "She wouldn't have a thing to do with me at first. I was carrying on around there with some other girls at the time. But, you know, I cut all that out. It's funny, ain't it, how you'll do that."

All I wanted to do was to keep on asking him questions. "How did you finally bring her around then?" I asked him.

"Oh, she come around all right in the end," he whispered, winking at me. "You can't keep the girls away from a good-looking fellow, uh?" His little grey eyes opened wide, and he nudged me.

"Ain't that right?" he added, laughing when I looked at him. "Of course I was just kidding, Bud," he said. "I guess I ain't no John Barrymore, all right."

He sounded so serious I had to laugh. "Sure, I knew that," I said.

I didn't mean it the way it sounded, but I was just as glad to let it go. I was so sick of his nudging me I could have hit him anyway. Besides, as I said, looking at his wife made me sore at things in general, and I guess I was taking it out on him. He wasn't really such a bad guy.

But he got over it all right, and pretty soon he laughed. "We was married in Brooklyn. She's a Catholic," he said.

"But how did it all happen?" I broke in on him, wanting to hear all I could. It seemed as if I had to.

"Well, I'll tell you how it was, Bud," he answered, sitting up again and crossing his legs, but keeping one hand on his wife's arm, "we got to keep awake, huh? But there ain't much to tell. There wasn't anything romantic about it or anything. I'd just been kidding around with her for a while—you know how it is—taking her to a show now and then without meaning much. She never let on one way or the other till the very end—but—but she said then she'd been crazy about me. Anyway I didn't hardly believe it myself for a long while. She was just a kid, see?"

"Oh, yeah, I see," I said.

He went right on. "She would be around the house cooking and dusting and so on and I'd just sneak up behind her and kiss her on the neck—that's about all. She was too tired for much gallavanting around most of the time usually."

I didn't like him telling me all this, and yet I kept egging him on. "Didn't she mind you kissing her like that?" I asked.

"Oh, no," he answered. "She wouldn't stand for a lot of fooling, but I wasn't never rough with her. I—I—she seemed to take it all right. Anyway we didn't court long. In fact it was just a month before I popped the question, like they say. It come on me like a bolt of lightning, but Mary said afterward the only thing that surprised her was—and worried her too, she said—was why I didn't get on to myself earlier."

"Yeah, go on," I said.

"Well, one night she was out in the kitchen and I was sort of helping around when my aunt come in. 'Mary,' she says, 'Mrs.

Link's out here with her baby. Come on out and take care of him while me and her go to the show, will you?' she says.

"So Mary and I went out and played with this kid for about half an hour. It was a cute kid—falling around. And then all of a sudden I felt something sort of come over me. It was the funniest feeling I ever had—like—like I wanted to pick her up and . . . Oh, well, anyway I stood up, see?—we were sitting on the floor— and Mary looked up at me as if she was surprised—the little bum. She wasn't no more surprised—but believe me I was. I was so surprised I was afraid if I opened my mouth I'd holler and act crazy. But then the first thing I knew I heard myself talking—like I was way away.

" 'Well, Kid,' I says, 'I guess you better set the date.' Right like that. 'Make it whenever you like,' I says, 'but the sooner the better.' That was all there was to it. I didn't mean to say it that way, believe me, but that's the way it was. Funny, how things happen so different from what you'd have said they would when you were thinking about it, ain't it? That was May, and we was married the following September. Mary carried roses."

I didn't say anything. I just took a quick look at his wife. Apparently the poor kid was sound asleep.

We were coming into a small town at the moment and stopped to gas up. Everybody that was awake piled out for a cup of coffee. I drank two. I was trying to think straight, but I guess I was too sleepy. The fellow and his wife both stayed in the bus.

When it came time to climb in again, I noticed it had gotten quite chilly while we were talking, so when I'd picked my way back to my seat, I told the fellow I was going to try to get a little sleep on the floor and his wife could stretch out and make herself comfortable. She was sitting up then and heard me. Neither one of them said anything, but the girl did stretch out, and he sat crunched up in one corner. I was hoping the girl would smile or something, but she didn't.

Pretty soon everybody else piled in and we started out again. The sailor and the two girls were just as full of pep as ever and began kidding around out loud. One of them said something funny, and my talkative friend let out another one of his horse laughs. I was feeling foolish still, so I took off my coat and put it over the girl's feet; she was coughing a little. Her husband already had his over her shoulders. He had the window open and I was glad it was warm on the floor. I asked him why he didn't put the window down, but he pointed to his wife, and shook his head. He was laughing so hard at the wisecrack from the seat in front he couldn't speak, but when he got through, he leaned over—I was stretched out on the floor in front of him then.

"Say, Bud, listen," he whispered, "did you ever hear the one about the Irishman and the girl in Hoboken?"

Well, I couldn't see him, but I knew just what he looked like. Something jumped up inside me, and I said, "No, damn it, and I don't want to, either."

He didn't say anything, but I could hear him sit back and move around trying to get comfortable. I was feeling so bad I could have killed him. Pretty soon I heard a kiss and some whispering, but from where I was, I couldn't tell whether it was in front or in back of me. That was all I knew for about three hours.

It was light when I woke up. I sat up on the floor and looked around. The girl was lying stretched out, fast asleep with her head in her husband's lap. When he saw me sit up, he winked at me, and grinned. I almost felt sorry for him—he looked so cold. I said, "How is she?"

He looked down at her and put his hand on her forehead. "Her cold's pretty bad," he whispered.

They got out at Harrisburg.

NORMAN O. BROWN

Unity

Is there a way out; an end to analysis; a cure; is there such a thing as health?

To heal is to make whole, as in wholesome; to make one again; to unify or reunify: this is Eros in action. Eros is the instinct that makes for union, or unification, and Thanatos, the death instinct, is the instinct that makes for separation, or division.

Crazy Jane in William Butler Yeats—Crazy Jane who is both the student and the teacher—says,

> Nothing can be sole or whole
> That has not been rent.

We have been rent; there is no health in us. We must acknowl-edge the rents, the tears, the splits, the divisions; and then we can pray, as Freud prays at the end of *Civilization and Its Discon-tents*, "that the other of the two heavenly forces, eternal Eros, will put forth his strength so as to maintain himself alongside his equally immortal adversary."

Yeats, "Crazy Jane Talks with the Bishop."

There is only one political problem in our world today: the unification of mankind. The Internationale shall be the human race. That they may be one—*ut unum sint*. This is Christ's last prayer before the crucifixion, which was also the last prayer of the late Pope John; it must be set beside Freud's prayer in *Civilization and Its Discontents*. For indeed they will not be one until Freud and Pope John are found to speak in unison; or Freud and Marx and Pope John: The thing is to bring them together. John X, 16:

Other sheep I have, which are not of this fold: them also must I bring, and they shall hear my voice; and there shall be one fold, and one shepherd.

John XVII, 21.

The unification of the human race: a mental fight, a struggle in and about men's minds. The rents, the tears, splits and divisions are mindmade; they are not based on the truth but on what the Buddhists call illusion, what Freud calls unconscious fantasies. The prevailing sense of reality, the prevailing forms of knowledge, are ruled by the instinct of aggression and divsion, are under the dominion of the death instinct. We are in Satan's kingdom; to build a Heaven in Hell's despite is to construct an erotic sense of reality.

To make in ourselves a new consciousness, an erotic sense of reality, is to become conscious of symbolism. Symbolism is mind making connections (correspondences) rather than distinctions (separations). Symbolism makes conscious interconnections and unions that were unconscious and repressed. Freud says, symbolism is on the track of a former identity, a lost unity: the lost continent, Atlantis, underneath the sea of life in which we live enisled; or perhaps even our union with the sea (Thalassa); oceanic consciousness; the unity of the whole cosmos as one living creature, as Plato said in the *Timaeus*.

Cf. Freud, "Interpretation of Dreams," 370.

Union and unification is of bodies, not souls. The erotic sense of reality unmasks the soul, the personality, the ego; because soul, personality and ego are what distinguish and separate us; they make us individuals, arrived at by dividing till you can divide no more—atoms. But psychic individuals, separate, unfissionable on the inside, impenetrable on the outside, are, like physical atoms, an illusion; in the twentieth century, in this age of fission, we can split the individual even as we can split the atom. Souls, personalities, and egos are masks, spectres, concealing our unity as body. For it is as one biological species that mankind is one—"the species-essence" that Karl Marx looked for; so that to become conscious of ourselves as body is to become conscious of mankind as one.

Cf. K. Marx and F. Engels, *Kleine ökonomische Schriften,* 42–166.

It is the erotic sense of reality that discovers the inadequacy of fraternity, or brotherhood. It is not adequate as a form for the re-unification of the human race: We must be either far more deeply unified, or not at all. The true form of unification—which can be found either in psychoanalysis or in Christianity, in Freud or Pope John, or Karl Marx—is: "We are all members of one body." The true form of the unification of the human race is not the brothers, Cain and Abel, but Adam the first man, and Christ the second man: for as in Adam all die, even so in Christ shall all be made alive.

I Corinthians XV, 22. Cf. Daniélou, *Origen,* 205: "When we expound the dogma of the Mystical Body we do not take the dogma itself from Karl Marx, but we do bring out the factors in it that correspond to what Karl Marx taught."

Christ is the second Adam; these two are one; there is only one man. This is not a new idea, but part of the great tradition, to be made new and alive today. St. Thomas Aquinas says, "many men are derived from Adam, as members of one body"—*tanquam membra unius corporis;* and, "the human race is to be considered as one body, which is called the mystical body, whose head is Christ himself, both with regard to the souls and with regard to the bodies"—*et quantum ad animas et quantum ad corpora.* The mystical body is not, because mystical, therefore non-bodily. And, St. Augustine: "The whole human race which was to become Adam's posterity through the first woman, was present in the first man." "We all existed in that one man, since, taken together, we were the one man who fell into sin." Even as in Hebrew *adham* is man and mankind in one; and the man Adam. "All mankind, whose life from Adam to the end of this world is as the life of one man."

St. Thomas Aquinas in Gierke, *Political Theories of the Middle Age,* 103, n. 7. Augustine, *De Civitate Dei,* XIII, 3–14, *de vera religione,* 27, 50. Cf. Pedersen, *Israel,* I, 110. Ladner, *The Idea of Reform,* 264–265.

And the resurrection is the resurrection of the body; but not the separate body of the individual, but the body of mankind as one body. The fall of man is the fall into division of the human race, the dismemberment of the first man, Adam; and the resurrection or rebirth through the second man, Christ, is to reconstitute the lost unity. "His fall into Division & his Resurrection to Unity"; till we all come to one perfect man. St. Athanasius, commenting on Christ's last prayer, "that they may be all one, as Thou in Me, and I in Thee," says it means that "born as it were by Me, they may all be one body and one spirit, and may combine to form one perfect man . . . so that, made divine, they may be one in us." The unification of mankind into one is also the unification of humanity and divinity; St. Gregory of Nyssa says, "Christ, by whom all mankind was united into divinity." Unification is deification.

Blake, *Night* I, 1. 21. Scheeben, *Mysteries*, 367n., 386n.
Cf. Augustine, *De Civitate Dei*, XXII, 17–18. Dante, *De Monarchia*, I, 8.
Ephesians IV, 13; John XVII, 21.

If we are all members of one body, then in that one body there is neither male nor female; or rather there is both: It is an androgynous or hermaphroditic body, containing both sexes. In this way St. Augustine explains that other old story: the creation of Eve out of the rib of Adam. "God did not wish to create the woman who was to be mated with man in the same way that He created man, but, rather, out of him, in order that the whole human race might be derived entirely from one single man." The division of the one man into two sexes is part of the fall; sexes are sections.

Galatians III, 28. Augustine, *De Civitate Dei*, XII, 21.

Hence according to the Epistle to the Ephesians the true meaning of the mystery of sexual intercourse is that it is a symbolic representation, or adumbration, of that mystical body in which we are all members of one body.

> So ought men to love their wives as their own bodies.
> He that loveth his wife loveth himself.
> For no man ever yet hated his own flesh; but nourisheth
> and cherisheth it, even as the Lord the church.

> For we are members of his body, of his flesh, and of his bones.
>
> For this cause shall a man leave his father and mother, and shall be joined unto his wife, and they two shall be one flesh.
>
> This is a great mystery: but I speak concerning Christ and the church.

Ephesians V, 28–32.

The fantastic hypothesis of Freud in *Beyond the Pleasure Principle* and Ferenczi in *Thalassa* turns out to be right after all. The tendency of the sexual instinct is to restore an earlier state of things, an earlier state of unity, before life was sexually differentiated; ultimately going back to a state "before living substance was torn apart into separate particles." Freud illustrated his hypothesis with the myth in Plato's *Symposium*, deriving sexual differentiation from the bisection of a primal hermaphroditic body.

Freud, *Beyond the Pleasure Principle*, 79–80.

What else is to be found in psychoanalysis, by those determined to find, about the one body, the mystical body? The truth, the healing truth, the wholesome truth, the truth that will make us whole, is not in individual psychology, nor in the currently so fashionable ego psychology, but in what the later Freud called "mass-psychology." Freud said his last work, *Moses and Monotheism*, was an attempt "to translate the concepts of individual psychology into mass-psychology." "Mass-psychology" is not mob psychology, but the psychology of mankind as a whole, as one mass, or one body. Mass, then, in the same sense as Augustine's *massa perditionis; universa massa in vitiata radice damnata.* The word "en-masse."

Cf. Augustine, *De Civitate Dei*, XIV, 26. Whitman, "One's-Self I Sing."

Psychoanalysis is always the discovery of the unconscious; the turn to mass-psychology corresponds to the discovery that the unconscious is collective. As early as *Totem and Taboo* (1913), Freud took as the basis of his whole position the existence of a "collective mind," or "mass-psyche"—the German is *Massenpsyche* —and he remained steadfast to that basis in *Massenpsychologie*

(1921) and *Moses* (1937): "a mass-psyche in which psychological processes occur as they do in the psyche of an individual." The defect in this statement is the implication that individual minds, as well as a group mind, are real. In *Moses and Monotheism* Freud disallows the term "collective unconscious," because it suggests that there might be some other kind of unconscious which is not collective; then comes his statement: "The content of the unconscious is collective anyhow, a general possession of all mankind." Since the true psychic reality is the unconscious, the true psychic reality is collective; there is only one psyche, a general possession of mankind.

Freud, *Moses and Monotheism*, 208; *Totem and Taboo*, 157.

The goal of psychotherapy is psychic integration; but there is no integration of the separate individual. The individual is obtained by division; integration of the individual is a strictly self-contradictory enterprise, as becomes evident in the futile attempts of the therapists to define "what we mean by mental health" in the individual person. The goal of "individuation," or of replacing the ego by the "self," deceitfully conceals the drastic break between the *principium individuationis* and the Dionysian, or drunken, principle of union, or communion, between man and man and between man and nature. The integration of the psyche is the integration of the human race, and the integration of the world with which we are inseparably connected. Only in one world can we be one. The inner voice, the personal salvation, the private experience are all based on an illusory distinction. Consciousness is as collective as the unconscious; there is only one psyche, ego-cosmic, in relation to which all conflict is endopsychic, all war intestine. Hence, when Cain slew Abel he slew himself: "For the soul, not belonging to the category of things separate from each other but under the category of things which form a single whole, must necessarily suffer what it seems to do."

Philo, *That the Worse Is Wont to Attack the Better*, XV.
Cf. Klein and Riviere, *Love, Hate and Reparation*, 61, 66, 68.

In the collective unconscious Freud finds what he calls an "archaic heritage," or "phylogenetic inheritance." "Phylogenetic inheritance," i.e., belonging to the "species-essence" of the human species; "archaic heritage," i.e., archetypes. At any rate, the phylo-genetic factor is the symbolic factor, the former identity or lost unity which symbolic consciousness recovers. "There probably exists in the mental life of the individual not only what he has experienced himself, but also what he brought with him at birth, fragments of a phylogenetic origin, an archaic heritage." Not in entire forgetfulness do we come. Freud comes to the conclusion that "the archaic heritage of mankind includes not only disposi-tions, but also ideational contents, memory traces of the experi-ences of former generations." The nucleus of neurosis turns out to be precisely in this phylogenetic factor: not in the individual's own murderous impulses against his individual father, but in the primal crime against the primal parent or parents. For Freud, then, in the end, as for Christianity, in Adam's fall we sinned all, and there is just that one collective sickness of the human race in all its genera-tions: we are all in the same boat, or body.

Freud, *Moses and Monotheism*, 157, 159; cf. 208–209.

Another signpost pointing in the same direction is the term *id*, which, in the later Freud, is the opposite of the term *ego*; as in the earlier Freud, consciousness is the opposite of the unconscious. The *id* is instinct; that Dionysian "cauldron of seething excite-ment," a sea of energy out of which the ego emerges like an island. The term *"id"*—*"it"*—taken from Nietzsche (via Grod-deck), is based on the intuition that the conduct through life of what we call our ego is essentially passive; it is not so much we who live, as that we are lived by unknown forces. The reality is instinct, and instinct is impersonal energy, an "it" who lives in us. I live, yet not I, but it lives in me; as in creation, *fiat*. Let it be; no "I," but an it. The "I-Thou" relationship is still a relation to Satan; the old Adversary; the Accuser; to whom we are responsible; or old Nobodaddy in the garden, calling, Adam, where art thou? Let there be no one to answer to.

Freud, *New Introductory Lectures*, 98; *The Ego and the Id*, 27.
Cf. Wilhelm and Jung, *Secret of the Golden Flower*, 131–132. Galatians II, 20.

The unconscious, then, is not a closet full of skeletons in the private house of the individual mind; it is not even, finally, a cave full of dreams and ghosts in which, like Plato's prisoners, most of us spend most of our lives—

The unconscious is rather that immortal sea which brought us hither; intimations of which are given in moments of "oceanic feeling"; one sea of energy or instinct; embracing all mankind, without distinction of race, language, or culture; and embracing all the generations of Adam, past, present, and future, in one phylogenetic heritage; in one mystical or symbolical body.

Cf. Freud, *Civilization and Its Discontents*, Ch. I.

ROBERT HOURIET

FROM *Getting Back Together* [1]

"Have you ever tried *not* observing . . . just experiencing . . . or do you always remain detached from whatever you're doing?" Man, this chick was what you call laying a trip! And of course all she said was true.

She concluded, "To catch the essence of communal life, you should put your notebook away, and then you may decide it is more important to live it than to write it." I thanked her for revealing my foibles, and we said good night.

January 16

This morning, I tried to start a conversation with Jean as she ground some flour (she baked a dozen loaves and they were eaten in two days), but she didn't respond to my openers. Instead she said, "I agree with everything Elaine told you last night," and paused to let it sink in, all the time continuing to grind, smiling and jiggling her earrings. "What you said during the meeting was with the tone of not caring about Peter or any of us. It was the tone of a ruthless curiosity, digging for a fact to fill out the story. It was your ego speaking."

There was more. She ground away. "I get the feeling when you talk that you are holding back. An aloofness. And that you don't dig the *feeling* of words, only their logical sense. And, you ask too many questions."

Wowwww. I shook my head dumbly and mumbled about hav-

[1] The following pages are excerpts from a journal, *Getting Back Together*, published in 1971, kept by Houriet while he was at a commune in Oregon.

ing to think over what she said and went off to dig a hole for a fruit tree.

Along the big brook, Peter had staked out spots where the fruit trees were to be transplanted. Beneath the topsoil the ground becomes red, gravelly and mixed with large rocks. I picked savagely at the gravel, sparks flying, and sometimes I jumped into the hole, scooping out the larger rocks by hand. I was angry: first, that Jean had overheard the conversation (Big Sister is listening) and angry at my own oversensitive reaction. On another level, I was watching myself being drawn into the interpersonal reality of the commune and away from my past well-practiced roles. It would be impossible to remain detached here and not to invest (and thus expose) my ego in the others. Small talk was out. I was being forced to justify myself. "Why write a book? Isn't it another ego trip? Aren't I using people like material?"

After lunch Peter asked if I'd help transplant the fruit trees. He had been paid in kind for his work at a local greenhouse—cherry, plum and apricot trees.

It was drizzling. Peter turned up the hood of his blue rain jacket. While I held the trees in place, he stood at a distance, like a painter, viewing the shape of the tree; then he stepped closer and pruned a branch until it was symmetrical. I told him about the exchange with Elaine and Jean. He was sympathetic, for we were much alike, both Geminis and intellectual Easterners. "It's impossible to stay here and not go through some heavy changes," he said. "I went through more changes here in five days than I would in five months somewhere else."

Peter was born in Connecticut. He graduated from Goddard, where he was much influenced by Gandhi's ideas of decentralized village democracy. He went to live for an isolated year in the small French-speaking towns of eastern Quebec. "I felt a need to find roots in some culture, but even the French-Canadian towns are being commercialized." He helped found the War Resisters League on the West Coast; earlier, he had been field secretary for a communal peace group living near Voluntown, Connecticut. "But I was running out of steam. How many times do you need to run your head against the wall to learn that society isn't going to change because of political demonstrations? You begin first by changing yourself, then your friends, and working outward. Creating a new life-style that speaks more strongly than political slogans. . . ."

The others had also reached the same point of frustration with society and had dropped out singly in despair. But now they were attempting a collective, more creative withdrawal. More than the five other founders of the commune, Peter insisted on giving it clearer structure by imposing a membership procedure and limiting its size. "From my anthropology course at Goddard I learned that the maximum size for most small groups to function is around twelve people." The rift between Peter and the rest of the group, however, was not due so much to his ideas as to the abstract way he expressed them. At first I couldn't see this because the trait was so much a part of myself. Now I knew one of the reasons why the two women had reacted the way they did.

While Peter held the tree in position, I filled the hole first with bonemeal, then black topsoil, and last the gravelly soil. Gently, as if sensing its vibrations, Peter tamped the soil around the base of the cherry tree.

Elaine wandered by, all bundled up. She had slept late. Peeking at the trees, she paused. "Hummm, I feel torn . . . I *know* the fruit trees will be good . . . but I hate to have the view blocked." She turned and plodded off, hands in her parka, eyes downward on the ground.

Peter leaned on his shovel, watching her walk toward the house. "She can't take any external limits, the kind of structure I need, because she can't set any limits within herself," he said. Again I felt a rush of panic at slipping into a different, more fluid reality, loosening my grasp on my inner handlebars. Through intuitive flashes, Peter had perceived Elaine's carefully guarded self. Why hadn't I noticed Peter's and Elaine's personalities before? Now, set before me, they seemed magnified. The going was getting very heavy.

Back in the house, Elaine had put on Crosby, Stills and Nash again, peeled off her clothes, and was dancing nude to "Judy Blue Eyes." The kids, who'd filled a big pot with popcorn, went about their playing oblivious to her gyrations—she who in the past had been a member of an intellectually elite group called "The Society for Creative Anachronisms," and who had danced topless in seedy San Francisco bars. That was Elaine—all extremes.

Reuben came in and squeezing by her murmured something like, "What a crazy chick." Elaine wheeled on him, her low-slung breasts still in motion, her hair spilling over her face, hissed, "Sometimes, Reuben, I think I could choke you," picked up her clothes, and stomped off. Reuben just stood there in his Robin Hood cap, with a long feather that looked like an antenna, his beetlelike eyes behind glasses even thicker than Elaine's. He just stood there and went uhhhhhhhhhh.

Reuben was the misfit. There's one or two in every commune. Or there should be. Reuben, whose real name was Irving, had been heavily into drugs (he could and did give you the pharmaceutical directions for making cocaine), and now it was yoga and the Eastern spiritual trip. He seemed perpetually on the edge of the family, spending much of his time meditating alone in the A-frame and continually annoying the others by diverting the conversation. Elaine, Peter and Jean disliked him intensely and had told him to leave, but he refused. He was allowed to stay because the rest of the commune was opposed on principle to obstructing the free flow by excluding anyone. But Jack felt that a policy of expelling undesirables was an admission that the community was unable to function naturally. "People should be able to select themselves, tell themselves that they don't belong here. I'd say we've had maybe thirty people who've done that. They stay for a week or two and decide that this isn't the spot or that they haven't any more to learn from the people here. Also, being closed would shut us off from change."

I once asked Peter if he felt communities bore a responsibility to take in some of the disturbed people who might otherwise end up in mental institutions. "Yeah, I dig how the commune is a kind of therapeutic institution. Certainly Reuben's better off here, he's improving a lot." Reuben was looked on as a burden, but he was accepted. His quirks, his oddities, his differences that bordered on schizophrenia, accepted, and for Reuben, that was a crucial step forward.

Peter was considering leaving the farm for a couple of weeks. He planned to go down to Berkeley to work in a greenhouse and, as he characteristically put it, "to reevaluate my role at the farm." Before he left, he heard a rumor that Andy, the owner of the general store, might donate some of his land for the construction of a hip church, meeting hall and school. Peter and I talked about the political problems that might be presented by hips organizing within a straight community. Later, during a conversation with Claudia and Elaine around the circular kitchen table, Peter tried to express his concern, knowing that he might not be around for a family discussion if Andy's proposal materialized. But he expressed himself rather abstractly: "It might be wise to contact a spokesman of the straight community"; and he dropped phrases like "anticipating their objections," "appointing a committee that would embrace a spectrum of society," etc.

Peter made sense to me, but his choice of words angered both Claudia and Elaine.

Claudia screamed, "It's not what you say, it's *how* you say it that makes me so mad."

Then Elaine took over. It was as if she were peeling an onion. "All the time I've known you I've had the notion you were trying to keep things from us . . . as if we were children and you were trying to spare us the pain of knowing all the cares that weighed on your shoulders. . . . It's a kind of insidious paternalism, and you're the leader. You had the foresight to press on and buy the land when everyone else was holding back. But now you try to influence us just by the tone of your voice. . . ." Elaine halted. Silence.

"Go on," said Peter.

Claudia: "Why don't you come out and tell us how you feel? Instead of using all this formal shit. I've very, very rarely seen you express the real *you*. The other night with the record player was one time. You were passionate, angry, frustrated, but it was you."

Peter (meekly): "This has been a very helpful conversation."

Claudia: "Fuck! There you go again. By the very *tone* of the words I can tell it hasn't sunk in."

Bill (who has been reading a how-to book on raising earthworms): "What are you all talking about?"

Peter (angry at last): "Why don't *you* get your head out of the sand? Why don't you ever say anything?"

Claudia and Elaine: "That's more like it."

Elaine (to Peter): "For as long as I've known you, I've thought you were always judging yourself and others. Every time we make music together [she plays the guitar, he the recorder] I can feel you criticizing . . . It destroys it for me. It makes me feel very unhappy. Why don't you throw away the report card you're always keeping? Take a vacation from school and teacher's dirty looks? Once I came into the kitchen when you and Claudia were talking, I don't remember when or about what, but I remember the tone . . . it was like hearing an interview between a social worker and his client. . . ."

Peter: "Well . . . thank you." He tried to say more, but Elaine hushed him with a kiss, and Claudia hugged him.

Elaine played the guitar, singing the melancholy Gordon Lightfoot song, "Early Morning Rain." I could empathize with her, but the gap between us was so great that there seemed no way to tell her that I felt the same way she did. I tried to build intellectual bridges between us. We talked. Of her ambivalence toward men, of Christian ritual, carnal love, community, but I was always driving her into some mind-fucking intellectual corner and she was always dodging me. I still pressed on, boring into her brain to get a photograph of it and match it with mine so that the differences could be analytically reconciled. Finally she became so overcome with inarticulate passion that her lips moved without any words coming out. She took my hand and led me to a beam by the kitchen counter where everyone had posted their favorite aphorisms and lines of poetry. The lines by Thomas Merton, transcribed elegantly in pen, were evidently Elaine's contribution:

> . . . to understand that one has nothing to say is to suddenly become free with a liberty that makes speech and silence equally easy. What one says will be something that probably has been said before. One need not trouble about being heard. The thing that is being said has been heard before . . . speech has only served us against the secret terror of not existing. Once the illusion is clear, man is delivered from the necessity of speaking in his own defense and henceforth speaks only for his brother's comfort.

What was there to say? We hugged and it was said. I took a flashlight and, leaving Elaine to her guitar, headed up toward the A-frame. After days of rain, the sky had finally cleared and the moon was out. It shimmered on the muddy puddles along the path. The flashlight was unnecessary. The moonlit meadow with moss hanging from the trees looked unearthly. What strange world was I moving through? A reality of reflected light, a house of twelve mirrors, each reflecting twelve images of the self. But which was the real image? Perhaps it was all nothing but reflection, image and fantasy—but to be sure, we were all in it together. There was a part of me in Peter that I could only see through Elaine. All three of us were Geminis. All of us were thwarted by different but similar blindnesses in the others.

January 17

The rain has settled in again, pelting evenly and intently, seemingly endless. I have a cold. My perceptions are as fogged in as the valley. The brook has backed up around the holding dams that were built last year to prevent it from eroding.

After breakfast I felt at loose ends. For the first time here, I craved some escape, like reading a newspaper or watching a movie or even TV, anything to assure myself that the dull, predictable outside world was still there.

The kids were uptight, too. Their unspent tensions and energies boomeranged through the house. The walls seemed to have shrunk. "Little" Roland teased Kathy about her braces. She parried with a "Fuck you" and chased him through the house. Finally she tripped him. He fell and knocked over the kitchen spice shelf.

The kids are a barometer of the general atmosphere. The grown-ups have also grown tense. The group mood could spiral up, attaining a collective high, and we could be Woodstock Nation again; or it could spiral downward into the darkness of Altamont.

This afternoon, Jean straightened and sorted through the shelves in the children's room. Each person has his own shelf for things like toothbrushes, combs, rings, papers and most clothes. Everything else goes into communal boxes and on communal shelves. Then she searched for a hand mirror missing from the common shelf. She found it on Peter's private shelf. He was sitting on a cushion in the main room when she came out, pissed off: "It really annoys me when you put the communal mirror on your shelf." Peter shrugged. Jean continued, "I spent a lot of time looking around for it, and it's happened before."

Trying to brighten the mood, I put on some Vivaldi concertos, but I forgot the unwritten rule that he who puts on a record must also return it to its cover and rack. Peter later discovered his records were left on the spindle, gathering dust, and chewed me out.

The phonograph played all day, but it never struck a common chord. Elaine cut off Vivaldi in midmovement and replaced it with Big Pink. Maureen turned the volume down. Elaine turned it back up.

The day before, Bill had had to go into town and the taillight on the pickup truck wasn't working. So he transferred the one from Maureen's truck (which was always referred to as Maureen's —she kept the keys) to the pickup and drove away. Today Maureen noticed the missing light and confronted Bill: "I could get busted for this, you know. It's not the first time something like this has happened. You're careless and you're. . . ."

Bill: "You get this straight, Maureen. As long as I'm in this commune, what you have is mine. You can't come in and dangle the keys over my head and say that as long as I'm a good boy you'll let me drive your car. I have every right to touch your car."

Maureen (shrilled): "You don't, you don't!"

Bill: "You're trying to push me but I'm not going to run away. Go ahead and hit me if you like it, but I'm not going to let you alone. If I see your kids doing something, I'll lay a hand on them."

Maureen: "You mean you'll act irresponsibly with them just the way you acted irresponsibly with my truck. Last summer you threw stones at them. Is that responsible?"

For a while I thought they might really come to blows. Finally, Bill picked up his flute and walked off playing it, into the rainy meadow.

Before dinner, J. D. and Jim, two guitarists from the House of Illusion, arrived to practice some spirituals and other songs for the community church to which we'd been invited by the local Pentecostal Church. We had just begun to get into the songs, which they strummed with a rock beat, "*What a friend we have in Jesus, all our fears and cares to bear,*" when Claudia stentoriously rang the gong and announced that it was meditation time and that we had to find some other place to sing.

Everyone was embarrassed by Claudia's rudeness. Jack took her aside to rap in the kitchen. She got angrier. Her face reddened. Meditation didn't develop. It wasn't the right day anyway. We were on a communal manic-depressive roller coaster, and now we were plunging downward with increasing momentum.

January 18

Much brighter and crisper. Elaine and I were talking across the room, still in our sleeping bags, when fat fluffy snow filled the bright sky and batted gaily against the windows.

After breakfast, Claudia asked me to help replant the Christmas trees. For sure. The snow came and went, alternating with a misty rain. A rainbow arched over the valley. The kids streamed out of the house, running toward it crying "happimiss, happimiss"—their word for joyous occasions. It originated with Woody's lisped pronunciation of "happiness."

Instead of following the yule custom of cutting down a tree, the commune had dug up two small firs, roots and all, and kept the roots wrapped in canvas while they were decorated. The true, pagan meaning of Christmas was a celebration of life's eternal renewal, Claudia explained, signifying that the winter solstice has been passed. So why kill trees in celebration?

I hefted one fir, its roots heavy with water, into the wheelbarrow and pushed off toward the meadow. Weighted down with trees, shovel and pick, the wheelbarrow plowed into the mud. I strained to push through it, puffing great balls of steam into the chilled air blown off the frozen mountains. At the compost heap, I paused to catch my breath.

The garbage from every meal is scraped into two plastic peanut butter jars and then emptied on the compost pile. Wood ash from the stove is sprinkled over it. Nearby is the gas-powered shredder used to chew the cornstalks into a fine mulch. From time to time the compost heap is turned over and mixed, revealing layer upon layer of decomposition and, near the bottom, a mass of pink, slithering worms. Jack loves to turn the pile over with a rake and see "how a corncob breaks back down to its component parts. Everything must break down before it can be reborn."

Claudia joined me. As we stood musing over the compost heap, Roland came toward us, his jeans, quilted with patches at the knees, tucked in his boots. He looked very much the farmer. He was able to answer some of my questions about the principles of organic farming. "After years of using chemical fertilizers, the nitrates seep into one layer of the ground and become deadly. The microorganisms are killed off and the soil loses fertility. Also, the ground gets very hard—it's the dead bodies of the organisms that keep the soil porous. So you have to use machinery to break it up every year.

"There are apple orchards in Washington State that have been so heavily sprayed with copper that they've had to be abandoned." To the organically-minded, the use of chemical fertilizers represents the imposition of man's ruthless will on nature. "You can plant just so much. Every seven years, the land should lie fallow so the natural processes can catch up. The commercial farmer takes far more than he naturally restores, and he tries to make up the difference with chemicals. What does the farmer in Nebraska with a thousand acres in wheat care if the land will be infertile in fifty years? By then he'll have sold out and moved to Florida."

Instead of chemicals, the farm uses lots of chicken shit, free for the hauling; rotten sawdust from any of several lumber yards; and seaweed such as kelp, high in minerals like iodine and potassium and also free for the taking along Oregon's ocean beaches. The farm was also planning a visit to one of the canneries to collect a load of fish scraps.

Roland led us over to the site of a new communal building, built on a gentle slope on the far side of the brook. We looked around for a place to transplant the Christmas trees. Before winter the men had sunk the building's supporting structure and dug a trench to keep the stream from eroding its underpinnings. "Erosion is one of our problems. We're going to plant some grass here to keep the slope from washing away, but it will have to be a special species that will be very tough and resistant to the dry, hot summer weather."

We selected a spot for the trees, a place where in some fifteen years they might be able to protect the front of the house from the torrid sun of August. In the summer, the streams become parched gullies and grasshoppers plague the farm. Last summer they chewed away a third of the fruit trees' new growth. The neighboring farmer scattered pesticide-tainted bait over his fields. "We found dead birds around. The irony is, of course, that the birds eat the grasshoppers." Rather than resort to pesticides, the farm decided to meet this year's assault with a natural predator. From a seed company, they ordered five boxes of praying mantises, who gorge themselves on their cousins, the grasshoppers. And to check the aphids, they sent away for an army of ladybugs.

After the holes were dug, we gently lowered the trees in place. "I always feel like saying a prayer after planting a tree," Claudia said.

"Go ahead," Roland urged.

"Grow!" was all she said.

Took a retreat to get my head together. I walked up the mountain to the cabin Laura was building for herself. It was about half finished. The floor was completed, and above it the rafters for the roof were nailed together. I sat on a box and pondered the view. The facing mountains were national forest land that had not been recently lumbered. The mountains had texture and color. In the ravines and hollows, the shaded trees were blue. Five miles away, the jagged spine of the mountain was so sharply etched against the sky that I could pick out the tips of individual trees. Even at this distance from the brook, the air was aroar with rushing water. Nature had pattern, gestalt. Man was beginning to see himself again as a part and passing stage instead of the be-all and end-all of evolution. Was there any kind of social ecology that united man to man as vitally as the aphid was linked to the cabbage and the moth? What was there to keep the people at the commune from going their individual ways? From replaying the old struggle of tooth and claw? Why should a dozen unrelated people remain together? Yesterday I had seen a natural force working in the commune—the antagonistic force of ego. And yet the commune went on. Why?

Methodically, I ticked off what *it* was not. *It* wasn't ideological. The family had left politics and revolution behind in Berkeley. *It* wasn't sexual freedom. They had no Reichian faith in orgasmic potency, no orgies, no group marriage structure. *It* wasn't cooperative economics: Outside the communes, hundreds of individuals and couples were surviving in the country by accepting a simpler standard of living—and food stamps.

Intellectually, I knew that *it* couldn't be grasped by man's analytical tools, his ologies: *It* was a consciousness totally different from that of analytical modern man, who always differentiated himself from his subject, categorically dividing Man from Nature, the Self from Society. *It* was a gestalt, a fresh vision, a . . . but my thoughts began to muddle. I was a would-be explorer, locked in a study, piecing together a map of a distant country I had not yet seen.

When Maureen returned from Berkeley, she brought some grass and several tabs of acid—Sunshine, she'd been told. This afternoon, when everyone was in the kitchen, she took one tab and offered the rest to anyone who wanted to trip along. Laura joined her.

"Robert?"

I declined. I wasn't ready yet. Would they mind if I accepted but didn't take it now? I might change my mind. For sure. Maureen gave me a tab wrapped in tinfoil. I put it in the top pocket of my wool shirt.

At the start of my travels, I had resolved not to take acid. I didn't want to lose my objectivity, freak out, return home wearing a hair shirt and having no coherent notes. I was afraid of changing, losing control, becoming submerged. I have never dived into water but have always eased in step by step.

They didn't press me, the conspicuous acid virgin of the group. No one here has the Timothy Leary compulsion to turn everyone on, or the dangerous faith that acid is everybody's cure-all. They respected my caution, but clearly doubted that I could write a good book without having tripped. While acid was not the commune's foundation of life, it was a common point of departure. They were trying to live the acid vision without the acid itself.

I am a cautious map reader who must know where I'm going and why. But I was beginning to learn that no trip turns out the way you planned it. Objectivity—philosophical and journalistic—affords only a partial account. Nothing—no person, no atomic particle—exists complete in itself, unaffected by the viewer. This is a fact of both physics and journalism. Reality is relationship.

After dinner we got into a rambling discussion and stumbled onto the topic of electricity. Elaine wanted to cut it off, sever the umbilical cord, secede altogether from the technology whose inevitable by-product was environmental pollution. Everyone agreed it would be good to disconnect. Someone switched off the overhead light and lit a homemade candle. Elaine continued rapping: They should also forsake toilet paper. With all the waste-paper in the world, produced at the cost of millions of trees a year, why not wipe with old newspapers?

Bill: "Where do you draw the line? How can anyone *exist* with-out taking away from nature? You're reasoning like the Catholic philosophers who argue backward from the existence of the soul to the conclusion that abortion is murder."

Elaine: "Well, it *is* murder."

(A gasp)

Bill: Don't you believe in contraception?"

Elaine: "It debases women to use the pill. It takes out all the joy when you're trying to keep your own nature under control."

Peter: "But how about all the other women in the world for whom the pill is an escape from unwanted children? Think of India. Are you speaking of all the women in India too?"

Elaine: "I'm speaking of how *I* feel. And it *is* a non-Western way of feeling. As Westerners, we look at India and see all the squalor and kids with matchstick legs and the dead bodies in the street, and we say that's hell. But the Indians don't. Death is a part of life, a part of the process. Death isn't as horrible for them. They have their children and their bodies and spirits pass on. Nothing is ever lost."

Roland: "It's true our bodies decompose just like corncobs. Unless you get sealed up in a casket where the bacterial action can't get. . . ."

Jack: "Maybe we should join a burial society and get cheap pine boxes for ourselves."

Peter: "Make our own."

Bill: "I read in *Whole Earth Catalogue* that you can make coffins out of papier-mâché."

Elaine: "I'd like to be composted."

Peter (laughing): "I don't know if I could take that every morn-ing, walking past the compost pile and noticing one of Elaine's eyeballs staring up at me."

Everyone laughed, then fell silent. Suddenly Maureen burst through the door with a handful of tan pups with closed eyes.

"Coffee's had her puppies!" she announced, and then, "Hey! Why do you have all the lights off?"

January 19

Today we visited another commune, the Onion Farm. We drove the two trucks, heading out late in the afternoon. J. D., the folk singer, came with us. It may have been the clear day and the distant purple mountains which prompted us to break unexpectedly into "America the Beautiful," surprised that we hadn't forgotten the words. We sang, "For purple mountains' majesty above the fruited plain," as we cruised down a canyon of tall firs.

"I sorta like that," said J. D. at the end. The song had once been the national anthem, he said, before the militarists had adopted "The Star-Spangled Banner." "Did you ever listen to those words?" he asked in his Tennessee twang. "Why, there's bombs a-bursting, rockets a-glaring . . . people dying to defend a piece of cloth." He took up his guitar again: "This Land Is Your Land. . . ." With Roland at the wheel of the old Dodge decorated with peace symbols, we crested a hill and drove past white water knifing through rock. On the far side of a green valley, we passed a lonely farm. A small boy on the farmhouse porch gave us a V sign as we coasted by. The flag of *our* vision was not a star-spangled, blood-soaked banner, but green, the color of grass.

The eighteen of us were arriving unannounced at dinner time, which was the custom among the communes. The Onion Farm's road was even ruttier and muddier than ours. We drove as far as we could and walked the rest of the way. The house looked like a sharecropper's on a *Bonnie and Clyde* set. Chickens roamed freely around the dusty yard.

Miraculously, there was enough food for dinner. We discovered that the farm was in the process of breaking up. One group was heading for British Columbia, and a few other couples were going to find their own houses in the valley.

After dinner J. D. led the singing. In his thirties, J. D. had seen pain. His hair was dirty blond. He wore a black leather jacket and boots. He had played in coffeehouses with Judi Collins and Tom Paxton and had turned down recording offers to go into the Mendocino Forest and compose his own music. He is a modern-day troubadour. The immediate contact live music brings between performer and audience is more fulfilling to him than cutting or listening to a record. Musically, J. D. has moved from acid rock into the heartland of American folk singing. "We've left the electrified mind behind. The country's always been there, but we had to go full circle to find it."

We smoked and sang folk songs. Three others from the Onion Farm joined J. D. and sang numbers like "It Takes A Worried Man To Sing A Worried Song." We stayed very late.

Trying to back down the road, one truck crashed through the thin sheet of ice over a rut and dug itself axle-deep in mud. Somebody went back to the house to see if we could borrow their four-wheel-drive truck and chain. The scene had been played before in my consciousness: a country road at night, engines racing, wheels spinning, the headlights catching clouds of steam and exhaust. The men crawled under the vehicle to attach chains. The women stood patiently, waiting, waiting, the stars very close overhead, singing to pass the time and soothe the children in their arms.

On the way home, the kids fell asleep in a tumble. Small towns emerged from the darkness, a scattering of houses, a bar and a darkened general store. In the front windows were reflected the pale-blue lights of TV's. The people inside were probably watching the eleven-o'clock news: the newest unemployment figures, casualty reports and Nixon policy statements. Nixon! He hardly mattered; he couldn't touch us. We had slipped away from 1970 and politics altogether. The President might as well be Calvin Coolidge. Let SDS try to change Nixon. We'd begin by changing ourselves, our own families, and then, maybe the valley. The frontier lay somewhere between the farm and the general store, across from which the longhairs might someday build their own church. A simple, plain kind of church based on a fundamental belief in God and man.

Claudia broke the silence. "I wish I'd thought to lay out the sleeping bags for the kids." While I was on a flight of fantasy, Claudia had been thinking ahead to the business of carrying the sleeping children into the dark house and clearing their shelves so they could be put to bed. The children always bring us back to earth, I thought, carrying a sleeping Woody over the washed-out culvert. We can go very far out, to the fringe, and live in the *now,* without schedules or plans, but the children bring us back. And if they don't, they cry. Their cries bring us down to the good earth.

January 21

Today's mail brought more of the typical queries, from college professors and disgruntled suburbanites. A lot send mimeographed questionnaires and form letters. Tacked to the bulletin board, most go unanswered.

Roland thumbed through. "It's disturbing that so many people think we can send them the secret formula for a working commune . . . they don't realize you just have to experience it— including the failure. I guess they really believe the world comes ready-made."

Bill decided to answer one of the form letters asking how to found a community, in a hundred words or less. He wrote:

> Principally, I am saying do not be bounded by old-fashioned ideas of success and failure. Do not be afraid of the possibility that your first attempt (or even second) will fall apart. In God's universe, there is no waste. If things do not follow the city-conceived ideas of how they should work, then know that you're not seeing enough. Everything has its place in the organism. Every experience is full of value. Do not be afraid of failing. Take the leap. Do it. Get on with it.

Claudia and I finished a day's accumulation of dishes. Drying and sorting, she stopped to hold a fork up to my attention. Most of the utensils were W. T. Grant's or university-purloined, but the one Claudia singled out was real, though battered, sterling silver. It was monogrammed. "It's from my wedding silver," she said and dropped it in a tin can with the others. Claudia recalled her marriage. The wedding had been conventional: bridesmaids, bouquets, champagne at the country club. She would never get married again. "It's putting all your eggs in one basket. You bank your emotion, hope and security on one other person and expect him to remain just the same, faithfully constant, till death do you part. It doesn't work that way. Everything changes and everything grows. Sometimes I have fantasies about Bill and me having some sort of ceremony, not a marriage ceremony, but something more like a love-in, out in the meadow with just the family. It would be nice to have some kind of ritual. . . ."

David had drifted into the kitchen. Though he and Marlena lived most of the time in Berkeley, they were awarded family status on their visits, due to their long acquaintance with people at the farm. He picked up the end of Claudia's fantasy. "Hip life changes too fast. But that's what we need, a few rituals. Like at Morningstar. After they planted their garden, they held a fertility dance and a fuck-in."

"Groovy, maybe that's what our tomatoes needed this year. Last year they were puny," Jean said.

David proposed a ritual to celebrate the birth of Claudia's child. "I heard that one commune in San Francisco collected the after-birth in a bowl and passed it around to be drunk, like communion."

Claudia had her own idea. "We could plant a tree." She thought a moment. "A persimmon."

Maureen elaborated on the fantasy. "And while you're in labor, Bill can dig the hole for the tree. Anxious fathers need something to do. Then we can take the placenta and drop it in before we transplant. That way, *nothing* is wasted."

January 23

There was a get-together of the valley's heads to practice for to-morrow's community sing at the Pentecostal Church. Four of us had attended last Sunday's service, and the minister had invited us to bring the rest along for the sing. It was held in the shed behind Morton's house. Morton is a patriarch of the long-hairs, one of the first to settle in the valley. He's a dropped-out econo-mist, who holds a doctorate and now supports his family by cut-ting firewood and collecting welfare.

Almost sixty heads and about ten local straight people had squeezed into the toolshed heated by a wood stove. John and J. D. and Jim and Steve, from a neighboring commune located on a mining claim, played guitars, banjo and a washtub base. They were joined by two straights, members of the church who sang spirituals and played the electric guitar. An older man in a cowboy hat sawed the electric fiddle. The wives of the church people were sitting around uneasily when the meeting began. There was an unspoken understanding among the hip people that no dope would be passed. Nevertheless, as it turned out, we got very, very high.

First we rehearsed the songs we'd sing the next day at the Four-Square Church: "What a Friend We Have in Jesus," "Heaven Is So High You Can't Get over It," "Get Together" (a contemporary rock song with wide appeal), "We Need a Whole Lot More of Jesus and a Lot Less Rock 'n' Roll," and "Jesus Met a Woman at the Well." There was some anxiety about making a good impression. Some of the straights were fearful that our musical ardor might in some way offend the churchgoers.

Since 1967, when the hip invasion of the valley began, relations between longhairs and local people had become tense. The critical summer, again, was 1968's. For a time, it looked to some of the straight residents as if the hippies were overrunning the valley. Teen-agers drove around taking shots at hippie shacks. Just once, the hippies shot back. In a wire-service story, the deputy sheriff was quoted as saying, "Every hippie is armed with rifles, pistols or knives. Even the girls have knives."

For a time it looked like a repeat of Oz versus Crawford County. A "betterment" association was organized to curb the influx and sponsored a mass meeting at which the association's president asserted that the county had no narcotics problem until the hippies arrived. "We'll get it whipped, and then we'll move in and clean up the rest," he said to loud applause. A Methodist minister who urged tolerance was booed. The sheriff's office began to make raids; the health inspectors made inspections, accompanied by police. On one, the deputy sheriff was knocked unconscious by a hippie defending himself against an illegal search. A manhunt ensued; roads to the area were blocked, but the hippie was not apprehended. The deputy sheriff, called Uncle Hal by the hippies, carried out a vendetta against longhairs, picking up and then busting hitchhikers going to and from the valley. Stores in the nearest town posted signs: WE DO NOT SOLICIT HIPPIE PATRONAGE.

But over the past year, the influx has slightly abated, and as the communes have taken root and made friends among the local people, relations between straights and hips have improved, how much no one here is quite sure. They may find out tomorrow at the community sing. It will be the first time a large group of hippies have met their straight neighbors face to face.

After the repertoire of spirituals had been exhausted, we sang old songs like "She'll Be Coming 'Round the Mountain" and "Oh, the Rock Island Line Is a Mighty Good Road. . . ." Clapping and stamping, the girls pulled up their long skirts to dance. Spontaneously, a square dance broke out. We whirled each other, arms locked, spinning around and then flying off to grab others. The fiddler picked it up immediately: "Swing your partner, do-si-do, right and left. . . ." Until then, the fiddler's middle-aged wife had held back. Now she was on her feet, demonstrating the Virginia reel.

We got higher and noisier. Elaine was in a frenzy, turning like a whirling dervish, making inarticulate sounds. People tripped and were caught, embraced and pulled back into the dance. I recalled how the Shakers, another communal sect, had gotten their name from the dances that sent them into ecstacies. We shook with the same frenzy. It came from within, unprompted by drugs, in a bare shed set in a valley of muddy roads, dark woods, prowling coyotes. I looked at the faces. Here were plain, simple folk who had found each other. It was inconceivable we could ever have been apart.

January 24

A perfect day at last. Blue sky feathered with high cirrus clouds. Everyone was excited and tense about the community sing. After breakfast Elaine and Maureen took sponge baths in the kitchen. Next, Roland dropped the kids, two or three at a time, into the washtub. Then Maureen combed their hair over cries of pained protest.

We donned our Sunday best. The kids wore hand-knit woolen sweaters. Kathy and Susan tied ribbons in their hair. Maureen reminded them not to piss on the church lawn. "Maureen, I know that!" Kathy exclaimed indignantly.

Laura put on one dress but felt uncomfortable in it. She finally chose a long red-and-white checked gingham. With her hair wound in a bun, she looked like a young schoolmarm, *circa* 1874. Joe wore deep-blue corduroys and a white tunic, with wide sleeves that Jean had trimmed with embroidery. Roland wore an orange corduroy shirt Elaine had made. Maureen put on an ankle-length gown and headband.

Just as we were all ready to leave, a car drove into the front yard. Two men wearing suits knocked at the door. They were police officers, conducting an investigation for the state attorney general's office into charges filed by the ACLU that the civil liberties of hippies were being violated by the local sheriff. Could they ask a few questions?

They sat on the sofa and took small notebooks out of their jackets. Their shoes were black and spit-shined.

Roland answered a few general questions and called Reuben, who had the most specific complaint. Last week he had been arrested in a nearby city for carrying a concealed weapon—the hunting knife he always carried. "I use it all the time, it's a drag to put it in a sheath," he said, showing them how easily he could pull it out from under his belt. The two officers made a note but added that the arrest seemed to be technically legal.

Maureen recalled the many times her truck had been stopped for license and registration checks. Morton, she said, had gotten seven tickets in three days. Roland told of some friends whose house had been illegally searched.

The officers took note of the search and said they would check it out. They asked about the commune's relations with the townspeople—shopkeepers and so on.

Maureen smiled. "Oh, that's different. We had a little trouble at first when the signs went up. We didn't want to make any trouble because we knew the Betterment Association pressured a lot of the shopowners into it. Like the laundromat. We stayed away for a year, until one day I went in with the kids and asked them—I went out of my way to be polite—if they minded if we washed our clothes there. They said, 'Don't pay any attention to the signs.' Since then we've gotten along real well. Last week the lady bought ice-cream cones for the kids."

Jack: "It's the people we *don't* know who make trouble. Almost everyone who comes out here and sees how we live goes away a lot more friendly. . . . Remember when Carol took the inspectors on a garden tour?" Everyone laughed. The incident occurred in the tense summer of 1968, when all the communes were inspected by health officials, county supervisors, the sheriff and members of the press. "Carol [a former member] blew their minds. She took all the supervisors out into the garden and led them from row to row, explaining how each one had been planted and naturally fertilized . . . and one supervisor, an old geezer who was a farmer himself, started giving her advice on how to use low-frequency sound to keep the rabbits out, and she smiled and listened. Later I overheard the supervisor saying, 'Shucks, these are just kids tryin' to farm.' "

The two officers laughed and closed their notebooks. They handed Roland a card and said to call their office with any complaints.

After they'd left, Jack said, "They seemed pretty fair."

Roland added, "It's good to know there are some cops like that around."

By now everyone was dressed and anxious to get on to the church.

First we headed over to the House of Illusion. The dogs followed, cutting across the meadow, running ahead and then falling behind as we gained the hard-top road. I sat in the back of the pickup, looking up at Maureen's profile against the rushing green background. Passing by the shacks along the river where hippies lived, we honked, cheered and whooped. Some of them followed us in their jalopies.

At the House of Illusion, J. D. and John led the way to a grove softly carpeted with needles, which was "down by the riverside." There were about thirty of us standing in a wide circle under tall firs with shafts of sun splintering through. As the guitars were tuned, the smoke went around. In his piercing, almost whining voice, J. D. sang the verses to an old folk song about heaven, while the rest of us did the chorus: "So high, you can't get over it, so low you can't get under it, so wide you can't go 'round it." I watched a girl gather up her long skirt and run along a rocky path slightly uphill from us, her body tilting gracefully from side to side, toward an A-frame.

We arrived at the church early, around fifty of us, exceeding half the church's seating capacity. I was afraid that the presence

of the longhairs would be a disaster in public relations. So was
Elaine, who talked of walking home. But Maureen was undanted.
"They'll love us. They *have* to love us," she said cheerily—as if
our smiling faces, glowing with inward grace, would win them
over.

Bob, the clean-shaven minister, arrived wearing a blue suit.
He took in our numbers, gulped, and invited us to take seats.

The interior was functional: linoleum floors and white-brick
walls. The congregation began to arrive. Men wore cufflinks and
monogrammed handkerchiefs in their breast pockets. Their wives,
high heels, teased hairdos and penciled eyebrows. They shot us
sideways glances. The minister welcomed everyone, including "the
bunch from T—" (the town nearest High Ridge Farm). He introduced the ministers from six local churches, who were there for the
sing. The congregation from each church sang a hymn. One contained a double chorus. "Praise the Lord!" sang the women, jumping up. "Hallelujah!" answered the men, springing up in turn like
jack-in-the-boxes. A girl in nylons and a purple sweater came up to
the stage with an accordion. Before playing, she spoke into the
microphone, saying that she loved "Jesus Christ more than anything else in the world." Then she began a lugubrious hymn:
"Silver was the price they paid to nail him to a tree. . . . He
could have sent ten thousand angels to destroy the world." Next
an older man played some spirituals on the saxophone. Then two
gray-haired sisters in long black dresses sang a duet: "On a hill far
away stood an old rugged cross."

It was our turn. There were too many of us to take the stage, so
we rose and grouped around J. D. and the others: "Je-sus met the
wo-man at the well, ah-el-el. . . ."[2] It was an old song known to
Baptists and heads alike, but we sang it with a new spirit that
effused as the song progressed. "He said: Wo-man, wo-man, where
is your husband. . . ." Elaine, in her flowered pajamas, glasses off,

[2] The spiritual is based on John 4:7–42, a passage that holds special significance
for hippies who've converted to Christianity, since it reveals Jesus as a social
revolutionary, as well as a mystic. The passage, involving an encounter between
Jesus and a Samaritan woman at Jacob's well, has been recast into hip language
by Wayout, Box 2329, Hollywood, California, one of many neoChristian
youth groups that developed on the West Coast during the late sixties as the
drug-hip subculture began to break down.

was doing her bumps and grinds. Reared a Jew, she believed in God but not the revengeful Yahveh who would send ten thousand angels to destroy a recalcitrant world.

"She said: Je-sus, Je-sus, ain't got no husband." Reuben, resplendent in beads, crosses and his Robin Hood hat with the freaky antenna, was shaking a tambourine and finger cymbals. He'd gone all through Meher Baba, Hare Krishna, Maharishi, Krishnamurti.

"And you don't know everything I've ever done."

As the fervor mounted, J. D.'s blond head thrashed from side to side. "He said, Wo-man, wo-man, you've got five husbands, he said. . . ." Maureen's face was radiant. Once she'd been buried nine hours in a mountain snowslide and felt that God had stayed with her, keeping her warm, until she was rescued. "And the one you've got now, he's not your own." Laura had discovered the joy and saving grace through acid. "This man, this man must be a prophet, she said. . . ." They had come to God by many paths. Now moved by a common spirit, not a doctrine but real experience. "Jesus met the wo-man at the well, ah-el-el, oh, yeah, And he told her everything she ever knew. . . ."

Afterward, coffee and cookies were served. Maureen tore chunks off a loaf of fresh bread she'd brought and offered them to the parishioners. Some politely refused. Others accepted. None seemed to understand the symbolism of the act. One prosperously dressed middle-aged man, with a fraternal society pin on his lapel, was grim-facedly engaged in conversation with Bob, the minister, who was apparently defending his decision to invite us. Most of the local people were friendly. The commune kids played with theirs. The church musicians made a date with J. D. for a down-country music session. An elderly couple struck up a conversation with Laura and asked her to do some housekeeping work for them.

Bob finished his long conversation with the hostile man, who drove off in a Chrysler, and then came over and spoke loudly enough so the whole congregation could hear: "I sure hope you can all come back next week and give us some more of that music." For sure, for sure, everyone answered.

January 28

Each morning I wake up and resolve to leave if nothing "new" happens to provide material for my notebook. Something "new" always does happen, nothing dramatic, small events that slowly deepen my insight into communal life.

I am torn between splitting and staying. The old reporter is anxious to leave, to get on with my cross-country itinerary, to put together a regional balance. A newer voice tells me to stay: One commune is all communes, nothing is "typical"; truth doesn't lie in a regional balance or averages or prototypes but is always here and now.

I've settled on a compromise plan: to go on a brief hitchhiking sidetrip to three communes north of here, then return to High Ridge Farm and decide not only where to go next but what to do about the acid still rolled in tinfoil in my breastpocket.

I've begun to ease myself into an acid trip, finishing Huxley's *Doors of Perception* and reading *The Teachings of Don Juan: A Yaqui Way of Knowledge,* by Carlos Castaneda. *Don Juan* is an account of the cosmology and spiritual beliefs of one American Indian who ritualistically took the natural hallucinogens, peyote, Jimson weed and the magic "mushroom." The book is really about Castaneda, who came to accept the existence of the supernatural while conducting his anthropological research.

Last night I sought advice from Jack about acid. We talked in the small alcove reserved for whoever was sleeping in with the kids. Should I take a full tab the first time? Jack was reluctant to advise me. Acid affected everyone differently, he said. For some, a full tab was good to take the first time. "It's better to wipe out all the garbage in your head, otherwise you get stuck halfway." He thought I was too honest to have a bad trip. People who repressed a lot found acid frightening.

The conversation gave me more confidence. I would be tripping among people I trusted. I decided to take the acid after I returned from my sidetrip.

Tonight Elaine was silent and communicated by notes. "I want to go along with you tomorrow," she wrote. "We can take my car."

I decided to leave the acid behind, putting it in a small pill container. With the trench shovel (used at night by people who couldn't make it to the outhouse) I dug a shallow hole and buried it under a fallen log.

February 2

An after-dinner meeting was called to rap about Maureen and Bill's differences. Everyone sat silently and tensely on the floor for about five minutes. Finally, Elaine spoke. "Why don't each of you tell us how you feel right now."

Softly crying and barely audible, Maureen said she felt insecurity, incompleteness, an anxiety partly arising from her relationship with Roland but which went all the way back to her mother. It was a rare thing to hear Maureen speak from her insides, anguished and broken. She had always been so cheery and superficial.

Bill: "What annoys me is that you're never here—you're always going down to Berkeley or over to the other communes. And you think of your kids as yours and your truck as yours."

Maureen: "They're security. I only get possessive when I feel other things slipping away. . . ." Claudia said she felt uncomfortable working in the kitchen with her because "I can't tell whether you want my help or just to be left alone. I wish you would come out frankly and say, 'Look, I want to make my own mistakes, so just let me do my own thing.' " Bill said Maureen's small talk annoyed him: "You come in bubbling about something that happened and it's like you don't care about me—you just bubble on . . . I feel like you don't recognize my existence, so I do things to hurt you. When I make you mad, you can't ignore me."

Roland, turning to Bill: "You mean you don't exist unless people recognize you? That's your problem, not Maureen's."

The meeting ended without any clear-cut resolution. The tensions, however, were more out front now. The meeting had been different from the usual encounter session, where people turn the candor on, only to turn it off again outside. At the commune, you couldn't change roles behind doors. Potentially, every minute was an encounter. There was no retreat. Your mumblings in your sleep could be overheard. Every little habit and personal idiosyncrasy was exposed. Everyone knew that Elaine loved to nibble sweets because her mother had deprived her of candy as a child. Every time we saw her furtively spooning brown sugar we would tell her she was an anxiety eater and that what she really needed was affection, not confection.

February 3

I woke deciding to drop the acid. It hadn't decomposed under the log. I walked down to the main building. People from the Bear Gulch commune had come to borrow the drill press. Some of them were retired dope dealers who'd put their savings into land.

After all the visitors had left, I asked if anyone wanted to share my half tab of acid, or else trip along. Laura said she'd trip if Roland did, but Roland was in a hard-work mood. Jerry asked the others if he should drop now or wait until he felt more at home. No one told him yes or no.

All the while, my heart was beating rapidly. I'd put the one tab on the table. It was orange and about the size of saccharine. I lost patience. With one gulp of coffee I washed it down, crumpled the tinfoil into a ball, and threw it across the room.

"He took it!" Cheers, applause.

I paced around grimly, like a father outside the delivery room. Nothing happened. I talked to Roland and to Bill. A half hour elapsed. Life in the room went on as usual. I stared out the window at the garden and the meadow, checking my perceptions for any sign of a change. At the garden's edge, jays and wrens hopped and stalked. Their existence suddenly seemed important.

I went to the bookcase and began flipping through an anthology of poems, but before I found the line I was searching for, it came to my lips: "The world is charged with the glory of God." As soon as I uttered it, a frightening wave of energy rushed through me. It was too much like drowning. Immediately I went over to Claudia and put my arms around her. She seemed the most stable and immediate point in the universe. The earthy smell of her sweat shirt was comforting. It was real. I asked her to stick around the kitchen. She understood.

I went to the sink and tried to look out the steamed-over window. I rubbed the condensation away, but it blurred and steamed up again. Laughing at my idiocy, I unlatched the window. The meadow was wet and glistening and colorful and charged with glory. Bending over the sink, I cried into the dishwater. What a convenient place to crack up! But between the sobs, the pain of breaking felt good. Death must be the same.

Jerry had put on a Simon and Garfunkel album and one line stuck in my head: "Blessed are the meek, for they shall inherit. . . ."

Somebody had made popcorn. It was celestially white. I took a handful, laid my head down on the circular table, and began to pulverize the popcorn with the heel of my hand, grinding it down into a mixture of tears, sweat and Mazola. I wiped my face with toilet paper, dying for the sins of the world, all the time grinding the popcorn. Everything must be reduced to its components.

Laura overheard my babblings: "This is a delivery ward." She and Gary split a tab. I wouldn't let Claudia out of the room. I could feel the new life in her and that was consolation, since I was dying, breaking down.

Under the counter the dogs lapped from their bowls. I had an impulse to join them on the floor and eat their food. When I looked at Claudia's face, it enlarged and assumed frightening power. Suddenly it revealed all the anger, love, passion and compassion she was capable of. I asked her if she believed in God.

In answer, she opened the door of the wood stove. Two or three pieces of wood burned over a bed of red coals. Wood changing to coals to heat, altering form but not dying. "I am God. You are God." Like the meadow, her face became too awesomely powerful and beautiful for me to behold. I dropped my head to the greasy pile of pulverized popcorn.

The dying took about an hour. Near the end, I gasped and shuddered and clung to the table. It subsided and was over. I—the ego, the self—had been busted.

I announced my intention to go outside. Would they let me go alone? No one seemed worried about my safety, so I went. Outdoors, I had to adjust myself to new dimensions of space and depth. The little bridge over the brook seemed like a high footbridge over the Himalayas. I knelt on it, an altar, and thanked God. My vision was sharp, stereoscopic. Fir trees, rising one above the other on the mountain, each had a definite position in space. Everything was alive and moving. The wood planks of the bridge crawled. From now on, I wouldn't tread so heavily on it.

Jerry came down from the meadow. He had begun his trip and

had seen monsters in the upper meadow. We calmly compared our trips, then returned to the house, agreeing that nature was too powerful.

Laura was tripping, too. She'd begun to paint the inside window frames bright yellow—the color of Van Gogh and Blake's sunflowers. By now, the sun had gone down, and the yellow seemed to have a light all its own.

Claudia, exhausted from delivering both Jerry and me through the throes of acid, lay snoring on the couch. Laura talked—to me, to herself—about her father and the absurdity of calling anything yours. "We don't possess anything." I watched her paint. A dab of blue paint was on her cheek, the color seeming to bleed over the rest of her face and her glasses. I told her she was beautiful. Upset and on the verge of tears, she gathered her paints and brushes and was going to leave the room. I implored her to stay and offered to leave instead. She understood how utterly alone I felt and remained.

We were on radically different trips. But that was always true. We were planets spinning in separate orbits. And all our orbits seemed to have a common center.

"I want someone to play with me," Laura said. We sat together and talked, alternating between intimate communication and utter aloneness.

"I wish," she said, "that there was some ritual we could perform now. I imagine us holding hands around a fire, chanting." Her description reminded me of the Druids. "Yes, a tribe," she said. She expanded the fantasy: After the cataclysm had destroyed the cities, the only survivors would live in tribes. "There will be mountain tribes, river tribes, valley tribes, and each of them will have their own customs and gods."

During Laura's trip, something clicked inside her that helped her concentrate her boundless energy. In a flash of insight, she chalked an aphorism on the blackboard that hung by the back kitchen door:

> FOR WAITING TO DO IT PERFECT,
> IT NEVER GETS DONE.

Then she took her paints into the children's room and began painting the walls and floor—artistically now. I stood apart and watched her, a butterfly that couldn't be grasped. Sometimes she'd step back from her work and appraise it from a distance, completely absorbed, looking, smiling and talking to herself. "That's how I see it," she said once. "That's what life looks like to me."

During the trip, I felt the futility of verbal communication. We send words across the great stellar distances, like radio signals between galaxies. By the time the messages are received the original meaning is lost. Better to use fewer words and suggest more.

Thumbtacked to the bookshelf was a postcard I had looked at many times without seeing. It was a reproduction of a painting, a Brueghel, that showed a boy up a tree, attempting to catch a bird. Under the trees walked a stout, stupid peasant carrying a hunting piece over his shoulder. He pointed at the boy, the expression on his face seeming to say, "*What a fool the boy is to try to catch a bird.*" He being as much a fool as the boy; and I, the viewer, as much a fool as the peasant.

The dinner of potatoes and vegetables was delicious. I used no salt or pepper, grooving instead on the essential taste of the potatoes. I grunted and slurped with gusto. What difference did it make? I took a sip of tea from Bill's cup. He didn't mind. His tea was my tea was our tea.

After dinner someone put on the first album of the Incredible String Band, an English group who use Jew's harps, whistles and hammer dulcimers to re-create tribal man's animistic vision. I had looked at the album cover before, a photograph of a freak family. Before they had looked weird. Now they were beautiful and no longer strange.

Then, I put on the first movement of Beethoven's Ninth Symphony and listened ear-up against the speaker. The beginning phrase was the most fundamental proposition of life: All must break down, down, all must die. The cadence of a dirge elevated to the cosmic scale; a rush of energy that stretched musical form to its limit. How could he have done that—to hear, and more, to capture the rush of the universe?

Jerry and I made a pact to stay up until dawn. I listened to the rest of the Ninth. Jerry did his macramé and talked of his parents, who deprecated everything he tried. He wanted to be reassured that he was having the right kind of trip and went into long descriptions of his thoughts and hallucinations. I could understand

and listen, but I couldn't reassure him. We were together but apart. The roosters crowed through the night, and we kept going outside to check for the dawn. Finally, the sky brightened. We lighted a lantern and started up the hill to the A-frame, being careful not to fall into gullies or awaken Jerry's meadow monsters.

February 4

When Jerry and I got down to the house, it was late in the afternoon. Betty told us the others had gone to buy a calf. A former member, now at Berkeley doing a PhD on Jean Cocteau, she had arrived last night. The three of us walked over to see Alice, a friend of Jerry's who lived a mile away across the valley. For once I didn't feel like initiating conversation. Alice was outside splitting wood when we arrived. Her old man was in Hawaii. We stayed for an hour and listened to a Carl Oglesby album that belonged to Betty.

When we got back to the farm, a sauna had begun on the hillside. It was just three steps down from the sauna to the brook. When I opened the door my lungs were sucked out by the hot, dry air, and I gasped. A fifty-gallon oil drum had been converted into a stove by blowtorching a door and a hole for the stovepipe. It was glowing red. I took off my clothes and hung them up in the dressing area on the same level as the stove. Then I stepped up to the hottest part of the sauna, under the low, sloping roof. A kerosene lamp hung from a rafter. It continually flared and then subsided, strobelike. About ten people were in the sauna. I squeezed into a space on the low bench.

Periodically, someone would toss water on the red-hot drum top. As it hit, it would vaporize with an explosive hiss. No one spoke. We sat separately stewing in our sweat. Our bodies seemed to have one skin of the same honey color. Yet our bodies were all different. Breasts had different tilts. Kneecaps could be smooth, chubby, or knobby.

Laura and I took turns rubbing backs. She spoke again of her tribal fantasies and of finding rituals "to get us all into the same space." I told her acid had suggested to me that unity of consciousness which she sought through ritual depended on some intermediary, a third being or presence.

Simultaneously we reached the unbearable point of heat and sweat. We opened the door and blinked at the light. In previous saunas, I had held myself back from immersing myself in the stream's deep current. But holding back enhanced the shock. This time I went under. Millions of open, relaxed sweat glands went wowwwwwww! and snapped shut. I bolted up. Laura lay in the streambed, buttocks and breasts rolling and twisting in the current. Then, seated on the pebbly bottom, she bubbled and spurted water like a naiad. With both hands she sleeked her wet-plastered hair back from her forehead.

We returned inside for another round. Jack began to om, softly at first, growing louder. We sweated and ommmmmmed. Silence —the rush of the stream. The lantern flickered.

Laura went to the water bucket, knelt and washed her hair, which had dried crisp. Maureen knelt beside her, and Laura cupped water and poured it over her head. Laura withdrew. Peter knelt down and Maureen washed his hair. Then Maureen fell into the intuitive sequence that had proceeded from the oming. No one spoke, yet we knew who the next to step forward would be. Jean washed my hair, and because I was the last, Laura returned to be washed by me, completing the circle.

We sat, drying on a tarpaulin spread out in the meadow. The sky was a dusky blue. A faint blush above the mountains. A slight scallop of a moon appeared, the eyelid of God. Against the music of the water, someone played strange improvisations on a flute. It was preharmonic music that evoked Druids worshiping at Stonehenge and the animistic world of gods and mystery; all the unity that had been lost on the way. We had to travel back in time, which was no time at all, to put the pieces back together, to put man back together, and to retrieve the original harmony.

Elaine, who'd been in seclusion all day, came down from the A-frame and we walked barefoot through the mud to the main house. A stew simmered on the stove. The Incredible String Band was on the phonograph singing their "Very Cellular Song." The last refrain bespeaks the vision of commonplace divinity infused into every particle of creation which only the very meek or the very stoned can see. It had been enshrined in crayoned letters on a wall of the commune.

CHAPTER FIVE

The Meditative Way: Spiritual Experience

*In a recent shaggy-dog story, abbreviated, a Westerner went in
search of the wisdom of the ancient Dalai Lama. After fording
untold rivers, climbing untold mountains, etc., etc., he finally
arrived at the appointed cave and asked the appointed question:
"What is the meaning of life, sage one?" "Running water flows
downhill." "Running water flows downhill!" the exasperated
Westerner exclaimed, apparently expecting greater wisdom. "Do
you mean it flows uphill?" came the sage one's reply.*

*The Orient has exercised its hold on the minds of great artists
and philosophers of the West for centuries, but only within the
last ten or fifteen years has it had any noticeable influence on
the lives of average Americans. In fact the influence is still too
imperceptible to be felt by more than a few. The story above
illustrates how for most of us the East remains a mysterious
reservoir of somehow profound, no doubt impractical, and
perhaps even dubious, wisdom. But very recently this wisdom—
or at least Western versions of it—has begun filtering into the
life styles of hundreds of thousands of Americans, young and old.
The influence of Eastern religion, with its heritage of peaceful
contemplativeness, has taken hold of the imaginations of many
who have rejected their Western religions but still need some
form of organized religious experience. Popularization of Eastern
thought may even be seen in the spreading influx of meditation
seminars, yoga sessions, occult theosophical sects, and alpha-wave
groups. Perhaps this sometimes murky religiosity may in many
cases be simply a faddish diversion for bored housewives and
distraught businessmen, but the influence of the East is much*

deeper and more pervasive on the life styles of youthful members of the counter culture than we may suspect.

At the center of the meditative strain stands Zen Buddhism. Although it is very difficult, and perhaps wrong-headed, to attempt to explain this elusive life style (for Zen represents a deeply assimilated attitude toward life, more than a codified philosophy or religion), we can at least point out several misconceptions about it. Probably the main areas of apprehension concern its privity, escapism, and asceticism. That is, it is thought to be beyond the understanding of the average person, unrealistic and irresponsible, and otherworldly to the point of denying the pleasures of the flesh. In our Western, work-oriented world all these values are viewed suspiciously. As for the first point—its supposed esoteric, incommunicable nature—nothing could be farther from the truth. For Zen is supremely simple; the only problem is that its very simplicity is a tremendous barrier to the Western mind, as Alan Watts points out in "On the Taboo against Knowing Who You Are." Zen seeks not a hidden key that unlocks the secrets of the universe, but a cultivation of the person's inner resources that allows him to see the divinity of the universe in the most commonplace object or event—a total simplicity captured in the poems "Yellow Afternoon" and "Yin and Yang." The second point is harder to counter, since Zen does represent a threat to Western man's preference for an active life over a life of contemplation. To a man who sees the world and human nature only scientifically, who values the supremacy of rational investigation (analysis and classification), and who places technological advancement ahead of everything else, Zen will always appear hopelessly escapist. (The point, of course, is that more and more people are coming to question the exclusive value of the "objective" consciousness—as Baba Ram Dass shows us in "The Transformation.") The third objection is the hardest to meet philosophically, but the easiest to explain practically. That is, in Zen Buddhism and other Eastern religions there is a certain asceticism, but it is difficult to dismiss as a simple renouncing of the passions for the emotionless state of the meditating mind. Fortunately, we needn't worry about this problem for, by and large, the mysticism which has been popularized is this-worldly; Zen teaches not rejection or corruption of the flesh, but an ecstasy of the human and the natural, an accepting joy that includes, rather than points away from, the sensory and sensual pleasures.

But does this mean that the meditative way is a good way for everyone? To be sure, its quiet, civilized, and often humorous way of teaching renders it comparatively "safe," yet there is a problem for the Westerner who naïvely rejects all Western values and willfully opts for the life of the spirit, as Jung suggests in his essay. For the fact remains that we are born and raised Westerners, and our culture sustains Western values. The snake who sheds his skin too soon or fails to grow another one in time freezes to death in the cold. Consciousness torn from its mother roots has Promethean freedom, but must be strong enough to survive a hostile climate. The selections in this section record successful and unsuccessful attempts to make the inner life the only life.

KENNETH REXROTH

Yin and Yang

It is spring once more in the Coast Range
Warm, perfumed, under the Easter moon.
The flowers are back in their places.
The birds back in their usual trees.
The winter stars set in the ocean.
The summer stars rise from the mountains.
The air is filled with atoms of quicksilver.
Resurrection envelops the earth.
Geometrical, blazing, deathless,
Animals and men march through heaven,   10
Pacing their secret ceremony.
The Lion gives the moon to the Virgin.
She stands at the crossroads of heaven,
Holding the full moon in her right hand,
A glittering wheat ear in her left.
The climax of the rite of rebirth
Has ascended from the underworld
Is proclaimed in light from the zenith.
In the underworld the sun swims
Between the fish called Yes and No.   20

WALLACE STEVENS

Yellow Afternoon

It was in the earth only
That he was at the bottom of things
And of himself. There he could say
Of this I am, this is the patriarch,

This it is that answers when I ask,
This is the mute, the final sculpture
Around which silence lies on silence.
This reposes alike in springtime
And, arbored and bronzed, in autumn.

He said I had this that I could love,   10
As one loves visible and responsive peace,
As one loves one's own being,
As one loves that which is the end
And must be loved, as one loves that
Of which one is a part as in a unity,
A unity that is the life one loves,
So that one lives all the lives that comprise it
As the life of the fatal unity of war.

Everything comes to him
From the middle of his field. The odor   20
Of earth penetrates more deeply than any word.
There he touches his being. There as he is
He is. The thought that he had found all this
Among men, in a woman—she caught his breath—
But he came back as one comes back from the sun
To lie on one's bed in the dark, close to a face
Without eyes or mouth, that looks at one and speaks.

DANIEL BERRIGAN

To Wallace Stevens

In each of us you live on, the lodged seed
of empiric imagination
from a great pod blown on death's virile wind.

You live in us; a life, creating dangers,
toppling the platitudes
that sink in mind and heart their flat denials.

Credo, we said, *credo*, mirror
to mirror, an inhumanity
before no god.

You are our puzzle. You, naked as we   10
amid the poverties of our world
—flowers, donkeys, angels meek as water—
cunningly
surpassed us in an hour. Refusing our credo
your marvelous method
made dawn, made a world, made marriage of light and flesh

without God, you said. But is decree of absence
final, when the imagination yields
like a god's brow
godlike men, armed, passionate for their world?   20

HERBERT LOMAS

Judas Speaks

Someone had to take a cool look at him.
Would-be martyr and messianic publicist,
He has everything to make you love him,
And everything to make you distrust him.
He stumps the country, lecturing to misfits,
Undeniably curing hysterics, staging theatrical
Performances of his message, leading starry-eyed followers
Into a nebulous mysticism, and they're believing,
Everyone's dropping into the delusion
That far-out truths are being revealed.   10

I love him, but someone's got to stop him,
Someone's got to take a cool look.
He doesn't want to compete, he spurns
The profit motive, despises what he considers
The rat-race, thinks we're being dehumanized
By an alienated society. He's disappointed
With politics and politicians, social rules,
Distrusts all authority and accuses the priests
Of being rotted by dogma and state allegiance.
Well, maybe they are, but someone,   20
Something's got to hold things together.
You can't turn all values upside down at once.
He adores spontaneity and improvisation,
But he finds work tedious, lives
Parasitically off the crumbs of the
Affluent Society. He wants a world
Where everyone is happy and loving.

He styles himself the Son of God
And proclaims the reign of Love Alone.
These new-style revolutionaries offer   30
No formulated theory or blueprint
For the future. He merely urges you
To live for the day and swallow prayer
As the ultimate panacea. He's excessively permissive,
And insofar as he has any political aims
These are, quite simply, to opt out of
"The world," meant pejoratively. His idea
Of redemption for the world is to
Change consciousness through love and such,
And thus change everything. New heaven, new earth!   40

So far his followers are still a minority
Among the quiet conforming majority
Who are creating the Affluent Society,
But he does twitch a contemporary nerve:
His philosophy may be full of holes
But his followers aren't philosophers
And he doesn't know what he's stirring up.
Their bizarre dress and behaviour are

Gaining currency and his sayings are
Slipping into the prevailing trendy jargon.   50
His followers don't work: they're apathetic,
Non-productive and irresponsible.
They stand for anarchy, nihilism and self-indulgence.
They're good-hearted but wrong-headed.
His version of Utopia is naïve and foolish,
But that doesn't disillusion the layabouts:
They lap it up, of course, like the stuff
He serves up at his love feasts.
And the health-hazard is patent.
He can produce disastrous panics,   60
Toppling the neurotic over the edge into madness,
Rendering the unwary so helplessly confused
That they physically do harm to themselves.
Deaths occur.

That being said, it would be unwise
To underestimate his long-term effects
On social security, crime, and the development
Of the Welfare State. The toleration
Of the Love Revolution would be a disaster
For the whole society. I have a responsibility   70
To my family, to my loved ones.
I don't deny he fooled me for a while
And in a way it's my duty to atone.
Of course, some people will call this a betrayal.
But let them. I can't help that.

HERMANN HESSE

Within and Without

There was once a man by the name of Frederick; he devoted himself to intellectual pursuits and had a wide range of knowledge. But not all knowledge was the same to him, nor was any thought as good as any other: he loved a certain type of thinking, and disdained and abominated the others. What he loved and revered was logic—that so admirable method—and, in general, what he called "science."

"Twice two is four," he used to say. "This I believe; and man must do his thinking on the basis of this truth."

He was not unaware, to be sure, that there were other sorts of thinking and knowledge; but they were not "science," and he held a low opinion of them. Although a freethinker, he was not intolerant of religion. Religion was founded on a tacit agreement among scientists. For several centuries their science had embraced nearly everything that existed on earth and was worth knowing, with the exception of one single province: the human soul. It had become a sort of custom, as time went on, to leave this to religion, and to tolerate its speculations on the soul, though without taking them seriously. Thus Frederick too was tolerant toward religion; but everything he recognized as superstition was profoundly odious and repugnant to him. Alien, uncultured, and retarded peoples might occupy themselves with it; in remote antiquity there might have been mystical or magical thinking; but since the birth of science and logic there was no longer any sense in making use of these outmoded and dubious tools.

So he said and so he thought; and when traces of superstition came to his attention he became angry and felt as if he had been touched by something hostile.

It angered him most of all, however, if he found such traces among his own sort, among educated men who were conversant with the principles of scientific thinking. And nothing was more painful and intolerable to him than that scandalous notion which lately he had sometimes heard expressed and discussed even by men of great culture—that absurd idea that "scientific thinking" was possibly not a supreme, timeless, eternal, foreordained, and unassailable mode of thought, but merely one of many, a transient way of thinking, not impervious to change and downfall. This irreverent, destructive, poisonous notion was abroad—even Frederick could not deny it; it had cropped up here and there as a result of the distress throughout the world brought about by war, revolution, and hunger, like a warning, like a white hand's ghostly writing on a white wall.

The more Frederick suffered from the fact that this idea existed and could so deeply distress him, the more passionately he assailed it and those whom he suspected of secretly believing in it. So far only a very few from among the truly educated had openly and frankly professed their belief in this new doctrine, a doctrine that seemed destined, should it gain in circulation and power, to destroy all spiritual values on earth and call forth chaos. Well, matters had not reached that point yet, and the scattered individuals who openly embraced the idea were still so few in number that they could be considered oddities and crotchety, peculiar fellows. But a drop of the poison, an emanation of that idea, could be perceived first on this side, then on that. Among the people and the half-educated no end of new doctrines could be found anyway, esoteric doctrines, sects, and discipleships; the world was full of them; everywhere one could scent out superstition, mysticism, spiritualistic cults, and other mysterious forces, which it was really necessary to combat, but to which science, as if from a private feeling of weakness, had for the present given free rein.

One day Frederick went to the house of one of his friends, with whom he had often studied. It so happened that he had not seen this friend for some time. While he was climbing the stairs of the house he tried to recall when and where it was that he had last been in his friend's company; but much as he could pride himself on his good memory for other things he could not remember. Because of this he fell imperceptibly into a certain vexation and ill humor, from which, as he stood before his friend's door, he was obliged forcibly to free himself.

Hardly had he greeted Erwin, his friend, when he noticed on his genial countenance a certain, as it were forbearing, smile, which it seemed to him he had never seen there before. And hardly had he seen this smile, which despite its friendliness he at once felt to be somehow mocking or hostile, when he immediately remembered what he had just been searching his memory for in vain—his last previous meeting with Erwin. He remembered that they had parted then without having quarreled, to be sure, but yet with a sense of inner discord and dissatisfaction, because Erwin, as it had seemed to him, had given far too little support to his attacks at that time on the realm of superstition.

It was strange. How could he have forgotten that entirely? And now he also knew that this was his only reason for not having sought out his friend for so long, merely this dissatisfaction, and that he had known this all the time, although he had invented for himself a host of other excuses for his repeated postponement of this visit.

Now they confronted one another; and it seemed to Frederick as if the little rift of that day had meantime tremendously widened. He felt that in this moment something was lacking between him and Erwin that had always been there before, an aura of solidarity, of spontaneous understanding—indeed, even of affection. Instead of these there was a vacuum. They greeted each other; spoke of the weather, their acquaintances, their health; and—God knows why! with every word Frederick had the disquieting sensation that he was not quite understanding his friend, that his friend did not really know him, that his words were missing their mark, that they could find no common ground for a real conversation. Moreover Erwin still had that friendly smile on his face, which Frederick was beginning almost to hate.

During a pause in the laborious conversation Frederick looked about the studio he knew so well and saw, pinned loosely on the wall, a sheet of paper. This sight moved him strangely and awakened ancient memories; for he recalled that, long ago in their student years, this had been a habit of Erwin's, a way he sometimes chose of keeping a thinker's saying or a poet's verse fresh in his mind. He stood up and went to the wall to read the paper.

There, in Erwin's beautiful script, he read the words: "Nothing is without, nothing is within; for what is without is within."

Blanching, he stood motionless for a moment. There it was! There he stood face to face with what he feared! At another time he would have let this leaf of paper pass, would have tolerated it charitably as a whim, as a harmless foible to which anyone was entitled, perhaps as a trifling sentimentality calling for indulgence. But now it was different. He felt that these words had not been set down for the sake of a fleeting poetic mood; it was not a vagary that Erwin had returned after so many years to a practice of his youth. What stood written here, as an avowal of his friend's concern at the moment, was mysticism! Erwin was unfaithful!

Slowly he turned to face him, whose smile was again radiant. "Explain this to me!" he demanded.

Erwin nodded, brimming with friendliness.

"Haven't you ever read this saying?"

"Certainly!" Frederick cried. "Of course I know it. It's mysticism, it's Gnosticism. It may be poetic, but—well, anyway, explain the saying to me, and why it's hanging on your wall!"

"Gladly," Erwin said. "The saying is a first introduction to an epistemology that I've been going into lately, and which has already brought me much happiness."

Frederick restrained his temper. He asked, "A new epistemology? Is there such a thing? And what is it called?"

"Oh," Erwin answered, "it's only new to me. It's already very old and venerable. It's called magic."

The word had been uttered. Profoundly astonished and startled by so candid a confession, Frederick, with a shudder, felt that he was confronted eye to eye with the arch-enemy, in the person of his friend. He did not know whether he was nearer rage or tears; the bitter feeling of irreparable loss possessed him. For a long time he remained silent.

Then, with a pretended decision in his voice, he began, "So now you want to become a magician?"

"Yes," Erwin replied unhesitatingly.

"A sort of sorcerer's apprentice, eh?"

"Certainly."

A clock could be heard ticking in the adjoining room, it was so quiet.

Then Frederick said, "This means, you know, that you are

abandoning all fellowship with serious science, and hence all fellowship with me."

"I hope that is not so," Erwin answered. "But if that's the way it has to be, what else can I do?"

"What else can you do?" Frederick burst out. "Why, break, break once and for all with this childishness, this wretched and contemptible belief in magic! That's what else you can do, if you want to keep my respect."

Erwin smiled a little, although he too no longer seemed cheerful.

"You speak as if," he said, so gently that through his quiet words Frederick's angry voice still seemed to be echoing about the room, "you speak as if that lay within my will, as if I had a choice, Frederick. That is not the case. I have no choice. It was not I that chose magic: magic chose me."

Frederick sighed deeply. "Then goodby," he said wearily, and stood up, without offering to shake hands.

"Not like that!" Erwin cried out. "No, you must not go from me like that. Pretend that one of us is lying on his deathbed— and that is so!—and that we must say farewell."

"But which of us, Erwin, is dying?"

"Today it is probably I, my friend. Whoever wishes to be born anew must be prepared to die."

Once more Frederick went up to the sheet of paper and read the saying about within and without.

"Very well," he said finally. "You are right, it won't do any good to part in anger. I'll do what you wish; I'll pretend that one of us is dying. Before I go I want to make a last request of you."

"I'm glad," Erwin said. "Tell me, what kindness can I show you on our leavetaking?"

"I repeat my first question, and this is also my request: explain this saying to me, as well as you can."

Erwin reflected a moment and then spoke:

"Nothing is without, nothing is within. You know the religious meaning of this: God is everywhere. He is in the spirit, and also in nature. All is divine, because God is all. Formerly this was called pantheism. Then the philosophic meaning: we are used to divorcing the within from the without in our thinking, but this is not necessary. Our spirit is capable of withdrawing behind the limits we have set for it, into the beyond. Beyond the pair of antitheses of which our world consists a new and different knowledge begins. . . . But, my dear friend, I must confess to you—since my thinking has changed there are no longer any unambiguous words and sayings for me: every word has tens and hundreds of meanings. And here what you fear begins—magic."

Frederick wrinkled his brow and was about to interrupt, but Erwin looked at him disarmingly and continued, speaking more distinctly, "Let me give you an example. Take something of mine along with you, any object, and examine it a little from time to time. Soon the principle of the within and the without will reveal one of its many means to you."

He glanced about the room, took a small clay figurine from a wall shelf, and gave it to Frederick, saying:

"*Take this with you as my parting gift. When this thing that I am now placing in your hands ceases to be outside you and is within you, come to me again! But if it remains outside you, the way it is now, forever, then this parting of yours from me shall also be forever!*"

Frederick wanted to say a great deal more; but Erwin took his hand, pressed it, and bade him farewell with an expression that permitted no further conversation.

Frederick left; descended the stairs (how prodigiously long ago he had climbed them!); went through the streets to his home, the little earthen figure in his hand, perplexed and sick of heart. In front of his house he stopped, shook the fist fiercely for a moment in which he was clutching the figurine, and felt a great urge to smash the ridiculous thing to the ground. He did not do so; he bit his lip and entered the house. Never before had he been so agitated, so tormented by conflicting emotions.

He looked for a place for his friend's gift, and put the figure on top of a bookcase. For the time being it stayed there.

Occasionally, as the days went by, he looked at it, brooding on it and on its origins, and pondering the meaning that this foolish thing was to have for him. It was a small figure of a man or a god or an idol, with two faces, like the Roman god Janus, modeled rather crudely of clay and covered with a burnt and somewhat cracked glaze. The little image looked coarse and insignificant; certainly it was not Roman or Greek workmanship; more likely it was the work of some backward, primitive race in Africa or the South Seas. The two faces, which were exactly alike, bore an apathetic, indolent, faintly grinning smile—it was downright ugly the way the little gnome squandered his stupid smile.

Frederick could not get used to the figure. It was totally unpleasant and offensive to him, it got in his way, it disturbed him. The very next day he took it down and put it on the stove, and a few days later moved it to a cupboard. Again and again it got in the path of his vision, as if it were forcing itself upon him; it laughed at him coldly and dull-wittedly, put on airs, demanded attention. After a few weeks he put it in the anteroom, between the photographs of Italy and the trivial little souvenirs which no one ever looked at. Now at least he saw the idol only when he was entering or leaving, and then he passed it quickly, without examining it more closely. But here too the thing still bothered him, though he did not admit this to himself.

With this shard, this two-faced monstrosity, vexation and torment had entered his life.

One day, months later, he returned from a short trip—he undertook such excursions now from time to time, as if something were driving him restlessly about; he entered his house, went through the anteroom, was greeted by the maid, and read the letters waiting for him. But he was ill at ease, as if he had forgotten something important; no book tempted him, no chair was comfortable. He began to rack his mind—what was the cause of this? Had he neglected something important? eaten something unsettling? In reflecting it occurred to him that this disturbing feeling had come over him as he had entered the apartment. He returned to the anteroom and involuntarily his first glance sought the clay figure.

A strange fright went through him when he did not see the idol. It had disappeared. It was missing. Had it walked away on its little crockery legs? Flown away? By magic?

Frederick pulled himself together, and smiled at his nervousness. Then he began quietly to search the whole room. When he found nothing he called the maid. She came, was embarrassed, and admitted at once that she had dropped the thing while cleaning up.

"Where is it?"

It was not there any more. It had seemed so solid, that little thing; she had often had it in her hands; and yet it had shattered to a hundred little pieces and splinters, and could not be fixed.

She had taken the fragments to a glazier, who had simply laughed at her; and then she had thrown them away.

Frederick dismissed the maid. He smiled. That was perfectly all right with him. He did not feel bad about the idol, God knows. The abomination was gone; now he would have peace. If only he had knocked the thing to pieces that very first day! What he had suffered in all this time! How sluggishly, strangely, craftily, evilly, satanically that idol had smiled at him! Well, now that it was gone he could admit it to himself: he had feared it, truly and sincerely feared it, this earthen god. Was it not the emblem and symbol of everything that was repugnant and intolerable to him, everything that he had recognized all along as pernicious, inimical, and worthy of suppression—an emblem of all superstitions, all darkness, all coercion of conscience and spirit? Did it not represent that ghastly power that one sometimes felt raging in the bowels of the earth, that distant earthquake, that approaching extinction of culture, that looming chaos? Had not this contemptible figure robbed him of his best friend—nay, not merely robbed, but made of the friend an enemy? Well, now the thing was gone. Vanished. Smashed to pieces. Done for. It was good so; it was much better than if he had destroyed it himself.

So he thought, or said. And he went about his affairs as before.

But it was like a curse. Now, just when he had got more or less used to that ridiculous figure, just when the sight of it in its usual place on the anteroom table had gradually become a bit familiar and unimportant to him, now its absence began to torment him! Yes, he missed it every time he went through that room; all he could see there was the empty spot where it had formerly stood, and emptiness emanated from the spot and filled the room with strangeness.

Bad days and worse nights began for Frederick. He could no longer go through the anteroom without thinking of the idol with the two faces, missing it, and feeling that his thoughts were tethered to it. This became an agonizing compulsion for him. And it was not by any means simply on the occasions when he went through that room that he was gripped by this compulsion—ah, no. Just as emptiness and desolation radiated from the now empty spot on the anteroom table, so this compulsive idea radiated within him, gradually crowded all else aside, rankling and filling him with emptiness and strangeness.

Again and again he pictured the figure with utmost distinctness, just to make it clear to himself how preposterous it was to grieve its loss. He could see it in all its stupid ugliness and barbarity, with its vacuous yet crafty smile, with its two faces—indeed, as if under duress, full of hatred and with his mouth drawn awry, he found himself attempting to reproduce that smile. The question pestered him whether the two faces were really exactly alike. Had not one of them, perhaps only because of a little roughness or a crack in the glaze, had a somewhat different expression? Something quizzical? Something sphinxlike? And how peculiar the color of that glaze had been! Green, and blue, and gray, but also red, were in it—a glaze that he now kept finding often in other objects, in a window's reflection of the sun or in the mirrorings of a wet pavement.

He brooded a great deal on this glaze, at night too. It also struck him what a strange, foreign, ill-sounding, unfamiliar, almost malignant word "glaze" was. He analyzed the word, and once he even reversed the order of its letters. Then it read "ezalg." Now where the devil did this word get its sound from? He knew this word "ezalg," certainly he knew it; moreover, it was an unfriendly and bad word, a word with ugly and disturbing connotations. For a long while he tormented himself with this question. Finally he hit upon it: "ezalg" reminded him of a book that he had bought and read many years ago on a trip, and that had dismayed, plagued, and yet secretly fascinated him; it had been entitled *Princess Ezalka*. It was like a curse: everything connected with the figurine —the glaze, the blue, the green, the smile—signified hostility, tormenting and poisoning him. And how very peculiarly *he*, Erwin, his erstwhile friend, had smiled as he had given the idol into his hand! How very peculiarly, how very significantly, how very hostily.

Frederick resisted manfully—and on many days not without success—the compulsive trend of his thoughts. He sensed the danger clearly: he did not want to go insane! No, it were better to die. Reason was necessary, life was not. And it occurred to him that perhaps *this* was magic, that Erwin, with the aid of that figure, had in some way enchanted him, and that he should fall as a sacrifice, as the defender of reason and science against these dismal powers. But if this were so, if he could even conceive of that as possible, then there *was* such a thing as magic, then there *was* sorcery. No, it were better to die!

A doctor recommended walks and baths; and sometimes, in search of amusement, he spent an evening at an inn. But it helped very little. He cursed Erwin; he cursed himself.

One night, as he often did now, he retired early and lay restlessly awake in bed, unable to sleep. He felt unwell and uneasy. He wanted to meditate; he wanted to find solace, wanted to speak sentences of some sort to himself, good sentences, comforting, reassuring ones, something with the straightforward serenity and lucidity of the sentence, "Twice two is four." Nothing came to mind; but, in a state almost of lightheadedness, he mumbled sounds and syllables to himself. Gradually words formed on his lips, and several times, without being sensible of its meaning, he said the same short sentence to himself, which had somehow taken form in him. He muttered it to himself, as if it might stupefy him, as if he might grope his way along it, as along a parapet, to the sleep that eluded him on the narrow, narrow path that skirted the abyss.

But suddenly, when he spoke somewhat louder, the words he was mumbling penetrated his consciousness. He knew them: they were, "Yes, now you are within me!" And instantly he knew. He knew what they meant—that they referred to the clay idol and that now, in this gray night hour, he had accurately and exactly fulfilled the prophecy Erwin had made on that unearthly day, that now the figure, which he had held contemptuously in his fingers then, was no longer outside him but within him! "For what is without is within."

Bounding up in a leap, he felt as if transfused with ice and fire. The world reeled about him, the planets stared at him insanely. He threw on some clothes, put on the light, left his house and ran in the middle of the night to Erwin's. There he saw a light burning in the studio window he knew so well; the door to the house was unlocked: everything seemed to be awaiting him. He rushed up the stairs. He walked unsteadily into Erwin's study, supported himself with trembling hands on the table. Erwin sat by the lamp, in its gentle light, contemplative, smiling.

Graciously Erwin arose. "You have come. That is good."

"Have you been expecting me?" Frederick whispered.

"I have been expecting you, as you know, from the moment you left here, taking my little gift with you. Has what I said then happened?"

"It has happened," Frederick said. "The idol is within me. I can't bear it any longer."

"Can I help you?" Erwin asked.

"I don't know. Do as you will. Tell me more of your magic! Tell me how the idol can get out of me again."

Erwin placed his hand on his friend's shoulder. He led him to an armchair and pressed him down in it. Then he spoke cordially to Frederick, smiling in an almost brotherly tone of voice:

"The idol will come out of you again. Have trust in me. Have trust in yourself. You have learned to believe in it. Now learn to love it! It is within you, but it is still dead, it is still a phantom to you. Awaken it, speak to it, question it! For it is you yourself! Do not hate it any longer, do not fear it, do not torment it—how you have tormented this poor idol, who was yet you yourself! How you have tormented yourself!"

"Is this the way to magic?" Frederick asked. He sat deep in the chair, as if he had grown older, and his voice was low.

"This is the way," Erwin replied, "and perhaps you have already taken the most difficult step. You have found by experience: the without can become the within. You have been beyond the pair of antitheses. It seemed hell to you; learn, my friend, it is heaven! For it is heaven that awaits you. Behold, this is magic: to interchange the without and the within, not by compulsion, not in anguish, as you have done it, but freely, voluntarily. Summon up the past, summon up the future: both are in you! Until today you have been the slave of the within. Learn to be its master. That is magic."

CARL JUNG

Commentary on
The Secret of the Golden Flower [1]

1. DIFFICULTIES ENCOUNTERED BY A EUROPEAN IN TRYING TO UNDERSTAND THE EAST

A thorough Westerner in feeling, I am necessarily deeply impressed by the strangeness of this Chinese text. It is true that some knowledge of Eastern religions and philosophies aids my intellect and intuition in understanding these ideas to a certain extent, just as I can understand the paradoxes of primitive beliefs in terms of "ethnology," or in terms of the "comparative history of religions." Indeed, this is the Western way of hiding one's heart under the cloak of so-called scientific understanding. We do it partly because of the *misérable vanité des savants* which fears and rejects with horror any sign of living sympathy, and partly because a sympathetic understanding might permit contact with an alien spirit to become a serious experience. So-called scientific objectivity would have reserved this text for the philological acuity of Sinologues, and would have guarded it jealously from any other interpretation. But Richard Wilhelm penetrated into the secret and mysterious vitality of Chinese wisdom too deeply to have allowed such a pearl of intuitive insight to disappear in the pigeonholes of the specialists. I am greatly honoured that his choice of a psychological commentator has fallen upon me.

This entails the risk, though, that this unique treasure will be

[1] The book this essay deals with is from ancient Chinese teachings which were transmitted orally until the eighth century A.D. As Jung's commentary reveals, the book discusses the relationship between psyche and cosmos.—*Eds.*

swallowed by still another special science. Nonetheless, anyone seeking to minimize the merits of Western science and scholarship is undermining the main support of the European mind. Science is not, indeed, a perfect instrument, but it is a superior and indispensable one that works harm only when taken as an end in itself. Scientific method must serve; it errs when it usurps a throne. It must be ready to serve all branches of science, because each, by reason of its insufficiency, has need of support from the others. Science is the tool of the Western mind and with it more doors can be opened than with bare hands. It is part and parcel of our knowledge and obscures our insight only when it holds that the understanding given by it is the only kind there is. The East has taught us another, wider, more profound, and higher understanding, that is, understanding through life. We know this way only vaguely, as a mere shadowy sentiment culled from religious terminology, and therefore we gladly dispose of Eastern "wisdom" in quotation marks and relegate it to the obscure territory of faith and superstition. But in this way we wholly misunderstand the "realism" of the East. This text, for instance, does not consist of exaggerated sentiment or overwrought mystical intuitions bordering on the pathological and emanating from ascetic cranks and recluses. It is based on the practical insights of highly evolved Chinese minds, which we have not the slightest justification for undervaluing.

This assertion may seem bold, perhaps, and is likely to be met with disbelief, but that is not surprising, considering how little is known about the material. Moreover, the strangeness of the material is so arresting that our embarrassment as to how and where the Chinese world of thought might be joined to ours is quite understandable. When faced with this problem of grasping the ideas of the East, the usual mistake of Western man is like that of the student in *Faust*. Misled by the Devil, he contemptuously turns his back on science, and, carried away by Eastern occultism, takes over yoga practices quite literally and becomes a pitiable imitator. (Theosophy is our best example of this mistake.) And so he abandons the one safe foundation of the Western mind and loses himself in a mist of words and ideas which never would have originated in European brains, and which can never be profitably grafted upon them.

An ancient adept has said: "If the wrong man uses the right

means, the right means work in the wrong way." This Chinese saying, unfortunately all too true, stands in sharp contrast to our belief in the "right" method irrespective of the man who applies it. In reality, in such matters everything depends on the man and little or nothing on the method. For the method is merely the path, the direction taken by a man. The way he acts is the true expression of his nature. If it ceases to be this, then the method is nothing more than an affectation, something artificially added, rootless and sapless, serving only the illegitimate goal of self-deception. It becomes a means of fooling oneself and of evading what may perhaps be the implacable law of one's being. This is far removed from the earth-born quality and sincerity of Chinese thought. On the contrary, it is the denial of one's own being, self-betrayal to strange and unclean gods, a cowardly trick for the purpose of usurping psychic superiority, everything in fact which is profoundly contrary to the meaning of the Chinese "method." For these insights result from a way of life that is complete, genuine, and true in the fullest sense; they are insights coming from that ancient, cultural life of China which has grown consistently and coherently from the deepest instincts, and which, for us, is forever remote and impossible to imitate.

Western imitation of the East is doubly tragic in that it comes from an unpsychological misunderstanding as sterile as are the modern escapades in Taos, the blissful South Sea Islands, and Central Africa, where "primitivity" is earnestly being played at while Western civilized man evades his menacing duties, his *Hic Rhodus hic salta*. It is not a question of our imitating, or worse still, becoming missionaries for what is organically foreign, but rather a question of building up our own Western culture, which sickens with a thousand ills. This has to be done on the spot, and by the real European as he is in his Western commonplaces, with his marriage problems, his neuroses, his social and political delusions, and his whole philosophical disorientation.

We should do well to confess at once that, fundamentally speaking, we do not understand the complete detachment from the world of a text like this, indeed, that we do not want to understand it. Have we, perhaps, an inkling that a mental attitude which can direct the glance inward to this extent can bring about such detachment only because these people have so completely fulfilled the instinctive demands of their natures that little or nothing prevents them from viewing the invisible essence of the world? Can it be, perhaps, that the premise of such vision is liberation from those ambitions and passions which bind us to the visible world, and does not this liberation result from the sensible fulfilment of instinctive demands, rather than from the premature or fear-born repression of them? Is it that our eyes are opened to the spirit only when the laws of earth are obeyed? Anybody who knows the history of Chinese culture and has also carefully studied the *I Ching*, that book of wisdom which for thousands of years has permeated all Chinese thought, will not pass over these questions lightly. He will know, moreover, that the views set forth in our text are nothing extraordinary from the Chinese point of view, but are actually inescapable, psychological conclusions.

In our Christian culture, spirit, and the passion of the spirit, were for a long time the greatest values and the things most worth striving for. Only after the decline of the Middle Ages, that is, in the course of the nineteenth century, when spirit began to degenerate into intellect, did a reaction set in against the unbearable dominance of intellectualism. This movement, it is true, at first committed the pardonable mistake of confusing intellect with spirit, and blaming the latter for the misdeeds of the former. Intellect does, in fact, harm the soul when it dares to possess itself of the heritage of the spirit. It is in no way fitted to do this, because spirit is something higher than intellect in that it includes not only the latter, but the feelings as well. It is a direction or principle of life that strives towards shining, suprahuman heights. In opposition to it stands the dark, the feminine, the earth-bound principle (yin), with its emotionality and instinctiveness that reach far back into the depths of time, and into the roots of physiological continuity. Without a doubt, these concepts are purely intuitive insights, but one cannot very well dispense with them if one is trying to understand the nature of the human soul. China could not do without them because, as the history of Chinese philosophy shows, it has never gone so far from central psychic facts as to lose itself in a one-sided overdevelopment and overvaluation of a single psychic function. Therefore, the Chinese have never failed to recognize the paradoxes and the polarity inherent in what is alive. The opposites always balanced one another—a sign of high culture. One-sidedness, though it lends momentum, is a mark of barbarism. The reaction which is now beginning in the West against the intellect in favour of feeling, or in favour of intuition, seems to me a mark of cultural advance, a widening of consciousness beyond the too narrow limits of a tyrannical intellect.

I have no wish to undervalue the tremendous differentiation of Western intellect; measured by it, Eastern intellect can be described as childish. (Obviously this has nothing to do with intelligence.) If we should succeed in elevating another or even a third psychic function to the dignity accorded intellect, then the West might expect to surpass the East by a very great margin. Therefore it is sad indeed when the European departs from his own nature and imitates the East or "affects" it in any way. The possibilities open to him would be so much greater if he would remain true to himself and develop out of his own nature all that the East has brought forth from its inner being in the course of the centuries.

In general, and looked at from the incurably external point of view of the intellect, it would seem as if the things so highly valued by the East were not desirable for us. Intellect alone cannot fathom at first the practical importance Eastern ideas might have for us, and that is why it can classify these ideas as philosophical and ethnological curiosities and nothing more. The lack of comprehension goes so far that even learned Sinologues have not understood the practical application of the *I Ching,* and have therefore looked on the book as a collection of abstruse magic spells.

2. MODERN PSYCHOLOGY OFFERS A POSSIBILITY OF UNDERSTANDING

Observations made in my practice have opened to me a quite new and unexpected approach to Eastern wisdom. But it must be well understood that I did not have a knowledge, however inadequate, of Chinese philosophy as a starting point. On the contrary, when I began my life-work in the practice of psychiatry and psychotherapy, I was completely ignorant of Chinese philosophy, and only later did my professional experience show me that in my technique I had been unconsciously led along that secret way which has been the preoccupation of the best minds of the East for centuries. This could be taken for a subjective fancy—one

reason for my previous reluctance to publish anything on the subject—but Richard Wilhelm, that great interpreter of the soul of
China, fully confirmed the parallel for me. Thus he gave me the
courage to write about a Chinese text which belongs entirely to
the mysterious shadows of the Eastern mind. At the same time,
and this is the extraordinary thing, in content it is a living parallel
to what takes place in the psychic development of my patients,
none of whom is Chinese.

In order to make this strange fact more intelligible to the
reader, it must be pointed out that just as the human body shows
a common anatomy over and above all racial differences, so, too,
the psyche possesses a common substratum transcending all differences in culture and consciousness. I have called this substratum
the collective unconscious. This unconscious psyche, common to
all mankind, does not consist merely of contents capable of becoming conscious, but of latent dispositions toward certain identical reactions. Thus the fact of the collective unconscious is
simply the psychic expression of the identity of brain-structure
irrespective of all racial differences. This explains the analogy,
sometimes even identity, between various myth-motifs and symbols, and the possibility of human beings making themselves
mutually understood. The various lines of psychic development
start from one common stock whose roots reach back into all the
strata of the past. This also explains the psychological parallelisms
with animals.

Taken purely psychologically, it means that mankind has common instincts of imagination and of action. All conscious imagination and action have been developed with these unconscious
archetypal images as their basis, and always remain bound up with
them. Especially is this the case when consciousness has not
attained any high degree of clarity, that is, when, in all its func-
tions, it is more dependent on the instincts than on the conscious
will, more governed by affect than by rational judgement. This
condition ensures a primitive health of the psyche, which, however, immediately becomes lack of adaptation as soon as circumstances arise calling for a higher moral effort. Instincts suffice only
for the individual embedded in nature, which, on the whole,
remains always the same. An individual who is more guided by
unconscious than by conscious choice tends therefore towards
marked psychic conservatism. This is the reason the primitive

does not change in the course of thousands of years, and it is also the reason why he fears everything strange and unusual. It might lead him to maladaptation, and thus to the greatest of psychic dangers, to a kind of neurosis in fact. A higher and wider consciousness, which comes about only through assimilation of the unfamiliar, tends towards autonomy, towards revolution against the old gods who are nothing other than those powerful, unconscious, archetypal images which have always held consciousness in thrall.

The more powerful and independent consciousness, and with it the conscious will, become, the more the unconscious is forced into the background. When this happens, it is easily possible for the conscious structures to detach themselves from the unconscious archetypes. Gaining thus in freedom, they break the chains of mere instinctiveness, and finally arrive at a state that is deprived of, or contrary to, instinct. Consciousness thus is torn from its roots and no longer able to appeal to the authority of the archetypal images; it has Promethean freedom, it is true, but also a godless *hybris*. It does indeed soar above the earth, even above mankind, but the danger of an upset is there, not for every individual, to be sure, but collectively for the weak members of such a society, who then, again like Prometheus, are chained to the Caucasus by the unconscious. The wise Chinese would say in the words of the *I Ching*: When yang has reached its greatest strength, the dark power of yin is born within its depths, for night begins at midday when yang breaks up and begins to change to yin.

A physician is in a position to see this peripeteia enacted literally in life. He sees, for instance, a successful businessman attaining all his desires, heedless of his peril, and then, having withdrawn from activity at the height of his success, falling in a short time into a neurosis, which changes him into a querulous old woman, fastens him to his bed, and thus finally destroys him. The picture is complete even to the change from a masculine to a womanish attitude. An exact parallel to this is the legend of Nebuchadnezzar in the Book of Daniel, and, indeed, Caesarean madness in general. Similar cases of one-sided exaggeration in the conscious standpoint, and of the corresponding yin reaction of the unconscious, form no small part of the practice of psychiatrists in our time which so overvalues the conscious will as to believe that "where there is a will there is a way." Not that I wish to detract in the least from the high moral value of conscious willing; consciousness and will may well continue to be considered the highest cultural achievements of humanity. But of what use is a morality that destroys the human being? To bring will and capacity into harmony seems to me to be a better thing than morality. Morality *à tout prix* is a sign of barbarism—more often wisdom is better—but perhaps I look at this through the professional glasses of the physician who has to mend the ills following in the wake of an exaggerated cultural achievement.

Be that as it may. In any case, it is a fact that consciousness, heightened by a necessary one-sidedness, gets so far out of touch with the archetypes that a breakdown follows. Long before the actual catastrophe, the signs of error announce themselves as absence of instinct, nervousness, disorientation, and entanglement in impossible situations and problems. When the physician comes to investigate, he finds an unconscious which is in complete rebellion against the values of the conscious, and which therefore cannot possibly be assimilated to the conscious, while the reverse, of course, is altogether out of the question. We are then confronted with an apparently irreconcilable conflict with which human reason cannot deal except by sham solutions or dubious compromises. If both these evasions are rejected, we are faced with the question as to what has become of the much needed unity of personality, and with the necessity of seeking it. And here we come to the path travelled by the East from time immemorial. Quite obviously, the Chinese owes the finding of this path to the fact that he was never able to force the opposites in human nature so far apart that all conscious connection between them was lost. The Chinese has such an all-inclusive consciousness because, as in the case of primitive mentality, the yea and the nay have remained in their original proximity. Nonetheless, he could not escape feeling the collision of the opposites, and therefore he sought out that way of life in which he would be what the Hindu terms *nirdvandva*, free of the opposites.

Our text is concerned with this way, and this same problem comes up with my patients also. There could be no greater mistake than for a Westerner to take up the direct practice of Chinese yoga, for it would be a matter of his will and his consciousness, and would only strengthen the latter against the unconscious, bringing about the very effect to be avoided. The neurosis would then simply be intensified. It cannot be sufficiently strongly empha-sized that we are not Orientals, and therefore have an entirely different point of departure in these things. It would also be a great mistake to assume that this is the path every neurotic must travel, or that it is the solution to be sought at every stage of the neurotic problem. It is appropriate only in those cases where the conscious has reached an abnormal degree of development, and has therefore diverged too far from the unconscious. This high degree of consciousness is the *conditio sine qua non*. Nothing would be more wrong than to wish to open this way to neurotics who are ill on account of an undue predominance of the uncon-scious. For the same reason, this way of development has scarcely any meaning before the middle of life (normally between the ages of thirty-five and forty); in fact, if entered upon too soon, it can be decidedly injurious.

As has been indicated, the reason for looking for a new way was the fact that the fundamental problem of the patient seemed insoluble to me unless violence was done to the one or the other side of his nature. I always worked with the temperamental con-viction that fundamentally there are no insoluble problems, and experience justified me insofar as I have often seen individuals simply outgrow a problem which had destroyed others. This "out-growing," as I formerly called it, on further experience was seen to consist in a new level of consciousness. Some higher or wider interest arose on the person's horizon, and through this widening of his view the insoluble problem lost its urgency. It was not solved logically in its own terms, but faded out when confronted with a new and stronger life-tendency. It was not repressed and made unconscious, but merely appeared in a different light, and so did indeed become different. What, on a lower level, had led to the wildest conflicts and to panicky outbursts of emotion, viewed from the higher level of the personality now seemed like a storm in the valley seen from a high mountaintop. This does not mean that the thunderstorm is robbed of its reality, but instead of being in it, one is now above it. However, since we are both valley and mountain with respect to the psyche, it might seem a vain illusion to feel oneself beyond what is human. One certainly does feel the affect and is shaken and tormented by it, yet at the same time one is aware of a higher consciousness, which prevents one from becoming identical with the affect, a consciousness which takes the affect objectively, and can say, "I know that I suffer." What our text says of indolence: "Indolence of which a man is conscious and indolence of which he is unconscious are a thousand miles apart," holds true in the highest degree of affect also.

Here and there it happened in my practice that a patient grew beyond himself because of unknown potentialities, and this became an experience of prime importance to me. I had learned in the meanwhile that the greatest and most important problems of life are all in a certain sense insoluble. They must be so because they express the necessary polarity inherent in every self-regulating system. They can never be solved, but only outgrown. I therefore asked myself whether this possibility of outgrowing, that is, further psychic development, was not the normal thing, and therefore remaining stuck in a conflict was what was pathological. Everyone must possess that higher level, at least in embryonic form, and in favourable circumstances must be able to develop this possibility. When I examined the way of development of those persons who quietly, and as if unconsciously, grew beyond themselves, I saw that their fates had something in common. The new thing came to them out of obscure possibilities either outside or inside themselves; they accepted it and developed further by means of it. It seemed to me typical that some took the new thing from outside themselves, others from within; or rather, that it grew into some persons from without, and into others from within. But the new thing never came exclusively either from within or from without. If it arose from outside, it became a deeply subjective experience; if it arose from within, it became an outer event. In no case was it conjured into existence through purpose and conscious willing, but rather seemed to be borne on the stream of time.

We are so greatly tempted to turn everything into purpose and method that I deliberately express myself in very abstract terms in order to avoid causing a prejudice in one direction or another. The new thing must not be pigeonholed under any heading, for then it becomes a recipe to be applied mechanically, and it would again be a case of the "right means" in the hands "of the wrong man." I have been deeply impressed with the fact that the new thing presented by fate seldom or never corresponds to conscious expectation. And still more remarkable, though the new thing contradicts deeply-rooted instincts as we have known them, it is a singularly appropriate expression of the total personality, an expression which one could not imagine in a more complete form.

What did these people do in order to achieve the development that liberated them? As far as I could see they did nothing (*wu wei*) [2] but let things happen. As Master Lü-tsu teaches in our text, the light rotates according to its own law, if one does not give up one's ordinary occupation. The art of letting things happen, action through nonaction, letting go of oneself, as taught by Meister Eckhart, became for me the key opening the door to the way. We must be able to let things happen in the psyche. For us, this actually is an art of which few people know anything. Consciousness is forever interfering, helping, correcting, and negating, and never leaving the simple growth of the psychic processes in peace. It would be simple enough, if only simplicity were not the most difficult of all things. To begin with, the task consists solely in objectively observing a fragment of a fantasy in its development. Nothing could be simpler, and yet right here the difficulties begin. No fantasy-fragment seems to appear—or yes, one does—but it is too stupid—hundreds of good reasons inhibit it. One cannot concentrate on it—it is too boring—what would it amount to—it is "nothing but," et cetera. The conscious mind raises prolific objections; in fact, it often seems bent upon blotting out the spontaneous fantasy-activity in spite of real insight, even of firm determination on the part of the individual to allow the psychic processes to go forward without interference. Often a veritable cramp of consciousness exists.

If one is successful in overcoming the initial difficulties, criticism is still likely to start in afterwards and attempt to interpret the fantasy, to classify, to aestheticize, or to depreciate it. The temptation to do this is almost irresistible. After complete and faithful observation, free rein can be given to the impatience of the conscious mind; in fact it must be given, else obstructing resistances develop. But each time the fantasy material is to be produced, the activity of consciousness must again be put aside.

In most cases the results of these efforts are not very encouraging at first. They usually consist of webs of fantasy which yield no clear knowledge of their origin or goal. Also, the way of getting at

[2] Action through nonaction.

the fantasies is individually different. For many people, it is easiest to write them; others visualize them, and others again draw and paint them with or without visualization. In cases of a high degree of conscious cramp, oftentimes the hands alone can fantasy; they model or draw figures that are often quite foreign to the conscious mind.

These exercises must be continued until the cramp in the conscious mind is released, or, in other words, until one can let things happen, which was the immediate goal of the exercise. In this way a new attitude is created, an attitude which accepts the non-rational and the incomprehensible, simply because it is what is happening. This attitude would be poison for a person who had already been overwhelmed by things that just happen, but it is of the highest value for one who chooses, with an exclusively conscious critique, only the things acceptable to his consciousness from among the things that happen, and thus is gradually drawn out of the stream of life into stagnant backwater.

At this point, the way travelled by the two types mentioned above seems to be separate. Both have learned to accept what comes to them. (As Master Lü-tsu teaches: "When occupations come to us we must accept them; when things come to us we must understand them from the ground up.") One man will chiefly take what comes to him from without, and the other what comes from within, and, according to the law of life, the one will have to take from the outside something he never could accept before from outside, and the other will accept from within things which would always have been excluded before.

This reversal of one's being means an enlargement, heightening, and enrichment of the personality when the previous values are retained along with the change, provided, of course, that these values are not mere illusions. If the values are not retained, the individual goes over to the other side, and passes from fitness to unfitness, from adaptation to the lack of it, from sense to non-sense, and even from rationality to mental disturbance. The way is not without danger. Everything good is costly, and the development of the personality is one of the most costly of all things. It is a question of yea-saying to oneself, of taking one's self as the most serious of tasks, of being conscious of everything one does, and keeping it constantly before one's eyes in all its dubious aspects—truly a task that taxes us to the utmost.

The Chinese can fall back upon the authority of his entire culture. If he starts on the long way, he does what is recognized as being the best of all the things he could do. But the Westerner who wishes to start upon this way, if he is truly serious about it, has all authority against him—intellectual, moral, and religious. That is why it is infinitely easier for a man to imitate the Chinese way and desert the troublesome European, or else to seek again the way back to the medievalism of the Christian Church and build up once more the European wall intended to separate true Christians from the poor heathen and the ethnographic curiosities dwelling outside. Aesthetic or intellectual flirtations with life and fate come to an abrupt end here. The step to higher consciousness leads us out and away from all rear-guard cover and from all safety measures. The individual must give himself to the new way completely, for it is only by means of his integrity that he can go further, and only his integrity can guarantee that his way does not turn out to be an absurd adventure.

Whether a person's fate comes to him from without or from within, the experiences and events of the way remain the same. Therefore I need say nothing about the manifold outer and inner events, the endless variety of which I could never exhaust in any case. To do so, moreover, would be irrelevant to the text under discussion. But there is much to be said of the psychic states that accompany the further development. These psychic states are expressed symbolically in our text, and in the very symbols which for many years have been familiar to me in my practice.

BABA RAM DASS

The Transformation:
Dr. Richard Alpert, Ph.D., into Baba Ram Dass

There are three stages in this journey that I have been on! The first, the social science stage; the second, the psychedelic stage; and the third, the yogi stage. They are summating—that is, each is contributing to the next. It's like the unfolding of a lotus flower. Now, as I look back, I realize that many of the experiences that made little sense to me at the time they occurred were pre-requisites for what was to come later. I want to share with you the parts of the internal journey that never get written up in the mass media: I'm not interested in the political parts of the story; I'm not interested in what you read in the *Saturday Evening Post* about LSD. This is the story of what goes on inside a human being who is undergoing all these experiences.

In 1961, the beginning of March, I was at perhaps the highest point of my academic career. I had just returned from being a visiting professor at the University of California at Berkeley: I had been assured of a permanent post that was being held for me at Harvard, if I got my publications in order. I held appointments in four departments at Harvard—the Social Relations Department, the Psychology Department, the Graduate School of Education, and the Health Service (where I was a therapist); I had research contracts with Yale and Stanford. In a worldly sense, I was making a great income and I was a collector of possessions.

I had an apartment in Cambridge that was filled with antiques and I gave very charming dinner parties. I had a Mercedes-Benz sedan and a Triumph 500 CC motorcycle and a Cessna 172 air-plane and an MG sports car and a sailboat and a bicycle. I vaca-tioned in the Caribbean where I did scuba-diving. I was living the way a successful bachelor professor is supposed to live in the American world of "he who makes it." I wasn't a genuine scholar, but I had gone through the whole academic trip. I had gotten my Ph.D.; I was writing books. I had research contracts. I taught courses in Human Motivation, Freudian Theory, Child Development. But what all this boils down to is that I was really a very good game player.

My lecture notes were the ideas of other men, subtly presented, and my research was all within the Zeitgeist—all that which one was supposed to research about.

In 1955 I had started doing therapy and my first therapy patient had turned me on to pot. I had not smoked regularly after that, but only sporadically, and I was still quite a heavy drinker. But this first patient had friends and they had friends and all of them became my patients. I became a "hip" therapist for the hip community at Stanford. When I'd go to the parties, they'd all say "Here comes the shrink" and I would sit in the corner looking superior. In addition, I had spent five years in psychoanalysis at a cool investment of something like $26,000.

Before March 6th, which was the day I took psylocybin, one of the psychedelics, I felt something was wrong in my world, but I couldn't label it in any way so as to get hold of it. I felt that the theories I was teaching in psychology didn't make it, that the psychologists didn't really have a grasp of the human condition, and that the theories I was teaching, which were theories of achievement and anxiety and defense mechanisms and so on, weren't getting to the crux of the matter.

My colleagues and I were 9:00 to 5:00 psychologists: We came to work every day and we did our psychology, just like you would do insurance or auto mechanics, and then at 5:00 we went home and were just as neurotic as we were before we went to work. Somehow, it seemed to me, if all of this theory were right, it should play more intimately into my own life. I understood the requirement of being "objective" for a scientist, but this is a most naïve concept in social sciences as we are finding out. And whatever the psychoanalysis did (and it did many things, I'm sure) I still was a neurotic at the end of those five years of psychoanalysis. Even my therapist thought so, because when I stopped analysis to go to Harvard, he said, "You are too sick to leave analysis." Those were his final words. But because I had been trained in Freudian

theory, I knew his game well enough to enjoy this terribly sophisticated, competitive relationship with my analyst, and I would say
to him, "Well in Freud's 1906 paper, don't you recall he said this,
and when I'm saying this you should be interpreting . . ." For
this I was paying $20 an hour!

Something was wrong. And the something wrong was that I just
didn't know, though I kept feeling all along the way that somebody else must know even though I didn't. The nature of life
was a mystery to me. All the stuff I was teaching was just like
little molecular bits of stuff but they didn't add up to a feeling
anything like wisdom. I was just getting more and more knowledgeable. And I was getting very good at bouncing three knowledge balls at once. I could sit in a doctoral exam, ask very sophisticated questions and look terribly wise. It was a hustle.

DISSATISFACTION

Now my predicament as a social scientist was that I was not
basically a scholar. I came out of a Jewish anxiety-ridden high-
achieving tradition. Though I had been through five years of psychoanalysis, still, every time I lectured, I would get extraordinary
diarrhea and tension. Lecturing five days a week made it quite a
complex problem to keep my stomach operating. But whatever
my motivations, they drove me so hard that despite the fact that I
was a very mediocre student (in fact, I could never get into
Harvard no matter how hard I tried, even using all my father's
political influence) I finally found myself on the faculty of the
"good" universities.

I could study ten hours and prepare a really good lecture on
Freud or Human Motivation, but it was all as if it were behind
a wall. It was theoretical. I theorized this or that. I espoused these
ideas, these intellectual concepts, quite apart from my own experi-
ential base. Although I could bring all kinds of emotional zeal to
bear on my presentation, there was a lack of validity in my guts
about what I was doing. And, to my suppressed dismay, I found
that this stance was considered acceptable by most of my colleagues who seemed, in their attempt to become "scientific," to
think of personality in terms of variables. Children were nothing
but ambulatory variables, and no matter how hard we tried, by

the time we got to the legitimacy of a highly operationally-defined
variable, it had lost its gut feeling. So the concepts we were working with were intellectual fun and games, but they weren't affect-
ing my life.

Here I was, sitting with the boys of the first team in cognitive
psychology, personality psychology, developmental psychology,
and in the midst of this I felt here were men and women who,
themselves, were not highly evolved beings. Their own lives were
not fulfilled. There was not enough human beauty, human fulfill-
ment, human contentment. I worked hard and the keys to the
kingdom were handed to me. I was being promised all of it. I had
felt I had got into whatever the inner circle meant: I could be
Program Chairman for Division 7 of the A.P.A. and I could be
on government committees, and have grants, and travel about
and sit on doctorate committees. But there was still that horrible
awareness that I didn't know something or other which made it
all fall together. And there was a slight panic in me that I was
going to spend the next forty years not knowing, and that apparently that was par for the course. And in off hours, we played
"Go," or poker, and cracked old jokes. The whole thing was too
empty. It was not honest enough.

And there was some point as a professor at Stanford and Harvard
when I experienced being caught in some kind of a meaningless
game in which the students were exquisite at playing the role of
students and the faculty were exquisite at playing the role of
faculty. I would get up and say what I had read in books and
they'd all write it down and give it back as answers on exams, but
nothing was happening. I felt as if I were in a sound-proof room.
Not enough was happening that mattered—that was real.

And as a therapist I felt caught in the drama of my own
theories. The research data showed that Rogerian patients ended
up saying positive statements, and Freudian patients ended up
talking about their mother because of subtle reinforcement clues—
it was so obvious. I would sit with my little notebook and when
the person would start talking about his mother, I'd make a note
and it didn't take long for the patient to realize that he got his
"note" taken, he got his pellet, every time he said certain things.
And pretty soon he would be "Freudianized."

In the face of this feeling of malaise, I ate more, collected more possessions, collected more appointments and positions and status, more sexual and alcoholic orgies, and more wildness in my life.

Every time I went to a family gathering, I was the boy who made it. I was a Professor at Harvard and everybody stood around in awe and listened to my every word, and all I felt was that horror that I knew inside that I didn't know. Of course, it was all such beautiful, gentle horror, because there was so much reward involved.

I had an empire in a place called Center for Research in Personality: a corner office in a building I'd helped design, with two secretaries and many graduate and undergraduate research assistants. I had done all this in about three years. I was really driven. Until you know a good, Jewish middle-class, upwardly mobile, anxiety-ridden neurotic, you haven't met a real achiever!

My Judaism was a political Judaism. I came out of a tradition of folk religion—the spirit escaped me somehow, although we did all the Yom Kippur and Passover Services. But Dad was on the Board of Trustees that hired and fired Rabbis, so how could I get into a feeling with a spiritual leader if my father was hiring and firing these guys.

Down the hall from my big empire, there was a little office. It had been a closet and they needed an extra office, so they cleared out the closet and put a desk in there and in that closet was Timothy Leary. He had been bicycling around Italy, bouncing checks, and David McClelland found him and brought him back as a creative gift to Western science. Tim and I became drinking buddies together. Then we started to teach courses together, such as the first year clinical course—practicum—on "Existential Transactional Behavior Change."

The more time I spent with Tim, the more I realized he had an absolutely extraordinary intellect. He really knew a lot. I found him extremely stimulating, and the students found him exciting to be around because of his openness to new ideas and his willingness to take wild risks in thinking.

One night when we were drinking together, we plotted a trip across North and South America, and when I said I flew a plane, he said, "Great, we'll fly in your plane."

And I said, "Wonderful," and neglected to tell him that I had only a student license.

So I secretly set about getting a license in order to meet him on August 1st in Cuernavaca, Mexico, where he was summering. There we would start our journey.

At that time I was a consultant for a School Mathematics Study Group, a mathematics program in Education at Stanford. I got my license and an airplane on the same day and flew to Mexico the next day in a death-defying leap. When I got there, I found that Timothy had done some other type of flying, just about the week before. Frank Baron, who was a psychologist at Cal, an old friend of Tim's, had introduced him to an anthropologist in Mexico and they had come to know about the Tionanactyl, the flesh of the Gods, the Magic Mushrooms of Mexico, which one obtained from Crazy Juanna, a woman up in the mountains who ate the mushrooms all the time. Contact was made with her and the mushrooms were obtained.

Tim had eaten nine of these mushrooms—so many male and so many female mushrooms—with a group of others around a swimming pool and had had a profound experience. He said, "I learned more in the six or seven hours of this experience than I had learned in all my years as a psychologist."

That is a strong statement!

When I arrived in Cuernavaca, the mushrooms were all gone, and so was the zeal to go on a trip across South America, because what was the sense in doing external journeying when obviously what Timothy had been looking for was inside his own head.

So I hung out in Tepetzlan with David McClelland and his family and in Cuernavaca with Tim and his entourage, and then flew back to the United States with Tim and Jackie, his son, and an iguana.

And I went to be a visiting professor at Cal and Tim went back to Harvard. And by the time I got back, Timothy had a large psychedelic project going.

He had consulted with Aldous Huxley, who was then visiting at M.I.T., and Aldous and Tim and a number of graduate students had contacted Sandoz, who produced a synthetic of the magic mushrooms called psylocybin, and they had gotten a test batch of this and were busy taking it and administering it. When I got back to Cambridge in the spring, I was invited to share in this bounty.

TURNING ON

The night that was chosen turned out to be the night of the biggest snowstorm of the year, and it was to be at Tim's home in Newton, a few blocks from the home of my parents where I had been visiting for dinner. I plowed through the snow, came in, and we sat around the kitchen table and there were about three or four of us and we passed the bottle of pills and I took my 10 milligrams. That was my preparation and my set and setting, but beyond that I trusted Timothy. I had seen that Timothy had had a profound experience and he was somebody with an intellect that I understood. I knew that he was not interpersonally destructive—he might be destructive of institutions, but not of individuals. He was a very loving person.

We took a very small dosage (later we were using five or ten times as much) and the first part of the experience was comparable to a strong pot-high, I'd say. A little more dramatic, a little more intense. Clearly though something happened.

During the first part of this experience with psylocybin, we got into a very low-level tragicomedy type thing. Tim's son's dog had been running in the snow and upon entering the warm kitchen lay gasping and panting. To our timeless minds, his struggle for breath continued too long and we thought he was about to expire. What could we do? We could hardly carry the dog through a blizzard in the early Sunday morning to the vet's, some four miles away, especially since we were all very high and thus not sure about the dog's state. It seemed our concern mounted and the dog passed into a nearby room where it appeared to collapse. We finally decided the only path was to summon 11-year-old Jackie from the Late TV show upstairs. Since he wasn't under a chemical influence, we would watch his interaction with the dog, rather than frighten him with our own suspicions.

Jackie was not pleased at being disturbed by us (merely to find out what he was watching on TV), but the problem was quickly solved by the dog, who, upon hearing Jackie's voice, leapt back to life, ready to play.

Now a few hours later I had gone off by myself to reflect upon these new feelings and senses. A deep calm pervaded my being.

The rug crawled and the pictures smiled, all of which delighted me. Then I saw a figure standing about eight feet away, where a moment before there had been none. I peered into the semi-darkness and recognized none other than myself, in cap and gown and hood, as a professor. It was as if that part of me, which was Harvard professor, had separated or disassociated itself from me.

"How interesting . . . an external hallucination," I thought. "Well, I worked hard to get that status but I don't really need it." Again I settled back into the cushions, separate now from my professorness, but at that moment the figure changed. Again I leaned forward straining to see. "Ah, me again." But now it was that aspect of me who was a social cosmopolite. "Okay, so that goes, too," I thought. Again and again the figure changed and I recognized over there all the different aspects I knew to be me . . . cellist, pilot, lover, and so on. With each new presentation, I again and again reassured myself that I didn't need that anyway.

Then I saw the figure become that in me which was Richard Alpert-ness, that is, my basic identity that had always been Richard. I associated the name with myself and my parents called me Richard: "Richard, you're a bad boy." So Richard has badness. Then "Richard, aren't you beautiful!" Then Richard has beauty. Thus develop all these aspects of self.

Sweat broke out on my forehead. I wasn't at all sure I could do without being Richard Alpert. Did that mean I'd have amnesia? Was that what this drug was going to do to me? Would it be permanent? Should I call Tim? Oh, what the hell—so I'll give up being Richard Alpert. I can always get a new social identity. At least I have my body . . . But I spoke too soon.

As I looked down at my legs for reassurance, I could see nothing below the kneecaps, and slowly, now to my horror, I saw the progressive disappearance of limbs and then torso, until all I could see with my eyes open was the couch on which I had sat. A scream formed in my throat. I felt that I must be dying, since there was nothing in my universe that led me to believe in life after leaving the body.

Doing without professorness or loverness, or even Richard Alpertness, okay, but I did NEED the body.

The panic mounted, adrenalin shot through my system—my mouth became dry, but along with this, a voice sounded inside—

inside what, I don't know—an intimate voice asked very quietly, and rather jocularly, it seemed to me, considering how distraught I was, ". . . but who's minding the store?"

When I could finally focus on the question, I realized that although everything by which I knew myself, even my body and this life itself, was gone, still I was fully aware! Not only that, but this aware "I" was watching the entire drama, including the panic, with calm compassion.

Instantly, with this recognition, I felt a new kind of calmness—one of a profundity never experienced before. I had just found that "I," that scanning device—that point—that essence—that place beyond. A place where "I" existed independent of social and physical identity. That which was I was beyond Life and Death. And something else—that "I" Knew—it really Knew. It was wise, rather than just knowledgeable. It was a voice inside that spoke truth. I recognized it, was one with it, and felt as if my entire life of looking to the outside world for reassurance—David Reisman's other-directed being, was over. Now I need only look within to that place where I Knew.

Fear had turned to exaltation. I ran out into the snow, laughing as the huge flakes swirled about me. In a moment the house was lost from view, but it was all right because inside I Knew.

Around five in the morning I walked back, plowing through the snow to my parents' home, and I thought, "Wouldn't it be nice; I'll shovel the walk—young tribal buck shovels the walk." So I started to shovel the walk and my parents' faces appeared at the upstairs window.

"Come to bed, you idiot. Nobody shovels snow at five in the morning."

And I looked up at them and I heard the external voice I had been listening to for 30 years, and inside me, something said, "It's all right to shovel snow and it's all right to be happy."

And I looked up at them and I laughed and did a jig and went back to shoveling snow. And they closed the windows and then I looked up and inside they were smiling too. That was my first experience of giving a contact high!

But also, you can see in that moment in the early morning the seeds of the breakaway. The seeds of the ability to be able to confront, and even disagree with, an existing institution and know and trust that inside place that says it's all right. It's something I could never have done without anxiety until that moment— until that day.

Now I thought at that moment, "Wow, I've got it made. I'm just a new beautiful being—I'm just an inner self—all I'll ever need to do is look inside and I'll know what to do and I can always trust it, and here I'll be forever."

But two or three days later I was talking about the whole thing in the past tense. I was talking about how I "experienced" this thing, because I was back being that anxiety-neurotic, in a slightly milder form, but still, my old personality was sneaking back up on me.

Well, the next day I had to give my lecture in Social Relations 143, Human Motivation, and it presented me with a bit of a problem because I couldn't find anywhere in the psychology teachings anything about what had happened to me the night before.

Now, what we did at first at Harvard was to tell all of our colleagues about this extraordinary thing that was happening to us, and they all shared our delight, as any scientists do when a fellow scientist finds a new avenue into the unknown. And so the first week they listened with delight. And then at the end of the first week we all went back into our experimental cell—the living room by the fire—and opened the bottle again and took some more psylocybin to chart this course further. And the next week we had shared a deeper experience and we came back and we spoke to our colleagues. Now they couldn't hear us quite as well. It wasn't that they were changing, it was that we were. We were developing a language among ourselves. If Admiral Byrd and an exploratory party are going deeper and deeper into the polar region, the things they think about and are concerned about and are interested in become less and less relevant to somebody living in New York City. This was our situation.

We had the choice along the way of stopping to bring everybody else along, or going on. But these experiences quickly became indescribable. I'd get to a point with my colleagues when I couldn't explain any further, because it came down to "To him who has had the experience no explanation is necessary; to him who has not, none is possible." And we would feel this frustration when they'd say, "It sounds very interesting." And we'd say,

"In order to know, you've got to try it." And they'd say, "No, that isn't scientific. It isn't appropriate to test your own product. You do it first on animals and then on graduate students . . ."

So then the next week we'd sit around on Saturday night and say, "What should we do?" and we all knew what we were going to do, and we would "turn on." We were exploring this inner realm of consciousness that we had been theorizing about all these years and suddenly we were traveling in and through and around it. At the same time, of course, by the second week, it was as though we had just been traveling in Tibet, and now, back in the school lunchroom, who do we hang out with? We hang out with the guy with whom we went to Tibet, because we shared this very powerful experience.

Pretty soon there were five or six of us and we were hanging out together and our colleagues said, "Ah ha, a cult is forming," which was true for us. A cult is a shared system of belief.

As to how to work with this stuff, Tim said, "We don't know what this is about yet and there are many models, but it would be best not to impose a model too soon, because a model that exists in the West for these states is pathological, and the model that exists in the primitive cultures is mystical and religious, and it's better we keep wide open . . ."

So we did what would be called a naturalistic study: We gave the psylocybin to maybe 200 people who were physically healthy enough and we said, "You take it under any conditions you want and all you've got to do is answer this questionnaire at the end, so we'll know what happened. You do it however you want to."

So we gave it to jazz musicians and physicists and philosophers and ministers and junkies and graduate students and social scientists. And at the end, we had these 200 protocols and the first analysis we did showed up very clearly that the reactions were a function of set and setting—a function of their expectations of what was going to happen and the environment in which they took the drug. If they had it in a very paranoid environment and they were expecting to have excitement, they tended to have paranoid excitement. All it did was intensify one's expectations.

However, the data also showed something else. Out of these first few hundred, you could see that there was some kind of a step ladder of experience. There was a kind of probablistic hierarchy of experience, so that the most likely experience everybody had was a heightened sensitivity to all of their five senses and speeding up of the thought process.

Then the next type of experience that people would frequently report was an interpersonal shift of figure and ground, where they would look at another person and see the way in which the other person was similar, rather than different from themselves. And it was as if the whole Western mind-training of individual differences had been made background instead of figure, so that you'd look at another human being and say, "Here we are." You'd see differences more as clothing, rather than as core stuff. This was a profound perceptual experience for many people.

For example, we had a Negro psychiatrist, Madison Presnell, working with us, and I had been trained to be a very liberal person about Negroes, which meant that you didn't have feelings. It was a phony kind of liberal thing. I went out of my way to be liberal. You know, that very self-conscious kind of equality. And Madison and I turned on together, and I looked at Madison and there we were, the same human beings. It was just that he was wearing that skin and I was wearing this skin. And it was no more or less than that. It was that shirt and this shirt and it had no more relevance than that. And I looked at that and suddenly there we were, whereas before I had been so busy with my superliberal reaction to color of skin, that I couldn't relax enough to share this unitive place.

Then there was a still less frequent type of experience reported: a oneness, in which subjects would say,

". . . I remember being in a dark room with another person and one of us spoke and one of us said, 'Who spoke, you or me?' It wasn't clear from who's mouth the words came."

And then there was a still less frequent experience where one looked at somebody and he started to see the other person as cellular structure or patterns of energy, rather than as a person.

And finally, a few subjects (maybe 3% or something like that) transcended all form and saw just pure energy—a homogeneous field. It has been called the White Light.

There was research being done by the group with prisoners, to try to change their rate of recidivism. And there were attempts with ministers: A study was run by Walter Pankhe and a group of the research community on Good Friday in Boston University chapel, with 20 ministers—advanced minister-training students—

ten received psylocybin and ten a placebo. It was a double-blind study on Good Friday in a chapel. It was absurd, because a double-blind study was absurd. Everybody knew something was happening. It was as if you were proving the obvious. Somebody who had taken the placebo which made their skin crawl reacted by saying, "Well, maybe something's happening," and then another minister would stagger into the room and say, "I see God! I see God!" and it was all too obvious in a short time who had had the psylocybin.

Now my own experiences were horrible and beautiful, and I kept working in different environments and settings, and, whenever anybody that I trusted brought along some new chemical, I would open my mouth and off I'd go. I was interested in doing this exploring.

For example, at one point I had been in the meditation room in the community house we had in Newton, and I was for four hours in a state of total homogeneous light, bliss, and then I recall starting to "come down" and this huge red wave rolled in across the room. It looked like a cross between a William Blake (that picture of the wave) sketch and a Hieronymous Bosch painting, and it was all my identities, all rolling in over me. I remember holding up my hand and saying, "NO, NO, I don't want to go back." It was like this heavy burden I was going to take on myself. And I realized I didn't have the key—I didn't know the magic words, like "Abracadabra" or "Hocus Pocus" or whatever it was going to be that would stop that wave, and it rolled in over me and then . . . "Oh, here I am again—Richard Alpert—what a drag!"

COMING DOWN

In these few years we had gotten over the feeling that one experience was going to make you enlightened forever. We saw that it wasn't going to be that simple.

And for five years I dealt with the matter of "coming down." The coming down matter is what led me to the next chapter of this drama. Because after six years I realized that no matter how ingenious my experimental designs were and how high I got, I came down.

At one point I took five people and we locked ourselves in a building for three weeks and we took 400 micrograms of LSD every four hours. That is 2400 micrograms of LSD a day, which sounds fancy, but after your first dose you build a tolerance; there's a refractory period. We finally were just drinking out of the bottle because it didn't seem to matter anymore. We'd just stay at a plateau. We were very high. What happened in those three weeks in that house, no one would ever believe, including us. And at the end of the three weeks we walked out of the house, and within a few days we came down!

And it was a terribly frustrating experience, as if you came into the kingdom of heaven and you saw how it all was and you felt these new states of awareness, and then you got cast out again and after two or 300 times of this began to feel an extraordinary kind of depression set in—a very gentle depression that whatever I knew still wasn't enough!

ENVIRONMENTAL CHANGES

Now at the same moment there were obvious changes going on, because that checking back, over and over again, to the inner place inside myself made me less and less attached to reassurance from the environment that I was all right. So I remember the moment when I was thrown out of Harvard . . .

There was a press conference and all of the reporters looked at me as if I was a prizefighter who had just lost a major fight and was headed for oblivion, that kind of look you have for losers—real losers! And they stood there looking at me that way. Everybody was looking at me that way, and inside I felt, "What I'm doing is all right."

Everybody—parents, colleagues, public—saw it as a horrible thing; I thought inside, "I must really be crazy now—because craziness is where everybody agrees about something—except you!" And yet I felt saner than I had ever felt, so I knew this was a new kind of craziness or perhaps a new kind of saneness. But the thing was, I always seemed to be able to skirt the line: to keep it together. I didn't ever DO anything quite crazy enough.

I was the guy that people would come to and say, "Look, would you calm Tim Leary—he's too far out. If you'll calm him and protect him" and so on. And I'd say, "I'll help him with pleasure 'cause he's that great a being." And I'd help raise money and run the kitchen and clean the house and raise the children . . .

Well, we realized then that what we needed to do was to create certain kinds of environments which would allow a person, after being into another state of consciousness, to retain a certain kind of environmental support for new ways of looking at himself. After all, if you see yourself as God and then you come back from this state and somebody says, "Hey, Sam, empty the garbage!," it catches you back into the model of "I'm Sam who empties the garbage." You can't maintain these new kinds of structures. It takes a while to realize that God can empty garbage.

Now in 1962 or 63, Tim and Ralph Metzer with him (I was just given author's credit because I took care of the kitchen) had come across the Tibetan Book of the Dead, which was a very close description of a number of these experiences. This book was 2500 years old, at least, and it had been used all those years for preparing Tibetan Lamas to die and be reincarnated. And when we opened it, we would find descriptions of the 49 days after death, before rebirth, that were perfect descriptions of sessions we were having with psychedelics.

How could this be? The parallel was so close. Tim rewrote the book as a manual called "The Psychedelic Experience," a manual for psychological death and rebirth, arguing that this was really a metaphor about psychological death and rebirth and not necessarily physical death and reincarnation.

Tim had gone to India, Ralph had gone to India, Allen Ginsberg had gone to India. I checked with everybody when they came back. There was Tim, being Tim, and there was Ralph, being Ralph, and there was Allen, being Allen—and I realized that they had all had lovely experiences and seen a beautiful country and so on, but they were not finished looking for something.

And by 1966–67, I was in the same predicament. I was aware that I didn't know enough to maintain these states of consciousness. And I was aware that nobody else around me seemed to know enough either. I checked with everybody I thought might know, and nobody seemed to know.

So I wasn't very optimistic about India or psychedelics. By 1967 I had shot my load! I had no more job as a psychologist in a respectable establishment, and I realized that we didn't know enough about psychedelics to use them profitably.

But at that time I was still lecturing around the country on psychedelics to such diverse groups as the Food and Drug Administration and the Hell's Angels.

Then along came a very lovely guy whom I had guided through some psychedelic sessions—an interesting guy who had gone to the University of Chicago in his early teens and had taught seminars in Chinese Economics, had started a company called Basic Systems, which had been sold to Xerox—and now he had retired. He was about 35 and he had retired and taken his five million dollars or whatever he made, and was now becoming a Buddhist. He wanted to make a journey to the East to look for holy men and he invited me to go along. He had a Land Rover imported into Teheran and this was my way out. What else was I going to do at this point?

So I left to go to India, and I took a bottle of LSD with me with the idea that I'd meet holy men along the way and I'd give them LSD and they'd tell me what LSD is. Maybe I'd learn the missing clue.

We started out from Teheran and for the next three months we had lovely guides and a most beautiful time, and we scored great hashish in Afghanistan, and at the end of three months I had seen the inside of the Land Rover, I had 1300 slides, many tape recordings of Indian music; I had drunk much bottled water, eaten many canned goods: I was a westerner traveling in India. That's what was happening to me when I got to Nepal.

We had done it all. We had gone to see the Dalai Lama, and we had gone on horseback up to Amanath Cave up in Kashmir; we had visited Benares, and finally we ended up in Katmandu, Nepal. I started to get extremely, extremely depressed. I'm sure part of it was due to the hashish. But also, part of it was because I didn't see what to do next.

I had done everything I thought I could do, and nothing new had happened. It was turning out to be just another trip. The despair got very heavy. We didn't know enough and I couldn't figure out how to socialize this thing about the new states of consciousness. And I didn't know what to do next. It wasn't like I didn't have LSD. I had plenty of LSD, but why take it? I knew what it was going to do, what it was going to tell me. It was going to show me that garden again and then I was going to be cast out, and that was it. And I never could quite stay. I was addicted to the experience at first, and then I even got tired of that. And the despair was extremely intense at that point.

We were sitting in a hippie restaurant, called the Blue Tibetan, and I was talking to some French hippies . . .

I had given LSD to a number of pundits around India and some reasonably pure men:

An old Buddhist Lama said, "It gave me a headache."

Somebody else said, "It's good, but not as good as meditation."

Somebody else said, "Where can I get more?"

And I got the same range of responses I'd get in America. I didn't get any great pearl of wisdom which would make me exclaim, "Oh, that's what it is—I was waiting for something that was going to do that thing!"

So I finally figured, "Well, it's not going to happen." We were about to go on to Japan, and I was pretty depressed because we were starting the return now and what was I returning to? What should I do now?

I decided I was going to come back and become a chauffeur. I wanted to be a servant and let somebody else program my consciousness. I could read holy books while I'd wait for whoever it was I was waiting for while they were at Bergdorf Goodman's, and I'd just change my whole style of life around. I could just get out of the whole drama of having to engineer my own ship for a while. This is a funny foreshadowing, as you'll see.

The despair was extremely intense at that point. I was really quite sad.

BHAGWAN DASS

I was in the Blue Tibetan with my friend and these other people, and in walked this very extraordinary guy, at least extraordinary with regard to his height. He was 6'7" and he had long blonde hair and a long blonde beard. He was a Westerner, an American, and was wearing holy clothes—a dhoti (a cloth Indian men wear instead of pants) and so on, and when he entered, he came directly over to our table and sat down.

Now, up until then, I had found this interesting thing that I

don't think I could have labeled until that moment. Once, when
I had met Gesha Wangyal at Freehold, N.J., I knew I was meeting a being who "Knew," but I couldn't get to it because I wasn't
ready, somehow. We were very close—we loved each other extraordinarily, but I hadn't been able to really absorb whatever I
needed to absorb. Now here was this young fellow and, again, I
had the feeling I had met somebody who "Knew."

I don't know how to describe this to you, except that I was
deep in my despair; I had gone through game, after game, after
game, first being a professor at Harvard, then being a psychedelic
spokesman, and still people were constantly looking into my eyes,
like "Do you know?" Just that subtle little look, and I was constantly looking into their eyes—"Do you know?" And there we
were, "Do you?" "Do you?" "Maybe he . . ." "Do you . . . ?"
And there was always that feeling that everybody was very close
and we all knew we knew, but nobody quite knew. I don't know
how to describe it, other than that.

And I met this guy and there was no doubt in my mind. It was
just like meeting a rock. It was just solid, all the way through.
Everywhere I pressed, there he was!

We were staying in a hotel owned by the King or the Prince
or something, because we were going first class, so we spirited
this fellow up to our suite in the Sewalti Hotel and for five days
we had a continuing seminar. We had this extraordinarily beautiful Indian sculptor, Harish Johari, who was our guide and friend.
Harish, this fellow, Bhagwan Dass, and David and I sat there
and, for five days high on Peach Melbas and hashish and mesca-
line, we had a seminar with Alexandra David Neehl's books and
Sir John Woodroffe's *Serpent Power*, and so on. At the end of
five days, I was still absolutely staggered by this guy. He had
started to teach me some mantras and working with beads. When
it came time to leave, to go to Japan, I had the choice of going
on to Japan on my first class route, or going off with this guy,
back into India on a temple pilgrimage. He had no money and
I had no money, and it was going to change my style of life con-
siderably. I thought, "Well, look, I came to India to find something and I still think this guy knows—I'm going to follow him."

But there was also the counter thought. "How absurd—who's
writing this bizarre script? Here I am—I've come half-way around

the world and I'm going to follow, through India, a 23-year-old guy from Laguna Beach, California."

I said to Harish and to David, "Do you think I'm making a mistake?" And Harish said, "No, he is a very high guy." And so I started to follow him—literally follow him.

Now, I'm suddenly barefoot. He has said, "You're not going to wear shoes, are you?" That sort of thing. And I've got a shoulder bag and my dhoti and blisters on my feet and dysentery, the likes of which you can't imagine, and all he says is, "Well, fast for a few days."

He's very compassionate, but no pity.

And we're sleeping on the ground, or on these wooden tables that you get when you stop at monasteries, and my hip bones ache. I go through an extraordinary physical breakdown, become very childlike, and he takes care of me. And we start to travel through temples—to Baneshwar and Konarak and so on.

I see that he's very powerful, so extraordinarily powerful—he's got an ectara, a one-stringed instrument, and I've got a little Tibetan drum, and we go around to the villages and people rush out and they touch our feet because we're holy men, which is embarrassing to me because I'm not a holy man—I'm obviously who I am—a sort of overage hippie, Western explorer—and I feel very embarrassed when they do that and they give us food. And he plays and sings and the Hindu people love him and revere him. And he's giving away all my money . . .

But I'm clinging tight to my passport and my return ticket to America, and a traveler's check that I'll need to get me to Delhi. Those things I'm going to hold on to. And my bottle of LSD, in case I should find something interesting.

And during these travels he's starting to train me in a most interesting way. We'd be sitting somewhere and I'd say,

"Did I ever tell you about the time that Tim and I . . ."

And he'd say, "Don't think about the past. Just be here now." Silence.

And I'd say, "How long do you think we're going to be on this trip?"

And he'd say, "Don't think about the future. Just be here now."

I'd say, "You know, I really feel crumby, my hips are hurting . . ."

"Emotions are like waves. Watch them disappear in the distance on the vast calm ocean."

He had just sort of wiped out my whole game. That was it— that was my whole trip—emotions, and past experiences, and future plans. I was, after all, a great story teller.

So we were silent. There was nothing to say.

He'd say, "You eat this" or, "Now you sleep here." And all the rest of the time we sang holy songs. That was all there was to do.

Or he would teach me Asanas—Hatha Yoga postures.

But there was no conversation. I didn't know anything about his life. He didn't know anything about my life. He wasn't the least bit interested in all of the extraordinary dramas that I had collected . . . He was the first person I couldn't seduce into being interested in all this. He just didn't care.

And yet, I never felt so profound an intimacy with another being. It was as if he were inside of my heart. And what started to blow my mind was that everywhere we went, he was at home.

If we went to a Thereavaden Buddhist monastery, he would be welcomed and suddenly he would be called Dharma Sara, a Southern Buddhist name, and some piece of clothing he wore, I suddenly saw, was also worn by all the other monks and I realized that he was an initiate in that scene, and they'd welcome him and he'd be in the inner temple and he knew all the chants and he was doing them.

We'd come across some Shavites, followers of Shiva, or some of the Swamis, and I suddenly realized that he was one of them. On his forehead would be the appropriate tilik, or mark, and he would be doing their chanting.

We'd meet Kargyupa lamas from Tibet and they would all welcome him as a brother, and he knew all their stuff. He had been in India for five years, and he was so high that everybody just welcomed him, feeling "he's obviously one of us."

I couldn't figure out what his scene was. All I personally felt was this tremendous pull toward Buddhism because Hinduism always seemed a little gauche—the paintings were a little too gross—the colors were bizarre and the whole thing was too melodramatic and too much emotion. I was pulling toward that clean, crystal-clear simplicity of the Southern Buddhists or the Zen Buddhists.

After about three months, I had a visa problem and we went

to Delhi, and I was still quite unsure of my new role as a holy man and so, when I got to Delhi, I took $4.00 out of my little traveler's check and bought a pair of pants and a shirt and a tie and took my horn-rimmed glasses out of my shoulder bag and stuck them back on and I became again Dr. Alpert, to go to the visa office. Dr. Alpert, who had a grant from the Folk Art Museum of New Mexico for collecting musical instruments, and I did my whole thing.

I kept my beads in my pocket. Because I didn't feel valid in this other role. And then the minute I got my visa fixed, he had to have his annual visa worked over and he had to go to a town nearby, which we went to, and we were welcomed at this big estate and given a holy man's house, and food brought to us, and he said, "You sit here. I'm going to see about my visa."

He told me just what to do. I was just like a baby. "Eat this." "Sit here." "Do this." And I just gave up. He knew. Do you know? I'll follow you.

He spoke Hindi fluently. My Hindi was very faltering. So he could handle it all.

We had spent a few weeks in a Chinese Buddhist monastery in Sarnath, which was extraordinarily powerful and beautiful, and something was happening to me but I couldn't grasp the total nature of it at all.

There was a strange thing about him. At night he didn't seem to sleep like I did. That is, any time I'd wake up at night, I'd look over and he would be sitting in the lotus position. And sometimes I'd make believe I was asleep and then open sort of a half-eye to see if he wasn't cheating—maybe he was sleeping Now—but he was always in the lotus posture.

Sometimes I'd see him lie down, but I would say that, 80% of the time when I would be sleeping heavily, he would be sitting in some state or other which he'd never describe to me. But he was not in personal contact—I mean, there was no wave or moving around, or nothing seemed to happen to him.

The night at that estate, I went out—I had to go to the bathroom and I went out under the stars and the following event happened . . .

The previous January 20th, at Boston in the Peter Bent Brigham Hospital, my mother had died of a spleen illness—the bone marrow stopped producing blood and the spleen took over and grew very large and they removed it and then she died. It had been a long illness and I had been with her through the week prior to her death and through it we had become extremely close. We had transcended mother-child and personalities and we had come into true contact. I spent days in the hospital just meditating. And I felt no loss when she died. Instead there was a tremendous continuing contact with her. And in fact, when I had been in Nepal, I had had a vision of her one night when I was going to bed. I saw her up on the ceiling and I was wondering whether to go to India or go on to Japan and she had a look that was the look of "You damn fool—you're always getting into hot water, but go ahead, and I think that's great." She looked peeved-pleased. It was like there were two beings in my mother. She was a middle-class woman from Boston, who wanted me to be absolutely responsible in the most culturally acceptable fashion, and then there was this swinger underneath—this spiritual being underneath who said, "—go, baby." And I felt these two beings in that look which supported my going back into India.

This night I'm under the stars, and I hadn't thought about her at all since that time. I'm under the stars, urinating, and I look up and the stars are very close because it's very dark and I suddenly experience a presence of mother, and I'm thinking about her—not about how she died or anything about that. I just feel her presence. It's very, very powerful. And I feel great love for her and then I go back to bed.

Of course, Bhagwan Dass is not the least interested in any of my life, so he'd be the last person I'd talk to about my thoughts or visions.

The next morning he says, "We've got to go to the mountains. I've got a visa problem. We've got to go see my Guru."

Now the term "Guru" had meant for me, in the West, a sort of high-grade teacher. There was a *Life* article about Allen Ginsberg—"Guru goes to Kansas"—and Allen was embarrassed and said, "I'm not really a Guru." And I didn't know what a Guru really was . . .

Bhagwan Dass also said we were going to borrow the Land Rover, which had been left with this sculptor, to go to the mountains. And I said, I didn't want to borrow the Land Rover. I'd just gotten out of that horrible blue box and I didn't want to get back into it, and I didn't want the responsibility. David had left it with this Indian sculptor and he wouldn't want to loan it to us anyway. I got very sulky. I didn't want to go see a guru—and suddenly I wanted to go back to America in the worst way.

I thought, "What am I doing? I'm following this kid and all he is . . ." But he says, "We've got to do this," and so we go to the town where the sculptor lives and within half an hour the sculptor says, "You have to go see your Guru? Take the Land Rover!"

Well, that's interesting.

We're in the Land Rover and he won't let me drive. So I'm sitting there sulking. He won't let me drive and we are in the Land Rover which I don't want to have and I'm now really in a bad mood. I've stopped smoking hashish a few days before because I'm having all kinds of reactions to it, and so I'm just in a very, very uptight, negative, paranoid state and all I want to do is go back to America, and suddenly I'm following this young kid who wants to drive and all he wanted me for was to get the Land Rover and now the whole paranoid con world fills my head. I'm full of it.

We go about 80 or 100 miles and we come to a tiny temple by the side of the road in the foothills of the Himalayas. We're stopping, and I think we're stopping because a truck's coming by, but when we stop, people surround the car, which they generally do, but they welcome him and he jumps out. And I can tell something's going to happen because, as we go up into the hills, he's starting to cry.

We're singing songs and tears are streaming down his face, and I know something's going on, but I don't know what.

We stop at this temple and he asks where the guru is and they point up on a hill, and he goes running up this hill and they're all following him, so delighted to see him. They all love him so much.

I get out of the car. Now I'm additionally bugged because everybody's ignoring me. And I'm following him and he's way ahead of me and I'm running after him barefoot up this rocky path and I'm stumbling—by now my feet are very tough—but still his legs are very long, and I'm running and people are ignoring me and I'm very bugged and I don't want to see the guru anyway and what the hell—

We go around this hill so that we come to a field which does not face on the road. It's facing into a valley and there's a little man in his 60's or 70's sitting with a blanket around him. And around him are eight or nine Hindu people and it's a beautiful tableau—clouds, beautiful green valley, lovely, lovely place—the foothills of the Himalayas.

And this fellow, Bhagwan Dass, comes up, runs to this man and throws himself on the ground, full-face doing "dunda pranam," and he's stretched out so his face is down on the ground, full-length and his hands are touching the feet of this man, who is sitting cross-legged. And he's crying and the man is patting him on the head and I don't know what's happening.

I'm standing on the side and thinking, "I'm not going to touch his feet. I don't have to. I'm not required to do that." And every now and then this man looks up at me and he twinkles a little. But I'm so uptight that I couldn't care less. Twinkle away, man!

Then he looks up at me—he speaks in Hindi, of which I understand maybe half, but there is a fellow who's translating all the time, who hangs out with him, and the Guru says to Bhagwan Dass, "You have a picture of me?"

Bhagwan Dass nods, "Yes."

"Give it to him," says the man, pointing at me.

"That's very nice," I think, "giving me a picture of himself," and I smile and nod appreciatively. But I'm still not going to touch his feet!

Then he says, "You came in a big car?" Of course that's the one thing I'm really uptight about.

"Yeah."

So he looks at me and he smiles and says, "You give it to me?"

I started to say, "Wha . . ." and Bhagwan Dass looks up—he's lying there—and he says, "Maharaji (meaning "great king"), if you want it you can have it—it's yours."

And I said, "No—now wait a minute—you can't give away David's car like that. That isn't our car . . . ," and this old man is laughing. In fact, everyone is laughing . . . except me.

Then he says, "You made much money in America?"

"Ah, at last he's feeding my ego," I think.

So I flick through all of my years as a professor and years as a smuggler and all my different dramas in my mind and I said, "Yeah."

"How much you make?"

"Well," I said, "at one time"—and I sort of upped the figure a bit, you know, my ego—"$25,000."

So they all converted that into rupees, which was practically half the economic base of India, and everybody was terribly awed by this figure, which was complete bragging on my part. It was phony —I never made $25,000. And he laughed again. And he said,

"You'll buy a car like that for me?"

And I remember what went through my mind. I had come out of a family of fund-raisers for the United Jewish Appeal, Brandeis, and Einstein Medical School, and I had never seen hustling like this. He doesn't even know my name and already he wants a $7,000 vehicle.

And I said, "Well, maybe . . ." The whole thing was freaking me so much.

And he said, "Take them away and give them food." So we were taken and given food—magnificent food—we were together still, and saddhus brought us beautiful food and then we were told to rest. Some time later we were back with the Maharaji and he said to me, "Come here. Sit." So I sat down and he looked at me and he said,

"You were out under the stars last night."

"Um-hum."

"You were thinking about your mother."

"Yes." ("Wow," I thought, "that's pretty good. I never mentioned that to anybody.")

"She died last year."

"Um-hum."

"She got very big in the stomach before she died."

. . . Pause . . . "Yes."

He leaned back and closed his eyes and said, "Spleen. She died of spleen."

Well, what happened to me at that moment, I can't really put into words. He looked at me in a certain way at that moment, and two things happened—it seemed simultaneous. They do not seem like cause and effect.

The first thing that happened was that my mind raced faster and faster to try to get leverage—to get a hold on what he had just done. I went through every super CIA paranoia I've ever had:

"Who is he?" "Who does he represent?"

"Where's the button he pushes where the file appears?" and "Why have they brought me here?"

None of it would jell.

It was just too impossible that this could have happened this way. The guy I was with didn't know all that stuff, and I was a tourist in a car, and the whole thing was just too far out. My mind went faster and faster and faster.

Up until then I had two categories for "psychic experience." One was "they happened to somebody else and they haven't happened to me, and they were terribly interesting and we certainly had to keep an open mind about it." That was my social science approach. The other one was, "well, man, I'm high on LSD. Who knows how it really is? After all, under the influence of a chemical, how do I know I'm not creating the whole thing?" Because, in fact, I had taken certain chemicals where I experienced the creation of total realities. The greatest example I have of this came about through a drug called JB 318, which I took in a room at Millbrook. I was sitting on the third floor and it seemed like nothing was happening at all. And into the room walked a girl from the community with a pitcher of lemonade and she said, would I like some lemonade, and I said that would be great, and she poured the lemonade, and she poured it and she kept pouring and the lemonade went over the side of the glass and fell to the floor and it went across the floor and up the wall and over the ceiling and down the wall and under my pants which got wet and it came back up into the glass—and when it touched the glass the glass disappeared and the lemonade disappeared and the wetness in my pants disappeared and the girl disappeared and I turned around to Ralph Metzner and I said,

"Ralph, the most extraordinary thing happened to me," and Ralph disappeared!

I was afraid to do anything but just sit. Whatever this is, it's not nothing. Just sit. Don't move, just sit!

So I had had experiences where I had seen myself completely create whole environments under psychedelics, and therefore I wasn't eager to interpret these things very quickly, because I, the observer, was, at those times, under the influence of the psychedelics.

But neither of these categories applied in this situation, and my mind went faster and faster and then I felt like what happens when a computer is fed an insoluble problem; the bell rings and the red light goes on and the machine stops. And my mind just gave up. It burned out its circuitry . . . its zeal to have an explanation. I needed something to get closure at the rational level and there wasn't anything. There just wasn't a place I could hide in my head about this.

And at the same moment, I felt this extremely violent pain in my chest and a tremendous wrenching feeling and I started to cry. And I cried and I cried and I cried. And I wasn't happy and I wasn't sad. It was not that kind of crying. The only thing I could say was it felt like I was home. Like the journey was over. Like I had finished.

Well, I cried, and they finally sort of spooned me up and took me to a temple about twelve miles away to stay overnight. That night I was very confused. A great feeling of lightness and confusion.

At one point in the evening I was looking in my shoulder bag and came across the bottle of LSD.

"Wow! I've finally met a guy who is going to Know! He will definitely know what LSD is. I'll have to ask him. That's what I'll do. I'll ask him." Then I forgot about it.

The next morning, at eight o'clock a messenger comes. "Maharaji wants to see you immediately." We went in the Land Rover the twelve miles to the other temple.

And I take one look at him, and it's like looking at the sun. I suddenly feel all warm. When I'm approaching him, he yells out at me, "Have you got a question?"

And he's very impatient with all of this nonsense, and he says, "Where's the medicine?"

I got a translation of this. He said medicine. I said, "Medicine?" I never thought of LSD as medicine! And somebody said, he must mean the LSD. "LSD?" He said, "Ah-cha—bring the LSD."

So I went to the car and got the little bottle of LSD and I came back.

"Let me see?"

So I poured it out in my hand—"What's that?"

"That's STP . . . That's librium and that's . . ." A little of everything. Sort of a little traveling kit.

He says, "Gives you siddhis?"

I had never heard the word "siddhi" before. So I asked for a translation and siddhi was translated as "power." From where I was at in relation to these concepts, I thought he was like a little old man, asking for power. Perhaps he was losing his vitality and wanted Vitamin B 12. That was one thing I didn't have and I felt terribly apologetic because I would have given him anything. If he wanted the Land Rover, he could have it. And I said, "Oh, no, I'm sorry"—I really felt bad I didn't have any—and put it back in the bottle.

He looked at me and extended his hand. So I put into his hand what's called a "White Lightning." This is an LSD pill and this one was from a special batch that had been made specially for me for traveling. And each pill was 305 micrograms and very pure. Very good acid. Usually you start a man over 60, maybe with 50 to 75 micrograms, very gently, so you won't upset him. 300 of pure acid is a very solid dose.

He looks at the pill and extends his hand further. So I put a second pill—that's 610 micrograms—then a third pill—that's 915 micrograms—into his palm.

That is sizeable for a first dose for anyone!

"Ah-cha."

And he swallows them! I see them go down. There's no doubt. And that little scientist in me says, "This is going to be very interesting!"

All day long I'm there, and every now and then he twinkles at me and nothing—nothing happens! That was his answer to my question. Now you have the data I have.

ASHTANGA YOGA

I was taken back to the temple. It was interesting. At no time was I asked, do you want to stay? Do you want to study? Everything was understood. There were no contracts. There were no promises. There were no vows. There was nothing.

The next day Maharaji instructed them to take me out and buy me clothes. They gave me a room. Nobody ever asked me for a nickel. Nobody ever asked me to spread the word. Nobody ever did anything. There was no commitment whatsoever required. It was all done internally. And that day I met a man who was to become my teacher, Hari Dass Baba.

This guru—Maharaji—has only his blanket. You see, he's in a place called SAHAJ SAMADHI and he's not identified with this world as most of us identify with it. If you didn't watch him, he'd just disappear altogether into the jungle or leave his body, but his devotees are always protecting him and watching him so they can keep him around. They've got an entourage around him and people come and bring gifts to the holy man because that's part of the way in which you gain holy merit in India. And money piles up, and so they build temples, or they build schools. He will walk to a place and there will be a saint who has lived in that place or cave and he'll say, "There will be a temple here," and then they build a temple. And they do all this around Maharaji. He does nothing.

As an example of Maharaji's style, I was once going through my address book and I came to Lama Govinda's name (he wrote *Foundations of Tibetan Mysticism* and *Way of the White Cloud*), and I thought, "Gee, I ought to go visit him. I'm here in the Himalayas and it wouldn't be a long trip and I could go and pay my respects. I must do that some time before I leave."

And the next day there is a message from Maharaji saying, "You are to go immediately to see Lama Govinda."

Another time, I had to go to Delhi to work on my visa and I took a bus. This was the first time after four months that they let me out alone. They were so protective of me. I don't know what they were afraid would happen to me, but they were always sending somebody with me . . . They weren't giving me elopement privileges, as they say in mental hospitals.

But they allowed me to go alone to Delhi and I took a twelve-hour bus trip. I went to Delhi and I was so high. I went through Connaught Place, which is the western hustle part of New Delhi. It's mostly BOAC and American Express and restaurants that serve ice cream sodas. The whole scene, which is right in the middle of India, has nothing to do with India particularly and all the Indians who hustle Westerners walk around in this block. And I went through that, barefoot, silent with my chalkboard—I was silent all the time. At American Express, writing my words, it was so high that not at one moment was there even a qualm or a doubt. I got so high that I went into some stores to buy things—

right in Connaught Place, which is designed to hustle Westerners
. . . And everybody knew I was a Westerner, and yet they insisted
on giving me the stuff free!

"You are a saddhu—it's a blessing to me that you'll take my
goods." That's how powerful the thing was that I was into at that
time.

So after all day long of doing my dramas with the Health
Department and so on, it came time for lunch. I had been on this
very fierce austere diet and I had lost 60 pounds. I was feeling
great—very light and very beautiful—but there was enough orality
still left in me to want to have a feast. I'll have a vegetarian feast,
I thought. So I went to a fancy vegetarian restaurant and I got a
table over in a corner and ordered their special deluxe vegetarian
dinner, from nuts to nuts, and I had the whole thing and the last
thing they served was vegetarian ice cream with two english biscuits
stuck into it. And those biscuits . . . the sweet thing has always
been a big part of my life, but I knew somehow, maybe I shouldn't
be eating those. They're so far out from my diet. It's not vegetables
—it's not rice. And so I was almost secretly eating the cookies in
this dark corner. I was feeling very guilty about eating these
cookies. But nobody was watching me. And then I went to a
Buddhist monastery for the night and the next day took the bus
back up to the mountain.

Two days later, we heard Maharaji was back—he had been up in
the mountains in another little village. He travels around a lot,
moves from place to place. I hadn't seen him in about a month
and a half—I didn't see much of him at all. We all went rushing
to see Maharaji and I got a bag of oranges to bring to him, and I
came and took one look at him and the oranges went flying and I
started to cry and I fell down and they were patting me. Maharaji was eating oranges as fast as he could, manifesting through
eating food the process of taking on the karma of someone else.

Women bring him food all day long. He just opens his mouth
and they feed him and he's taking on karma that way. And he
ate eight oranges right before my eyes. I had never seen anything
like that. And the principal of the school was feeding me oranges
and I was crying and the whole thing was very maudlin, and he
pulls me by the hair and I look up and he says to me, "How did
you like the biscuits?"

I'd be at my temple. And I'd think about arranging for a beautiful lama in America to get some money, or something like that. Then I'd go to bed and pull the covers over my head and perhaps have a very worldly thought; I would think about what I'd do with all my powers when I got them; perhaps a sexual thought. Then when next I saw Maharaji he would tell me something like, "You want to give money to a lama in America." And I'd feel like I was such a beautiful guy. Then suddenly I'd be horrified with the realization that if he knew that thought, then he must know that one, too . . . ohhhhh . . . and that one, too! Then I'd look at the ground. And when I'd finally steal a glance at him, he'd be looking at me with such total love.

Now the impact of these experiences was very profound. As they say in the Sikh religion—once you realize God knows everything, you're free. I had been through many years of psychoanalysis and still I had managed to keep private places in my head—I wouldn't say they were big, labeled categories, but they were certain attitudes or feelings that were still very private. And suddenly I realized that he knew everything that was going on in my head, all the time, and that he still loved me. Because who we are is behind all that.

I said to Hari Dass Baba, "Why is it that Maharaji never tells me the bad things I think?," and he says, "It does not help your sadhana—your spiritual work. He knows it all, but he just does the things that help you."

The sculptor had said he loved Maharaji so much, we should keep the Land Rover up there. The Land Rover was just sitting around and so Maharaji got the Land Rover after all, for that time. And then one day I was told we were going on an outing up in the Himalayas for the day. This was very exciting, because I never left my room in the temple. Now in the temple, or around Maharaji, there were eight or nine people. Bhagwan Dass and I were the only Westerners. In fact, at no time that I was there did I see any other Westerners. This is clearly not a Western scene and, in fact, I was specifically told when returning to the United States that I was not to mention Maharaji's name or where he was, or anything.

The few people that have slipped by this net and figured out from clues in my speech and their knowledge of India where he was and have gone to see him, were thrown out immediately . . . very summarily dismissed, which is very strange. All I can do is pass that information on to you. I think the message is that you don't need to go to anywhere else to find what you are seeking.

So there were eight or nine people and, whenever there was a scene, I walked last. I was the lowest man on the totem pole. They all loved me and honored me and I was the novice, like in a karate or judo class where you stand at the back until you learn more. I was always in the back and they were always teaching me.

So we went in the Land Rover. Maharaji was up in the front—Bhagwan Dass was driving. Bhagwan Dass turned out to be very high in this scene. He was very, very highly thought of and honored. He had started playing the sitar; he was a fantastic musician and the Hindu people loved him. He would do bhajan—holy music—so high they would go out on it. So Bhagwan Dass was driving and I was way in the back of the Land Rover camper with the women and some luggage.

And we went up into the hills and came to a place where we stopped and were given apples in an orchard and we looked at a beautiful view. We stayed about ten minutes and then Maharaji says, "We've got to go on."

We got in the car, went further up the hill, and came to a Forestry camp. Some of his devotees are people in the Forestry Department, so they make this available to him.

So we got to this place and there was a building waiting and a caretaker—"Oh, Maharaji, you've graced us with your presence." He went inside with the man that is there to take care of him or be with him all the time—and we all sat on the lawn.

After a little while, a message came out, "Maharaji wants to see you." And I got up and went in and sat down in front of him. He looked at me and said,

"You make many people laugh in America?"

I said, "Yes, I like to do that."

"Good . . . You like to feed children?"

"Yes. Sure."

"Good."

He asked a few more questions like that, which seemed to be nice questions, but . . . ? Then he smiled and he reached forward and he tapped me right on the forehead, just three times. That's all.

Then the other fellow came along and lifted me and walked me out the door. I was completely confused. I didn't know what had happened to me—why he had done it—what it was about.

When I walked out, the people out in the yard said that I looked as if I were in a very high state. They said tears were streaming down my face. But all I felt inside was confusion. I have never felt any further understanding of it since then. I don't know what it was all about. It was not an idle movement, because the minute that was over, we all got back in the car and went home.

I pass that on to you. You know now what I know about that. Just an interesting thing. I don't know what it means, yet.

Hari Dass Baba was my teacher. I was taught by this man with a chalkboard in the most terse way possible. I would get up early, take my bath in the river or out of a pail with a lota (a bowl). I would go in and do my breathing exercises, my pranayam and my hatha yoga, meditate, study, and, around 11:30 in the morning, this man would arrive and with chalkboard he would write something down:

"If a pickpocket meets a saint, he sees only his pockets."

Then he'd get up and leave. Or he'd write,

"If you wear shoeleather, the whole earth is covered with leather."

These were his ways of teaching me about how motivation affects perception. His teaching seemed to be no teaching because he always taught from within . . . that is, his lessons aroused in me just affirmation . . . as if I knew it all already.

When starting to teach me about what it meant to be "ahimsa" or nonviolent, and the effect on the environment around you of the vibrations—when he started to teach me about energy and vibrations, his opening statement was "Snakes Know Heart." "Yogis in jungle need not fear." Because if you're pure enough, cool it, don't worry. But you've got to be very pure.

So his teaching was of this nature. And it was not until a number of months later that I got hold of Vivekananda's book "Raja Yoga" and I realized that he had been teaching me Raja Yoga, very systematically—an exquisite scientific system that had been originally enunciated somewhere between 500 B.C. and 500 A.D. by Patanjali, in a set of sutras, or phrases, and it's called Ashtanga Yoga or eight-limbed yoga—and also known as Raja or

Kingly yoga. And this beautiful yogi was teaching me this wisdom with simple metaphor and brief phrase.

Now, though I am a beginner on the path, I have returned to the West for a time to work out karma or unfulfilled commitment. Part of this commitment is to share what I have learned with those of you who are on a similar journey. One can share a message through telling "our-story" as I have just done, or through teaching methods of yoga, or singing, or making love. Each of us finds his unique vehicle for sharing with others his bit of wisdom.

For me, this story is but a vehicle for sharing with you the true message . . . the living faith in what is possible.

ALAN W. WATTS

FROM *The Book:*
On the Taboo against Knowing Who You Are

This book explores an unrecognized but mighty taboo—our tacit conspiracy to ignore who, or what, we really are. Briefly, the thesis is that the prevalent sensation of oneself as a separate ego enclosed in a bag of skin is a hallucination which accords neither with Western science nor with the experimental philosophy-religions of the East—in particular the central and germinal Vedanta philosophy of Hinduism. This hallucination underlies the misuse of technology for the violent subjugation of man's natural environment and, consequently, its eventual destruction. . . .

It is said that humanity has evolved one-sidedly, growing in technical power without any comparable growth in moral integrity, or, as some would prefer to say, without comparable progress in education and rational thinking. Yet the problem is more basic. The root of the matter is the way in which we feel and conceive ourselves as human beings, our sensation of being alive, of individual existence and identity. We suffer from a hallucination, from a false and distorted sensation of our own existence as living organisms. Most of us have the sensation that "I myself" is a separate center of feeling and action, living inside and bounded by the physical body—a center which "confronts" an "external" world of people and things, making contact through the senses with a universe both alien and strange. Everyday figures of speech reflect this illusion. "I came into this World." "You must *face* reality." "The conquest of nature."

This feeling of being lonely and very temporary visitors in the universe is in flat contradiction to everything known about man (and all other living organisms) in the sciences. We do not "come into" this world; we come *out* of it, as leaves from a tree. As the ocean "waves," the universe "peoples." Every individual is an expression of the whole realm of nature, a unique action of the total universe. . . .

The hostile attitude of conquering nature ignores the basic interdependence of all things and events—that the world beyond the skin is actually an extension of our own bodies—and will end in destroying the very environment from which we emerge and upon which our whole life depends. . . .

. . . The sensation of "I" as a lonely and isolated center of being is so powerful and common-sensical, and so fundamental to our modes of speech and thought, to our laws and social institutions, that we cannot experience selfhood except as something superficial in the scheme of the universe. I seem to be a brief light that flashes but once in all the eons of time—a rare, complicated, and all-too-delicate organism on the fringe of biological evolution, where the wave of life bursts into individual, sparkling, and multicolored drops that gleam for a moment only to vanish forever. Under such conditioning it seems impossible and even absurd to realize that myself does not reside in the drop alone, but in the whole surge of energy which ranges from the galaxies to the nuclear fields in my body. At this level of existence "I" am immeasurably old; my forms are infinite and their comings and goings are simply the pulses or vibrations of a single and eternal flow of energy.

The difficulty in realizing this to be so is that conceptual thinking cannot grasp it. It is as if the eyes were trying to look at themselves directly, or as if one were trying to describe the color of a mirror in terms of colors reflected in the mirror. Just as sight is something more than all things seen, the foundation or "ground" of our existence and our awareness cannot be understood in terms of things that are known. We are forced, therefore, to speak of it through myth—that is, through special metaphors, analogies, and images which say what it is *like* as distinct from what it *is*. At one extreme of its meaning, "myth" is fable, falsehood, or superstition. But at another, "myth" is a useful and fruitful image by which we make sense of life in somewhat the same way that we can explain electrical forces by comparing them with the behavior of water or air. Yet "myth," in this second sense, is not to be taken literally, just as electricity is not to be confused with air or water. Thus in using myth one must take care not to confuse image with fact, which would be like climbing up the signpost instead of following the road.

Myth, then, is the form in which I try to answer when children ask me those fundamental metaphysical questions which come so readily to their minds: "Where did the world come from?" "Why did God make the world?" "Where was I before I was born?" "Where do people go when they die?" Again and again I have found that they seem to be satisfied with a simple and very ancient story, which goes something like this:

"There was never a time when the world began, because it goes round and round like a circle, and there is no place on a circle where it begins. Look at my watch, which tells the time; it goes round, and so the world repeats itself again and again. But just as the hour-hand of the watch goes up to twelve and down to six, so, too, there is day and night, waking and sleeping, living and dying, summer and winter. You can't have any one of these without the other, because you wouldn't be able to know what black is unless you had seen it side-by-side with white, or white unless side-by-side with black.

"In the same way, there are times when the world is, and times when it isn't, for if the world went on and on without rest for ever and ever, it would get horribly tired of itself. It comes and it goes. Now you see it; now you don't. So because it doesn't get tired of itself, it always comes back again after it disappears. It's like your breath: It goes in and out, in and out, and if you try to hold it in all the time you feel terrible. It's also like the game of hide-and-seek, because it's always fun to find new ways of hiding, and to seek for someone who doesn't always hide in the same place.

"God also likes to play hide-and-seek, but because there is nothing outside God, he has no one but himself to play with. But he gets over this difficulty by pretending that he is not himself. This is his way of hiding from himself. He pretends that he is you and I and all the people in the world, all the animals, all the plants, all the rocks, and all the stars. In this way he has strange and wonderful adventures, some of which are terrible and frightening. But these are just like bad dreams, for when he wakes up they will disappear.

"Now when God plays hide and pretends that he is you and I, he does it so well that it takes him a long time to remember where and how he hid himself. But that's the whole fun of it—just what he wanted to do. He doesn't want to find himself too quickly, for that would spoil the game. That is why it is so difficult for you and me to find out that we are God in disguise, pretending not to be himself. But when the game has gone on long enough, all of us will wake up, stop pretending, and remember that we are all one single Self—the God who is all that there is and who lives for ever and ever.

"Of course, you must remember that God isn't shaped like a person. People have skins and there is always something outside our skins. If there weren't, we wouldn't know the difference between what is inside and outside our bodies. But God has no skin and no shape because there isn't any outside to him. [With a sufficiently intelligent child, I illustrate this with a Mobius strip— a ring of paper tape twisted once in such a way that it has only one side and one edge.] The inside and the outside of God are the same. And though I have been talking about God as 'he' and not 'she,' God isn't a man or a woman. I didn't say 'it' because we usually say 'it' for things that aren't alive.

"God is the Self of the world, but you can't see God for the same reason that, without a mirror, you can't see your own eyes, and you certainly can't bite your own teeth or look inside your head. Your self is that cleverly hidden because it is God hiding.

"You may ask why God sometimes hides in the form of horrible people, or pretends to be people who suffer great disease and pain. Remember, first, that he isn't really doing this to anyone but himself. Remember, too, that in almost all the stories you enjoy there have to be bad people as well as good people, for the thrill of the tale is to find out how the good people will get the better of the bad. It's the same as when we play cards. At the beginning of the game we shuffle them all into a mess, which is like the bad things in the world, but the point of the game is to put the mess into good order, and the one who does it best is the winner. Then we shuffle the cards once more and play again, and so it goes with the world."

"The Ultimate Ground of Being" is Paul Tillich's decontaminated term for "God" and would also do for "the Self of the world" as I put it in my story for children. But the secret which my story slips over to the child is that the Ultimate Ground of Being is you. Not, of course, the everyday you which the Ground is assuming, or "pretending" to be, but that inmost Self which escapes inspection because it's always the inspector. This, then, is the taboo of taboos: You're IT! . . .

Hitherto the poets and philosophers of science have used the vast expanse and duration of the universe as a pretext for reflections on the unimportance of man, forgetting that man with "that enchanted loom, the brain" is precisely what transforms this immense electrical pulsation into light and color, shape and sound, large and small, hard and heavy, long and short. In knowing the world we humanize it, and if, as we discover it, we are astonished at its dimensions and its complexity, we should be just as astonished that we have the brains to perceive it. . . .

The people we are tempted to call clods and boors are just those who seem to find nothing fascinating in being human; their humanity is incomplete, for it has never astonished them. . . .

How is it possible that a being with such sensitive jewels as the eyes, such enchanted musical instruments as the ears, and such a fabulous arabesque of nerves as the brain can experience itself as anything less than a god? And, when you consider that this incalculably subtle organism is inseparable from the still more marvelous patterns of its environment—from the minutest electrical designs to the whole company of the galaxies—how is it conceivable that this incarnation of all eternity can be bored with being?

CHAPTER SIX

The Lay of the Land: Through Nature

"Smile O voluptuous cool-breath'd earth! . . . Earth of the vitreous pour of the full moon just tinged with blue! . . . Smile, for your lover comes," Whitman wrote more than a century ago, expressing modern man's desire to return to nature. We return for many reasons—to lose ourselves, to find ourselves, to forget, to learn. And just as many different conditions drive us out of our cities and into the countryside, many things seem to happen once we reach the hallowed ground. But almost everyone seems to agree that nothing happens unless we are attentive to it. Nothing much seems to happen to the tourists who make their annual treks to gape passively at the vast stretches of the Grand Canyon, although for some strange reason the average American's preconditioned taste for the "sublime" landscape doesn't disappear. But visiting the national monuments is not the reason so many young people are putting on backpacks and hitchhiking to the mountains. They might not even know why they're going, but it's not to look at the countryside, it's to be in it. One may wonder if part of the reason for the mass exodus to the mountains and seashore doesn't have less to do with nature than with a thirst for excitement—for that unexpected adversity that not only passes the time but also challenges inner resources. Be this as it may, they go, and something happens to them. As Thoreau said last century, "Not till we are lost, in other words not till we have lost the world, do we begin to find ourselves, and realize where we are and the infinite extent of our relations." William O. Douglas' "Wilderness Beach" invites us to consider these infinite relations.

E. B. White's letter to Thoreau is a depressing measure of

327

what has already been lost. This chapter, therefore, implicitly raises questions addressed to the ecological crisis. Yet its main theme has to do more with what we can receive from the nature we now have, than with the pressing question of how we can preserve what we have. Modern art continually depicts our sickness: We are getting bored with endless parades of anxiety-ridden lost souls living computer existences in crowded cities. But our great prophetic and visionary poets have long been proclaiming a very simple cure: Let go. Stop seizing life and learn how to attend to what simply is. Daydream on the trail with Gary Snyder. Enter the still space of Denise Levertov's poems. Become an animal again: Think not with your head, but with your whole body; see not with your eyes, but with your soul, as Loren Eiseley bids us. Awaken your mind not by losing it to general truths, but by focusing it on a particular—this particular flower or tree in this particular place. Attend to nature's presences —the subtle, mysterious miracles of light, color, form, texture. Recapture the childlike vision that sees nature not for what can be made of it, but for what it is. Letting go means resisting our natural tendency to attribute human meaning or purpose to the nonhuman, and instead allowing the world patiently to give up its own presences. Such visionary insight is captured by the two poems, "Wales Visitation" and "Poem in October." In Blake's famous phrase, "If the doors of perception were cleansed, every thing would appear to man as it is, infinite." Simple is this wisdom and yet hard for production-oriented Western man to understand and incorporate into his life style. As long as we continue gazing out, like the tourist at the Grand Canyon, we will not see what lies at our feet. And we will not be rooted to the earth in the way that Momaday shows the American Indians were in "Eagles of the Valle Grande" and "The Bear and the Colt."

DYLAN THOMAS

Poem in October

It was my thirtieth year to heaven
Woke to my hearing from harbour and neighbour wood
    And the mussel pooled and the heron
        Priested shore
      The morning beckon
With water praying and call of seagull and rook
And the knock of sailing boats on the net webbed wall
    Myself to set foot
      That second
In the still sleeping town and set forth.   10

    My birthday began with the water-
Birds and the birds of the winged trees flying my name
    Above the farms and the white horses
        And I' rose
      In rainy autumn
And walked abroad in a shower of all my days.
High tide and the heron dived when I took the road
    Over the border
      And the gates
Of the town closed as the town awoke.   20

    A springful of larks in a rolling
Cloud and the roadside bushes brimming with whistling
    Blackbirds and the sun of October
        Summery
      On the hill's shoulder,
Here were fond climates and sweet singers suddenly
Come in the morning where I wandered and listened
    To the rain wringing
      Wind blow cold
In the wood faraway under me.   30

    Pale rain over the dwindling harbour
And over the sea wet church the size of a snail

With its horns through mist and the castle
            Brown as owls
            But all the gardens
Of spring and summer were blooming in the tall tales
Beyond the border and under the lark full cloud.
            There could I marvel
            My birthday
Away but the weather turned around.   40

        It turned away from the blithe country
And down the other air and the blue altered sky
        Streamed again a wonder of summer
                    With apples
            Pears and red currants
And I saw in the turning so clearly a child's
Forgotten mornings when he walked with his mother
            Through the parables
            Of sun light
And the legends of the green chapels   50

        And the twice told fields of infancy
That his tears burned my cheeks and his heart moved in
                                        mine.
        These were the woods the river and sea
                Where a boy
            In the listening
Summertime of the dead whispered the truth of his joy
To the trees and the stones and the fish in the tide.
            And the mystery
            Sang alive
Still in the water and singingbirds.   60

        And there could I marvel my birthday
Away but the weather turned around. And the true
        Joy of the long dead child sang burning
                In the sun.
            It was my thirtieth
Year to heaven stood there then in the summer noon
Though the town below lay leaved with October blood.

O may my heart's truth
Still be sung
On this high hill in a year's turning.   70

ALLEN GINSBERG

Wales Visitation

White fog lifting & falling on mountain-brow
Trees moving in rivers of wind
The clouds arise
as on a wave, gigantic eddy lifting mist
above teeming ferns exquisitely swayed
along a green crag
glimpsed thru mullioned glass in valley raine—

Bardic, O Self, Visitacione, tell naught
but what seen by one man in a vale in Albion,
of the folk, whose physical sciences end in Ecology,   10
the wisdom of earthly relations,
of mouths & eyes interknit ten centuries visible,
orchards of mind language manifest human,
of the satanic thistle that raises its horned symmetry
flowering above sister grass-daisies' small pink
bloomlets angelic as lightbulbs—

Remember 160 miles from London's symmetrical thorned
tower
& network of TV pictures flashing bearded your Self
the Lambs on the tree-nooked hillside this day bleating
heard in Blake's old ear, & the silent thought of
Wordsworth in   20
eld Stillness

clouds passing through skeleton arches of Tintern Abbey—
         Bard Nameless as the Vast, babble to Vastness!

All the Valley quivered, one extended motion, wind
              undulating on mossy hills
   a giant wash that sank white fog delicately down red
                                          runnels
                 on the mountainside
   whose leaf-branch tendrils moved asway
              in granitic undertow down—
and lifted the floating Nebulous upward, and lifted the arms
                                    of the trees   30
       and lifted the grasses an instant in balance
            and lifted the lambs to hold still
       and lifted the green of the hill, in one solemn wave.

A solid mass of Heaven, mist-infused, ebbs thru the vale,
   a wavelet of Immensity, lapping gigantic through Llan-
                                thony Valley,
   the length of all England, valley upon valley under Heaven's
                          ocean tonned with cloud-hang,
         Heaven balanced on a grassblade,
Roar of the mountain wind slow, sigh of the body,
   One Being on the mountainside stirring gently   40
   Exquisite scales trembling everywhere in balance, one
                                    motion
              on the cloudy sky-floor shifting through a million
                                 footed daisies,
              pheasant croaking up steep meadows,
one Majesty the motion that stirred wet grass quivering
   to the farthest tendril of white fog poured down
              through shivering flowers on the mountain's
                                    head—

No imperfection in the budded mountain,
   Valleys breathe, heaven and earth move together,   50
   daisies push inches of yellow air, vegetables tremble,
         green atoms shimmer in grassy mandalas,
sheep speckle the mountainside, revolving their jaws with
                                    empty eyes,

horses dance in the warm rain,
tree-lined canals network through live farmland,
blueberries fringe house walls
on hills nippled with white rock,
meadow-bellies haired with fern—

Out, out on the hillside, into the ocean sound, delicate gusts
of wet air,   60
Fall on the ground, O great Wetness, O mother, No harm
on your body!
Stare close, no imperfection in the grass,
each flower Buddha-eye, repeating the story, the
myriad-formed soul—
Kneel before the foxglove raising green buds, mauve bells
drooped
doubled down the stem trembling antennae,
look in the eyes of the branded lambs that stare
breathing stockstill under dripping hawthorn—
I lay down mixing my beard with the wet hair of the mountainside,
smelling the brown vagina-moist ground, harmless,   70
tasting the violet thistle-hair, sweetness—
One being so balanced, so vast, that its softest breath
moves every floweret in stillness on the valley floor,
trembles lamb-hair hung gossamer rain-beaded in the grass,
lifts trees on their roots, birds in the great draught
hiding their strength in the rain, bearing same weight,

Groan thru breast and neck, a great Oh! to earth heart
Calling our Presence together
The great secret is no secret
Senses fit the winds,   80
Visible is visible,
rain-mist curtains wave through the bearded vale,
gray atoms wet the wind's Kaballah
Crosslegged on a rock in dusk rain,
rubber-booted in soft grass, mind moveless,
breath trembles in white daisies by the roadside,
Heaven breath and my own symmetric
Airs wavering thru antlered green fern

drawn in my navel, same breath as breathes thru
                              Capel-y-Ffn,
            Sounds of Aleph and Aum   90
                through forests of gristle,
        my skull and Lord Hereford's Knob equal,
                    All Albion one.

What did I notice? Particulars! The
        vision of the great One is myriad—
    smoke curls upward from ash tray,
            house fire burned low,
The night, still wet & moody black heaven
                    starless
        upward in motion with wet wind.   100

CHARLES TOMLINSON

Saving the Appearances

The horse is white. Or it
appears to be under this
November light that could
well be October. It goes
as nimbly as a spider does
but it is gainly: the great
field makes it small
so that it seems
to crawl out of the distance
and to grow not larger   10
but less slow. Stains
on its sides show where
the mud is and the power
now overmasters the fragility
of its earlier bearing. Tall
it shudders over one and bends

a full neck, cropping
the foreground, blotting
the whole space back
behind those pounding feet.   20
Mounted, one feels the sky
as much the measure of the event
as the field had been, and all
the divisions of the indivisible
unite again, or seem
to do as when the approaching
horse was white, on this
November unsombre day
where what appears, is.

GARY SNYDER

Daydreaming on the Trail

A lonely stretch, in the bind of poor fishing & drouth,
following the ocean
crossing pass after pass,
fields of wild reeds,
I've come this far alone.

dozing in the pale sun
on the sand of a dried-up riverbed
back and shoulder chilled
something bothering me—
I think at that last quartzite pass   10
I left the oak gate in the fence
of the cowpasture open
probably because I was hurrying—
            a white gate—
did I close it or not?

light cool sky,
mistletoe on chestnut floats in vision
manylayered clouds upriver
cool lattice of sunlight
some unknown big bird   calling   20
faintly, crork   crork

DENISE LEVERTOV

The Breathing

An absolute
patience.
Trees stand
up to their knees in
fog. The fog
slowly flows
uphill.
        White
cobwebs, the grass
leaning where deer   10
have looked for apples.
The woods
from brook to where
the top of the hill looks
over the fog, send up
not one bird.
So absolute, it is
no other than
happiness itself, a breathing
too quiet to hear.   20

DENISE LEVERTOV

Come into Animal Presence

Come into animal presence.
No man is so guileless as
the serpent. The lonely white
rabbit on the roof is a star
twitching its ears at the rain.
The llama intricately
folding its hind legs to be seated
not disdains but mildly
disregards human approval.

What joy when the insouciant   10
armadillo glances at us and doesn't
quicken his trotting
across the track into the palm brush.

What is this joy? That no animal
falters, but knows what it must do?
That the snake has no blemish,
that the rabbit inspects his strange surroundings
in white star-silence? The llama
rests in dignity, the armadillo
has some intention to pursue in the palm-forest.   20
Those who were sacred have remained so,
holiness does not dissolve, it is a presence
of bronze, only the sight that saw it
faltered and turned from it.
An old joy returns in holy presence.

N. SCOTT MOMADAY

The Eagles of the Valle Grande

The Eagle Watchers Society was the principal ceremonial organization of the Bahkyush. Its chief, Patiestewa, and all its members
were direct descendants of those old men and women who had
made that journey along the edge of oblivion. There was a look
about these men, even now. It was as if, conscious of having
come so close to extinction, they had got a keener sense of humility than their benefactors, and paradoxically a greater sense of
pride. Both attributes could be seen in such a man as old Patiestewa. He was hard, and he appeared to have seen more of life
than had other men. In their uttermost peril long ago, the
Bahkyush had been fashioned into seers and soothsayers. They
had acquired a tragic sense, which gave to them as a race so much
dignity and bearing. They were medicine men; they were rain-
makers and eagle hunters.

He was not thinking of the eagles. He had been walking since
daybreak down from the mountain where that year he had broken
a horse for the rancher John Raymond. By the middle of the
morning he was on the rim of the Valle Grande, a great volcanic
crater that lay high up on the western slope of the range. It was
the right eye of the earth, held open to the sun. Of all places that
he knew, this valley alone could reflect the great spatial majesty
of the sky. It was scooped out of the dark peaks like the well of a
great, gathering storm, deep umber and blue and smoke-colored.
The view across the diameter was magnificent; it was an unbelievably great expanse. As many times as he had been there in
the past, each new sight of it always brought him up short, and
he had to catch his breath. Just there, it seemed, a strange and
brilliant light lay upon the world, and all the objects in the land-

scape were washed clean and set away in the distance. In the morning sunlight the Valle Grande was dappled with the shadows of clouds and vibrant with rolling winter grass. The clouds were always there, huge, sharply described, and shining in the pure air. But the great feature of the valley was its size. It was almost too great for the eye to hold, strangely beautiful and full of distance. Such vastness makes for illusion, a kind of illusion that comprehends reality, and where it exists there is always wonder and exhilaration. He looked at the facets of a boulder that lay balanced on the edge of the land, and the first thing beyond, the vague misty field out of which it stood, was the floor of the valley itself, pale and blue-green, miles away. He shifted the focus of his gaze, and he could just make out the clusters of dots that were cattle grazing along the river in the faraway plain.

Then he saw the eagles across the distance, two of them, riding low in the depths and rising diagonally toward him. He did not know what they were at first, and he stood watching them, their far, silent flight erratic and wild in the bright morning. They rose and swung across the skyline, veering close at last, and he knelt down behind the rock, dumb with pleasure and excitement, holding on to them with his eyes.

They were golden eagles, a male and a female, in their mating flight. They were cavorting, spinning and spiraling on the cold, clear columns of air, and they were beautiful. They swooped and hovered, leaning on the air, and swung close together, feinting and screaming with delight. The female was full-grown, and the span of her broad wings was greater than any man's height. There was a fine flourish to her motion; she was deceptively, incredibly fast, and her pivots and wheels were wide and full-blown. But her great weight was streamlined and perfectly controlled. She carried a rattlesnake; it hung shining from her feet, limp and curving out in the trail of her flight. Suddenly her wings and tail fanned, catching full on the wind, and for an instant she was still, widespread and spectral in the blue, while her mate flared past and away, turning around in the distance to look for her. Then she began to beat upward at an angle from the rim until she was small in the sky, and she let go of the snake. It fell slowly, writhing and rolling, floating out like a bit of silver thread against the wide backdrop of the land. She held still above, buoyed up on the cold current, her crop and hackles gleaming like copper in the sun. The male swerved and sailed. He was younger than she and a little more than half as large. He was quicker, tighter in his moves. He let the carrion drift by; then suddenly he gathered himself and stooped, sliding down in a blur of motion to the strike. He hit the snake in the head, with not the slightest deflection of his course or speed, cracking its long body like a whip. Then he rolled and swung upward in a great pendulum arc, riding out his momentum. At the top of his glide he let go of the snake in turn, but the female did not go for it. Instead she soared out over the plain, nearly out of sight, like a mote receding into the haze of the far mountain. The male followed, and Abel watched them go, straining to see, saw them veer once, dip and disappear.

Now there was the business of the society. It was getting on toward the end of November, and the eagle hunters were getting ready to set forth to the mountains. He brooded for a time, full of a strange longing; then one day he went to old Patiestewa and told him of what he had seen. "I think you had better let me go," he said. The old chief closed his eyes and thought about it for a long time. Then he answered: "Yes, I had better let you go."

The next day the Bahkyush eagle watchers started out on foot, he among them, northward through the canyon and into the high timber beyond. They were gone for days, holding up here and there at the holy places where they must pray and make their offerings. Early in the morning they came out of the trees on the edge of the Valle Grande. The land fell and reached away in the early light as far as the eye could see, the hills folding together and the gray grass rolling in the plain, and they began the descent. At midmorning they came to the lower meadows in the basin. It was clear and cold, and the air was thin and sharp like a shard of glass. They needed bait, and they circled out and apart, forming a ring. When the circle was formed, they converged slowly toward the center, clapping and calling out in a high, flat voice that carried only a little way. And as they closed, rabbits began to jump up from the grass and bound. They got away at first, many of them, while the men were still a distance apart, but gradually the ring grew small and the rabbits crept to the center and hid away in the brush. Now and then one of them tried to break away, and the nearest man threw his stick after it. These weapons were small curved clubs, and they were thrown with deadly accuracy by the eagle hunters, so that when the ring was of a certain size and the men only a few feet apart, very few of the animals got away.

He bent close to the ground, his armed cocked and shaking with tension. A great jack-rabbit buck bounded from the grass, straight past him. It struck the ground beyond and sprang again, nearly thirty feet through the air. He spun around and hurled the stick. It struck the jack rabbit a glancing blow just as it bounded again, and the animal slumped in the air and fell heavily to the ground.

The clapping and calling had stopped. He could feel his heart beating and the sweat growing cold on his skin. There was something like remorse or disappointment now that the rabbits were still and strewn about on the ground. He picked one of the dead animals from the brush—it was warm and soft, its eyes shining like porcelain, full of the luster of death—then the great buck, which was not dead but only stunned and frozen with fear. He felt the warm living weight of it in his hands; it was brittle with life, taut with hard, sinewy strength.

When he had bound the bait together and placed it in the sack, he gathered bunches of tall grass and cut a number of evergreen boughs from a thicket in the plain; these he tied in a bundle and carried in a sling on his back. He went to the river and washed his head in order to purify himself. When all was ready, he waved to the others and started off alone to the cliffs. When he came to the first plateau, he rested and looked out across the valley. The sun was high, and all around there was a pale, dry uniformity of light, a winter glare on the clouds and peaks. He could see a crow circling low in the distance. Higher on the land, where a great slab of white rock protruded from the mountain, he saw the eagle-hunt house; he headed for it. The house was a small tower of stone, built around a pit, hollow and open at the top. Near it was a shrine, a stone shelf in which there was a slight depression. There he placed a prayer offering. He got into the house, and with boughs he made a latticework of beams across the top and covered it with grass. When it was finished, there was a small opening at the center. Through it he raised the rabbits and laid them down on the boughs. He could see here and there through the screen, but his line of vision was vertical, or nearly so, and his quarry would come from the sun. He began to sing, now and then calling out, low in his throat.

The eagles soared southward, high above the Valle Grande. They were almost too high to be seen. From their vantage point the land below reached away on either side to the long, crooked tributaries of the range; down the great open corridor to the south were the wooded slopes and the canyon, the desert and the far end of the earth bending on the sky. They caught sight of the rabbits and were deflected. They veered and banked, lowering themselves into the crater, gathering speed. By the time he knew of their presence, they were low and coming fast on either side of the pit, swooping with blinding speed. The male caught hold of the air and fell off, touching upon the face of the cliff in order to flush the rabbits, while the female hurtled in to take her prey on the run. Nothing happened; the rabbits did not move. She overshot the trap and screamed. She was enraged and she hurled herself around in the air. She swung back with a great clamor of her wings and fell with fury on the bait. He saw her in the instant she struck. Her foot flashed out and one of her talons laid the jack rabbit open the length of its body. It stiffened and jerked, and her other foot took hold of its skull and crushed it. In that split second, when the center of her weight touched down upon the trap, he reached for her. His hands closed upon her legs and he drew her down with all his strength. For one instant only did she recoil, splashing her great wings down upon the beams and boughs—and she very nearly broke from his grasp; but then she was down in the darkness of the well, hooded, and she was still.

At dusk he met with the other hunters in the plain. San Juanito, too, had got an eagle, but it was an aged male and poor by comparison. They gathered around the old eagle and spoke to it, bidding it return with their good will and sorrow to the eagles of the crags. They fixed a prayer plume to its leg and let it go. He watched it back away and stoop, flaring its wings on the ground, glowering, full of fear and suspicion. Then it took leave of the ground and beat upward, clattering through the still shadows of the valley. It gathered speed, driving higher and higher until it reached the shafts of reddish-gold final light that lay like bars across the crater. The light caught it up and set a dark blaze upon it. It leveled off and sailed. Then it was gone from sight, but he looked after it for a time. He could see it still in the mind's eye and hear in his memory the awful whisper of its flight on the wind. It filled him with longing. He felt the great weight of the bird which he held in the sack. The dusk was fading quickly into night, and the others could not see that his eyes were filled with tears.

That night, while the others ate by the fire, he stole away to look at the great bird. He drew the sack open; the bird shivered, he thought, and drew itself up. Bound and helpless, his eagle seemed drab and shapeless in the moonlight, too large and ungainly for flight. The sight of it filled him with shame and disgust. He took hold of its throat in the darkness and cut off its breath.

N. SCOTT MOMADAY

The Bear and the Colt

They were old enough then, and he took his grandsons out at
first light to the old Campo Santo, south and west of the Middle.
He made them stand just there, above the point of the low white
rock, facing east. They could see the black mesa looming on the
first light, and he told them there was the house of the sun. They
must learn the whole contour of the black mesa. They must know
it as they knew the shape of their hands, always and by heart.
The sun rose up on the black mesa at a different place each day.
It began there, at a point on the central slope, standing still for
the solstice, and ranged all the days southward across the rise and
fall of the long plateau, drawing closer by the measure of mornings and moons to the lee, and back again. They must know the
long journey of the sun on the black mesa, how it rode in the
seasons and the years, and they must live according to the sun
appearing, for only then could they reckon where they were,
where all things were, in time. There, at the rounder knoll, it was
time to plant corn; and there, where the highest plane fell away,
that was the day of the rooster race, six days ahead of the black
bull running and the little horse dancing, seven ahead of the Pecos
immigration; and there, and there, and there, the secret dances,
every four days of fasting in the kiva, the moon good for hoeing
and the time for harvest, the rabbit and witch hunts, all the
proper days of the clans and societies; and just there at the saddle,
where the sky was lower and brighter than elsewhere on the high
black land, the clearing of the ditches in advance of the spring
rains and the long race of the black men at dawn.

These things he told to his grandsons carefully, slowly and at
length, because they were old and true, and they could be lost

forever as easily as one generation is lost to the next, as easily as one old man might lose his voice, having spoken not enough or not at all. But his grandsons knew already; not the names or the strict position of the sun each day in relation to its house, but the larger motion and meaning of the great organic calendar itself, the emergency of dawn and dusk, summer and winter, the very cycle of the sun and of all the suns that were and were to come. And he knew they knew, and he took them with him to the fields and they cut open the earth and touched the corn and ate sweet melons in the sun.

He was a young man, and he rode out on the buckskin colt to the north and west, leading the hunting horse, across the river and beyond the white cliffs and the plain, beyond the hills and the mesas, the canyons and the caves. And once, where the horses could not go because the face of the rock was almost vertical and unbroken and the ancient handholds were worn away to shadows in the centuries of wind and rain, he climbed among the walls and pinnacles of rock, adhering like a vine to the face of the rock, pressing with no force at all his whole mind and weight upon the sheer ascent, running the roots of his weight into invisible hollows and cracks, and he heard the whistle and moan of the wind among the crags, like ancient voices, and saw the horses far below in the sunlit gorge. And there were the caves. He came suddenly upon a narrow ledge and stood before the mouth of a cave. It was sealed with silver webs, and he brushed them away. He bent to enter and knelt down on the floor. It was dark and cool and close inside, and smelled of damp earth and dead and ancient fires, as if centuries ago the air had entered and stood still behind the web. The dead embers and ashes lay still in a mound upon the floor, and the floor was deep and packed with clay and glazed with the blood of animals. The chiseled dome was low and encrusted with smoke, and the one round wall was a perfect radius of rock and plaster. Here and there were earthen bowls, one very large, chipped and broken only at the mouth, deep and fired within. It was beautiful and thin-shelled and fragile-looking, but he struck the nails of his hand against it, and it rang like metal. There was a black metate by the door, the coarse, igneous grain of the shallow bowl forever bleached with meal, and in the ashes of the fire were several ears and cobs of corn, each no bigger than his thumb, charred and brittle, but whole and hard as wood. And there among the things of the dead he listened in the stillness all around and heard only the lowing of the wind . . . and then the plummet and rush of a great swooping bird—out of the corner of his eye he saw the awful shadow which hurtled across the light—and the clatter of wings on the cliff, and the small, thin cry of a rodent. And in the same instant the huge wings heaved with calm, gathering up the dead weight, and rose away.

All afternoon he rode on toward the summit of the blue mountain, and at last he was high among the falls and the steep timbered slopes. The sun fell behind the land above him and the dusk grew up among the trees, and still he went on in the dying light, climbing up to the top of the land. And all afternoon he had seen the tracks of wild animals and heard the motion of the dead leaves and the breaking of branches on either side. Twice he had seen deer, motionless, watching, standing away in easy range, blended with light and shadow, fading away into the leaves and the land. He let them be, but remembered where they were and how they stood, reckoning well and instinctively their notion of fear and flight, their age and weight.

He had seen the tracks of wolves and mountain lions and the deep prints of a half-grown bear, and in the last light he drew up in a small clearing and made his camp. It was a good place, and he was lucky to have come upon it while he still could see. A dead tree had fallen upon a bed of rock; it was clear of the damp earth and the leaves, and the wood made an almost smokeless fire. The timber all around was thick, and it held the light and the sound of the fire within the clearing. He tethered the horses there in the open, as close to the fire as he could, and opened the blanket roll and ate. He slept sitting against the saddle, and kept the fire going and the rifle cocked across his waist.

He awoke startled to the stiffening of the horses. They stood quivering and taut with their heads high and turned around upon the dark and nearest wall of trees. He could see the whites of their eyes and the ears laid back upon the bristling manes and the almost imperceptible shiver and bunch of their haunches to the spine. And at the same time he saw the dark shape sauntering among the trees, and then the others, sitting all around, motionless, the short pointed ears and the soft shining eyes, almost kindly and discreet, the gaze of the gray heads bidding only welcome and wild good will. And he was young and it was the first time he had come among them and he brought the rifle up and made no sound. He swung the sights slowly around from one to another of the still, shadowy shapes, but they made no sign except to cock their heads a notch, sitting still and away in the darkness like a litter of pups, full of shyness and wonder and delight. He was hard on the track of the bear; it was somewhere close by in the night, and it knew of him, had been ahead of him for hours in the afternoon and evening, holding the same methodical pace, unhurried, certain of where it was and where he was and of every step of the way between, keeping always and barely out of sight, almost out of hearing. And it was there now, off in the blackness, standing still and invisible, waiting. And he did not want to break the stillness of the night, for it was holy and profound; it was rest and restoration, the hunter's offering of death and the sad watch of the hunted, waiting somewhere away in the cold darkness and breathing easily of its life, brooding around at last to forgiveness and consent; the silence was essential to them both, and it lay out like a bond between them, ancient and inviolable. He could neither take nor give any advantage of cowardice where no cowardice was, and he laid the rifle down. He spoke low to the horses and soothed them. He drew fresh wood upon the fire and the gray shapes crept away to the edge of the light, and in the morning they were gone.

It was gray before the dawn and there was a thin frost on the leaves, and he saddled up and started out again, slowly, after the track and into the wind. At sunrise he came upon the ridge of the mountain. For hours he followed the ridge, and he could see for miles across the land. It was late in the autumn and clear, and the great shining slopes, green and blue, rose out of the shadows on either side, and the sunlit groves of aspen shone bright with clusters of yellow leaves and thin white lines of bark, and far below in the deep folds of the land he could see the tops of the black pines swaying. At mid-morning he was low in a saddle of the ridge, and he came upon a huge outcrop of rock and the track was lost. An ancient watercourse fell away like a flight of stairs to the left, the falls broad and shallow at first, but ever more narrow and deep farther down. He tied the horses and started down the rock on foot, using the rifle to balance himself. He went slowly, quietly down until he came to a deep open funnel in the rock. The ground on either side sloped sharply down to a broad ravine and the edge of the timber beyond, and he saw the scored earth where the bear had left the rock and gone sliding down, and the swath in the brush of the ravine. He thought of going the same way; it would be quick and easy, and he was close to the kill, closing in and growing restless. But he must make no sound of hurry. The bear knew he was coming, knew better than he how close he was, was even now watching him from the wood, waiting, but still he must make no sound of hurry. The walls of the funnel were deep and smooth, and they converged at the bank of the ravine some twenty feet below, and the ravine was filled with sweet clover and paintbrush and sage. He held the rifle out as far as he could reach and let it go; it fell upon a stand of tall sweet clover with scarcely any sound, and the dull stock shone and the long barrel glinted among the curving green and yellow stalks. He let himself down into the funnel, little by little, supported only by the tension of his strength against the walls. The going was hard and slow, and near the end his arms and legs began to shake, but he was young and strong and he dropped from the point of the rock to the sand below and took up the rifle and went on, not hurrying but going only as fast as the bear had gone, going even in the bear's tracks, across the ravine and up the embankment and through the trees, unwary now, sensible only of closing in, going on and looking down at the tracks.

And when at last he looked up, the timber stood around a pool of light, and the bear was standing still and small at the far side of the brake, careless, unheeding. He brought the rifle up, and the bear raised and turned its head and made no sign of fear. It was small and black in the deep shade and dappled with light, its body turned three-quarters away and standing perfectly still, and the flat head and the small black eyes that were fixed upon him hung around upon the shoulder and under the hump of the spine. The bear was young and heavy with tallow, and the underside of the body and the backs of its short, thick legs were tufted with winter hair, longer and lighter than the rest, and dull as dust. His hand tightened on the stock and the rifle bucked and the sharp report rang upon the walls and carried out upon the slopes, and he heard the sudden scattering of birds overhead and saw the darting shadows all around. The bullet slammed into the flesh and jarred the whole black body once, but the head remained motionless and the eyes level upon him. Then, and for one instant only, there was a sad and meaningless haste. The bear turned away and lumbered, though not with fear, not with any hurt, but haste, slightly reflexive, a single step, or two, or three, and it was overcome. It shuddered and looked around again and fell.

The hunt was over, and only then could he hurry; it was over and well done. The wound was small and clean, behind the foreleg and low on the body, where the fur and flesh were thin, and there was no blood at the mouth. He took out his pouch of pollen and made yellow streaks above the bear's eyes. It was almost noon, and he hurried. He disemboweled the bear and laid the flesh open with splints, so that the blood should not run into the fur and stain the hide. He ate quickly of the bear's liver, taking it with him, thinking what he must do, remembering now his descent upon the rock and the whole lay of the land, all the angles of his vision from the ridge. He went quickly, a quarter of a mile or more down the ravine, until he came to a place where the horses could keep their footing on the near side of the ridge. The blood of the bear was on him, and the bear's liver was warm and wet in his hand. He came upon the ridge and the colt grew wild in its eyes and blew, pulling away, and its hoofs clattered on the rock and the skin crawled at the roots of its mane. He approached it slowly, talking to it, and took hold of the reins. The hunting horse watched, full of age and indifference, switching its tail. There was no time to lose. He held hard to the reins, turning down the bit in the colt's mouth, and his voice rose a little and was edged. Slowly he brought the bear's flesh up to the flaring nostrils of the colt and smeared the muzzle with it.

And he rode the colt back down the mountain, leading the hunting horse with the bear on its back, and, like the old hunting horse and the young black bear, he and the colt had come of age and were hunters, too. He made camp that night far down in the peneplain and saw the stars and heard the coyotes away by the river. And in the early morning he rode into the town. He was a man then, and smeared with the blood of a bear. He shouted, and the men came out to meet him. They came with rifles, and he gave them strips of the bear's flesh, which they wrapped around the barrels of their guns. And soon the women came with switches, and they spoke to the bear and laid the switches to its hide. The men and women were jubilant and all around, and he rode stonefaced in their midst, looking straight ahead.

E. B. WHITE

Walden—June 1939

Miss Nims, take a letter to Henry David Thoreau. Dear Henry: I thought of you the other afternoon as I was approaching Concord doing fifty on Route 62. That is a high speed at which to hold a philosopher in one's mind, but in this century we are a nimble bunch.

On one of the lawns in the outskirts of the village a woman was cutting the grass with a motorized lawn mower. What made me think of you was that the machine had rather got away from her, although she was game enough, and in the brief glimpse I had of the scene it appeared to me that the lawn was mowing the lady. She kept a tight grip on the handles, which throbbed violently with every explosion of the one-cylinder motor, and as she sheered around bushes and lurched along at a reluctant trot behind her impetuous servant, she looked like a puppy who had grabbed something that was too much for him. Concord hasn't changed much, Henry; the farm implements and the animals still have the upper hand.

I may as well admit that I was journeying to Concord with the deliberate intention of visiting your woods; for although I have never knelt at the grave of a philosopher nor placed wreaths on moldy poets, and have often gone a mile out of my way to avoid some place of historical interest, I have always wanted to see Walden Pond. The account which you left of your sojourn there is, you will be amused to learn, a document of increasing pertinence; each year it seems to gain a little headway, as the world loses ground. We may all be transcendental yet, whether we like it or not. As our common complexities increase, any tale of individual simplicity (and yours is the best written and the cockiest) acquires a new fascination; as our goods accumulate, but not our well-being, your report of an existence without material adorn-ment takes on a certain awkward credibility.

My purpose in going to Walden Pond, like yours, was not to live cheaply or to live dearly there, but to transact some private business with the fewest obstacles. Approaching Concord, doing forty, doing forty-five, doing fifty, the steering wheel held snug in my palms, the highway held grimly in my vision, the crown of the road now serving me (on the righthand curves), now defeating me (on the lefthand curves), I began to rouse myself from the stupefaction which a day's motor journey induces. It was a delicious evening, Henry, when the whole body is one sense, and imbibes delight through every pore, if I may coin a phrase. Fields were richly brown where the harrow, drawn by the stripped Ford, had lately sunk its teeth; pastures were green; and overhead the sky had that same everlasting great look which you will find on Page 144 of the Oxford Pocket Edition. I could feel the road entering me, through tire, wheel, spring, and cushion; shall I not have intelligence with earth too? Am I not partly leaves and vegetable mold myself?—a man of infinite horsepower, yet partly leaves.

Stay with me on 62 and it will take you into Concord. As I say, it was a delicious evening. The snake had come forth to die in a bloody S on the highway, the wheel upon its head, its bowels flat now and exposed. The turtle had come up too to cross the road and die in the attempt, its hard shell smashed under the rubber blow, its intestinal yearning (for the other side of the road) forever squashed. There was a sign by the wayside which announced that the road had a "cotton surface." You wouldn't know what that is, but neither, for that matter, did I. There is a cryptic ingredient in many of our modern improvements—we are awed and pleased without knowing quite what we are enjoying. It is something to be traveling on a road with a cotton surface.

The civilization round Concord today is an odd distillation of city, village, farm, and manor. The houses, yards, fields look not quite suburban, not quite rural. Under the bronze beech and the blue spruce of the departed baron grazes the milch goat of the heirs. Under the porte-cochère stands the reconditioned station wagon; under the grape arbor sit the puppies for sale. (But why do men degenerate ever? What makes families run out?)

It was June and everywhere June was publishing her immemorial stanza: in the lilacs, in the syringa, in the freshly edged paths and the sweetness of moist beloved gardens, and the little wire wickets that preserve the tulips' front. Farmers were already moving the fruits of their toil into their yards, arranging the rhubarb, the asparagus, the strictly fresh eggs on the painted stands under the little shed roofs with the patent shingles. And though it was almost a hundred years since you had taken your ax and started cutting out your home on Walden Pond, I was interested to observe that the philosophical spirit was still alive in Massachusetts: in the center of a vacant lot some boys were assembling the framework of a rude shelter, their whole mind and skill concentrated in the rather inauspicious helter-skeleton of studs and rafters. They too were escaping from town, to live naturally, in a rich blend of savagery and philosophy.

That evening, after supper at the inn, I strolled out into the twilight to dream my shapeless transcendental dreams and see that the car was locked up for the night (first open the right front door, then reach over, straining, and pull up the handles of the left rear and the left front till you hear the click, then the handle of the right rear, then shut the right front but open it again, remembering that the key is still in the ignition switch, remove the key, shut the right front again with a bang, push the tiny keyhole cover to one side, insert key, turn, and withdraw). It is what we all do, Henry. It is called locking the car. It is said to confuse thieves and keep them from making off with the laprobe. Four doors to lock behind one robe. The driver himself never uses a laprobe, the free movement of his legs being vital to the operation of the vehicle; so that when he locks the car it is a pure and unselfish act. I have in my life gained very little essential heat from laprobes, yet I have ever been at pains to lock them up.

The evening was full of sounds, some of which would have stirred your memory. The robins still love the elms of New England villages at sundown. There is enough of the thrush in them to make song inevitable at the end of day, and enough of the tramp to make them hang round the dwellings of men. A robin, like many another American, dearly loves a white house with green blinds. Concord is still full of them.

Your fellow-townsmen were stirring abroad—not many afoot, most of them in their cars; and the sound which they made in

Concord at evening was a rustling and a whispering. The sound lacks steadfastness and is wholly unlike that of a train. A train, as you know who lived so near the Fitchburg line, whistles once or twice sadly and is gone, trailing a memory in smoke, soothing to ear and mind. Automobiles, skirting a village green, are like flies that have gained the inner ear—they buzz, cease, pause, start, shift, stop, halt, brake, and the whole effect is a nervous polytone curiously disturbing.

As I wandered along, the toc-toc of ping-pong balls drifted from an attic window. In front of the Reuben Brown house a Buick was drawn up. At the wheel, motionless, his hat upon his head, a man sat, listening to Amos and Andy on the radio (it is a drama of many scenes and without an end). The deep voice of Andrew Brown, emerging from the car, although it originated more than two hundred miles away, was unstrained by distance. When you used to sit on the shore of your pond on Sunday morning, listening to the church bells of Acton and Concord, you were aware of the excellent filter of the intervening atmosphere. Science has attended to that, and sound now maintains its intensity without regard for distance. Properly sponsored, it goes on forever.

A fire engine, out for a trial spin, roared past Emerson's house, hot with readiness for public duty. Over the barn roofs the martins dipped and chittered. A swarthy daughter of an asparagus grower, in culottes, shirt, and bandanna, pedaled past on her bicycle. It was indeed a delicious evening, and I returned to the inn (I believe it was your house once) to rock with the old ladies on the concrete veranda.

Next morning early I started afoot for Walden, out Main Street and down Thoreau, past the depot and the Minute Man Chevrolet Company. The morning was fresh, and in a bean field along the way I flushed an agriculturalist, quietly studying his beans. Thoreau Street soon joined Number 126, an artery of the State. We number our highways nowadays, our speed being so great we can remember little of their quality or character and are lucky to remember their number. (Men have an indistinct notion that if they keep up this activity long enough all will at length ride somewhere, in next to no time.) Your pond is on 126.

I knew I must be nearing your woodland retreat when the Golden Pheasant lunchroom came into view—Sealtest ice cream, toasted sandwiches, hot frankfurters, waffles, tonics, and lunches. Were I the proprietor, I should add rice, Indian meal, and molasses—just for old time's sake. The Pheasant, incidentally, is for sale: a chance for some nature lover who wishes to set himself up beside a pond in the Concord atmosphere and live deliberately, fronting only the essential facts of life on Number 126. Beyond the Pheasant was a place called Walden Breezes, an oasis whose porch pillars were made of old green shutters sawed into lengths. On the porch was a distorting mirror, to give the traveler a comical image of himself, who had miraculously learned to gaze in an ordinary glass without smiling. Behind the Breezes, in a sun-parched clearing, dwelt your philosophical descendants in their trailers, each trailer the size of your hut, but all grouped together for the sake of congeniality. Trailer people leave the city, as you did, to discover solitude and in any weather, at any hour of the day or night, to improve the nick of time; but they soon collect in villages and get bogged deeper in the mud than ever. The camp behind Walden Breezes was just rousing itself to the morning. The ground was packed hard under the heel, and the sun came through the clearing to bake the soil and enlarge the wry smell of cramped housekeeping. Cushman's bakery truck had stopped to deliver an early basket of rolls. A camp dog, seeing me in the road, barked petulantly. A man emerged from one of the trailers and set forth with a bucket to draw water from some forest tap.

Leaving the highway I turned off into the woods toward the pond, which was apparent through the foliage. The floor of the forest was strewn with dried old oak leaves and *Transcripts*. From beneath the flattened popcorn wrapper (*granum explosum*) peeped the frail violet. I followed a footpath and descended to the water's edge. The pond lay clear and blue in the morning light, as you have seen it so many times. In the shallows a man's water-logged shirt undulated gently. A few flies came out to greet me and convoy me to your cove, past the No Bathing signs on which the fellows and the girls had scrawled their names. I felt strangely excited suddenly to be snooping around your premises, tiptoeing along watchfully, as though not to tread by mistake upon the intervening century. Before I got to the cove I heard something which seemed to me quite wonderful: I heard your frog, a full, clear *troonk*, guiding me, still hoarse and solemn, bridging the years as the robins had bridged them in the sweetness of the village evening. But he soon quit, and I came on a couple of young boys throwing stones at him.

Your front yard is marked by a bronze tablet set in a stone. Four small granite posts, a few feet away, show where the house was. On top of the tablet was a pair of faded blue bathing trunks with a white stripe. Back of it is a pile of stones, a sort of cairn, left by your visitors as a tribute I suppose. It is a rather ugly little heap of stones, Henry. In fact the hillside itself seems faded, browbeaten; a few tall skinny pines, bare of lower limbs, a smattering of young maples in suitable green, some birches and oaks, and a number of trees felled by the last big wind. It was from the bole of one of these fallen pines, torn up by the roots, that I extracted the stone which I added to the cairn—a sentimental act in which I was interrupted by a small terrier from a nearby picnic group, who confronted me and wanted to know about the stone.

I sat down for a while on one of the posts of your house to listen to the bluebottles and the dragonflies. The invaded glade sprawled shabby and mean at my feet, but the flies were tuned to the old vibration. There were the remains of a fire in your ruins, but I doubt that it was yours; also two beer bottles trodden into the soil and become part of earth. A young oak had taken root in your house, and two or three ferns, unrolling like the ticklers at a banquet. The only other furnishings were a DuBarry pattern sheet, a page torn from a picture magazine, and some crusts in wax paper.

Before I quit I walked clear round the pond and found the place where you used to sit on the N.E. side to get the sun in the fall, and the beach where you got sand for scrubbing your floor. On the eastern side of the pond, where the highway borders it, the State has built dressing rooms for swimmers, a float with diving towers, drinking fountains of porcelain, and rowboats for hire. The pond is in fact a State Preserve, and carries a twenty-dollar fine for picking wild flowers, a decree signed in all solemnity by your fellow-citizens Walter C. Wardwell, Erson B. Barlow, and Nathaniel I. Bowditch. There was a smell of creosote where they had been building a wide wooden stairway to the road and the parking area. Swimmers and boaters were arriving; bodies splashed vigorously into the water and emerged wet and beautiful in the bright air. As I left, a boatload of town boys were splashing about in mid-pond, kidding and fooling, the young fellows singing at the tops of their lungs in a wild chorus:

> Amer-ica, A-mer-i-ca, God shed his grace on thee,
> And crown thy good with brotherhood
> From sea to shi-ning sea!

I walked back to town along the railroad, following your custom. The rails were expanding noisily in the hot sun, and on the slope of the roadbed the wild grape and the blackberry sent up their creepers to the track.

The expense of my brief sojourn in Concord was:

Canvas shoes	$1.95	
Baseball bat	.25 ⎤	gifts to take back
Left-handed fielder's glove	1.25 ⎦	to a boy
Hotel and meals	4.25	
In all	$7.70	

As you see, this amount was almost what you spent for food for eight months. I cannot defend the shoes or the expenditure for shelter and food: they reveal a meanness and grossness in my nature which you would find contemptible. The baseball equipment, however, is the sort of impediment with which you were never on even terms. You must remember that the house where you practiced the sort of economy which I respect was haunted only by mice and squirrels. You never had to cope with a shortstop.

WILLIAM O. DOUGLAS

Wilderness Beach

On a summer's day this wilderness beach is a bit of paradise. The stars are bright at night; and if one has chosen his time wisely, he will find the moon shining over waters that gently touch the beaches. By morning, fog that is thick and low has swallowed the entire coastline. A person disappears from view at camp's edge or walks as a ghostly figure. Rocks and islands that lie offshore come and go in the swirling mist. The logs piled high along the shore assume strange and grotesque forms. Everything seems out of focus. As the ceiling moves upward, patches of fog still blur the vision, making offshore islands disappear and then come magically back into view. The place seems unreal—a part of some far-off place of mystery. The Hole in the Rock is at these times the most fascinating of all. It lies near the take-out point of the hike, above the Quillayute River near the northern edge of Rialto Beach. A huge granite cliff forms a shoulder that protrudes into the Pacific, blocking passage on foot. Wind and sand have worn a hole through it, a large arching cave that finally broke the barricade. Hard, glistening sand packs the beach. The cliffs rise high behind it. In the fog this opening in the rock is a keyhole to the supernal land where rolling mists form weird shapes and only the sound of surf is familiar to man.

The sun is always high when the fog has gone. Some days a fresh wind blows from the northwest. At other times there is no breath of air to make the alder leaves glisten. At these times I like to put my pack under a spruce and lie in the grass above the beach, watching the waves come in from Asia. When the wind is high there is always a booming sound from the nearby point. When the air is breathless, the waves are soft and gentle and faraway. Then

357

the quiet of the bench above the beach is so deep I have heard the pods of the brome grass breaking—a faint, crackling sound that the ear can hear only when there is deep quiet. Time passes quickly in these idle hours of dreaming. I dream of far-off peoples who share the Pacific with us. I think of time and the universe and the unseen forces that have made the earth of which we are a part. I realize how small and minute man is in the cosmic scheme. Yet how bold and aggressive and dangerous he has become. Now he has unlocked the secrets and can destroy and sterilize for eons the good earth from which we all came. Earth, the hard sand below me, the waves that make it, the alder and spruce above me, the ferns and brome grass that envelop me—all this seems newly precious, almost sacred. We look to the heavens for help and up-lift, but it is to the earth we are chained; it is from the earth that we must find our sustenance; it is on the earth that we must find solutions to the problems that promise to destroy all life here.

LOREN EISELEY

The Judgment of the Birds

It is a commonplace of all religious thought, even the most primitive, that the man seeking visions and insight must go apart from his fellows and live for a time in the wilderness. If he is of the proper sort, he will return with a message. It may not be a message from the god he set out to seek, but even if he has failed in that particular, he will have had a vision or seen a marvel, and these are always worth listening to and thinking about.

The world, I have come to believe, is a very queer place, but we have been part of this queerness for so long that we tend to take it for granted. We rush to and fro like Mad Hatters upon our peculiar errands, all the time imagining our surroundings to be dull and ourselves quite ordinary creatures. Actually, there is nothing in the world to encourage this idea, but such is the mind of man, and this is why he finds it necessary from time to time to send emissaries into the wilderness in the hope of learning of great events, or plans in store for him, that will resuscitate his waning taste for life. His great news services, his worldwide radio network, he knows with a last remnant of healthy distrust will be of no use to him in this matter. No miracle can withstand a radio broadcast, and it is certain that it would be no miracle if it could. One must seek, then, what only the solitary approach can give—a natural revelation.

Let it be understood that I am not the sort of man to whom is entrusted direct knowledge of great events or prophecies. A naturalist, however, spends much of his life alone, and my life is no exception. Even in New York City there are patches of wilderness, and a man by himself is bound to undergo certain experiences falling into the class of which I speak. I set mine down, therefore: a mat-

ter of pigeons, a flight of chemicals, and a judgment of birds, in
the hope that they will come to the eye of those who have retained
a true taste for the marvelous, and who are capable of discerning
in the flow of ordinary events the point at which the mundane
world gives way to quite another dimension.

New York is not, on the whole, the best place to enjoy the
downright miraculous nature of the planet. There are, I do not
doubt, many remarkable stories to be heard there and many strange
sights to be seen, but to grasp a marvel fully it must be savored
from all aspects. This cannot be done while one is being jostled
and hustled along a crowded street. Nevertheless, in any city
there are true wildernesses where a man can be alone. It can happen in a hotel room, or on the high roofs at dawn.

One night on the twentieth floor of a midtown hotel I awoke in
the dark and grew restless. On an impulse I climbed upon the
broad old-fashioned window sill, opened the curtains and peered
out. It was the hour just before dawn, the hour when men sigh in
their sleep, or, if awake, strive to focus their wavering eyesight
upon a world emerging from the shadows. I leaned out sleepily
through the open window. I had expected depths, but not the
sight I saw.

I found I was looking down from that great height into a series
of curious cupolas or lofts that I could just barely make out in the
darkness. As I looked, the outlines of these lofts became more distinct because the light was being reflected from the wings of pigeons who, in utter silence, were beginning to float outward upon
the city. In and out through the open slits in the cupolas passed
the white-winged birds on their mysterious errands. At this hour
the city was theirs, and quietly, without the brush of a single wing
tip against stone in that high, eerie place, they were taking over
the spires of Manhattan. They were pouring upward in a light
that was not yet perceptible to human eyes, while far down in the
blackness of the alleys it was still midnight.

As I crouched half asleep across the sill, I had a moment's illusion that the world had changed in the night, as in some immense snowfall, and that if I were to leave, it would have to be
as these other inhabitants were doing, by the window. I should
have to launch out into that great bottomless void with the
simple confidence of young birds reared high up there among
the familiar chimney pots and interposed horrors of the abyss.

I leaned farther out. To and fro went the white wings, to and fro. There were no sounds from any of them. They knew man was asleep and this light for a little while was theirs. Or perhaps I had only dreamed about man in this city of wings—which he could surely never have built. Perhaps I, myself, was one of these birds dreaming unpleasantly a moment of old dangers far below as I teetered on a window ledge.

Around and around went the wings. It needed only a little courage, only a little shove from the window ledge to enter that city of light. The muscles of my hands were already making little premonitory lunges. I wanted to enter that city and go away over the roofs in the first dawn. I wanted to enter it so badly that I drew back carefully into the room and opened the hall door. I found my coat on the chair, and it slowly became clear to me that there was a way down through the floors, that I was, after all, only a man.

I dressed then and went back to my own kind, and I have been rather more than usually careful ever since not to look into the city of light. I had seen, just once, man's greatest creation from a strange inverted angle, and it was not really his at all. I will never forget how those wings went round and round, and how, by the merest pressure of the fingers and a feeling for air, one might go away over the roofs. It is a knowledge, however, that is better kept to oneself. I think of it sometimes in such a way that the wings, beginning far down in the black depths of the mind, begin to rise and whirl till all the mind is lit by their spinning, and there is a sense of things passing away, but lightly, as a wing might veer over an obstacle.

To see from an inverted angle, however, is not a gift allotted merely to the human imagination. I have come to suspect that within their degree it is sensed by animals, though perhaps as rarely as among men. The time has to be right; one has to be, by chance or intention, upon the border of two worlds. And sometimes these two borders may shift or interpenetrate and one sees the miraculous.

I once saw this happen to a crow.

This crow lives near my house, and though I have never injured him, he takes good care to stay up in the very highest trees and, in general, to avoid humanity. His world begins at about the limit of my eyesight.

On the particular morning when this episode occurred, the whole countryside was buried in one of the thickest fogs in years. The ceiling was absolutely zero. All planes were grounded, and even a pedestrian could hardly see his outstretched hand before him.

I was groping across a field in the general direction of the railroad station, following a dimly outlined path. Suddenly out of the fog, at about the level of my eyes, and so closely that I flinched, there flashed a pair of immense black wings and a huge beak. The whole bird rushed over my head with a frantic cawing outcry of such hideous terror as I have never heard in a crow's voice before, and never expect to hear again.

He was lost and startled, I thought, as I recovered my poise. He ought not to have flown out in this fog. He'd knock his silly brains out.

All afternoon that great awkward cry rang in my head. Merely being lost in a fog seemed scarcely to account for it—especially in a tough, intelligent old bandit such as I knew that particular crow to be. I even looked once in the mirror to see what it might be about me that had so revolted him that he had cried out in protest to the very stones.

Finally, as I worked my way homeward along the path, the solution came to me. It should have been clear before. The borders of our worlds had shifted. It was the fog that had done it. That crow, and I knew him well, never under normal circumstances flew low near men. He had been lost all right, but it was more than that. He had thought he was high up, and when he encountered me looming gigantically through the fog, he had perceived a ghastly and, to the crow mind, unnatural sight. He had seen a man walking on air, desecrating the very heart of the crow kingdom, a harbinger of the most profound evil a crow mind could conceive of—air-walking men. The encounter, he must have thought, had taken place a hundred feet over the roofs.

He caws now when he sees me leaving for the station in the morning, and I fancy that in that note I catch the uncertainty of a mind that has come to know things are not always what they seem. He has seen a marvel in his heights of air and is no longer as other crows. He has experienced the human world from an unlikely perspective. He and I share a viewpoint in common: Our worlds have interpenetrated, and we both have faith in the miraculous.

It is a faith that in my own case has been augmented by two remarkable sights. As I have hinted previously, I once saw some very odd chemicals fly across a waste so dead it might have been upon the moon, and once, by an even more fantastic piece of luck, I was present when a group of birds passed a judgment upon life.

On the maps of the old voyageurs it is called *Mauvaises Terres*, the evil lands, and, slurred a little with the passage through many minds, it has come down to us anglicized as the Badlands. The soft shuffle of moccasins has passed through its canyons on the grim business of war and flight, but the last of those slight disturbances of immemorial silences died out almost a century ago. The land, if one can call it a land, is a waste as lifeless as that valley in which lie-the kings of Egypt. Like the Valley of the Kings, it is a mausoleum, a place of dry bones in what once was a place of life. Now it has silences as deep as those in the moon's airless chasms.

Nothing grows among its pinnacles; there is no shade except under great toadstools of sandstone whose bases have been eaten to the shape of wine glasses by the wind. Everything is flaking, cracking, disintegrating, wearing away in the long, imperceptible weather of time. The ash of ancient volcanic outbursts still sterilizes its soil, and its colors in that waste are the colors that flame in the lonely sunsets on dead planets. Men come there but rarely, and for one purpose only, the collection of bones.

It was a late hour on a cold, wind-bitten autumn day when I climbed a great hill spined like a dinosaur's back and tried to take my bearings. The tumbled waste fell away in waves in all directions. Blue air was darkening into purple along the bases of the hills. I shifted my knapsack, heavy with the petrified bones of long-vanished creatures, and studied my compass. I wanted to be out of there by nightfall, and already the sun was going sullenly down in the west.

It was then that I saw the flight coming on. It was moving like a little close-knit body of black specks that danced and darted and closed again. It was pouring from the north and heading toward me with the undeviating relentlessness of a compass needle. It streamed through the shadows rising out of monstrous gorges. It rushed over towering pinnacles in the red light of the sun, or momentarily sank from sight within their shade. Across that desert of eroding clay and wind-worn stone they came with a faint wild twittering that filled all the air about me as those tiny living bullets hurtled past into the night.

It may not strike you as a marvel. It would not, perhaps, unless you stood in the middle of a dead world at sunset, but that was where I stood. Fifty million years lay under my feet, fifty million years of bellowing monsters moving in a green world now gone so utterly that its very light was traveling on the farther edge of space. The chemicals of all that vanished age lay about me in the ground. Around me still lay the shearing molars of dead titanotheres, the delicate sabers of soft-stepping cats, the hollow sockets that had held the eyes of many a strange outmoded beast. Those eyes had looked out upon a world as real as ours; dark, savage brains had roamed and roared their challenges into the steaming night.

Now they were still here, or, put it as you will, the chemicals that made them were here about me in the ground. The carbon that had driven them ran blackly in the eroding stone. The stain of iron was in the clays. The iron did not remember the blood it had once moved within, the phosphorus had forgot the savage brain. The little individual moment had ebbed from all those strange combinations of chemicals as it would ebb from our living bodies into the sinks and runnels of oncoming time.

I had lifted up a fistful of that ground. I held it while that wild flight of south-bound warblers hurtled over me into the oncoming dark. There went phosphorus, there went iron, there went carbon, there beat the calcium in those hurrying wings. Alone on a dead planet I watched that incredible miracle speeding past. It ran by some true compass over field and waste land. It cried its individual ecstasies into the air until the gullies rang. It swerved like a single body, it knew itself and, lonely, it bunched close in the racing darkness, its individual entities feeling about them the rising night. And so, crying to each other their identity, they passed away out of my view.

I dropped my fistful of earth. I heard it roll inanimate back into the gully at the base of the hill: iron, carbon, the chemicals of life. Like men from those wild tribes who had haunted these hills before me seeking visions, I made my sign to the great darkness. It was not a mocking sign, and I was not mocked. As I walked into my camp late that night, one man, rousing from his blankets beside the fire, asked sleepily, "What did you see?"

"I think, a miracle," I said softly, but I said it to myself. Behind me that vast waste began to glow under the rising moon.

I have said that I saw a judgment upon life, and that it was not passed by men. Those who stare at birds in cages or who test minds by their closeness to our own may not care for it. It comes from far away out of my past, in a place of pouring waters and green leaves. I shall never see an episode like it again if I live to be a hundred, nor do I think that one man in a million has ever seen it, because man is an intruder into such silences. The light must be right, and the observer must remain unseen. No man sets up such an experiment. What he sees, he sees by chance.

You may put it that I had come over a mountain, that I had slogged through fern and pine needles for half a long day, and that on the edge of a little glade with one long, crooked branch extending across it, I had sat down to rest with my back against a stump. Through accident I was concealed from the glade, although I could see into it perfectly.

The sun was warm there, and the murmurs of forest life blurred softly away into my sleep. When I awoke, dimly aware of some commotion and outcry in the clearing, the light was slanting down through the pines in such a way that the glade was lit like some vast cathedral. I could see the dust motes of wood pollen in the long shaft of light, and there on the extended branch sat an enormous raven with a red and squirming nestling in his beak.

The sound that awoke me was the outraged cries of the nestling's parents, who flew helplessly in circles about the clearing. The sleek black monster was indifferent to them. He gulped, whetted his beak on the dead branch a moment, and sat still. Up to that point the little tragedy had followed the usual pattern. But suddenly, out of all that area of woodland, a soft sound of complaint began to rise. Into the glade fluttered small birds of half a dozen varieties drawn by the anguished outcries of the tiny parents.

No one dared to attack the raven. But they cried there in some instinctive common misery, the bereaved and the unbereaved. The glade filled with their soft rustling and their cries. They fluttered as though to point their wings at the murderer. There was a dim intangible ethic he had violated, that they knew. He was a bird of death.

And he, the murderer, the black bird at the heart of life, sat on there, glistening in the common light, formidable, unmoving, unperturbed, untouchable.

The sighing died. It was then I saw the judgment. It was the judgment of life against death. I will never see it again so forcefully presented. I will never hear it again in notes so tragically prolonged. For in the midst of protest, they forgot the violence. There, in that clearing, the crystal note of a song sparrow lifted hesitantly in the hush. And finally, after painful fluttering, another took the song, and then another, the song passing from one bird to another, doubtfully at first, as though some evil thing were being slowly forgotten. Till suddenly they took heart and sang from many throats joyously together as birds are known to sing. They sang because life is sweet and sunlight beautiful. They sang under the brooding shadow of the raven. In simple truth they had forgotten the raven, for they were the singers of life, and not of death.

I was not of that airy company. My limbs were the heavy limbs of an earthbound creature who could climb mountains, even the mountains of the mind, only by a great effort of will. I knew I had seen a marvel and observed a judgment, but the mind which was my human endowment was sure to question it and to be at me day by day with its heresies until I grew to doubt the meaning of what I had seen. Eventually darkness and subtleties would ring me round once more.

And so it proved until, on the top of a stepladder, I made one more observation upon life. It was cold that autumn evening, and, standing under a suburban street light in a spate of leaves and beginning snow, I was suddenly conscious of some huge and hairy shadows dancing over the pavement. They seemed attached to an odd, globular shape that was magnified above me. There was no mistaking it. I was standing under the shadow of an orb-weaving spider. Gigantically projected against the street, she was about her spinning when everything was going underground. Even her cables were magnified upon the sidewalk and already I was half-entangled in their shadows.

"Good Lord," I thought, "she has found herself a kind of minor sun and is going to upset the course of nature."

I procured a ladder from my yard and climbed up to inspect the situation. There she was, the universe running down around her, warmly arranged among her guy ropes attached to the lamp supports—a great black and yellow embodiment of the life force, not giving up to either frost or stepladders. She ignored me and went on tightening and improving her web.

I stood over her on the ladder, a faint snow touching my cheeks, and surveyed her universe. There were a couple of iridescent green beetle cases turning slowly on a loose strand of web, a fragment of luminescent eye from a moth's wing and a large indeterminable object, perhaps a cicada, that had struggled and been wrapped in silk. There were also little bits and slivers, little red and blue flashes from the scales of anonymous wings that had crashed there.

Some days, I thought, they will be dull and gray and the shine will be out of them; then the dew will polish them again and drops hang on the silk until everything is gleaming and turning in the light. It is like a mind, really, where everything changes but remains, and in the end you have these eaten-out bits of experience like beetle wings.

I stood over her a moment longer, comprehending somewhat reluctantly that her adventure against the great blind forces of winter, her seizure of this warming globe of light, would come to nothing and was hopeless. Nevertheless it brought the birds back into my mind, and that faraway song which had traveled with growing strength around a forest clearing years ago—a kind of heroism, a world where even a spider refuses to lie down and die if a rope can still be spun on to a star. Maybe man himself will fight like this in the end, I thought, slowly realizing that the web and its threatening yellow occupant had been added to some luminous store of experience, shining for a moment in the fog-bound reaches of my brain.

The mind, it came to me as I slowly descended the ladder, is a very remarkable thing; it has gotten itself a kind of courage by looking at a spider in a street lamp. Here was something that ought to be passed on to those who will fight our final freezing battle with the void. I thought of setting it down carefully as a message to the future: *In the days of the frost seek a minor sun.*

But as I hesitated, it became plain that something was wrong. The marvel was escaping—a sense of bigness beyond man's power to grasp, the essence of life in its great dealings with the universe. It was better, I decided, for the emissaries returning from the wilderness, even if they were merely descending from a stepladder, to record their marvel, not to define its meaning. In that way it would go echoing on through the minds of men, each grasping at that beyond out of which the miracles emerge, and which, once defined, ceases to satisfy the human need for symbols.

In the end I merely made a mental note: One specimen of Epeira observed building a web in a street light. Late autumn and cold for spiders. Cold for men, too. I shivered and left the lamp glowing there in my mind. The last I saw of Epeira she was hauling steadily on a cable. I stepped carefully over her shadow as I walked away.

CHAPTER SEVEN

Visions for the Future

So where do we go from here? The safest rule to follow in thinking about the future is to expect the unexpected. Our only real certainty is that the future rarely, if ever, comes in the shapes we predict for it. Perhaps this is best, for where would be the excitement of the future once its mystery were lost? It may be that it is precisely the sense of mystery itself, a mystery Creeley's poem subtly evokes, which we need most to recover if we are to have any future at all. We require the very inscrutability of the future for a screen where we may project those visions of hope which make it possible to go on with existence. In the wisdom of the Old Testament, "We see as through a glass darkly."

In his poem, "Advice to a Prophet," Richard Wilbur reminds us that our current fascination with apocalyptic predictions of doom by fashionable disciples of despair makes it easy for us to forget some old truisms. As Edmund Bacon has written in his recent book, Design of Cities, *"we are in danger of losing one of the most important concepts of mankind, that the future is what we make it." Or perhaps Yeats said it best: "In dreams begin responsibilities." If it is true that men turn to violence as a way of dramatizing their inner vacancies, then our present agitation is itself a sign of the urgent need to search out visions with which we can live. As Roger Zelazny's story suggests, our present needs are twofold: We must first believe that a future is possible at all, and then we must be prepared to take responsibility for the kinds of visions by which we choose to shape this future.*

The words of Alan McGlashan best sum up the distance covered in going from the first section of this anthology to the last. In The Savage and Beautiful Country, *he points us in the direction of "an unimaginable Beyond" which has always invited man to transcend himself. In our restlessness lies our redemption.*

> *Today we live in an atmosphere which is pervaded by a growing and extremely uncomfortable conviction that something is about to burst. By the great majority this possibility is referred to the external world, where indeed it may very well occur. The big bang may be a multimegaton H-bomb, or some space experiment which calls down upon us a brief, annihilating gesture of cosmic irritation. But it is also possible that our external anxieties may be projections of an approaching explosion within ourselves. Man may be about to burst from his psychological swaddling clothes—an event as crucial and as perilous as any that could occur in the external world. Something of the sort is already happening. Psyche, the immortal butterfly, is struggling within her cocoon. Spiritually as well as physically man begins suddenly to feel the world he lives in is too small for him, suddenly to realize the intolerable crampedness of the human situation. With the blind urgency of an embryo that has reached its term, man strains to escape, to burst through to an unimaginable Beyond, making unconsciously, as he does so, some noble, some foolish, some dangerous, some ludicrous movements.*

We seek, first and foremost, attitudes and orientations—not destinations. Marshall McLuhan chides us for steering the great automobile of our culture into the future while we gaze through the rearview mirror. But perhaps this backward gaze is precisely what is called for. It might be that the clues to our salvation lie mainly in our "primitive" past. The anthropologists have become our current intellectual heroes, as Susan Sontag reports, mainly because such researchers as Claude Lévi-Strauss, Mircea Eliade, Lucien Lévy-Bruhl, Bronislaw Malinowski, and Margaret Mead have shown us how full of the awareness of Being the sacralized consciousness of primitive man is, compared to modern man's desecrated vision. In this final chapter, Laurens van der Post's description of the Kalahari Bushman ushers us into such a primitive world-view. Aboriginal natives can see; they can experience so much more than we because their world is charged with a sense of the numinous. Where we can only see a blank, they see a universe permeated with the Life Spirit. Their world is alive in a way that reveals ours as dead and inert. Their world is overflowing with presences, mystery, awe, and reverence. Ours is an empty vacuum. Modern man's great hubris is that he thought to become superior by divesting himself of all the superstitions and myths deluding the "backward" areas of the world. The anthropologists are beginning to teach us how by desacralizing the universe we lost an appreciation of its wholeness. Man must surpass what he is or die, Nietzsche said. He must ever fling himself into the mystery of a Beyond. Perhaps the transcendence we most require today lies in a recovery of that consciousness man once knew at the dawn of creation. Perhaps our future rests in a repossession of our earliest past. It very well may be that tomorrow is the beginning of the world.

PHILIP BOOTH

First Lesson

Lie back, daughter, let your head
be tipped back in the cup of my hand.
Gently, and I will hold you. Spread
your arms wide, lie out on the stream
and look high at the gulls. A dead-
man's float is face down. You will dive
and swim soon enough where this tidewater
ebbs to the sea. Daughter, believe
me, when you tire on the long thrash
to your island, lie up, and survive.   10
As you float now, where I held you
and let go, remember when fear
cramps your heart what I told you:
lie gently and wide to the light-year
stars, lie back, and the sea will hold you.

ROBERT CREELEY

For No Clear Reason

I dreamt last night
the fright was over, that
the dust came, and then water,
and women and men, together
again, and all was quiet
in the dim moon's light.

A paean of such patience—
laughing, laughing at me,
and the days extend over

the earth's great cover,   10
grass, trees, and flower-
ing season, for no clear reason.

HERBERT LOMAS

The Underground Revolution

Beer bottles are getting broken
In Holborn and Camden Town.
At this moment
In King's Road and Covent Garden
Thousands of Indian shamen
Are breaking beer bottles.

At this moment
Just off Sloane Square
The squaws are on the warpath
And thousands of Indian shamen   10
Are breaking beer bottles
In Notting Hill Gate.

This revolution in consciousness
Happened on the fourth dimension
When thousands of Indian shamen
Murdered in America
Walked into Blake's London
And started living in the houses.

With their superior agelessness
All those Red Indian guides   20
Who appeared so inexplicably
In the Spiritualist Movement
Are breaking beer bottles
Near Charing Cross Road.

Englishmen, disguised as Americans,
Wiped out the wigwam,
And now the Red Men, disguised as Englishmen,
Are coming down to Holborn,
Breaking beer bottles
And smoking pot.   30

You can't put new pot into old bottles,
But the tribes are coming back,
Educating the white man,
Breaking his beer bottles,
And thousands of Indian shamen
Are creating an empire, gently.

Gently they are coming down
As the so-called young,
As the sons of Albion
And the daughters of Beulah,   40
In clouds of weird smoke
They are breaking the beer bottles.

RICHARD WILBUR

Advice to a Prophet

When you come, as you soon must, to the streets of our city,
Mad-eyed from stating the obvious,
Not proclaiming our fall but begging us
In God's name to have self-pity,

Spare us all word of the weapons, their force and range,
The long numbers that rocket the mind;
Our slow, unreckoning hearts will be left behind,
Unable to fear what is too strange.

Nor shall you scare us with talk of the death of the race.
How should we dream of this place without us?—   10
The sun mere fire, the leaves untroubled about us,
A stone look on the stone's face?

Speak of the world's own change. Though we cannot con-
    ceive
Of an undreamt thing, we know to our cost
How the dreamt cloud crumbles, the vines are blackened by
    frost,
How the view alters. We could believe,

If you told us so, that the white-tailed deer will slip
Into perfect shade, grown perfectly shy,
The lark avoid the reaches of our eye,
The jack-pine lose its knuckled grip   20

On the cold ledge, and every torrent burn
As Xanthus once, its gliding trout
Stunned in a twinkling. What should we be without
The dolphin's arc, the dove's return,

These things in which we have seen ourselves and spoken?
Ask us, prophet, how we shall call
Our natures forth when that live tongue is all
Dispelled, that glass obscured or broken

In which we have said the rose of our love and the clean
Horse of our courage, in which beheld   30
The singing locust of the soul unshelled,
And all we mean or wish to mean.

Ask us, ask us whether with the worldless rose
Our hearts shall fail us; come demanding
Whether there shall be lofty or long standing
When the bronze annals of the oak-tree close.

JOHN BARTH

Night-Sea Journey

"One way or another, no matter which theory of our journey is correct, it's myself I address; to whom I rehearse as to a stranger our history and condition, and will disclose my secret hope though I sink for it.

"Is the journey my invention? Do the night, the sea, exist at all, I ask myself, apart from my experience of them? Do I myself exist, or is this a dream? Sometimes I wonder. And if I am, who am I? The Heritage I supposedly transport? But how can I be both vessel and contents? Such are the questions that beset my intervals of rest.

"My trouble is, I lack conviction. Many accounts of our situation seem plausible to me—where and what we are, why we swim and wither. But implausible ones as well, perhaps especially those, I must admit as possibly correct. Even likely. If at times, in certain humors—striking in unison, say, with my neighbors and chanting with them 'Onward! Upward!'—I have supposed that we have after all a common Maker, Whose nature and motives we may not know, but Who engendered us in some mysterious wise and launched us forth toward some end known but to Him—if (for a moodslength only) I have been able to entertain such notions, very popular in certain quarters, it is because our night-sea journey partakes of their absurdity. One might even say: I can believe them *because* they are absurd.

"Has that been said before?

"Another paradox: it appears to be these recesses from swimming that sustain me in the swim. Two measures onward and upward, flailing with the rest, then I float exhausted and dispirited, brood upon the night, the sea, the journey, while the flood bears me a measure back and down: slow progress, but I live, I live, and make my way, aye, past many a drownèd comrade in the end, stronger, worthier than I, victims of their unremitting *joie de nager*. I have seen the best swimmers of my generation go under. Numberless the number of the dead! Thousands drown as I think this thought, millions as I rest before returning to the swim. And scores, hundreds of millions have expired since we surged forth, brave in our innocence, upon our dreadful way. 'Love! Love!' we sang then, a quarter-billion strong, and churned the warm sea white with joy of swimming! Now all are gone down—the buoyant, the sodden, leaders and followers, all gone under, while wretched I swim on. Yet these same reflective intervals that keep me afloat have led me into wonder, doubt, despair—strange emotions for a swimmer!—have led me, even, to suspect . . . that our night-sea journey is without meaning.

"Indeed, if I have yet to join the hosts of the suicides, it is because (fatigue apart) I find it no meaningfuller to drown myself than to go on swimming.

"I know that there are those who seem actually to enjoy the night-sea; who claim to love swimming for its own sake, or sincerely believe that 'reaching the Shore,' 'transmitting the Heritage' (*Whose* Heritage, I'd like to know? And to whom?) is worth the staggering cost. I do not. Swimming itself I find at best not actively unpleasant, more often tiresome, not infrequently a torment. Arguments from function and design don't impress me: granted that we can and do swim, that in a manner of speaking our long tails and streamlined heads are 'meant for' swimming; it by no means follows—for me, at least—that we *should* swim, or otherwise endeavor to 'fulfill our destiny.' Which is to say, Someone Else's destiny, since ours, so far as I can see, is merely to perish, one way or another, soon or late. The heartless zeal of our (departed) leaders, like the blind ambition and good cheer of my own youth, appalls me now; for the death of my comrades I am inconsolable. If the night-sea journey has justification, it is not for us swimmers ever to discover it.

"Oh, to be sure, 'Love!' one heard on every side: 'Love it is that drives and sustains us!' I translate: we don't know *what* drives and sustains us, only that we are most miserably driven and, imperfectly, sustained. *Love* is how we call our ignorance of what whips us. 'To reach the Shore,' then: but what if the Shore exists in the fancies of us swimmers merely, who dream it to account for the dreadful fact that we swim, have always and only swum, and continue swimming without respite (myself excepted) until we die? Supposing even that there *were* a Shore—that, as a cynical companion of mine once imagined, we rise from the drowned to discover all those vulgar superstitions and exalted metaphors to be literal truth: the giant Maker of us all, the Shores of Light beyond our night-sea journey!—whatever would a swimmer do there? The fact is, when we imagine the Shore, what comes to mind is just the opposite of our condition: no more night, no more sea, no more journeying. In short, the blissful estate of the drowned.

" 'Ours not to stop and think; ours but to swim and sink. . . .' Because a moment's thought reveals the pointlessness of swimming. 'No matter,' I've heard some say, even as they gulped their last: 'The night-sea journey may be absurd, but here we swim, will-we nill-we, against the flood, onward and upward, toward a Shore that may not exist and couldn't be reached if it did.' The thoughtful swimmer's choices, then, they say, are two: give over thrashing and go under for good, or embrace the absurdity; affirm in and for itself the night-sea journey; swim on with neither motive nor destination, for the sake of swimming, and compassionate moreover with your fellow swimmer, we being all at sea and equally in the dark. I find neither course acceptable. If not even the hypothetical Shore can justify a sea-full of drownèd comrades, to speak of the swim-in-itself as somehow doing so strikes me as obscene. I continue to swim—but only because blind habit, blind instinct, blind fear of drowning are still more strong than the horror of our journey. And if on occasion I have assisted a fellow-thrasher, joined in the cheers and songs, even passed along to others strokes of genius from the drownèd great, it's that I shrink by temperament from making myself conspicuous. To paddle off in one's own direction, assert one's independent right-of-way, overrun one's fellows without compunction, or dedicate oneself entirely to pleasures and diversions without regard for conscience—I can't finally condemn those who journey in this wise; in half my moods I envy them and despise the weak vitality that keeps me from following their example. But in reasonabler moments I remind myself that it's their very freedom and self-responsibility I reject, as more dramatically absurd, in our senseless circumstances, than tailing along in conventional fashion. Suicides, rebels, affirmers of the paradox—nay-sayers and yea-sayers alike to our fatal journey—I finally shake my head at them. And splash sighing past their corpses, one by one, as past a hundred sorts of others: friends, enemies, brothers; fools, sages, brutes —and nobodies, million upon million. I envy them all.

"A poor irony: that I, who find abhorrent and tautological the doctrine of survival of the fittest (*fitness* meaning, in my experience, nothing more than survival-ability, a talent whose only demonstration is the fact of survival, but whose chief ingredients seem to be strength, guile, callousness), may be the sole remaining swimmer! But the doctrine is false as well as repellent: Chance drowns the worthy with the unworthy, bears up the unfit with the fit by whatever definition, and makes the night-sea journey essentially *haphazard* as well as murderous and unjustified.

" 'You only swim once.' Why bother, then?

" 'Except ye drown, ye shall not reach the Shore of Light.' Poppycock.

"One of my late companions—that same cynic with the curious fancy, among the first to drown—entertained us with odd conjectures while we waited to begin our journey. A favorite theory of his was that the Father does exist, and did indeed make us and the sea we swim—but not a-purpose or even consciously; He made us, as it were, despite Himself, as we make waves with every tail-thrash, and may be unaware of our existence. Another was that He knows we're here but doesn't care what happens to us, inasmuch as He creates (voluntarily or not) other seas and swimmers at more or less regular intervals. In bitterer moments, such as just before he drowned, my friend even supposed that our Maker wished us unmade; there was indeed a Shore, he'd argue, which could save at least some of us from drowning and toward which it was our function to struggle—but for reasons unknowable to us He wanted desperately to prevent our reaching that happy place and fulfilling our destiny. Our 'Father,' in short, was our adversary and would-be killer! No less outrageous, and offensive to traditional opinion, were the fellow's speculations on the nature of our Maker: that He might well be no swimmer Himself at all, but some sort of monstrosity, perhaps even tailless; that He might be stupid, malicious, insensible, perverse, or asleep and dreaming; that the end for which He created and launched us forth, and which we flagellate ourselves to fathom, was perhaps immoral, even obscene. Et cetera, et cetera: there was no end to the chap's conjectures, or the impoliteness of his fancy; I have reason to suspect that his early demise, whether planned by 'our Maker' or not, was expedited by certain fellow-swimmers indignant at his blasphemies.

"In other moods, however (he was as given to moods as I), his theorizing would become half-serious, so it seemed to me, especially upon the subjects of Fate and Immortality, to which our youthful conversations often turned. Then his harangues, if no less fantastical, grew solemn and obscure, and if he was still baiting us, his passion undid the joke. His objection to popular opinions of the hereafter, he would declare, was their claim to general validity. Why need believers hold that *all* the drownèd rise to be judged at journey's end, and non-believers that drowning is final without exception? In *his* opinion (so he'd vow at least), nearly everyone's fate was permanent death; indeed he took a sour pleasure in supposing that every 'Maker' made thousands of separate seas in His creative lifetime, each populated like ours with millions of swimmers, and that in almost every instance both sea and swimmers were utterly annihilated, whether accidentally or by malevolent design. (Nothing if not pluralistical, he imagined there might be millions and billions of 'Fathers,' perhaps in some 'night-sea' of their own!) However—and here he turned infidels against him with the faithful—he professed to believe that in possibly a single night-sea per thousand, say, one of its quarter-billion swimmers (that is, one swimmer in two hundred fifty billions) achieved a qualified immortality. In some cases the rate might be slightly higher; in others it was vastly lower, for just as there are swimmers of every degree of proficiency, including some who drown before the journey starts, unable to swim at all, and others created drowned, as it were, so he imagined what can only be termed impotent Creators, Makers unable to Make, as well as uncommonly fertile ones and all grades between. And it pleased him to deny any necessary relation between a Maker's productivity and His other virtues—including, even, the quality of His creatures.

"I could go on (*he* surely did) with his elaboration of these mad notions—such as that swimmers in other night-seas needn't be of our kind; that Makers themselves might belong to different *species,* so to speak; that our particular Maker mightn't Himself be immortal, or that we might be not only His emissaries but His 'immortality,' continuing His life and our own, transmogrified, beyond our individual deaths. Even this modified immortality (meaningless to me) he conceived as relative and contingent, subject to accident or deliberate termination: his pet hypothesis was that Makers and swimmers *each generate the other*—against all odds, their number being so great—and that any given 'immortality-chain' could terminate after any number of cycles, so that what was 'immortal' (still speaking relatively) was only the cyclic process of incarnation, which itself might have a beginning and an end. Alternatively he liked to imagine cycles within cycles, either finite or infinite: for example, the 'night-sea,' as it were, in which Makers 'swam' and created night-seas and swimmers like ourselves, might be the creation of a larger Maker, Himself one of many, Who in turn et cetera. Time itself he regarded as relative to our experience, like magnitude: who knew but what, with each thrash of our tails, minuscule seas and swimmers, whole eternities, came to pass—as ours, perhaps, and our Maker's Maker's, was elapsing between the strokes of some supertail, in a slower order of time?

"Naturally I hooted with the others at this nonsense. We were young then, and had only the dimmest notion of what lay ahead; in our ignorance we imagined night-sea journeying to be a positively heroic enterprise. Its meaning and value we never questioned; to be sure, some must go down by the way, a pity no doubt, but to win a race requires that others lose, and like all my fellows I took for granted that I would be the winner. We milled and swarmed, impatient to be off, never mind where or why, only to try our youth against the realities of night and sea; if we indulged the skeptic at all, it was as a droll, half-contemptible mascot. When he died in the initial slaughter, no one cared.

"And even now I don't subscribe to all his views—but I no longer scoff. The horror of our history has purged me of opinions, as of vanity, confidence, spirit, charity, hope, vitality, everything— except dull dread and a kind of melancholy, stunned persistence. What leads me to recall his fancies is my growing suspicion that I, of all swimmers, may be the sole survivor of this fell journey, tale-bearer of a generation. This suspicion, together with the recent sea-change, suggests to me now that nothing is impossible,

not even my late companion's wildest visions, and brings me to
a certain desperate resolve, the point of my chronicling.

"Very likely I have lost my senses. The carnage at our setting
out; our decimation by whirlpool, poisoned cataract, sea-convul-
sion; the panic stampedes, mutinies, slaughters, mass suicides; the
mounting evidence that none will survive the journey—add to
these anguish and fatigue; it were a miracle if sanity stayed afloat.
Thus I admit, with the other possibilities, that the present sweet-
ening and calming of the sea, and what seems to be a kind of
vasty presence, song, or summons from the near upstream, may
be hallucinations of disordered sensibility. . . .

"Perhaps, even, I am drowned already. Surely I was never meant
for the rough-and-tumble of the swim; not impossibly I perished
at the outset and have only imaged the night-sea journey from
some final deep. In any case, I'm no longer young, and it is we
spent old swimmers, disabused of every illusion, who are most
vulnerable to dreams.

"Sometimes I think I am my drownèd friend.

"Out with it: I've begun to believe, not only that *She* exists,
but that She lies not far ahead, and stills the sea, and draws me
Herward! Aghast, I recollect his maddest notion: that our destination (which existed, mind, in but one night-sea out of hundreds
and thousands) was no Shore, as commonly conceived, but a mysterious being, indescribable except by paradox and vaguest figure:
wholly different from us swimmers, yet our complement; the death
of us, yet our salvation and resurrection; simultaneously our journey's end, mid-point, and commencement; not membered and
thrashing like us, but a motionless or hugely gliding sphere of unimaginable dimension; self-contained, yet dependent absolutely,
in some wise, upon the chance (always monstrously improbable)
that one of us will survive the night-sea journey and reach . . .
Her! *Her*, he called it, or *She*, which is to say, Other-than-a-he.
I shake my head; the thing is too preposterous; it is myself I talk
to, to keep my reason in this awful darkness. There is no She!
There is no You! I rave to myself; it's Death alone that hears and
summons. To the drowned, all seas are calm. . . .

"Listen: my friend maintained that in every order of creation
there are two sorts of creators, contrary yet complementary, one
of which gives rise to seas and swimmers, the other to the Night-
which-contains-the-sea and to What-waits-at-the-journey's-end: the

former, in short, to destiny, the latter to destination (and both profligately, involuntarily, perhaps indifferently or unwittingly). The 'purpose' of the night-sea journey—but not necessarily of the journeyer or of either Maker!—my friend could describe only in abstractions: *consummation, transfiguration, union of contraries, transcension of categories.* When we laughed, he would shrug and admit that he understood the business no better than we, and thought it ridiculous, dreary, possibly obscene. 'But one of you,' he'd add with his wry smile, 'may be the Hero destined to complete the night-sea journey and be one with Her. Chances are, of course, you won't make it.' He himself, he declared, was not even going to try; the whole idea repelled him; if we chose to dismiss it as an ugly fiction, so much the better for us; thrash, splash, and be merry, we were soon enough drowned. But there it was, he could not say how he knew or why he bothered to tell us, any more than he could say what would happen after She and Hero, Shore and Swimmer, 'merged identities' to become something both and neither. He quite agreed with me that if the issue of that magical union had no memory of the night-sea journey, for example, it enjoyed a poor sort of immortality; even poorer if, as he rather imagined, a swimmer-hero plus a She equaled or became merely another Maker of future night-seas and the rest, at such incredible expense of life. This being the case—he was persuaded it was—the merciful thing to do was refuse to participate; the genuine heroes, in his opinion, were the suicides, and the hero of heroes would be the swimmer who, in the very presence of the Other, refused Her proffered 'immortality' and thus put an end to at least one cycle of catastrophes.

"How we mocked him! Our moment came, we hurtled forth, pretending to glory in the adventure, thrashing, singing, cursing, strangling, rationalizing, rescuing, killing, inventing rules and stories and relationships, giving up, struggling on, but dying all, and still in darkness, until only a battered remnant was left to croak 'Onward, upward,' like a bitter echo. Then they too fell silent—victims, I can only presume, of the last frightful wave— and the moment came when I also, utterly desolate and spent, thrashed my last and gave myself over to the current, to sink or float as might be, but swim no more. Whereupon, marvelous to tell, in an instant the sea grew still! Then warmly, gently, the great tide turned, began to bear me, as it does now, onward and upward will-I nill-I, like a flood of joy—and I recalled with dismay my dead friend's teaching.

"I am not deceived. This new emotion is Her doing; the desire that possesses me is Her bewitchment. Lucidity passes from me; in a moment I'll cry 'Love!' bury myself in Her side, and be 'transfigured.' Which is to say, I die already; this fellow transported by passion is not I; *I am he who abjures and rejects the night-sea journey!* I. . . .

"I am all love. 'Come!' She whispers, and I have no will.

"You who I may be about to become, whatever You are: with the last twitch of my real self I beg You to listen. It is *not* love that sustains me! No; though Her magic makes me burn to sing the contrary, and though I drown even now for the blasphemy, I will say truth. What has fetched me across this dreadful sea is a single hope, gift of my poor dead comrade: that You may be stronger-willed than I, and that by sheer force of concentration I may transmit to You, along with Your official Heritage, a private legacy of awful recollection and negative resolve. Mad as it may be, my dream is that some unimaginable embodiment of myself (or myself plus Her if that's how it must be) will come to find itself expressing, in however garbled or radical a translation, some reflection of these reflections. If against all odds this comes to pass, may You to whom, through whom I speak, do what I cannot: terminate this aimless, brutal business! Stop Your hearing against Her song! Hate love!

"Still alive, afloat, afire. Farewell then my penultimate hope: that one may be sunk for direct blasphemy on the very shore of the Shore. Can it be (my old friend would smile) that only utterest nay-sayers survive the night? But even that were Sense, and there is no sense, only senseless love, senseless death. Whoever echoes these reflections: be more courageous than their author! An end to night-sea journeys! Make no more! And forswear me when I shall forswear myself, deny myself, plunge into Her who summons, singing . . .

" 'Love! Love! Love!' "

ROGER ZELAZNY

A Rose for Ecclesiastes

I

I was busy translating one of my *Madrigals Macabre* into Martian on the morning I was found acceptable. The intercom had buzzed briefly, and I dropped my pencil and flipped on the toggle in a single motion.

"Mister G," piped Morton's youthful contralto, "the old man says I should 'get hold of that damned conceited rhymer' right away, and send him to his cabin.—Since there's only one damned conceited rhymer . . ."

"Let not ambition mock thy useful toil." I cut him off.

So, the Martians had finally made up their minds! I knocked an inch and a half of ash from a smouldering butt, and took my first drag since I had lit it. The entire month's anticipation tried hard to crowd itself into the moment, but could not quite make it. I was frightened to walk those forty feet and hear Emory say the words I already knew he would say; and that feeling elbowed the other one into the background.

So I finished the stanza I was translating before I got up.

It took only a moment to reach Emory's door. I knocked twice and opened it, just as he growled, "Come in."

"You wanted to see me?" I sat down quickly to save him the trouble of offering me a seat.

"That was fast. What did you do, run?"

I regarded his paternal discontent:

Little fatty flecks beneath pale eyes, thinning hair, and an Irish nose; a voice a decibel louder than anyone else's . . .

Hamlet to Claudius: "I was working."

"Hah!" he snorted. "Come off it. No one's ever seen you do any of that stuff."

I shrugged my shoulders and started to rise.

"If that's what you called me down here—"

"Sit down!"

He stood up. He walked around his desk. He hovered above me and glared down. (A hard trick, even when I'm in a low chair.)

"You are undoubtedly the most antagonistic bastard I've ever had to work with!" he bellowed, like a belly-stung buffalo. "Why the hell don't you act like a human being sometime and surprise everybody? I'm willing to admit you're smart, maybe even a genius, but—oh, Hell!" He made a heaving gesture with both hands and walked back to his chair.

"Betty has finally talked them into letting you go in." His voice was normal again. "They'll receive you this afternoon. Draw one of the jeepsters after lunch, and get down there."

"Okay," I said.

"That's all, then."

I nodded, got to my feet. My hand was on the doorknob when he said:

"I don't have to tell you how important this is. Don't treat them the way you treat us."

I closed the door behind me.

I don't remember what I had for lunch. I was nervous, but I knew instinctively that I wouldn't muff it. My Boston publishers expected a Martian Idyll, or at least a Saint-Exupéry job on space flight. The National Science Association wanted a complete report on the Rise and Fall of the Martian Empire.

They would both be pleased. I knew.

That's the reason everyone is jealous—why they hate me. I always come through, and I can come through better than anyone else.

I shoveled in a final anthill of slop, and made my way to our car barn. I drew one jeepster and headed it toward Tirellian.

Flames of sand, lousy with iron oxide, set fire to the buggy. They swarmed over the open top and bit through my scarf; they set to work pitting my goggles.

The jeepster, swaying and panting like a little donkey I once rode through the Himalayas, kept kicking me in the seat of the pants. The Mountains of Tirellian shuffled their feet and moved toward me at a cockeyed angle.

Suddenly I was heading uphill, and I shifted gears to accommodate the engine's braying. Not like Gobi, not like the Great Southwestern Desert, I mused. Just red, just dead . . . without even a cactus.

I reached the crest of the hill, but I had raised too much dust to see what was ahead. It didn't matter, though, I have a head full of maps. I bore to the left and downhill, adjusting the throttle. A cross-wind and solid ground beat down the fires. I felt like Ulysses in Malebolge—with a terza-rima speech in one hand and an eye out for Dante.

I sounded a rock pagoda and arrived.

Betty waved as I crunched to a halt, then jumped down.

"Hi," I choked, unwinding my scarf and shaking out a pound and a half of grit. "Like, where do I go and who do I see?"

She permitted herself a brief Germanic giggle—more at my starting a sentence with "like" than at my discomfort—then she started talking. (She is a top linguist, so a word from the Village Idiom still tickles her!)

I appreciated her precise, furry talk; informational, and all that. I had enough in the way of social pleasantries before me to last at least the rest of my life. I looked at her chocolate-bar eyes and perfect teeth, at her sun-bleached hair, close-cropped to the head (I hate blondes!), and decided that she was in love with me.

"Mr. Gallinger, the Matriarch is waiting inside to be introduced. She has consented to open the Temple records for your study." She paused here to pat her hair and squirm a little. Did my gaze make her nervous?

"They are religious documents, as well as their only history," she continued, "sort of like the Mahabharata. She expects you to observe certain rituals in handling them, like repeating the sacred words when you turn pages—she will teach you the system."

I nodded quickly, several times.

"Fine, let's go in."

"Uh—" she paused. "Do not forget their Eleven Forms of Politeness and Degree. They take matters of form quite seriously—and do not get into any discussions over the equality of the sexes—"

"I know all about their taboos," I broke in. "Don't worry. I've lived in the Orient, remember?"

She dropped her eyes and seized my hand. I almost jerked it away.

"It will look better if I enter leading you."

I swallowed my comments and followed her, like Samson in Gaza.

Inside, my last thought met with a strange correspondence. The Matriarch's quarters were a rather abstract version of what I imagine the tents of the tribes of Israel to have been like. Abstract, I say, because it was all frescoed brick, peaked like a huge tent, with animal-skin representations, like gray-blue scars, that looked as if they had been laid on the walls with a palette knife.

The Matriarch, M'Cwyie, was short, white-haired, fiftyish, and dressed like a Gypsy queen. With her rainbow of voluminous skirts she looked like an inverted punch bowl set atop a cushion.

Accepting my obeisances, she regarded me as an owl might a rabbit. The lids of those black, black eyes jumped upwards as she discovered my perfect accent.—The tape recorder Betty had carried on her interviews had done its part, and I knew the language reports from the first two expeditions, verbatim. I'm all hell when it comes to picking up accents.

"You are the poet?"

"Yes," I replied.

"Recite one of your poems, please."

"I'm sorry, but nothing short of a thorough translating job would do justice to your language and my poetry, and I don't know enough of your language yet."

"Oh?"

"But I've been making such translations for my own amusement, as an exercise in grammar," I continued. "I'd be honored to bring a few of them along one of the times that I come here."

"Yes. Do so."

Score one for me!

She turned to Betty.

"You may go now."

Betty muttered the parting formalities, gave me a strange sidewise look, and was gone. She apparently had expected to stay and "assist" me. She wanted a piece of the glory, like everyone else.

But I was the Schliemann at this Troy, and there would be only one name on the Association report!

M'Cwyie rose, and I noticed that she gained very little height by standing. But then I'm six-six and look like a poplar in October: thin, bright red on top, and towering above everyone else.

"Our records are very, very old," she began. "Betty says that your word for their age is 'millennia.' "

I nodded appreciatively.

"I'm very eager to see them."

"They are not here. We will have to go into the Temple—they may not be removed."

I was suddenly wary.

"You have no objections to my copying them, do you?"

"No. I see that you respect them, or your desire would not be so great."

"Excellent."

She seemed amused. I asked her what was funny.

"The High Tongue may not be so easy for a foreigner to learn."

It came through fast.

No one on the first expedition had gotten this close. I had no way of knowing that this was a double-language deal—a classical as well as a vulgar. I knew some of their Prakrit, now I had to learn all their Sanskrit.

"Ouch! and damn!"

"Pardon, please?"

"It's nontranslatable, M'Cwyie. But imagine yourself having to learn the High Tongue in a hurry, and you can guess at the sentiment."

She seemed amused again, and told me to remove my shoes.

She guided me through an alcove . . .

. . . and into a burst of Byzantine brilliance!

No Earthman had ever been in this room before, or I would have heard about it. Carter, the first expedition's linguist, with the help of one Mary Allen, M.D., had learned all the grammar and vocabulary that I knew while sitting cross-legged in the antechamber.

We had had no idea this existed. Greedily, I cast my eyes about. A highly sophisticated system of esthetics lay behind the décor. We would have to revise our entire estimation of Martian culture.

For one thing, the ceiling was vaulted and corbeled; for another, there were side columns with reverse flutings; for another—oh hell! The place was big. Posh. You could never have guessed it from the shaggy outsides.

I bent forward to study the gilt filigree on a ceremonial table. M'Cwyie seemed a bit smug at my intentness, but I'd still have hated to play poker with her.

The table was loaded with books.

With my toe, I traced a mosaic on the floor.

"Is your entire city within this one building?"

"Yes, it goes far back into the mountain."

"I see," I said, seeing nothing.

I couldn't ask her for a conducted tour, yet.

She moved to a small stool by the table.

"Shall we begin your friendship with the High Tongue?"

I was trying to photograph the hall with my eyes, knowing I would have to get a camera in here, somehow, sooner or later. I tore my gaze from a statuette and nodded, hard.

"Yes, introduce me."

I sat down.

For the next three weeks alphabet-bugs chased each other behind my eyelids whenever I tried to sleep. The sky was an unclouded pool of turquoise that rippled calligraphies whenever I swept my eyes across it. I drank quarts of coffee while I worked and mixed cocktails of Benzedrine and champagne for my coffee breaks.

M'Cwyie tutored me two hours every morning, and occasionally for another two in the evening. I spent an additional fourteen hours a day on my own, once I had gotten up sufficient momentum to go ahead alone.

And at night the elevator of time dropped me to its bottom floors . . .

I was six again, learning my Hebrew, Greek, Latin, and Aramaic. I was ten, sneaking peeks at the *Iliad*. When Daddy wasn't spreading hellfire, brimstone, and brotherly love, he was teaching me to dig the Word, like in the original.

Lord! There are so many originals and so *many* words! When I was twelve I started pointing out the little differences between what he was preaching and what I was reading.

The fundamentalist vigor of his reply brooked no debate. It

was worse than any beating. I kept my mouth shut after that and learned to appreciate Old Testament poetry.

—Lord, I am sorry! Daddy—Sir—I am sorry!—It couldn't be! It couldn't be . . .

On the day the boy graduated from high school, with the French, German, Spanish, and Latin awards, Dad Gallinger had told his fourteen-year-old, six-foot scarecrow of a son that he wanted him to enter the ministry. I remember how his son was evasive:

"Sir," he had said, "I'd sort of like to study on my own for a year or so, and then take pre-theology courses at some liberal-arts university. I feel I'm still sort of young to try a seminary, straight off."

The Voice of God: "But you have the gift of tongues, my son. You can preach the Gospel in all the lands of Babel. You were born to be a missionary. You say you are young, but time is rushing by you like a whirlwind. Start early, and you will enjoy added years of service."

The added years of service were so many added tails to the cat repeatedly laid on my back. I can't see his face now, I never can. Maybe it is because I was always afraid to look at it then.

And years later, when he was dead, and laid out, in black, amidst bouquets, amidst weeping congregationalists, amidst prayers, red faces, handkerchiefs, hands patting your shoulders, solemn-faced comforters . . . I looked at him and did not recognize him.

We had met nine months before my birth, this stranger and I. He had never been cruel—stern, demanding, with contempt for everyone's shortcomings—but never cruel. He was also all that I had had of a mother. And brothers. And sisters. He had tolerated my three years at St. John's, possibly because of its name, never knowing how liberal and delightful a place it really was.

But I never knew him, and the man atop the catafalque demanded nothing now; I was free not to preach the Word.

But now I wanted to, in a different way. I wanted to preach a word that I could never have voiced while he lived.

I did not return for my Senior year in the fall. I had a small inheritance coming, and a bit of trouble getting control of it since I was still under eighteen. But I managed.

It was Greenwich Village I finally settled upon.

Not telling any well-meaning parishioners my new address, I

entered into a daily routine of writing poetry and teaching myself Japanese and Hindustani. I grew a fiery beard, drank espresso, and learned to play chess. I wanted to try a couple of the other paths to salvation.

After that, it was two years in India with the Old Peace Corps—which broke me of my Buddhism, and gave me my *Pipes of Krishna* lyrics and the Pulitzer they deserved.

Then back to the States for my degree, grad work in linguistics, and more prizes.

Then one day a ship went to Mars. The vessel settling in its New Mexico nest of fires contained a new language.—It was fantastic, exotic, and esthetically overpowering. After I had learned all there was to know about it, and written my book, I was famous in new circles.

"Go, Gallinger. Dip your bucket in the well, and bring us a drink of Mars. Go, learn another world—but remain aloof, rail at it gently like Auden—and hand us its soul in iambics."

And I came to the land where the sun is a tarnished penny, where the wind is a whip, where two moons play at hot-rod games, and a hell of sand gives you the incendiary itches whenever you look at it.

I rose from my twistings on the bunk and crossed the darkened cabin to a port. The desert was a carpet of endless orange, bulging from the sweepings of centuries beneath it.

"I a stranger, unafraid—This is the land—I've got it made!"

I laughed.

I had the High Tongue by the tail already—or the roots, if you want your puns anatomical, as well as correct.

The High and Low Tongues were not so dissimilar as they had first seemed. I had enough of the one to get me through the murkier parts of the other. I had the grammar and all the commoner irregular verbs down cold; the dictionary I was constructing grew by the day, like a tulip, and would bloom shortly. Every time I played the tapes, the stem lengthened.

Now was the time to tax my ingenuity, to really drive the lessons home. I had purposely refrained from plunging into the major texts until I could do justice to them. I had been reading minor commentaries, bits of verse, fragments of history. And one thing had impressed me strongly in all that I read.

They wrote about concrete things: rocks, sand, water, winds; and the tenor couched within these elemental symbols was fiercely pessimistic. It reminded me of some Buddhist texts, but even more so, I realized from my recent *recherches*, it was like parts of the Old Testament. Specifically it reminded me of the Book of Ecclesiastes.

That, then, would be it. The sentiment, as well as the vocabulary, was so similar that it would be a perfect exercise. Like putting Poe into French. I would never be a convert to the Way of Malann, but I would show them that an Earthman had once thought the same thoughts, felt similarly.

I switched on my desk lamp and sought King James amidst my books.

Vanity of vanities, saith the Preacher, vanity of vanities; all is vanity. What profit hath a man . . .

My progress seemed to startle M'Cwyie. She peered at me, like Sartre's Other, across the tabletop. I ran through a chapter in the Book of Locar. I didn't look up, but I could feel the tight net her eyes were working about my head, shoulders, and rapid hands. I turned another page.

Was she weighing the net, judging the size of the catch? And what for? The books said nothing of fishers on Mars. Especially of men. They said that some god named Malann had spat, or had done something disgusting (depending on the version you read), and that life had gotten underway as a disease in inorganic matter. They said that movement was its first law, its first law, and that the dance was the only legitimate reply to the inorganic . . . the dance's quality its justification,—fication . . . and love is a disease in organic matter—Inorganic matter?

I shook my head. I had almost been asleep.

"M'narra."

I stood and stretched. Her eyes outlined me greedily now. So I met them, and they dropped.

"I grow tired. I want to rest awhile. I didn't sleep much last night."

She nodded, Earth's shorthand for "yes," as she had learned from me.

"You wish to relax, and see the explicitness of the doctrine of Locar in its fullness?"

"Pardon me?"

"You wish to see a Dance of Locar?"

"Oh." Their damned circuits of form and periphrasis here ran worse than the Koreans! "Yes. Surely. Any time it's going to be done, I'd be happy to watch."

I continued, "In the meantime, I've been meaning to ask you whether I might take some pictures—"

"Now is the time. Sit down. Rest. I will call the musicians."

She bustled out through a door I had never been past.

Well now, the dance was the highest art, according to Locar, not to mention Havelock Ellis, and I was about to see how their centuries-dead philosopher felt it should be conducted. I rubbed my eyes and snapped over, touching my toes a few times.

The blood began pounding in my head, and I sucked in a couple deep breaths. I bent again and there was a flurry of motion at the door.

To the trio who entered with M'Cwyie I must have looked as if I were searching for the marbles I had just lost, bent over like that.

I grinned weakly and straightened up, my face red from more than exertion. I hadn't expected them *that* quickly.

Suddenly I thought of Havelock Ellis again in his area of greatest popularity.

The little redheaded doll, wearing, sari-like, a diaphanous piece of the Martian sky, looked up in wonder—as a child at some colorful flag on a high pole.

"Hello," I said, or its equivalent.

She bowed before replying. Evidently I had been promoted in status.

"I shall dance," said the red wound in that pale, pale cameo, her face. Eyes, the color of dream and her dress, pulled away from mine.

She drifted to the center of the room.

Standing there, like a figure in an Etruscan frieze, she was either meditating or regarding the design on the floor.

Was the mosaic symbolic of something? I studied it. If it was, it eluded me; it would make an attractive bathroom floor or patio, but I couldn't see much in it beyond that.

The other two were paint-spattered sparrows like M'Cwyie, in their middle years. One settled to the floor with a triple-stringed instrument faintly resembling a *samisen*. The other held a simple woodblock and two drumsticks.

M'Cwyie disdained her stool and was seated upon the floor before I realized it. I followed suit.

The *samisen* player was still tuning up, so I leaned toward M'Cwyie.

"What is the dancer's name?"

"Braxa," she replied, without looking at me, and raised her left hand, slowly, which meant yes, and go ahead, and let it begin.

The stringed thing throbbed like a toothache, and a tick-tocking, like ghosts of all the clocks they had never invented, sprang from the block.

Braxa was a statue, both hands raised to her face, elbows high and outspread.

The music became a metaphor for fire.

Crackle, purr, snap . . .

She did not move.

The hissing altered to splashes. The cadence slowed. It was water now, the most precious thing in the world, gurgling clear then green over mossy rocks.

Still she did not move.

Glissandos. A pause.

Then, so faint I could hardly be sure at first, the tremble of the winds began. Softly, gently, sighing and halting, uncertain. A pause, a sob, then a repetition of the first statement, only louder.

Were my eyes completely bugged from my reading, or was Braxa actually trembling, all over, head to foot.

She was.

She began a microscopic swaying. A fraction of an inch right, then left. Her fingers opened like the petals of a flower, and I could see that her eyes were closed.

Her eyes opened. They were distant, glassy, looking through me and the walls. Her swaying became more pronounced, merged with the beat.

The wind was sweeping in from the desert now, falling against Tirellian like waves on a dike. Her fingers moved, they were the gusts. Her arms, slow pendulums, descended, began a counter-movement.

The gale was coming now. She began an axial movement and

her hands caught up with the rest of her body, only now her shoulders commenced to writhe out a figure eight.

The wind! The wind, I say. O wild, enigmatic! O muse of St.-John Perse!

The cyclone was twisting round those eyes, its still center. Her head was thrown back, but I knew there was no ceiling between her gaze, passive as Buddha's, and the unchanging skies. Only the two moons, perhaps, interrupted their slumber in that elemental Nirvana of uninhabited turquoise.

Years ago, I had seen the Devadasis in India, the street dancers, spinning their colorful webs, drawing in the male insect. But Braxa was more than this: she was a Ramadjany, like those votaries of Rama, incarnation of Vishnu, who had given the dance to man: the sacred dancers.

The clicking was monotonously steady now; the whine of the strings made me think of the stinging rays of the sun, their heat stolen by the wind's halations; the blue was Sarasvati and Mary, and a girl named Laura. I heard a sitar from somewhere, watched this statue come to life, and inhaled a divine afflatus.

I was again Rimbaud with his hashish, Baudelaire with his laudanum, Poe, De Quincy, Wilde, Mallarmé, and Aleister Crowley. I was, for a fleeting second, my father in his dark pulpit and darker suit, the hymns and the organ's wheeze transmuted to bright wind.

She was a spun weather vane, a feathered crucifix hovering in the air, a clothesline holding one bright garment lashed parallel to the ground. Her shoulder was bare now, and her right breast moved up and down like a moon in the sky, its red nipple appearing momently above a fold and vanishing again. The music was as formal as Job's argument with God. Her dance was God's reply.

The music slowed, settled; it had been met, matched, answered. Her garment, as if alive, crept back into the more sedate folds it originally held.

She dropped low, lower, to the floor. Her head fell upon her raised knees. She did not move.

There was silence.

I realized, from the ache across my shoulders, how tensely I had been sitting. My armpits were wet. Rivulets had been running down my sides. What did one do now? Applaud?

I sought M'Cwyie from the corner of my eye. She raised her right hand.

As if by telepathy the girl shuddered all over and stood. The musicians also rose. So did M'Cwyie.

I got to my feet, with a charley horse in my left leg, and said, "It was beautiful," inane as that sounds.

I received three different High Forms of "thank you."

There was a flurry of color and I was alone again with M'Cwyie.

"That is the one hundred seventeenth of the two thousand two hundred twenty-four dances of Locar."

I looked down at her.

"Whether Locar was right or wrong, he worked out a fine reply to the inorganic."

She smiled.

"Are the dances of your world like this?"

"Some of them are similar. I was reminded of them as I watched Braxa—but I've never seen anything exactly like hers."

"She is good," M'Cwyie said. "She knows all the dances."

A hint of her earlier expression which had troubled me . . .

It was gone in an instant.

"I must tend to my duties now." She moved to the table and closed the books. "M'narra."

"Good-bye." I slipped into my boots.

"Good-bye, Gallinger."

I walked out the door, mounted the jeepster, and roared across the evening into night, my wings of risen desert flapping slowly behind me.

II

I had just closed the door behind Betty, after a brief grammar session, when I heard the voices in the hall. My vent was opened a fraction, so I stood there and eavesdropped:

Morton's fruity treble: "Guess what? He said 'hello' to me a while ago."

"Hmmph!" Emory's elephant lungs exploded. "Either he's slipping, or you were standing in his way and he wanted you to move."

"Probably didn't recognize me. I don't think he sleeps any more, now he has that language to play with. I had night watch last week, and every night I passed his door at 0300—I always heard that recorder going. At 0500, when I got off, he was still at it."

"The guy *is* working hard," Emory admitted, grudgingly. "In fact, I think he's taking some kind of dope to keep awake. He looks sort of glassy-eyed these days. Maybe that's natural for a poet, though."

Betty had been standing there, because she broke in then:

"Regardless of what you think of him, it's going to take me at least a year to learn what he's picked up in three weeks. And I'm just a linguist, not a poet."

Morton must have been nursing a crush on her bovine charms. It's the only reason I can think of for his dropping his guns to say what he did.

"I took a course in modern poetry when I was back at the university," he began. "We read six authors—Yeats, Pound, Eliot, Crane, Stevens, and Gallinger—and on the last day of the semester, when the prof was feeling a little rhetorical, he said, 'These six names are written on the century, and all the gates of criticism and Hell shall not prevail against them.'"

"Myself," he continued. "I thought his *Pipes of Krishna* and his *Madrigals* were great. I was honored to be chosen for an expedition he was going on.

"I think he's spoken two dozen words to me since I met him," he finished.

The Defense: "Did it ever occur to you," Betty said, "that he might be tremendously self-conscious about his appearance? He was also a precocious child, and probably never even had school friends. He's sensitive and very introverted."

"Sensitive? Self-conscious?" Emory choked and gagged. "The man is as proud as Lucifer, and he's a walking insult machine. You press a button like 'Hello' or 'Nice day' and he thumbs his nose at you. He's got it down to a reflex."

They muttered a few other pleasantries and drifted away.

Well, bless you, Morton boy. You little pimple-faced, Ivy-bred connoisseur! I've never taken a course in my poetry, but I'm glad someone said that. The Gates of Hell. Well, now! Maybe Daddy's prayers got heard somewhere, and I am a missionary, after all!

Only . . .

. . . Only a missionary needs something to convert people *to*. I have my private system of esthetics, and I suppose it oozes an ethical by-product somewhere. But if I ever had anything to preach, really, even in my poems, I wouldn't care to preach it to such lowlifes as you. If you think I'm a slob, I'm also a snob, and there's no room for you in Heaven—it's a private place, where Swift, Shaw, and Petronius Arbiter come to dinner.

And oh, the feasts we have! The Trimalchio's, the Emory's we dissect!

We finish you with the soup, Morton!

I turned and settled at my desk. I wanted to write something. Ecclesiastes could take a night off. I wanted to write a poem, a poem about the one hundred seventeenth dance of Locar; about a rose following the light, traced by the wind, sick, like Blake's rose, dying . . .

I found a pencil and began.

When I had finished I was pleased. It wasn't great—at least, it was no greater than it needed to be—High Martian not being my strongest tongue. I groped, and put it into English, with partial rhymes. Maybe I'd stick it in my next book. I called it *Braxa*:

> In a land of wind and red,
> where the icy evening of Time
> freezes milk in the breasts of Life,
> as two moons overhead—
> cat and dog in alleyways of dream—
> scratch and scramble agelessly my flight . . .
> This final flower turns a burning head.

I put it away and found some phenobarbital. I was suddenly tired.

When I showed my poem to M'Cwyie the next day, she read it through several times, very slowly.

"It is lovely," she said. "But you used three words from your own language. 'Cat' and 'dog,' I assume, are two small animals with a hereditary hatred for one another. But what is 'flower'?"

"Oh," I said. "I've never come across your word for 'flower,' but I was actually thinking of an Earth flower, the rose."

"What is it like?"

"Well, its petals are generally bright red. That's what I meant, on one level, by 'burning head.' I also wanted it to imply fever, though, and red hair, and the fire of life. The rose, itself, has a thorny stem, green leaves, and a distinct, pleasant aroma."

"I wish I could see one."

"I suppose it could be arranged. I'll check."

"Do it, please. You are a—" She used the word for "prophet," or religious poet, like Isaiah or Locar. "—and your poem is inspired. I shall tell Braxa of it."

I declined the nomination, but felt flattered.

This, then, I decided, was the strategic day, the day on which to ask whether I might bring in the microfilm machine and the camera. I wanted to copy all their texts, I explained, and I couldn't write fast enough to do it.

She surprised me by agreeing immediately. But she bowled me over with her invitation.

"Would you like to come and stay here while you do this thing? Then you can work night and day, any time you want—except when the Temple is being used, of course."

I bowed.

"I should be honored."

"Good. Bring your machines when you want, and I will show you a room."

"Will this afternoon be all right?"

"Certainly."

"Then I will go now and get things ready. Until this afternoon . . ."

"Good-bye."

I anticipated a little trouble from Emory, but not much. Everyone back at the ship was anxious to see the Martians, talk with the Martians, poke needles in the Martians, ask them about Martian climate, diseases, soil chemistry, politics, and mushrooms (our botanist was a fungus nut, but a reasonably good guy)—and only four or five had actually gotten to see them. The crew had been spending most of its time excavating dead cities and their acropolises. We played the game by strict rules, and the natives were as fiercely insular as the nineteenth-century Japanese. I figured I would meet with little resistance, and I figured right.

In fact, I got the distinct impression that everyone was happy to see me move out.

I stopped in the hydroponics room to speak with our mushroom master.

"Hi, Kane. Grow any toadstools in the sand yet?"

He sniffed. He always sniffs. Maybe he's allergic to plants.

"Hello, Gallinger. No, I haven't had any success with toadstools, but look behind the car barn next time you're out there. I've got a few cacti going."

"Great," I observed. Doc Kane was about my only friend aboard, not counting Betty.

"Say, I came down to ask you a favor."

"Name it."

"I want a rose."

"A what?"

"A rose. You know, a nice red American Beauty job—thorns, pretty smelling—"

"I don't think it will take in this soil. *Sniff, sniff*."

"No, you don't understand. I don't want to plant it, I just want the flowers."

"I'd have to use the tanks." He scratched his hairless dome. "It would take at least three months to get you flowers, even under forced growth."

"Will you do it?"

"Sure, if you don't mind the wait."

"Not at all. In fact, three months will just make it before we leave." I looked about at the pools of crawling slime, at the trays of shoots. "—I'm moving up to Tirellian today, but I'll be in and out all the time. I'll be here when it blooms."

"Moving up there, eh? Moore said they're an in-group."

"I guess I'm 'in' then."

"Looks that way—I still don't see how you learned their language, though. Of course, I had trouble with French and German for my PhD, but last week I heard Betty demonstrate it at lunch. It just sounds like a lot of weird noises. She says speaking it is like working a *Times* crossword and trying to imitate birdcalls at the same time."

I laughed, and took the cigarette he offered me.

"It's complicated," I acknowledged. "But, well, it's as if you suddenly came across a whole new class of mycetae here—you'd dream about it at night."

His eyes were gleaming.

"Wouldn't that be something! I might, yet, you know."

"Maybe you will."

He chuckled as we walked to the door.

"I'll start your roses tonight. Take it easy down there."

"You bet. Thanks."

Like I said, a fungus nut, but a fairly good guy.

My quarters in the Citadel of Tirellian were directly adjacent to the Temple, on the inward side and slightly to the left. They were a considerable improvement over my cramped cabin, and I was pleased that Martian culture had progressed sufficiently to discover the desirability of the mattress over the pallet. Also, the bed was long enough to accommodate me, which *was* surprising.

So I unpacked and took sixteen thirty-five mm shots of the Temple, before starting on the books.

I took 'stats until I was sick of turning pages without knowing what they said. So I started translating a work of history.

"Lo. In the thirty-seventh year of the Process of Cillen the rains came, which gave rise to rejoicing, for it was a rare and untoward occurrence, and commonly construed a blessing.

"But it was not the life-giving semen of Malann which fell from the heavens. It was the blood of the universe, spurting from an artery. And the last days were upon us. The final dance was to begin.

"The rains brought the plague that does not kill, and the last passes of Locar began with their drumming . . ."

I asked myself what the hell Tamur meant, for he was an historian and supposedly committed to fact. This was not their Apocalypse.

Unless they could be one and the same . . . ?

Why not? I mused. Tirellian's handful of people were the remnant of what had obviously once been a highly developed culture. They had had wars, but no holocausts; science, but little technology. A plague, a plague that did not kill . . . ? Could that have done it? How, if it wasn't fatal?

I read on, but the nature of the plague was not discussed. I turned pages, skipped ahead, and drew a blank.

M'Cwyie! M'Cwyie! When I want to question you most, you are not around!

Would it be a *faux pas* to go looking for her? Yes, I decided. I was restricted to the rooms I had been shown, that had been an implicit understanding. I would have to wait to find out.

So I cursed long and loud, in many languages, doubtless burning Malann's sacred ears, there in his Temple.

He did not see fit to strike me dead, so I decided to call it a day and hit the sack.

I must have been asleep for several hours when Braxa entered my room with a tiny lamp. She dragged me awake by tugging at my pajama sleeve.

I said hello. Thinking back, there is not much else I could have said.

"Hello."

"I have come," she said, "to hear the poem."

"What poem?"

"Yours."

"Oh."

I yawned, sat up, and did things people usually do when awakened in the middle of the night to read poetry.

"That is very kind of you, but isn't the hour a trifle awkward?"

"I don't mind," she said.

Someday I am going to write an article for the *Journal of Semantics*, called "Tone of Voice: An Insufficient Vehicle for Irony."

However, I was awake, so I grabbed my robe.

"What sort of animal is that?" she asked, pointing at the silk dragon on my lapel.

"Mythical," I replied. "Now look, it's late. I am tired. I have much to do in the morning. And M'Cwyie just might get the wrong idea if she learns you were here."

"Wrong idea?"

"You know damned well what I mean!" It was the first time I had had an opportunity to use Martian profanity, and it failed.

"No," she said, "I do not know."

She seemed frightened, like a puppy being scolded without knowing what it has done wrong.

I softened. Her red cloak matched her hair and lips so perfectly, and those lips were trembling.

"Here now, I didn't mean to upset you. On my world there are certain, uh, mores, concerning people of different sex alone together in bedrooms, and not allied by marriage . . . Um, I mean, you see what I mean?"

"No."

They were jade, her eyes.

"Well, it's sort of . . . Well, it's sex, that's what it is."

A light was switched on in those jade lamps.

"Oh, you mean having children!"

"Yes. That's it! Exactly."

She laughed. It was the first time I had heard laughter in Tirellian. It sounded like a violinist striking his high strings with the bow, in short little chops. It was not an altogether pleasant thing to hear, especially because she laughed too long.

When she had finished she moved closer.

"I remember, now," she said. "We used to have such rules. Half a Process ago, when I was a child, we had such rules. But," she looked as if she were ready to laugh again, "there is no need for them now."

My mind moved like a tape recorder played at triple speed.

Half a Process! HalfaProcessaProcessaProcess! No! Yes!

Half a Process was two hundred forty-three years, roughly speaking!

—Time enough to learn the two thousand two hundred twenty-four dances of Locar.

—Time enough to grow old, if you were human.

—Earth-style human, I mean.

I looked at her again, pale as the white queen in an ivory chess set.

She was human, I'd stake my soul—alive, normal, healthy, I'd stake my life—woman, my body . . .

But she was two and a half centuries old, which made M'Cwyie Methuselah's grandma. It flattered me to think of their repeated complimenting of my skills, as linguist, as poet. These superior beings!

But what did she mean 'there is no such need for them now'? Why the near-hysteria? Why all those funny looks I'd been getting from M'Cwyie?

I suddenly knew I was close to something important, besides a beautiful girl.

"Tell me," I said, in my Casual Voice, "did it have anything to do with 'the plague that does not kill,' of which Tamur wrote?"

"Yes," she replied, "the children born after the Rains could have no children of their own, and—"

"And what?" I was leaning forward, memory set at "record."

"—and the men had no desire to get any."

I sagged backward against the bedpost. Racial sterility, masculine impotence, following phenomenal weather. Had some vagabond cloud of radioactive junk from God knows where penetrated their weak atmosphere one day? One day long before Schiaparelli saw the canals, mythical as my dragon, before those "canals" had given rise to some correct guesses for all the wrong reasons, had Braxa been alive, dancing, here—damned in the womb since blind Milton had written of another paradise, equally lost?

I found a cigarette. Good thing I had thought to bring ashtrays. Mars had never had a tobacco industry either. Or booze. The ascetics I had met in India had been Dionysiac compared to this.

"What is that tube of fire?"

"A cigarette. Want one?"

"Yes, please."

She sat beside me, and I lighted it for her.

"It irritates the nose."

"Yes. Draw some into your lungs, hold it there, and exhale."

A moment passed.

"Ooh," she said.

A pause, then, "Is it sacred?"

"No, it's nicotine," I answered, "a very *ersatz* form of divinity."

Another pause.

"Please don't ask me to translate 'ersatz'."

"I won't. I get this feeling sometimes when I dance."

"It will pass in a moment."

"Tell me your poem now."

An idea hit me.

"Wait a minute," I said, "I may have something better."

I got up and rummaged through my notebooks, then I returned and sat beside her.

"These are the first three chapters of the Book of Ecclesiastes," I explained. "It is very similar to your own sacred books."

I started reading.

I got through eleven verses before she cried out, "Please don't read that! Tell me one of yours!"

I stopped and tossed the notebook onto a nearby table. She was shaking, not as she had quivered that day she danced as the wind,

but with the jitter of unshed tears. She held her cigarette awk-
wardly, like a pencil. Clumsily, I put my arm about her shoulders.

"He is so sad," she said, "like all the others."

So I twisted my mind like a bright ribbon, folded it, and tied
the crazy Christmas knots I love so well. From German to Martian, with love, I did an impromptu paraphrasal of a poem about
a Spanish dancer. I thought it would please her. I was right.

"Ooh," she said again. "Did you write that?"

"No, it's by a better man than I."

"I don't believe you. You wrote it."

"No, a man named Rilke did."

"But you brought it across to my language.—Light another
match, so I can see how she danced."

I did.

" 'The fires of forever,' " she mused, "and she stamped them
out, 'with small, firm feet.' I wish I could dance like that."

"You're better than any Gypsy," I laughed, blowing it out.

"No, I'm not. I couldn't do that."

Her cigarette was burning down, so I removed it from her fingers
and put it out, along with my own.

"Do you want me to dance for you?"

"No," I said. "Go to bed."

She smiled, and before I realized it, had unclasped the fold of
red at her shoulder.

And everything fell away.

And I swallowed, with some difficulty.

"All right," she said.

So I kissed her, as the breath of fallen cloth extinguished the
lamp.

III

The days were like Shelley's leaves: yellow, red, brown, whipped
in bright gusts by the west wind. They swirled past me with the
rattle of microfilm. Almost all the books were recorded now. It
would take scholars years to get through them, to properly assess
their value. Mars was locked in my desk.

Ecclesiastes, abandoned and returned to a dozen times, was almost ready to speak in the High Tongue.

I whistled when I wasn't in the Temple. I wrote reams of poetry I would have been ashamed of before. Evenings I would walk with Braxa, across the dunes or up into the mountains. Sometimes she would dance for me; and I would read something long, and in dactylic hexameter. She still thought I was Rilke, and I almost kidded myself into believing it. Here I was, staying at the Castle Duino, writing his *Elegies*.

> . . . It is strange to inhabit the Earth no more,
> to use no longer customs scarce acquired,
> nor interpret roses . . .

No! Never interpret roses! Don't. Smell them (sniff, Kane!), pick them, enjoy them. Live in the moment. Hold to it tightly. But charge not the gods to explain. So fast the leaves go by, are blown . . .

And no one ever noticed us. Or cared.

Laura. Laura and Braxa. They rhyme, you know, with a bit of clash. Tall, cool, and blonde was she (I hate blondes!), and Daddy had turned me inside out, like a pocket, and I thought she could fill me again. But the big, beat word-slinger, with Judas-beard and dog-trust in his eyes, oh, he had been a fine decoration at her parties. And that was all.

How the machine cursed me in the Temple! It blasphemed Malann and Gallinger. And the wild west wind went by and something was not far behind.

The last days were upon us.

A day went by and I did not see Braxa, and a night.

And a second. A third.

I was half-mad. I hadn't realized how close we had become, how important she had been. With the dumb assurance of presence, I had fought against questioning roses.

I had to ask. I didn't want to, but I had no choice.

"Where is she, M'Cwyie? Where is Braxa?"

"She is gone," she said.

"Where?"

"I do not know."

I looked at those devil-bird eyes. Anathema maranatha rose to my lips.

"I must know."

She looked through me.

"She has left us. She is gone. Up into the hills, I suppose. Or the desert. It does not matter. What does anything matter? The dance draws to a close. The Temple will soon be empty."

"Why? Why did she leave?"

"I do not know."

"I must see her again. We lift off in a matter of days."

"I am sorry, Gallinger."

"So am I," I said, and slammed shut a book without saying "m'narra."

I stood up.

"I will find her."

I left the Temple. M'Cwyie was a seated statue. My boots were still where I had left them.

All day I roared up and down the dunes, going nowhere. To the crew of the *Aspic* I must have looked like a sandstorm, all by myself. Finally, I had to return for more fuel.

Emory came stalking out.

"Okay, make it good. You look like the abominable dust man. Why the rodeo?"

"Why, I, uh, lost something."

"In the middle of the desert? Was it one of your sonnets? They're the only thing I can think of that you'd make such a fuss over."

"No, dammit! It was something personal."

George had finished filling the tank. I started to mount the jeep-ster again.

"Hold on there!" He grabbed my arm.

"You're not going back until you tell me what this is all about."

I could have broken his grip, but then he could order me dragged back by the heels, and quite a few people would enjoy doing the dragging. So I forced myself to speak slowly, softly:

"It's simply that I lost my watch. My mother gave it to me and it's a family heirloom. I want to find it before we leave."

"You sure it's not in your cabin, or down in Tirellian?"

"I've already checked."

"Maybe somebody hid it to irritate you. You know you're not the most popular guy around."

I shook my head.

"I thought of that. But I always carry it in my right pocket. I think it might have bounced out going over the dunes."

He narrowed his eyes.

"I remember reading on a book jacket that your mother died when you were born."

"That's right," I said, biting my tongue. "The watch belonged to her father and she wanted me to have it. My father kept it for me."

"Hmph!" he snorted. "That's a pretty strange way to look for a watch, riding up and down in a jeepster."

"I could see the light shining off it that way," I offered, lamely.

"Well, it's starting to get dark," he observed. "No sense looking any more today.

"Throw a dust sheet over the jeepster," he directed a mechanic.

He patted my arm.

"Come on in and get a shower, and something to eat. You look as if you could use both."

Little fatty flecks beneath pale eyes, thinning hair, and an Irish nose; a voice a decibel louder than anyone else's . . .

His only qualifications for leadership!

I stood there, hating him. Claudius! If only this were the fifth act!

But suddenly the idea of a shower, and food, came through to me. I could use both badly. If I insisted on hurrying back immediately, I might arouse more suspicion.

So I brushed some sand from my sleeve.

"You're right. That sounds like a good idea."

"Come on, we'll eat in my cabin."

The shower was a blessing, clean khakis were the grace of God, and the food smelled like Heaven.

"Smells pretty good," I said.

We hacked up our steaks in silence. When we got to the dessert and coffee, he suggested:

"Why don't you take the night off? Stay here and get some sleep."

I shook my head.

"I'm pretty busy. Finishing up. There's not much time left."

"A couple days ago you said you were almost finished."

"Almost, but not quite."

"You also said they'll be holding a service in the Temple tonight."

"That's right. I'm going to work in my room."

He shrugged his shoulders.

Finally, he said, "Gallinger," and I looked up because my name means trouble.

"It shouldn't be any of my business," he said, "but it is. Betty says you have a girl down there."

There was no question mark. It was a statement hanging in the air. Waiting.

—Betty, you're a bitch. You're a cow and a bitch. And a jealous one, at that. Why didn't you keep your nose where it belonged, shut your eyes? Your mouth?

"So?" I said, a statement with a question mark.

"So," he answered it, "it is my duty, as head of this expedition, to see that relations with the natives are carried on in a friendly, and diplomatic, manner."

"You speak of them," I said, "as though they are aborigines. Nothing could be further from the truth."

I rose.

"When my papers are published, everyone on Earth will know that truth. I'll tell them things Doctor Moore never even guessed at. I'll tell the tragedy of a doomed race, waiting for death, resigned and disinterested. I'll tell why, and it will break hard, scholarly hearts. I'll write about it, and they will give me more prizes, and this time I won't want them.

"My God!" I exclaimed. "They had a culture when our ancestors were clubbing the sabre-tooth and finding out how fire works!"

"*Do* you have a girl down there?"

"Yes!" I said. *Yes, Claudius! Yes, Daddy! Yes, Emory!* "I do. But I'm going to let you in on a scholarly scoop now. They're already dead. They're sterile. In one more generation there won't be any Martians."

I paused, then added, "Except in my papers, except on a few pieces of microfilm and tape. And in some poems, about a girl who did give a damn and could only bitch about the unfairness of it all by dancing."

"Oh," he said.

After awhile:

"You *have* been behaving differently these past couple months. You've even been downright civil on occasion, you know. I couldn't help wondering what was happening. I didn't know anything mattered that strongly to you."

I bowed my head.

"Is she the reason you were racing around the desert?"

I nodded.

"Why?"

I looked up.

"Because she's out there, somewhere. I don't know where, or why. And I've got to find her before we go."

"Oh," he said again.

Then he leaned back, opened a drawer, and took out something wrapped in a towel. He unwound it. A framed photo of a woman lay on the table.

"My wife," he said.

It was an attractive face, with big, almond eyes.

"I'm a Navy man, you know," he began. "Young officer once. Met her in Japan.

"Where I come from it wasn't considered right to marry into another race, so we never did. But she was my wife. When she died I was on the other side of the world. They took my children, and I've never seen them since. I couldn't learn what orphanage, what home, they were put into. That was long ago. Very few people know about it."

"I'm sorry," I said.

"Don't be. Forget it. But," he shifted in his chair and looked at me, "if you do want to take her back with you—do it. It'll mean my neck, but I'm too old to ever head another expedition like this one. So go ahead."

He gulped his cold coffee.

"Get your jeepster."

He swiveled the chair around.

I tried to say "thank you" twice, but I couldn't. So I got up and walked out.

"Sayonara, and all that," he muttered behind me.

"Here it is, Gallinger!" I heard a shout.

I turned on my heel and looked back up the ramp.

"Kane!"

He was limned in the port, shadow against light, but I had heard him sniff.

I returned the few steps.

"Here what is?"

"Your rose."

He produced a plastic container, divided internally. The lower half was filled with liquid. The stem ran down into it. The other half, a glass of claret in this horrible night, was a large, newly opened rose.

"Thank you," I said, tucking it into my jacket.

"Going back to Tirellian, eh?"

"Yes."

"I saw you come aboard, so I got it ready. Just missed you at the Captain's cabin. He was busy. Hollered out that I could catch you at the barns."

"Thanks again."

"It's chemically treated. It will stay in bloom for weeks."

I nodded. I was gone.

Up into the mountains now. Far. Far. The sky was a bucket of ice in which no moons floated. The going became steeper, and the little donkey protested. I whipped him with the throttle and went on. Up. Up. I spotted a green, unwinking star, and felt a lump in my throat. The uncased rose beat against my chest like an extra heart. The donkey brayed, long and loudly, then began to cough. I lashed him some more and he died.

I threw the emergency brake on and got out. I began to walk.

So cold, so cold it grows. Up here. At night? Why? Why did she do it? Why flee the campfire when night comes on?

And I was up, down around, and through every chasm, gorge, and pass, with my long-legged strides and an ease of movement never known on Earth.

Barely two days remain, my love, and thou hast forsaken me. Why?

I crawled under overhangs. I leapt over ridges. I scraped my knees, an elbow. I heard my jacket tear.

No answer, Malann? Do you really hate your people this much? Then I'll try someone else. Vishnu, you're the Preserver. Preserve her, please! Let me find her.

Jehovah?

Adonis? Osiris? Thammuz? Manitou? Legba? Where is she?

I ranged far and high, and I slipped.

Stones ground underfoot and I dangled over an edge. My fingers so cold. It was hard to grip the rock.

I looked down.

Twelve feet or so. I let go and dropped, landed rolling.

Then I heard her scream.

I lay there, not moving, looking up. Against the night, above, she called.

"Gallinger!"

I lay still.

"Gallinger!"

And she was gone.

I heard stones rattle and knew she was coming down some path to the right of me.

I jumped up and ducked into the shadow of a boulder.

She rounded a cut-off, and picked her way, uncertainly, through the stones.

"Gallinger?"

I stepped out and seized her shoulders.

"Braxa."

She screamed again, then began to cry, crowding against me. It was the first time I had ever heard her cry.

"Why?" I asked. "Why?"

But she only clung to me and sobbed.

Finally, "I thought you had killed yourself."

"Maybe I would have," I said. "Why did you leave Tirellian? And me?"

"Didn't M'Cwyie tell you? Didn't you guess?"

"I didn't guess, and M'Cwyie said she didn't know."

"Then she lied. She knows."

"What? What is it she knows?"

She shook all over, then was silent for a long time. I realized suddenly that she was wearing only her flimsy dancer's costume. I pushed her from me, took off my jacket, and put it about her shoulders.

"Great Malann!" I cried. "You'll freeze to death!"

"No," she said, "I won't."

I was transferring the rose case to my pocket.

"What is that?" she asked.

"A rose," I answered. "You can't make it out much in the dark.
I once compared you to one. Remember?"

"Yu-Yes. May I carry it?"

"Sure." I stuck it in the jacket pocket.

"Well? I'm still waiting for an explanation."

"You really do not know?" she said.

"No!"

"When the Rains came," she said, "apparently only our men
were affected, which was enough. . . . Because I—wasn't—affected
—apparently—"

"Oh," I said. "Oh."

We stood there, and I thought.

"Well, why did you run? What's wrong with being pregnant on
Mars? Tamur was mistaken. Your people can live again."

She laughed, again that wild violin played by a Paganini gone
mad. I stopped her before it went too far.

"How?" she finally asked, rubbing her cheek.

"Your people live longer than ours. If our child is normal it will
mean our races can intermarry. There must still be other fertile
women of your race. Why not?"

"You have read the Book of Locar," she said, "and yet you ask
me that? Death was decided, voted upon, and passed, shortly
after it appeared in this form. But long before, the followers of
Locar knew. They decided it long ago. 'We have done all things,'
they said, 'we have seen all things, we have heard and felt all
things. The dance was good. Now let it end.'"

"You can't believe that."

"What I believe does not matter," she replied. "M'Cwyie and
the Mothers have decided we must die. Their very title is now a
mockery, but their decisions will be upheld. There is only one
prophecy left, and it is mistaken. We will die."

"No," I said.

"What, then?"

"Come back with me, to Earth."

"No."

"All right, then. Come with me now."

"Where?"

"Back to Tirellian. I'm going to talk to the Mothers."

"You can't! There is a Ceremony tonight!"

I laughed.

"A ceremony for a god who knocks you down, and then kicks you in the teeth?"

"He is still Malann," she answered. "We are still his people."

"You and my father would have gotten along fine," I snarled. "But I am going, and you are coming with me, even if I have to carry you—and I'm bigger than you are."

"But you are not bigger than Ontro."

"Who the hell is Ontro?"

"He will stop you, Gallinger. He is the Fist of Malann."

IV

I scudded the jeepster to a halt in front of the only entrance I knew, M'Cwyie's. Braxa, who had seen the rose in a headlamp, now cradled it in her lap, like our child, and said nothing. There was a passive, lovely look on her face.

"Are they in the Temple now?" I wanted to know.

The Madonna expression did not change. I repeated the question. She stirred.

"Yes," she said, from a distance, "but you cannot go in."

"We'll see."

I circled and helped her down.

I led her by the hand, and she moved as if in a trance. In the light of the new-risen moon, her eyes looked as they had the day I met her, when she had danced. I snapped my fingers. Nothing happened.

So I pushed the door open and led her in. The room was half-lighted.

And she screamed for the third time that evening:

"Do not harm him, Ontro! It is Gallinger!"

I had never seen a Martian man before, only women. So I had no way of knowing whether he was a freak, though I suspected it strongly.

I looked up at him.

His half-naked body was covered with moles and swellings. Gland trouble, I guessed.

I had thought I was the tallest man on the planet, but he was seven feet tall and overweight. Now I knew where my giant bed had come from!

"Go back," he said. "She may enter. You may not."

"I must get my books and things."

He raised a huge left arm. I followed it. All my belongings lay neatly stacked in the corner.

"I must go in. I must talk with M'Cwyie and the Mothers."

"You may not."

"The lives of your people depend on it."

"Go back," he boomed. "Go home to *your* people, Gallinger. Leave *us!*"

My name sounded so different on his lips, like someone else's. How old was he? I wondered. Three hundred? Four? Had he been a Temple guardian all his life? Why? Who was there to guard against? I didn't like the way he moved. I had seen men who moved like that before.

"Go back," he repeated.

If they had refined their martial arts as far as they had their dances, or, worse yet, if their fighting arts were a part of the dance, I was in for trouble.

"Go on in," I said to Braxa. "Give the rose to M'Cwyie. Tell her that I sent it. Tell her I'll be there shortly."

"I will do as you ask. Remember me on Earth, Gallinger. Goodbye."

I did not answer her, and she walked past Ontro and into the next room, bearing her rose.

"Now will you leave?" he asked. "If you like, I will tell her that we fought and you almost beat me, but I knocked you unconscious and carried you back to your ship."

"No," I said, "either I go around you or go over you, but I am going through."

He dropped into a crouch, arms extended.

"It is a sin to lay hands on a holy man," he rumbled, "but I will stop you, Gallinger."

My memory was a fogged window, suddenly exposed to fresh air. Things cleared. I looked back six years.

I was a student of Oriental Languages at the University of Tokyo. It was my twice-weekly night of recreation. I stood in a thirty-foot circle in the Kodokan, the *judogi* lashed about my high hips by a brown belt. I was *Ikkyu*, one notch below the lowest degree of expert. A brown diamond above my right breast said "Jiu-Jitsu" in Japanese, and it meant *atemiwaza*, really, because of the one striking technique I had worked out, found unbelievably suitable to my size, and won matches with.

But I had never used it on a man, and it was five years since I had practiced. I was out of shape, I knew, but I tried hard to force my mind *tsuki no kokoro*, like the moon, reflecting the all of Ontro.

Somewhere, out of the past, a voice said, "*Hajime*, let it begin."

I snapped into my *neko-ashi-dachi* cat stance, and his eyes burned strangely. He hurried to correct his own position—and I threw it at him!

My one trick!

My long left leg lashed up like a broken spring. Seven feet off the ground my foot connected with his jaw as he tried to leap backward.

His head snapped back and he fell. A soft moan escaped his lips. *That's all there is to it*, I thought. *Sorry, old fellow.*

And as I stepped over him, somehow, groggily, he tripped me, and I fell across his body. I couldn't believe he had strength enough to remain conscious after that blow, let alone move. I hated to punish him any more.

But he found my throat and slipped a forearm across it before I realized there was a purpose to his action.

No! Don't let it end like this!

It was a bar of steel across my windpipe, my carotids. Then I realized that he was still unconscious, and that this was a reflex instilled by countless years of training. I had seen it happen once, in *shiai*. The man had died because he had been choked unconscious and still fought on, and his opponent thought he had not been applying the choke properly. He tried harder.

But it was rare, so very rare!

I jammed my elbows into his ribs and threw my head back in his face. The grip eased, but not enough. I hated to do it, but I reached up and broke his little finger.

The arm went loose and I twisted free.

He lay there panting, face contorted. My heart went out to the fallen giant, defending his people, his religion, following his orders. I cursed myself as I had never cursed before, for walking over him, instead of around.

I staggered across the room to my little heap of possessions. I sat on the projector case and lit a cigarette.

I couldn't go into the Temple until I got my breath back, until I thought of something to say.

How do you talk a race out of killing itself?

Suddenly—

—Could it happen? Would it work that way? If I read them the Book of Ecclesiastes—if I read them a greater piece of literature than any Locar ever wrote—and as somber—and as pessimistic—and showed them that our race had gone on despite one man's condemning all of life in the highest poetry—showed them that the vanity he had mocked had borne us to the Heavens—would they believe it?—would they change their minds?

I ground out my cigarette on the beautiful floor, and found my notebook. A strange fury rose within me as I stood.

And I walked into the Temple to preach the Black Gospel according to Gallinger, from the Book of Life.

There was silence all about me.

M'Cwyie had been reading Locar, the rose set at her right hand, target of all eyes.

Until I entered.

Hundreds of people were seated on the floor, barefoot. The few men were as small as the women, I noted.

I had my boots on.

Go *all the way*, I figured. *You either lose or you win—everything!*

A dozen crones sat in a semicircle behind M'Cwyie. The Mothers.

The barren earth, the dry wombs, the fire-touched.

I moved to the table.

"Dying yourselves, you would condemn your people," I addressed them, "that they may not know the life you have known—the joys, the sorrows, the fullness.—But it is not true that you all must die." I addressed the multitude now. "Those who say this lie. Braxa knows, for she will bear a child—"

They sat there, like rows of Buddhas. M'Cwyie drew back into the semicircle.

"—my child!" I continued, wondering what my father would have thought of this sermon.

". . . And all the women young enough may bear children. It is only your men who are sterile.—And if you permit the doctors of the next expedition to examine you, perhaps even the men may be helped. But if they cannot, you can mate with the men of Earth.

"And ours is not an insignificant people, an insignificant place," I went on. "Thousands of years ago, the Locar of our world wrote a book saying that it was. He spoke as Locar did, but we did not lie down, despite plagues, wars, and famines. We did not die. One by one we beat down the diseases, we fed the hungry, we fought the wars, and, recently, have gone a long time without them. We may finally have conquered them. I do not know.

"But we have crossed millions of miles of nothingness. We have visited another world. And our Locar had said, 'Why bother? What is the worth of it? It is all vanity, anyhow.'

"And the secret is," I lowered my voice, as at a poetry reading, "he was right! It *is* vanity, it *is* pride! It is the *hybris* of rationalism to always attack the prophet, the mystic, the god. It is our blasphemy which has made us great, and will sustain us, and which the gods secretly admire in us.—All the truly sacred names of God are blasphemous things to speak!"

I was working up a sweat. I paused dizzily.

"Here is the Book of Ecclesiastes," I announced, and began:

" 'Vanity of vanities, saith the Preacher, vanity of vanities; all is vanity. What profit hath a man . . . ' "

I spotted Braxa in the back, mute, rapt.

I wondered what she was thinking.

And I wound the hours of night about me, like black thread on a spool.

Oh, it was late! I had spoken till day came, and still I spoke. I finished Ecclesiastes and continued Gallinger.

And when I finished, there was still only a silence.

The Buddhas, all in a row, had not stirred through the night. And after a long while M'Cwyie raised her right hand. One by one the Mothers did the same.

And I knew what that meant.

It meant no, do not, cease, and stop.

It meant that I had failed.

I walked slowly from the room and slumped beside my baggage.

Ontro was gone. Good that I had not killed him . . .

After a thousand years M'Cwyie entered.

She said, "Your job is finished."

I did not move.

"The prophecy is fulfilled," she said. "My people are rejoicing. You have won, holy man. Now leave us quickly."

My mind was a deflated balloon. I pumped a little air back into it.

"I'm not a holy man," I said, "just a second-rate poet with a bad case of *hybris*."

I lit my last cigarette.

Finally, "All right, what prophecy?"

"The Promise of Locar," she replied, as though the explaining were unnecessary, "that a holy man would come from the heavens to save us in our last hours, if all the dances of Locar were completed. He would defeat the Fist of Malann and bring us life."

"How?"

"As with Braxa, and as the example in the Temple."

"Example?"

"You read us his words, as great as Locar's. You read to us how there is 'nothing new under the sun.' And you mocked his words as you read them—showing us a new thing.

"There has never been a flower on Mars," she said, "but we will learn to grow them.

"You are the Sacred Scoffer," she finished. "He-Who-Must-Mock-in-the-Temple—you go shod on holy ground."

"But you voted 'no'," I said.

"I voted not to carry out our original plan, and to let Braxa's child live instead."

"Oh." The cigarette fell from my fingers. How close it had been! How little I had known!

"And Braxa?"

"She was chosen half a Process ago to do the dances—to wait for you."

"But she said that Ontro would stop me."

M'Cwyie stood there for a long time.

"She had never believed the prophecy herself. Things are not well with her now. She ran away, fearing it was true. When you completed it and we voted, she knew."

"Then she does not love me? Never did?"

"I am sorry, Gallinger. It was the one part of her duty she never managed."

"Duty," I said flatly. . . . Dutydutyduty! Tra-la!

"She has said good-bye, she does not wish to see you again.

". . . and we will never forget your teachings," she added.

"Don't," I said, automatically, suddenly knowing the great paradox which lies at the heart of all miracles. I did not believe a word of my own gospel, never had.

I stood, like a drunken man, and muttered "M'narra."

I went outside, into my last day on Mars.

I have conquered thee, Malann—and the victory is thine! Rest easy on thy starry bed. God damned!

I left the jeepster there and walked back to the *Aspic*, leaving the burden of life so many footsteps behind me. I went to my cabin, locked the door, and took forty-four sleeping pills.

But when I awakened, I was in the dispensary, and alive.

I felt the throb of engines as I slowly stood up and somehow made it to the port.

Blurred Mars hung like a swollen belly above me, until it dissolved, brimmed over, and streamed down my face.

ARTHUR C. CLARKE

Brain and Body

A safe and practical form of suspended animation—which involves no medical impossibility and may indeed be regarded as an extension of anesthesia—could have major effects upon society. Men suffering from incurable diseases might choose to leapfrog ten or twenty years, in the hope that medical science might have caught up with their condition. The insane, and criminals beyond our present powers of redemption, might also be sent forward in time, in the expectation that the future could salvage them. Our descendants might not appreciate this legacy, of course; but at least they could not send it back.

All this assumes—though no one has yet proved it—that the legend of Rip van Winkle is scientifically sound, and that the processes of aging would be slowed down, or even checked, during suspended animation. Thus a sleeping man could travel down the centuries, stopping from time to time and exploring the future as today we explore space. There are always misfits in every age who might prefer to do this, if they were given the opportunity, so that they could see the world that will exist far beyond their normal span of life.

And this brings us to what is, perhaps, the greatest enigma of all. *Is* there a normal span of life, or do all men really die by accident? Though we now live, on the average, far longer than our ancestors, the absolute limit does not seem to have altered since records became available. The Biblical three-score-years-and-ten is still as valid today as it was four thousand years ago.

No human being has been proved to have lived more than 115 years; the much higher figures often quoted are almost certainly due to fraud or error. Man, it seems, is the longest lived of all the mammals, but some fish and tortoises may attain their second century. And trees, of course, have incredible life-spans; the oldest known living organism is a small and unprepossessing bristlecone pine in the foothills of the Sierra Nevada. It has been growing, though hardly flourishing, for 4,600 years.

Death (though not aging) is obviously essential for progress, both social and biological. Even if it did not perish from over-population, a world of immortals would soon stagnate. In every sphere of human activity, one can find examples of the stultifying influence of men who have outlived their usefulness. Yet death—like sleep—does not appear to be biologically inevitable, even if it is an evolutionary necessity.

Our bodies are not like machines; they never wear out, because they are continually rebuilt from new materials. If this process were uniformly efficient, we would be immortal. Unfortunately, after a few decades something seems to go wrong in the repair-and-maintenance department; the materials are as good as ever, but the old plans get lost or ignored, and vital services are not properly restored when they break down. It is as if the cells of the body can no longer remember the jobs they once did so well.

The way of avoiding a failure of memory is to keep better records, and perhaps one day we will be able to help our bodies to do just that. The invention of the alphabet made mental for-getfulness no longer inevitable; the more sophisticated tools of future medicine may cure physical forgetfulness, by allowing us to preserve, in some suitable storage device, the ideal prototypes of our bodies. Deviations from the norm could then be checked from time to time and corrected, before they became serious.

Because biological immortality and the preservation of youth are such potent lures, men will never cease to search for them, tantalized by the examples of creatures who live for centuries and undeterred by the unfortunate experience of Dr. Faust. It would be foolish to imagine that this search will never be successful, down all the ages that lie ahead. Whether success would be desir-able is quite another matter.

The body is the vehicle of the brain, and the brain is the seat of the mind. In the past, this triad has been inseparable, but it will not always be so. If we cannot prevent our bodies from dis-integrating, we may replace them while there is yet time.

The replacement need not be another body of flesh and blood;

it could be a machine, and this may represent the next stage in evolution. Even if the brain is not immortal, it could certainly live much longer than the body, whose diseases and accidents eventually bring it low. Many years ago, in a famous series of experiments, Russian surgeons kept a dog's head alive for some days by purely mechanical means. I do not know if they have yet succeeded with men, but I shall be surprised if they have not tried.

If you think that an immobile brain would lead a very dull sort of life, you have not fully understood what has already been said about the senses. A brain connected by wire or radio links to suitable organs could participate in any conceivable experience, real or imaginary. When you touch something, are you *really* aware that your brain is not at your fingertips, but three feet away? And would you notice the difference, if that three feet were three thousand miles? Radio waves make such a journey more swiftly than the nervous impulses can travel along your arm.

One can imagine a time when men who still inhabit organic bodies are regarded with pity by those who have passed on to an infinitely richer mode of existence, capable of throwing their consciousness or sphere of attention instantaneously to any point on land, sea, or sky where there is a suitable sensing organ. In adolescence we leave childhood behind; one day there may be a second and more portentous adolescence, when we bid farewell to the flesh.

But even if we can keep the brain alive indefinitely, surely in the end it would be clogged with memories, overlaid like a palimpsest with so many impressions and experiences that there would be no room for more? Eventually, perhaps yes, though I would repeat again that we have no idea of the ultimate capacity of a well-trained mind, even without the mechanical aids which will certainly become available. As a good round figure, a thousand years would seem to be about the ultimate limit for continuous human existence—though suspended animation might spread this millennium across far longer vistas of time.

Yet there may be a way past even this barrier, as I suggested in the novel *The City and the Stars*. This was an attempt to envisage a virtually eternal society, in the closed city of Diaspar a billion years from now. I would like to end by quoting the words in which my hero learns the facts of life from his old tutor, Jeserac:

> A human being, like any other object, is defined by its structure—its pattern. The pattern of a man is incredibly complex; yet Nature was once able to pack that pattern into a tiny cell, too small for the eye to see.
>
> What Nature can do, Man can do also, in his own way. We do not know how long the task took. A million years, perhaps—but what is that? In the end our ancestors learned to analyse and store the information that would define any specific human being—and to use that information to recreate the original. . . .
>
> The way in which information is stored is of no importance; all that matters is the information itself. It may be in the form of written words on paper, of varying magnetic fields, or patterns of electric charge. Men have used all these methods of storage, and many others. Suffice to say that long ago they were able to store themselves—or, to be more precise, the disembodied patterns from which they could be called back into existence. . . .
>
> In a little while, . . . I shall prepare to leave this life. I shall go back through my memories, editing them and cancelling those I do not wish to keep. Then I shall walk into the Hall of Creation, but through a door that you have never seen. This old body will cease to exist, and so will consciousness itself. Nothing will be left of Jeserac but a galaxy of electrons frozen in the heart of a crystal.
>
> I shall sleep, . . . and without dreams. Then one day, perhaps a hundred thousand years from now, I shall find myself in a new body, meeting those who have been chosen to be my guardians. . . . At first I will know nothing of Diaspar and will have no memories of what I was before. Those memories will slowly return, at the end of my infancy, and I will build upon them as I move forward into my new cycle of existence.
>
> This is the pattern of our lives. . . . We have all been here many, many times before, though as the intervals of nonexistence vary according to random laws, this present population will never repeat itself. The new Jeserac will have new and different friends and interests, but the old Jeserac—as much of him as I wish to save—will still exist. . . .

At any moment only a hundredth of the citizens of Diaspar live and walk in its streets. The vast majority slumber in the memory banks, waiting for the signal that will call them forth on to the stage of existence once again. And so we have continuity, yet change—immortality, but not stagnation. . . .

Is this fantasy? I do not know; but I suspect that the truths of the far future will be stranger still.

LAURENS VAN DER POST

Love, the Aboriginal Tracker

I recalled something written many years ago: "Love is the aboriginal tracker, the Bushman on the faded desert spoor of our lost selves." [1] There was a great lost world to be rediscovered and rebuilt, not in the Kalahari but in the wasteland of our spirit where we had driven the first things of life, as we had driven the little Bushman into the desert of Southern Africa. There was indeed a cruelly denied and neglected first child of life, a Bushman in each of us. I remembered how audiences all over the world reacted when I spoke about the Bushman. Without exception their imaginations were, at the first description of his person, immediately alert. They were audiences of such different histories, cultures and races as Spanish, Swiss, Italian, Indian, French, Japanese, Finnish, German, Scandinavian, American, and assorted British. I felt the Bushman could not have excited the interest of them all unless he represented some elemental common denominator in such diversity of spirit. Most significant, perhaps, was the large number of people who wrote to me saying they had dreamt about the Bushman after first hearing me talk about him. Many letters would begin in the same way: "I must tell you: It is so strange. I hardly ever dream, but the night after your talk I had a dream about a Bushman."

One dream moved me so much that I have remembered it in some detail. It was that of a Spaniard, who told me: "I have not

[1] The Bushmen are regarded by ethnologists as the aborigines of central and southern Africa, related to the Pygmies. The few who remain of this ancient race live nomadically in remote wastes of the Kalahari desert, where Colonel van der Post discovered them and lived with them for several weeks, recording their rich folklore. They are extraordinarily skilled trackers and hunters, their only weapon the bow and arrow.

had a dream for years, but last night after the talk I dreamt I was in a great dilapidated building rather like a neglected castle I once knew. Somewhere inside it a woman was weeping as if her heart would break. I rushed from room to room along corridor after corridor and down stair after stair, trying to find her so that I could comfort her. Everywhere I went was empty; the dust thick on the floor and cobwebs on the wall. I was in despair of ever finding her, though the sound of her weeping grew louder and more pitiful in my ears. Suddenly one of your little Bushmen appeared in a window. He beckoned to me urgently with his bow, indicating that he would lead me to the woman. I started out to follow him, but immediately there was a growl behind me. To my horror one of the fiercest of the wolfhounds, which I let loose in the grounds of my own house as watchdogs every night, leapt forward and dashed straight at the Bushman. I tried to call the hound back but I could not find my voice. In the struggle to find it, I woke up in great distress and could not sleep again. In fact I have felt out of sorts with myself the whole of today. Now what do you say to that?"

What indeed could one say about it, even now, except that although these great plains and mountains of South Africa through which I travelled on my way to the sea may know the Bushman no more, "the prophetic soul of the wide world dreaming on things to come," as Shakespeare put it, knew him still and was glad to meet him again on the lips of living men? Anything that set a dreamless heart dreaming again was not to be despised. For the dream is the keeper of the wonder of which I have spoken. It is there that we must go to "take upon ourselves the mystery of things as if we were God's spies." The first time I came across this great cry which would deliver Lear from imprisonment in his own anguish, not by removing his suffering, but by giving it a meaning, the word spies troubled me greatly. After the trumpet call of the opening phrase it sounded oddly pejorative to me. Now I realized it could not have been more apt. Intimation of the new meaning to be lived never comes by battalions, but by single spies. It comes as an improbable summons in some lonely, seemingly ill-equipped and often suffering individual heart, operating far ahead of the armies of new life, like a spy behind the lines of the totalitarian spirit of its day. The mystery we must take upon ourselves in order to free our arrested being is that of the first things of life, which our twentieth-century civilization puts last, but of which the Bushman gives us so consummate an image, representing the child before whom we are commanded to humble ourselves and to become like if we are to enter the Kingdom.

I thought, therefore, I would begin by trying to serve the first things in myself, to turn to the point of origin in myself, to my own moment of innocence when the first things of Africa came over the rim of imagination like starlight out of the night so dearly beloved by my native continent. I realized that earliest and latest, old and new, primitive and civilized had met in my life in a way which was perhaps unique. I had experienced primitive Africa, the first life of the land. If I succeeded in rediscovering my own first experience of the first things of Africa, if I honoured them in myself, I might help others to rediscover and honour the same things in themselves. It would not matter that I possessed no expert training or special knowledge. Consciously or unconsciously, one lives not only one's own life but also the life of one's time. What was valid in my own experience would be valid in a measure also for my own day. I could let my experience of the primitive pattern of creation speak for me, since I have taken part in the most ancient working of the human spirit as it had been transmitted from the lives of the first people of Africa. I would merely be the bridge between the first pattern of things and my own time. I would use what knowledge I had of the first Africa, in particular the little I had now learnt of the Bushman, his mind and way of life in the desert, merely to interpret the experience into a contemporary idiom and so try to make it accessible to the modern imagination. That, however amateurish or small, could be the beginning of better things, because what the world lacks today is not so much knowledge of these first things as experience of them.

We know so much intellectually, indeed, that we are in danger of becoming the prisoners of our knowledge. We suffer from a hubris of the mind. We have abolished superstition of the heart only to install a superstition of the intellect in its place. We behave as if there were some magic in mere thought, and we use thinking for purposes for which it was never designed. As a result we are no longer sufficiently aware of the importance of what we cannot know intellectually, what we must know in other ways, of the living experience before and beyond our transitory knowledge. The passion of the spirit, which would inspire man to live his finest hour dangerously on the exposed frontier of his knowledge, seemed to me to have declined into a vague and arid restlessness hiding behind an arrogant intellectualism, as a child of arrested development behind the skirts of its mother.

Intellectually, modern man knows almost all there is to know about the pattern of creation in himself, the forms it takes, the surface designs it describes. He has measured the pitch of its rhythms and carefully recorded all the mechanics. From the outside he sees the desirable first object of life more clearly perhaps than man has ever seen it before. But less and less does he experience the process within. Less and less is he capable of committing himself body and soul to the creative experiment that is continually seeking to fire him and to charge his little life with great objective meaning. Cut off by accumulated knowledge from the heart of his own living experience, he moves among a comfortable rubble of material possession, alone and unbelonging, sick, poor, starved of meaning. How different the naked little Bushman, who could carry all he possessed in one hand! Whatever his life lacked, I never felt it was meaning. Meaning for him died only when we bent him to our bright twentieth-century will. Otherwise, he was rich where we were poor; he walked clear-cut through my mind, clothed in his own vivid experience of the dream of life within him. By comparison most of the people I saw on my way to the sea were blurred, and like the knight at arms in Keats' frightening allegory, "palely loitering" through life.

The essence of all this was put to me once by a great hunter, who was born in Africa, and who died thereafter having wandered all over it for seventy years, from the trembling Bushveld of the Transvaal to where the baroque mountains of Abyssinia dwindle down in dead hills to the Red Sea. Africa, he told me, was truly God's country—the last in the world perhaps with a soul of its own; and the difference between those born of its great earth and those who invaded it from Europe and Asia was simply the difference between *being* and *having*. He said the natural child of Africa *is*; the European or Asian *has*. He was not alone in this assessment of the conflict: The primitive keepers of the soul of Africa were keenly aware of its dangers to the being of man. I could give many instances of this awareness manifesting itself tragically in the history of Africa, from the time my ancestors landed at the Cape of Good Hope three hundred years ago, to Mau Mau in Kenya, and the latest series of ritual murders; but I prefer to give an illustration from my own life.

Soon after leaving school I heard that a new prophet had arisen among the great Zulu nation of South Africa. I was greatly excited by the news. Africa was still profoundly an Old Testament country, and the appearance of a prophet seemed not only natural and right but also an event that might always be of some cosmic importance. I went to see him as soon as I could. He lived in a round kraal, grass beehive huts on a hill standing among the complex of chasms and gorges of a deep and intricate valley in Natal. It was early summer; one of those days that come over the edge of time charged with a meaning of their own. The valley was overflowing with light, sensitive and trembling like a heart with its first apprehension of love. On the slope of the hill a long line of women were hoeing the magenta earth. They were naked to the waist; their strong bodies and full breasts were aubergine-coloured in the sun. As they worked they sang together in soft voices a song of the earth, with rhythm so in accord with the pulse of the light and the water-wheel-turn of the day in the blue sky that it made one great round of summer music. From the slopes beyond came the clear bright voices of the young boys herding the cattle and talking easily to one another, often a mile apart. Sometimes, too, one heard a cow calling for her calf, a goat's bright bleat, or a donkey's shattering plea for compassion, but the sound of the singing set to the rhythm of the day dominated the valley.

The first indication I had that the prophet was coming to meet us was when the singing stopped abruptly. The women ceased hoeing and turned to look down the hill behind them. From the bed of the stream below, a man emerged. He was tall, dressed in a white gown that fell to his feet, and with a long staff in his hand he slowly climbed the hill towards us, as if deep in thought. The women watched him with such close attention that one felt every step he took was fateful. At one moment I thought the women were going to break off working altogether and form up in a body behind him to escort him back to his kraal: but he made a gesture with his long arm, dignified and imperative, which immediately set them to work again, hoeing with such a will that the dust flickered like fire around their feet. Noticing this my guide, a Zulu chief himself, smiled with a dark satisfaction and remarked, "Not by the men, but by the women who flock to him and their obedience, shall you first know the true prophet."

When the seer stood before us at last, raising his hand palm-outwards in the ancient Zulu greeting, I thought I had never seen a more beautiful person. His head was round and shapely, his forehead broad, his features sensitive; the face as a whole naturally ascetic without being either austere or fanatic. His eyes were big and well-spaced, having the look of a personality in whom nothing was hidden. His hands were those of an artist, and he used them delicately to point his words. On his head he wore the round ring which among his people is a sign that the man is complete. He wore his ring so naturally that it did not seem to be imposed from without, but rather to emanate from him like a halo from a saint.

Outside his kraal there was a large wild fig tree whose dark green leaves were wet with light. We sat down in its shade and talked until the sun went down red behind the blue rim of the valley filled with evening smoke. The more we talked, the more I felt that I was not in the twentieth century but some early Biblical hour. We talked about a great many things of immense interest—I shall refer to them later—yet about the subject that mattered most to me I was disappointed. When I begged him to speak of the first spirit of the Zulu nation, Umkulunkulu, the Great One, he shook his beautiful old head and said with infinite sadness, "We do not speak of Umkulunkulu any longer. His praise-names are forgotten. People now talk only of things that are useful to them."

Recalling this conversation, which took place nearly thirty-five years ago, I realized that the situation which I believe we are all facing in the world today was one which the primitive world, the past life of Africa, knew only too well. It is a loss of first spirit, or to put it in the old-fashioned way, a loss of soul. Before my day with the Zulu prophet was over, I knew that he regarded this as the greatest calamity that could come to human beings. Other examples flooded my mind of how the keepers of man's first spirit in Africa constantly warned him against this peril. Indeed, the primitive world regarded the preservation of first spirit as the greatest, most urgent of all its tasks. It designed elaborate ritual, ceaselessly fashioned myths, legends, stories and music, to contain the meaning and feed the fire of the creative soul.

Here, from far back in my childhood, the memory of one of the servants in our large patriarchal household joined the Zulu seer. She was the lowest in the long hierarchy of black and coloured servants; yet, when we were hurt or distressed, she was the one we used to go to for comfort. One cold winter's evening when I could not sleep, she told me this story.

There was once, she said, a man of the early race who possessed a wonderful herd of cattle: Every beast in the herd matched the others in coats of black and white stipples. She stressed the colour of the cattle repeatedly. Even then, young as I was, I had an idea how important the matter of colour was. Cattle were never mere cattle to primitive men, but creatures full of rare and ancient spirit. As he listened to them lowing in his kraal after the lion's roar or the leopard's cough, he heard again the accents of his ancestors. When they were born he regarded the colour of their coats closely because it showed some meaning, some degree of favour or disfavour on the part of the great spirit over all. He had single adjectives for describing each combination of colour, and was never compelled to use a phrase like "a sort of strawberry roan" to designate an animal: There was one exact word to do it for him. As a child I knew eight such adjectives for which we had no single equivalent in any European tongue.

This combination of black and white in cattle was the greatest and most significant colour scheme of all, and the word for it had profound mystical associations. For instance, I was once with our black herdsmen when a cow was safely delivered of a black and white stippled calf: The cry of joy, reverence and gratitude to creation for so great a favour which broke from their deep throats, was one of the most wonderful sounds I have ever heard. I knew too a tribe who, when a man among them died, brought the finest white and black stippled cow in his possession to the side of the open grave. There they made it lower its head so that it would look its dead master in the face for the last time. Thereafter it belonged utterly to the spirits, and no one in the dead man's family would ever dream of killing or selling it.

There was meaning in everything for the first people—from the birth of a calf to the death of a man and beyond; and enclosing all, there was an overwhelming sense that every living thing shared in the process of creation. When our servant told me how this man of the early race possessed cattle with such numinous hides, my child imagination anticipated a story of more than usual significance, and I could not keep still in bed for excitement.

This man of the early race, therefore, she told me, dearly loved his black and white cattle. He always took them out into the veld himself, chose the best possible grazing for them, and watched over them like a mother over her children, seeing that no wild animals came near to hurt or disturb them. In the evening he would bring them back to his kraal, seal the entrance carefully with branches of the toughest thorn, and watching them contentedly chewing the cud, think, "In the morning I shall have a wonderful lot of milk to draw from them." One morning, however, when he went into his kraal expecting to find the udders of the cows full and sleek with milk, he was amazed to see they were slack, wrinkled, and empty. He thought with immediate self-reproach he had chosen their grazing badly, and took them to better grass. He brought them home in the evening and again thought, "Tomorrow for a certainty I shall get more milk than ever before." But again in the morning the udders were slack and dry. For the second time he changed their grazing, and yet again the cows had no milk. Disturbed and suspicious, he decided to keep a watch on the cattle throughout the dark.

In the middle of the night he was astonished to see a cord of finely-woven fibre descending from the stars; and down this cord, hand over hand, one after another came some young women of the people of the sky. He saw them, beautiful and gay, whispering and laughing softly among themselves, steal into the kraal and milk his cattle dry with calabashes. Indignant, he jumped out to catch them, but they scattered cleverly so that he did not know which way to run. In the end he did manage to catch one; but while he was chasing her the rest, calabashes and all, fled up the sky, withdrawing the cord after the last of them so that he could not follow. However, he was content because the young woman he had caught was the loveliest of them all. He made her his wife and from that moment he had no more trouble from the women of the people of the sky.

His new wife now went daily to work in the fields for him while he tended his cattle. They were happy and they prospered. There was only one thing that worried him. When he caught his wife she had a basket with her. It was skilfully woven, so tight that he could not see through it, and was always closed firmly on top with a lid that fitted exactly into the opening. Before she would marry him, his wife had made him promise that he would never lift the lid of the basket and look inside until she gave him permission to do so. If he did, a great disaster might overtake them both. But as the months went by, the man began to forget his promise. He became steadily more curious, seeing the basket so near day after day, with the lid always firmly shut. One day when he was alone he went into his wife's hut, saw the basket standing there in the shadows, and could bear it no longer. Snatching off the lid, he looked inside. For a moment he stood there unbelieving, then burst out laughing.

When his wife came back in the evening she knew at once what had happened. She put her hand to her heart, and looking at him with tears in her eyes, she said, "You've looked in the basket."

He admitted it with a laugh, saying, "You silly woman. You silly, silly creature. Why have you made such a fuss about this basket? There's nothing in it at all."

"Nothing?" she said, hardly finding the strength to speak.

"Yes, nothing," he answered emphatically.

At that she turned her back on him, walking away straight into the sunset, and vanished. She was never seen on earth again.

To this day I can hear the old black servant woman saying to me, "And do you know why she went away, my little master? Not because he had broken his promise but because, looking into the basket, he had found it empty. She went because the basket was not empty: It was full of beautiful things of the sky she stored there for them both, and because he could not see them and just laughed, there was no use for her on earth any more and she vanished."

That story seems to me an accurate image of our predicament in the World now, both as individuals and as nations. The primitive spirit stands in rags and tatters, rejected by the contemporary mind, offering us such warnings. Laughing, unaware of peril, we lift the lids of our own particular baskets and, blindly declaring them to be empty, we lose our soul, of which woman is the immemorial image.

It is true there is no resolution, only tragedy and a warning, in this African tale. But the woman who walked into the bloodred sunset of Africa to vanish, the servant in rags and tatters still haunting the corridors of my own mind, the woman abandoned and weeping in the ruined castle in the dream of the Spaniard, and indeed the naked, demented Bushman woman [2] whimpering in the summer sunlight of the desert, each in her own way seemed to serve a single meaning. They all drew attention to the denial of something vital in the human spirit. The denial might be caused, as in the African tale, by the unawareness of man whose vision is so tied to the world *without* that he is incapable of seeing the spiritual content of his own inner world. It might be caused by the cruelty of man, who trespasses against his own humanity in doing violence to earth's children; or by mere inability to control that fierce watchdog of our daylight selves—the mind narrowed to an aggressive materialistic rationalism, as in the dream of the Spaniard who could not call back the wolfhound he kept to guard his home and treasured possessions.

The general state of neglect can be symbolized by a ruined castle, a desert in Southern Africa, or a despised basket in the shadows of an African hut. But they all conveyed only one thing to me—the peril of man when divorced from the first things in himself. Cut off from them for long, he loses his meaning just as that man of the early race, blind to the contents of the basket, lost his lovely lady of the starry sky. Only those who have seen the stars of Africa can know how terrible such a loss must have been. This peril appeared so active in the world around me that I felt I could say of it, as Dabé [3] said of the Bushman woman at Gemsbok Pan, "The Time of the Hyaena is upon us."

However, once I had discovered the kinship of these images, so far apart in their origins yet so closely related in their meaning, I began to consider more carefully the rest of the pattern of the first things of Africa. In particular, I examined the pattern of the Bushman as experienced through my own life and imagination. It was so much older than even the earliest known pattern of the most primitive of black races in Africa. It was, as far as I knew, the purest manifestation of life lived in the beginning according

[2] A reference to an earlier incident in the book. Van der Post had seen this woman at a truck stop in the desert, and learned her history. She had been captured and raped by a white man and thenceforth, in a demented condition, was similarly treated by others.

[3] Dabé was van der Post's Bushman guide on the expedition into the Kalahari. Among all the numinous animals in Bushman folklore, the hyena is the only one with an absolutely evil role.

to life's own design rather than man's wilful and one-sided plan for it. It is true, I was not without prejudice in the matter, for I had a private hope of the utmost importance to me. The Bushman's physical shape combined those of a child and a man: I surmised that examination of his inner life might reveal a pattern which reconciled the spiritual opposites in the human being and made him whole.

More immediately, his tragedy was the only one I knew in Africa for which White and Black shared an equal guilt. In the long and terrible history of Africa, it was the one mirror wherein both White and Black could clearly view not the unreal and conflicting abstractions they have made of one another, but what is so tragically hidden from them—their common, fallible, and bewildered human faces. If that could be done, it might start the first movement towards a reconciliation, first in their imagination and then in their lives. But apart from these private rationalizations, I was compelled toward the Bushman like someone who walks in his sleep, obedient to a dream of finding in the dark what the day had denied him.

So I collected all I could discover of what has been written about the Bushman. I had read it all many times before in my life. It had become part of my imaginative experience: But, knowing how different just one of the Bushman legends had appeared to me after my journey into the desert, I was determined to take nothing for granted. I would pool all I had learnt in the past with what I had brought back with me from the desert, and see what came out of it at leisure on the long voyage back to England by sea.

A 3
B 4
C 5
D 6
E 7
F 8
G 9
H 0
I 1
J 2